ALFRED HERBERT LTD AND THE BRITISH MACHINE TOOL INDUSTRY, 1887-1983

T0300528

Modern Economic and Social History Series

General Editor: Derek H. Aldcroft

Titles in this series include:

Alfred Herbert Ltd and the British Machine Tool Industry, 1887-1983

ROGER LLOYD-JONES AND M.J. LEWIS
Sheffield Hallam University, UK

Routledge
Taylor & Francis Group
LONDON AND NEW YORK

First published 2006 by Ashgate Publishing

2 Park Square, Milton Park, Abingdon, Oxfordshire OX14 4RN
711 Third Avenue, New York, NY 10017

Routledge is an imprint of the Taylor & Francis Group, an informa business

First issued in paperback 2017

British Library Cataloguing in Publication Data
Lloyd-Jones, Roger, 1944–
  Alfred Herbert Ltd and the British machine tool industry, 1887-1983. – (Modern economic and social history)
  1. Alfred Herbert Ltd. 2. Machine-tool industry – Great Britain – History – 20th century
  I. Title II. Lewis, M.J. (Myrddin John), 1957–
  338.4'7621902'0941'0904

Library of Congress Cataloging-in-Publication Data
Lloyd-Jones, Roger, 1944–
  Alfred Herbert Ltd. and the British machine tool industry, 1887-1983 / Roger Lloyd-Jones and M.J. Lewis.
        p. cm.—(Modern economic and social history)
    Includes bibliographical references and index.
    ISBN 0-7546-0523-X (alk. paper)
    1. Alfred Herbert Ltd.—History. 2. Machine-tool industry—Great Britain—History. I. Lewis, M.J. (Myrddin John), 1957– II. Title. III. Series: Modern economic and social history series.

    HD9703.G74A44 2005
    338.7'61621902'0941—dc22

                                                      2005013239

ISBN 13: 978-0-7546-0523-2 (hbk)
ISBN 13: 978-1-138-27417-4 (pbk)

For Abby, Emily, Alistair, Phoebe, Mason, Robert

Contents

List of Figure and Tables

Modern Economic and Social History Series
General Editor's Preface

Economic and social history has been a flourishing subject of scholarly study during recent decades. Not only has the volume of literature increased enormously but the range of interest in time, space and subject matter has broadened considerably so that today there are many sub-branches of the subject which have developed considerable status in their own right.

One of the aims of this series is to encourage the publication of scholarly monographs on any aspect of modern economic and social history. The geographical coverage is world-wide and contributions on the non-British themes will be especially welcome. While emphasis will be placed on works embodying original research, it is also intended that the series should provide the opportunity to publish studies of a more general thematic nature which offer a reappraisal or critical analysis of major issues of debate.

Derek H. Aldcroft
University of Leicester

Acknowledgements

We would like to thank the following: Professor Derek Aldcroft for his encouragement of our research work on the British machine tool industry; Simon Brown and his staff at Lancaster Gate, London, who allowed us to use the private papers of the Machine Tool Trade Association. The professionalism of the staff at Coventry Archive was a great aid in our long labours on the Alfred Herbert papers. Also we would like to thank the staff of the West Yorkshire Archive Service, Leeds and Halifax, the Glasgow University Archives and Business Research Centre, and the Bodleian Library, University of Oxford. The research was supported by sabbatical leave granted by the Humanities Research Centre at Sheffield Hallam University. Our appreciation to the following for putting up with our long discussions on the machine tool industry: Professor Peter Cain, Professor Josephine Maltby, and Dr. Mark Matthews. Colleagues at various conferences where we gave papers on aspects of the project also produced valuable advice. Finally, I am sure that our wives are relieved that our obsession with the machine tool industry is more or less complete.

CHAPTER ONE

Introduction

The machine tool industry formed a small but vital part of Britain's manufacturing sector, and this study examines its development over the twentieth century. The importance of the industry's contribution to the health and efficiency of the manufacturing economy was reflected in the influential Mitchell Report of 1960. While the report was a public condemnation of the industry's technical record, it nevertheless recognised that the British machine tool industry had developed a reputation 'throughout the world as an excellent producer of standard machine tools of all categories: it supplies almost the whole home demand for such machine tools and exports approximately 30 per cent of its production'.[1] The industry exerted an influence far greater than its actual size, and consequently its analysis requires an engagement, at various points, with broad themes associated with the performance of British industry in the twentieth century. In particular, the industry is located within debates over Britain's long-run manufacturing decline and issues of modernisation, which from the late 1950s envisaged institutional reform, involving co-operation between business, labour and the state as a panacea for the declining competitiveness of manufacturing.[2] The machine tool industry at various stages of its evolution received scathing criticism over its performance, but, as we shall demonstrate, it also produced positive outcomes that marked it as an important sector of the British manufacturing economy.

The broad approach of this book is to examine the industry's development through the lens of its largest firm, Alfred Herbert Ltd. of Coventry, founded in 1887. In the years before the First World War Herbert's grew to be the largest machine tool maker in Europe, and by the 1950s claimed to be the largest machine tool organisation in the world. The role of this company is suggestive of Nelson's metaphor of the 'player and the game', and this is used in a reflective sense to generally inform the relationship between the firm, the industry, and the market-cum-technological environment.[3] Nelson acknowledges that 'what firms do often matters significantly', but in order to fully 'understand the players there is a need

---

[1] Sir Steuart Mitchell (hereafter Mitchell Report), *The Machine Tool Industry: A Report by the Sub-Committee of the Machine Tool Advisory Council* (London, H.M.S.O, 1960), p. 32.

[2] For a broad general survey of these issues see M. Dintenfass, 'Converging Accounts, Misleading Metaphors and Persistent Doubts: Reflections on the Historiography of Britain's Decline', in J-P. Dormois and M. Dintenfass (eds), *The British Industrial Decline* (London, Routledge, 1999).

[3] R. Nelson, 'The Role of Firms in Technical Advance: A Perspective from Evolutionary Theory', in G. Dosi, R. Gionettie, and P. A. Toninelli (eds), *Technology and Enterprise in Historical Perspective* (Oxford, Oxford University Press, 1992), pp. 165-8.

to specify the game that is being played'.[4] Business does not work in a 'vacuum',[5] and to explore its evolution requires an understanding of how the firm evolves within the changing market, technical and institutional environment, which is the province of both the business and economic historian.[6] For example, one of the most astute observations of the British machine tool industry was made by Sir Alfred Herbert, the founder of the company, who claimed that 'nearly all machine tool makers were strong individualists, who preferred the private company with its many advantages of direct control and immediate response to stimuli'.[7] This observation reflects the long-run pattern of ownership and control in the industry, which fits Chandler's perception of the retention of personal capitalism in British industry.[8] By the 1950s, there was a general belief that large firms would provide the opportunity for greater productive efficiency, increase the level of standardisation, and would enable a rising curve of technological development to enhance the competitive performance of British manufacturing companies. Such assumptions underpinned the Anglo-American Productivity Teams of the early 1950s, a report of 1953 on the machine tool industry concluding that what was required was wholesale rationalisation leading to a significant reduction in 'the number of independent companies in the industry'. Large-scale business was seen as a counter to a business culture that protected its 'individuality and independence'.[9]

Yet a sub-committee of the Machine Tool Trade Association (MTTA), the main body representing the industry, while adhering to some of the recommendations of the report, nevertheless condemned a process of rationalisation. Echoing the views of Sir Alfred Herbert, expressed in the 1930s, the sub-committee accepted that individualism was deeply embedded in the industry, but that recommendations for a significant reduction in the number of firms suggested 'a certain degree of tolerance for the idea of the establishment of a monopoly'.[10] Rationalisation was a sensitive matter for an industry composed of large numbers of small firms, but even large companies such as Alfred Herbert remained committed to personal and independent control. While providing a balanced assessment of the industry in 1960, the Mitchell Report nevertheless highlighted a business culture which celebrated independence and resulted in a highly fragmented business structure.[11] In the same year the MTTA acknowledged that the large number of small firms in the industry were 'handicapped

---

[4] Ibid., p. 165.
[5] D. J. Jeremy, *A Business History of Britain 1900-1990s* (Oxford, Oxford University Press, 1998), p. 1.
[6] For an explanation of the study of the business firm in the context of the market-cum-technological environment, see J. F. Wilson, *British Business History 1720-1914* (Manchester, Manchester University Press, 1995), pp. 83-4, 87-8.
[7] Machine Tool Trade Association (MTTA), Annual Report, 1935.
[8] A. D. Chandler, *Scale and Scope: The Dynamics of Industrial Capitalism* (Cambridge, Mass., Belknap Press, 1990), pp. 235-94.
[9] *Productivity Team Report on Metalworking Machine-Tools by Anglo-American Council on Productivity* (London, H.M.S.O., 1953), p. 46.
[10] *Engineer*, 26 June 1963, pp. 93-4.
[11] Mitchell Report, p. 21.

when it came to reducing costs of production, rationalising design, and marketing their goods in the most efficient manner'.[12] The process of rationalisation and concentration did not accelerate until the 1960s, and from 1945 to the late 1950s the number of firms in the industry remained more or less constant. A small number of firms employed in excess of 300 employees, while the vast majority employed less than 300. Large numbers of small, often family controlled firms, characterised the industry, and even in 1959 there were 200 firms in the industry with an average turnover of only £40,000 per annum.[13] As late as 1983 Kenneth Baker, the Minister of Information Technology, commented that a fundamental characteristic of the machine tool industry 'is that there are large numbers of family firms which tended to be dominated by strong characters', to which he added the proviso that there was 'nothing wrong with that as long as they move with the times'.[14]

Apart from the small-scale structure of the industry, the machine tool sector also displayed three other structural features, which are emphasised throughout this exploration of its business history. First, machine tool firms were not only makers of machines, but also acted as factorers for the products of other firms, both at home and abroad. This is strongly emphasised in our focus on Herbert's, which from its origins in the late 1880s developed an extensive network of sales agency relations. Second, machine tool firms transacted with each other for machine tools, and also engaged in extensive sub-contracting arrangements. Sub-contracting was particularly important in periods of high demand pressure, as we shall see in the case of Herbert's and other machine tool firms during the First World War, the recovery phase from the depression after 1934, and during the Second World War. Finally, machine tool firms evolved a relationship with customers that strongly emphasised the importance of meeting customer need, and leading manufacturers such as Herbert's placed an emphasis upon design based upon the requirements of British engineering.

The structural features of the industry set a context for exploring its performance, which itself opens up issues about British industrial decline. As Tomlinson has pointed out 'the idea that the British economy has in some sense declined in the past century informs most recent historical writing, especially economic'.[15] In particular, this applies to manufacturing,[16] and the centrality of

---

[12] MTTA, Council Minute Books, 1946-70, 6 October 1960, 'Report on British Machine Tool Exports'.

[13] E. W. Evans, 'Some Problems of Growth in the Machine Tool Industry', *Yorkshire Bulletin of Economic and Social Research*, Vol. 18 (1966), pp. 46-7; H. A. Breeley and G. W. Troup, 'The Machine Tool Industry', in D. Burn (ed.), *The Structure of British Industry: A Symposium*, Vol. 1 (Cambridge, Cambridge University Press, 1958), p. 363; MTTA, Machine Tool Directory, 1966, produced by Miln and Robinson for private circulation, pp. 12-13.

[14] *Third Report of the Industry and Trade Committee: Machine Tools and Robotics*, Session 1982-3, p. 14.

[15] J. Tomlinson, 'Inventing "Decline": The Falling Behind of the British Economy in the Postwar Years', *Economic History Review*, Vol. 49, No. 4 (1996), p. 731.

[16] A classic example of this is contained in S. Pollard, *The Wasting of the British Economy* (London, Croom Helm, 1982).

machine tools to this sector positions the industry in this debate. Yet as Tomlinson argues, 'concern' with decline in the past is 'episodic rather than continuous', and the notion of a century of decline 'is the product of retrospective judgements'. Decline was specific to particular eras from the late nineteenth century, and was not a 'homogeneous problem'.[17] Our study confirms Tomlinson's proposition; the machine tool industry, despite the fact that it was emasculated by the 1980s, did not experience a slow linear decline. Prior to the 1970s, after which the industry and its largest producer Herbert's faced mounting problems, periods of business difficulties were followed by periods of renewal and optimism. For example we will show in Chapter Two that the industry did respond to the growing American challenge of the 1890s, and made positive advancements in the Edwardian years. Again, machine tool firms made positive contributions to munitions supply during the two world wars, explored in Chapters Three and Six. Without an adequate supply of machine tools, there could not have been an increasing production of shells and other munitions and armaments that characterised the two conflicts. Indeed, by the 1950s Britain could boast that in Alfred Herbert it had a national asset, the largest machine tool organisation in the world making a vital contribution to the nation's export drive. Our study of the industry highlights other examples of business success, and consequently notions of gradual long-term decline are not tenable. The industry defies a simple narrative framework and provides a reminder to the historian of the dangers of pursuing a teleological search for final causes.

Assessing the performance of the industry, and key firms such as Herbert's, is also complicated by the fact that the industry faced a number of constraints which were outside its control. A recurring problem concerned the shortage of skilled labour, especially during the upturn of economic activity. During periods of economic downturn, the obverse occurred, with firms facing difficulties in retaining their teams of skilled workers. The problem of labour supply was most acute during the First World War, the brief post-war boom, rearmament in the late 1930s and in the Second World War, and during the long boom of the 1950s and 1960s when it became a matter of deep concern to the industry's leaders. Even in the 1980s, when the industry was facing rapid decline, there were complaints that 'One of the factors holding back the U.K. machine tool industry is the shortage of trained personnel'.[18] Labour shortages reflected a long-term constraint facing the industry, relating to the cyclical pattern of demand. The historical evidence suggests that during recessions the level of orders for machine tools could be less than half that achieved during periods of rising economic activity, and the switch from downswing to upswing representing the volatility of the cycle was 'quicker' than in other industries.[19] This meant that firms were vulnerable to short-term movements in demand with its consequent volatility for turnover, profits and investment. The impact of the cycle on investment decisions

---

[17] Tomlinson, 'Inventing', p. 732.
[18] *Industry and Trade Committee: Machine Tools*, 1982-3, p. xix.
[19] Ibid., p. 29.

was a long-term characteristic of the industry, and machine tool firms were frequently criticised for their failure to invest sufficiently during downturns in demand to create sufficient productive capacity to take advantage of rising orders during the subsequent upswing. Consequently, during periods of prosperity, potential customers faced lengthening delivery times and rising prices and firms such as Herbert's used their factoring and sub-contracting operations in an attempt to meet user need. Over the long-term, the cyclical pattern of ordering facing the industry had a ratchet effect. In each successive upswing British machine tool makers struggled to meet demand, and this led progressively to growing import penetration. The issue of import penetration was raised by users and makers of machine tools in the 1890s, and again became a matter of concern in the inter war years. By the 1950s and 1960s the degree of imports had become a major issue in the assessment of the industry's competitive performance, and a focal point for discussion at the industry level. Chapters Seven and Eight show that imports were central to the national debate over modernisation and the involvement of government in the industry's affairs.

The cyclical pattern of demand provided a convenient defence for the industry against its critics. A repeated complaint of British machine tool makers was that users tended to bunch their demand for machines during upturns in the cycle, a common feature of the industry's relations with an important customer, the motor vehicle industry. For example, between 1955 and 1957 British car firms were committed to heavy investment programmes in new plant, and their large and concentrated demand for machine tools meant that domestic suppliers were unable to meet orders, with the obvious consequence that delivery dates lengthened and foreign imports rose. In addition, British machine makers claimed that their customers in the engineering industries failed to modernise plant, illustrated in Chapter Four by problems in creating markets for British built special-purpose and automatic machine tools, in increasing demand by continuous production industries such as automobiles. This criticism reflected an important distinction characterising the products of the machine tool industry. General-purpose machine tools were regarded as the 'backbone' of the British engineering industry, as they could be adapted to a wide variety of uses. Conversely, special-purpose machines were designed 'either to perform one type of operation or to produce one type of component'.[20] The criticism of the customer by machine tool makers did not go unanswered. For example, C. R. F. Engelbach of Austin Motors complained in 1927 that machine tool firms were 'backward' in supplying modern equipment to British engineering.[21] In addition, the evidence from the inter-war years suggests that the trend towards the production of standard general-purpose machines by British makers was reinforced, opening a gap in the market for the inflow of American and also German special-purpose machines. Debates on the technical competency of the industry again resurfaced in the 1950s and 1960s, when it came under increasing scrutiny concerning its relative competitive position. Complaints abounded that the British industry was slow to develop modern machine

---

[20] *Machine Tool Review* (published by Alfred Herbert Ltd.), Vol. 47, 1959, p. 3.

[21] *American Machinist*, 8 October 1927, p. 104E.

technology, only to be countered by makers who responded that the machine tool industry was constrained by the limited investment of the engineering industry in modern equipment. Indeed, the maker's allegations were supported by a National Economic Development Council (NEDC) report on investment in machine tools in 1965, which observed that 'Methods of investment appraisal in use by most of the companies in the engineering industry are either non-existent or inaccurate or misleading'. The report also expressed 'surprise' at the lack of knowledge of users concerning tax incentives for purchasing modern machine tools.[22]

By the 1960s a particular concern involved the slow diffusion in Britain of numerically controlled machine tools, which limited the opportunities of domestic makers in this field. The NEDC report concluded that 'many firms in the engineering industry are failing to recognise worthwhile investments and are thus not availing themselves of the benefits which greater use of modern machine tools would bring'.[23] At times, the voice of the machine tool industry itself could take on a strident tone. As E. N. Addison, the chairman of Addison Tools Ltd., complained in 1983, 'it is not the machine tool industry that is inefficient, but the engineering industry. We cannot sell to them because they do not know how to produce. There is no demand because the engineering industry ... is run by accountants'.[24] Addison's statement symbolised the strong engineering traditions of the businessmen who managed the industry, as well as representing a long standing condemnation of the inadequacies of British engineering practices. With the industry facing crisis in the early 1980s, J. L. D. Gailey, the president of the MTTA had no doubt 'that a national engineering industry tends to get a machine tool industry as good as it deserves'.[25]

There is some justification in Gailey's complaint, but the blame for the industry's shortcomings should not simply be laid to rest with the users of machine tools. There is little evidence to suggest that the British machine tool industry was a technological leader, pushing user industries towards the technological frontier. Rather, it was essentially adaptive, responding to the needs of users via a path of incremental improvements to machine design. In the case of Herbert's, the company gradually evolved its technology through a process of experimentation, which by the inter-war years was already leading to issues at the boardroom level concerning their capability to build machines of original design. Incremental design improvements symbolised the company's technical policy in the 1920s, which adapted to customer needs, and this trend continued into the 1960s. By the late 1950s, Herbert's joint managing director, J. C. Blair, praised the accumulation of technical knowledge held in a 'Board of engineers', and the company's ability to respond to the changing demands of its customers.[26] The leading firm in the

---

[22] National Economic Development Council, *Investment in Machine Tools. A Survey by the Management Consultants' Association* (London, H.M.S.O, 1965), pp. 2, 15.

[23] Ibid., p. 21.

[24] *Industry and Trade Committee: Machine Tools*, 1982-3, p. 38.

[25] Ibid., p. 44.

[26] Coventry Archive, 926/1/1/1, Minute Book of the Board of Directors of Alfred Herbert Ltd., 1944-60, 5 June 1957.

industry thus followed a pattern of 'design creativity and variety', which characterised British engineering practice in general, and forewent 'American style production engineering'.[27]

An adaptive response to design by British machine tool firms is also shown by their concentration of output on general-purpose machines, which could be adapted to a wide variety of uses. A consequence of this historical pattern of production was a reliance on imports of special-purpose machines by British users.[28] Indeed, the industry reinforced market specialisation, with merchant firms such as Charles Churchill & Co. and Burton, Griffiths & Co. acting as agents for imported machine tools, and machine makers themselves, notably Herbert's developing an organisational structure that reflected its role both as a manufacturing and factoring company. Herbert's developed market networks for the import of foreign, especially American machine tools, and this was a common feature of the industry. In turn, this reflected a strong commitment to the principles of free trade, and while American machine makers were not slow to call for protection at various times, the response in Britain was muted. Throughout the 1920s the industry remained committed to free trade, and only conceded on this point during the world depression of the early 1930s. The move to protection in 1932, however, did not settle the question, and as shown in Chapter Five the 'deficiency' of machine tools in the rearmament drive from the mid-1930s opened up the issue of importing vital equipment via the Import Duties Advisory Committee. The industry remained committed to free imports, and in 1964, when the Labour Government imposed a surcharge on imports the MTTA was bitterly opposed. This view persisted, the MTTA commenting in 1983 that the industry had a long-term commitment to defend 'free trade measures', ensuring that British manufacturing industry had 'access to the best available machine tools world wide'.[29] Such beliefs legitimated the international specialisation pursued by British machine makers, and tended to reinforce the position of the industry as primarily a provider of general-purpose machine tools designed to satisfy customer needs.

The 'game' facing British machine tool makers in the course of the twentieth century was conditioned by the relationships with user industries, the cyclical pattern of demand, a deep commitment to international specialisation via free trade, and a constantly changing technological environment. The 'players', notably Britain's leading maker Alfred Herbert, did believe that they made a positive contribution to the 'game', providing for customer needs and justifying international specialisation by asserting that it provided a major contribution to national industrial efficiency. Such a broad generalisation is open to question in the examination of the long-term development of the industry, but certainly it did respond with vitality during both world wars. During both conflicts there was a heavy reliance upon imported American machine tools, facilitated by the factoring

---

[27] J. K. Brown, 'Design Plans, Working Drawings, National Styles. Engineering Practices in Great Britain and the United States, 1775-1945', *Technology and Culture*, Vol. 41, No. 2 (2000), pp. 224-6.

[28] *Machine Tool Review*, Vol. 47, 1959, p. 25.

[29] *Industry and Trade Committee: Machine Tools*, 1982-3, p. 29.

services of British firms such as Herbert's, but at the same time domestic makers did substantially increase output, which made a vital contribution to the war effort. For example, by 1944 American machine tool imports represented only 14.4 per cent of U.K. production, compared to 53.3 per cent in 1940, leading Sir Alfred Herbert to proclaim that 'there is no longer a possibility of the progress of the war being hampered by a lack of machine tools'.[30] In addition, firms did develop closer, if at times somewhat fraught relations, with the state. For example, during the Great War Sir Alfred Herbert promoted closer links between the industry and the Ministry of Munitions through his role as director of machine tool supply. Although this raised the national profile of the industry, there is little evidence that the war stimulated major technological advances amongst machine tool makers. As Joseph Pickin, a Herbert director, stated at the end of the war, amongst the company's machines 'there are none of any striking originality'.[31] Makers adapted to the intense demands of war, but radical technical change was limited. A similar pattern can be detected during the Second World War. Between September 1936 and the summer of 1944 the British machine tool industry 'built as many machines as were manufactured in the preceding 40 years',[32] but its capability to manufacture special-purpose machines was variable. By the end of the war there was a surplus of general-purpose machines but a continued serious deficiency in specials. As Chapters Three and Six show, the wars raised a whole series of other issues relating to the deployment of female workers, the initial reluctance of firms to invest in sufficient capacity, the problems of retaining a skilled labour force, and the sometimes volatile nature of industrial relations.

During the three peace-time phases, 1890s to 1914, the inter-war years, and post-1945, the machine tool industry made a positive contribution to exports, provided a wide range of services to engineering, and placed a high priority on meeting customer needs. Where firms were less successful was in developing organisational capabilities in response to the growing competitive pressures induced by the changing market and technological environment. The industry's long-term commitment to personal capitalism lends support to Chandler's allegations concerning the reluctance of British industrialists to build managerial hierarchies.[33] Business firms, according to Nelson, 'have a considerable range of freedom regarding whether, or just how, they can take advantage of the opportunities the environment affords'.[34] In turn, this raises questions about the capabilities of firms to adequately respond to their external environment. By the 1960s the leading British firm of Herbert's was characterised by a set of

---

[30] M. M. Postan, *British War Production* (London, H.M.S.O and Longman and Green, 1952), p. 207; Coventry Archive, 586/11, Alfred Herbert, General Minute Book, 1894-1950, 16 July 1944.

[31] Coventry Archive, 926/1/4/1-3, Alfred Herbert Ltd., Minute Books of the Departmental Board of Directors, 1911-41, 9 September 1918.

[32] *Machinist*, 19 August 1944, p. 115E.

[33] See Chandler, *Scale and Scope*, pp. 235-6.

[34] R. Nelson, *The Sources of Economic Growth* (Cambridge, Mass., Harvard University Press, 2000), p. 104.

managerial and organisational deficiencies, which created problems for the company in meeting the challenges of changing markets, increasing foreign competition, and new technological developments. From the late 1950s, the 'game' changed rapidly, and the following two decades saw a sharp contraction in the industry as firms were absorbed into larger engineering groups or simply disappeared altogether.

The business history of Herbert's from the 1960s is one of frustrated ambitions. Its policy of acquisition, notably the take-over of the machine tool interests of Birmingham Small Arms (BSA) in 1965, and its development of numerical control through an association with the American company Ingersoll in 1967, proved quickly to be failures. The Herbert management were unable to re-organise the BSA companies, and they became a financial millstone around their necks, and the anticipated commercial success of the new Herbert-Ingersoll machines proved to be a major miscalculation. The British machine tool industry's flagship company, a symbol of the industry's ingenuity during the twentieth century, fell into a dramatic and sudden decline. In the mid-1960s the company's market capitalisation was £43.4 million, but by 1975 it had been acquired by the National Enterprise Board for £1 million, in fact a generous settlement given that the market value of its shares now totalled just £800,000. The demise of Herbert's fits the observations of Zollo and Winter that business success is determined by the ability of top management to understand 'the causal links between the actions' they take and 'the performance outcomes' they obtain.[35] Management expectations of a new era of progress for the company in the 1960s did not match performance outcomes. On the technical front, the capabilities of the Herbert management had been built upon the accumulation of tacit knowledge, which had enabled the company to follow a path of incremental product development with more or less stable business routines. However, by the 1960s and 1970s the company faced a rapidly changing technological and competitive environment, and were unable to adapt their organisational capabilities to meet the challenge. As Zollo and Winter observe, when 'technological ... and competitive conditions are subject to rapid change, persistence in the same operational routines become hazardous'.[36] Despite the search for strategies to survive, Herbert's lacked the managerial competencies to extract itself from its downward spiral.

Its fall symbolised the general decline of the British machine tool industry. During the 1970s there was a general reduction in both the number and the size of British machine tool firms, and Britain's share of world machine tool output fell from 8 per cent in 1971 to 5 per cent in 1977, and to just 3 per cent in 1981. Correspondingly, employment contracted from 53,000 workers in 1976 to 36,000 in 1982, a drop of 32 per cent. The reduction of the industry's capacity was accompanied by rising import penetration. Domestic makers were unable to meet demand and this led to a doubling of the proportion of imports in domestic

---

[35] M. Zollo and S. G. Winter, 'Deliberate Learning and the Evolution of Dynamic Capabilities', *Organisation Science*, Vol. 13, No. 3 (2002), p. 340.

[36] Ibid., p. 341.

consumption over the 1970s.[37] By the early 1980s the industry was described as 'technologically rather backward', and 'too slow' in the development of advanced numerically controlled machine technology.[38] While a slow-down of world economic activity in the 1970s undoubtedly had a negative impact on Britain's machine tool makers, the British industry nevertheless performed relatively poorly compared to their major competitors. For example, a cross-national survey praised the Swiss machine tool industry for 'a timely introduction of new technologies', enabling them 'to remain in a leading position in the world market, whereas Britain's machine tool industry had 'with a few exceptions ... almost disappeared'.[39]

The gloom shrouding the British machine tool industry was evident in the findings of the Trade and Industry Committee of the House of Commons in 1983, which concluded that it was 'clear that the decline of the U.K. machine tool industry is only partly attributable to the current world recession'. Failures of management, innovation and marketing have resulted in a lack of competitiveness before the end of the last decade'.[40] By the end of the 1990s, the U.K. was highly dependent upon imports, the proportion of machine tool imports to total consumption standing at 82 per cent in 1997.[41] Nevertheless, the process by which the industry had reached this state of affairs was by no means straightforward, or a simple case of linear decline. In the course of the twentieth century the British machine tool industry had achieved some notable successes, faced formidable challenges and, despite its small size, played a strategically important role in the nation's manufacturing economy.

---

[37] H. Arnold, 'The Recent History of the Machine Tool Industry and the Effects of Technological Change', University of Munich, Institute for Innovation Research and Technology Management (2001), p. 3; *Industry and Trade Committee: Machine Tools, 1982-3*, pp. x, 32.

[38] A. Daley and D. J. Jones, 'The Machine Tool Industry in Britain, Germany and the United States, *National Institute Economic Review*, No. 92 (1980).

[39] C. Ackerman and J. Harrop, 'The Management of Technological Innovation in the Machine Tool Industry: A Cross-National Regional Survey of Britain and Switzerland', *R&D Management*, Vol. 15, No. 3 (1985), pp. 207-18.

[40] *Industry and Trade Committee: Machine Tools, 1982-3*, p. xix.

[41] W. Ip and K. Vowels, 'The Machine Tool Market in the U.K.' (June 1999), www.dfait-maecl.ca/english/geo/europe@4208-e.htm

Technological and Business Development: British Machine Tools and the American Challenge, 1890-1914

'America beats the world.'

Introduction

This view of American technological superiority in machine tools, made by an informed immigrant engineer, Von Mayenberg, symbolised Britain's alleged backwardness in a key engineering industry.[1] On this side of the Atlantic, machine tool entrepreneurs, with knowledge of American practices, were equally critical of Britain's competitive performance. Charles Churchill, an American who had marketed and sold machine tools in London since 1865, alleged that the USA manufactured the finest lathes, planers, milling machines, and those tools used in the manufacture of other machines. In contrast, British makers were 'conservative and careful', and displayed 'very little disposition or inclination to copy American machine design'.[2] From the mid-1890s the British market was flooded with American machine imports, a response to the domestic boom in Britain, which was driven by investment in residential building, public utilities especially electricity and tramways, and the growth of new industries such as bicycles.[3] In this expansionary environment, what form did the American challenge take, were they better equipped to exploit the British market for machine tools, were domestic makers 'conservative' in their attitude to technological change, and how did British producers respond to the erosion of their competitive position?

British Industry and American Machine Tools

European manufacturing industry expanded rapidly in the mid-1890s, and machine tools were 'being bought in great quantities'. Unable to meet the demand, the European market provided American machine makers with a great opportunity,

---

[1] *American Machinist*, 4 March 1897, p. 182.

[2] *American Machinist*, 12 October 1896, p. 987.

[3] See E. Sigsworth and J. Blackman, 'The Home Boom of the 1890s', *Yorkshire Bulletin of Economic and Social Research*, Vol. 16/17 (1965/1966), pp. 75, 82.

which was reinforced by the preference of European manufacturers for American designs. American machine tool exports rose sharply, especially from 1895, and kept American machine tool shops 'busy'. The British Tariff Commission,[4] an unofficial committee of manufacturers formed in 1904, considered that American machine tool imports had achieved a considerable hold on the British market. In 1908 Britain imported from the U.S.A. 798 tons of machine tools valued at £99,014, compared to just 189 tons valued at £16,494 from all other countries.[5] German competition also intensified, and together with rising American exports into European and third world markets, the upswing in economic activity after 1895 represented a major opportunity for the diffusion of new machine tools. This, it has been argued, was given an added impetus by the boom in bicycle sales in Britain and Europe.[6] The mid-1890s therefore marked a sudden change in the foreign trading pattern for American makers, and before this date the impact of American machine tools on 'British engineering practice ... was minimal'.[7] Charles Churchill, who imported large numbers of American machine tools through his London business, could claim that prior to the 1890s the trade had mainly consisted of single orders, or at best a few machines for an individual machine shop, but by the mid-1890s invoices 'often took the form of complete equipments for the production of a certain machine or article'. In 1896, for example, the Cleveland Machine Screw Co. sold 50 machine tools to an English manufacturer for installation in a single plant, and their sales in the English market were expected to be around 200 during the year.[8] The rapid expansion of American machine tools in North-West European markets in the 1890s is graphically represented by the sales of two leading American producers, shown in Table 2.1.

American imports opened up questions about the technical competence of British machine tool makers. *The American Machinist* commented that 'it is at least possible that the relative merits of English and American machine tools have an important bearing on the fact that our tools go to England, but that English tools do not come here'.[9] American superiority was carefully considered by Charles Churchill, who believed that British makers were 'conservative', preferring to embody their own ideas into machine tool design. Further, British production methods were unable to build machines which could compete in price with that of American makers. Britain's competitive disadvantage, claimed Churchill, was related to the insufficient scale of production in British machine tool shops, which meant that they could not match the lower costs of American makers. Indeed,

---

[4] See A. Marrison, *British Business and Protectionism 1903-1932* (Oxford, Clarendon Press, 1996), Ch. 2.

[5] *American Machinist*, 4 March 1897, p. 182.

[6] J. Zeitlin, 'The Labour Strategies of British Engineering Employers, 1890-1922', in H. Gospel and C. R. Littler (eds), *Managerial Strategies and Industrial Relations* (London, Heinemann, 1983), p. 29; R. Floud, *The British Machine Tool Industry, 1850-1914* (Cambridge, Cambridge University Press, 1976), p. 73.

[7] Zeitlin, 'Labour Strategies, p. 29.

[8] *American Machinist*, 12 October 1896, p. 286; 12 July 1909, p. 987.

[9] *American Machinist*, 3 March 1898, p. 171.

Churchill was surprised at the inadequacies of the British in certain machine lines. For over 30 years, he claimed, his company had been distributing a variety of American drill and lathe chucks into the British market, selling between 500 to 800 per month, but he professed to know that there was not 'a single chuck maker in England'.[10] Churchill, as an American, may well have drawn too sharp a contrast between American and British practices, but he was not alone in his criticisms of the British industry.

Table 2.1
Foreign Shipments to North-West Europe of Machine Tools by Two American Machine Tool Firms, 1880-99

Brown & Sharpe		Bullard	
1880-4	84	1881-4	7
1885-9	633	1885-9	13
1890-4	431	1890-4	7
1895-9	2,560	1895-9	446

Source: Floud, *British Machine Tool Industry*, p. 82.

Joseph Horner, a practising engineer, was alarmed about the extent to which 'American machine tool builders had invaded the British market', especially to meet the rapidly growing demands of the booming bicycle industry.[11] Growing business confidence in the mid-1890s triggered a substantial rise in the number of bicycle factories from 497 in 1895 to 991 by 1897, and there was a corresponding doubling of the workforce from 20,923 to 42,775.[12] The bicycle boom opened up the market for American machine tool imports, but Horner was not impressed with the opinion that British makers were 'too busy to supply the requirements of the bicycle factories'. Passing this off as a 'mere excuse', he dismissed the allegation that British engineers and mechanics lacked the necessary skills and capabilities to compete with the Americans. Horner offered four reasons why the British machine tool industry seemed less adept at seizing the opportunity opened up by the bicycle boom.[13]

Firstly, Horner pointed out that in a world of growing international competition, in which Britain formed 'but one section of the world's workshops', it was not possible to maintain competitive advantage simply by relying on an endowment of mechanical genius'. A key capability of the machine tool maker was the importance attached to studying the 'precise work of users', and 'to cater for those wants as carefully as possible, unhindered by preconceived ideas and conservative prejudices'. Such an approach required concentrating on genuine

---

[10] *American Machinist*, 12 October 1896, p. 987.
[11] *American Machinist*, 30 December 1897, p. 969.
[12] R. Lloyd-Jones and M. J. Lewis, *Raleigh and the British Bicycle Industry, 1880-1960: An Economic and Business History* (Aldershot, Ashgate, 2000), p. 10.
[13] *American Machinist*, 30 December 1897, p. 969.

designs and a sharp attention to detail, and this included machine tool accessories, feeds and machine movements. The overall attention given to user needs would save time and contribute to raising the efficiency of machine tool manufacture. A second factor was the need to search for continuous improvement, and Horner urged British makers to recognise, as their American counterparts had apparently done, that there was 'no machine which is so good, but that it may be improved upon'.[14] Improvement innovations, a key feature of the process of technological change,[15] involved changes not only to the actual technical performance of the machine tool itself, but also to drawings, patterns, stamps and special tools which contributed to the overall efficiency of the final product. Thirdly, and echoing a comment of Charles Churchill, Horner stressed the importance of the relationship between the mechanical evolution of the machine and the scale of production. As mechanical complexity evolved, so an increase in the scale of production was needed to facilitate the implementation 'of a perfect shop system'. In turn, this would enable machine tool makers to develop the inter-changeability of parts, which would lower labour costs per unit of output. Fourthly, the available evidence showed that American machine shops were becoming increasingly specialised at a rate far greater than that of the British equivalent. American makers tended to focus their energies on a few types of machine tools, and Horner gave the examples of Warner & Swasey, brass-finishing tools, Gisholt & Co., heavy turret lathes, and Pratt & Whitney, lathes and screwing machines. In contrast, Horner cited the example of Tangye of Birmingham who, in addition to making machine tools, also manufactured 'cranes, engines, pumps, boilers and many other articles'. According to Horner, specialisation facilitated both innovatory improvement and more effective marketing. American firms accepted that there was no 'finality of design', and by dedicated marketing of machine brands innovative American firms, such as Cincinnati Grinders, 'became as well known by name and number as the Whitworth thread and the Morse tapers'.[16] In contrast, many of Britain's older machine tool firms by the late nineteenth century had evolved from general engineering concerns and continued to combine machine tool production with the manufacture of other tools, equipment and engineering products. In the British case, 'there is very little evidence of increasing specialisation on machine tool production alone'.[17]

The consequence of British deficiencies was an American assault on the domestic market. Horner, for example, claimed that not only had American makers ousted British screwing machines from the bicycle shops, but they were also able to supply a range of automatic machine tools which could be operated without skilled labour. Comparatively, British machine tool designs, to secure the best results, still depended upon the deployment of skilled operatives. As Horner

---

[14] *American Machinist*, 30 December 1896, p. 969.

[15] N. Rosenberg, *Perspectives on Technology* (Cambridge, Cambridge University Press, 1976), p. 73.

[16] *American Machinist*, 30 December 1896, p. 969.

[17] Floud, *British Machine Tool Industry*, p. 42. See also S. B. Saul, 'The Machine Tool Industry in Britain to 1914', *Business History*, Vol. 10 (1968).

observed, Britain's hopes of recovering market share depended upon long-term investment in designing 'superior machines', and this meant they had 'a long leeway to make up' as it 'is vastly easier to lose a market than to recover it'. The Stanley Show of 1897, the main trade fair of the bicycle industry, demonstrated the competitive pressure on the British maker, the light lathes on display being mainly of American design. Horner observed that the American machines incorporated the latest designs, while the small numbers of British models displayed were 'much as they were 30 years ago'. More innovative British firms were not represented, and Horner noted that the best British lathes were made by firms who built their machines to 'a greater or lesser degree to American design', and followed 'American methods'. Welcoming the fact that replication of American practices had 'grown up in recent years', Horner also accepted that it illustrated 'the adage that imitation is the sincerest form of flattery'.[18] Assimilation of American technology, as we shall see later, was an important factor in the evolution of Britain's largest machine tool maker, Alfred Herbert.

Nevertheless, contemporary opinion in the 1890s projected an unflattering image of the British machine tool industry. Compared to their American competitors, the British were allegedly conservative in design, generalist rather than specialist, over-reliant on skilled labour inputs, slow to reap the benefits of economies of scale, and lacking in innovatory drive and marketing skills. Further, progressive firms in the industry were mere imitators of American designs and practices. Indeed, the American invasion set in motion 'some decidingly plain talk ... by English engineers'.[19] One such engineer, Herbert Austin, who in 1898 was the works manager of the Wolsely Sheep Shearing Co. of Birmingham, which he had joined in 1893 following a period in Australia where he had managed an engineering company, was to design the first Wolsley car in 1895, and in 1901 to combine machine tool manufacture with that of motor cars.[20] Austin did not mince his words when he remarked that the 'continued prattling about the ignorant conservatism of the English and the wonderful adaptability of the American is enough to make a man sick'. Accusations of conservatism, Austin claimed, were contradictory when British engineering firms purchased large numbers of 'improved' American machine tools. The British, he claimed, were not 'blind protectionists ... purchasing tools only of local make'. Cosmopolitanism, consistent with the principles of orthodox free traders, was Austin's vision: 'If the Americans have all the best factories for making tools, by all means let them make them and we will be content to use them'.[21]

Commenting on debates about the performance of the late nineteenth century engineering industry in Britain, Zeitlin has argued that the introduction of automatic machines can be 'seen as exemplifying a progressive entrepreneurial

---

[18] *American Machinist*, 30 December 1896, p. 970.

[19] *American Machinist*, 20 June 1898, p. 59.

[20] Floud, *British Machine Tool Industry*, p. 44.

[21] *American Machinist*, 3 March 1898, p. 164. For a discussion on free trade orthodoxy see A. Howe, 'Free Trade and the Victorians', in A. Marrison (ed.), *Free Trade and its Reception, 1815-1960: Vol. 1, Freedom and Trade* (London, Routledge, 1998).

response to foreign competition'.[22] Indeed, James Vose, a Manchester engineer, commenting on the recent introduction of American machine tools, observed that 'I do not find any real jealousy of them on the part of most tool makers here'. British makers, he claimed, were quite prepared to accept the superiority of American machines in terms of design, but they were also able to show equally commendable aspects of British ingenuity. British machine shops widely employed American machines, and Vose saw this as good practice because 'the importation of American machines ... has caused and will continue to cause, discussion on the principles of tool making and tends to improve the design of tools on both sides of the Atlantic'. Implicitly raising the issue of technological transfer, Vose strongly advocated 'the best tools for any purpose can generally be selected from either one source or the other'.[23] The alleged conservatism of British makers was clearly challenged by contemporaries, and this is supported by Floud's examination of new entrants into the British machine tool industry at the end of the nineteenth century. Entrepreneurs such as Alfred Herbert, Coventry, James Archdale, Birmingham, William Asquith, Halifax, James Smith of Dean, Smith and Grace, Keighley, and Thomas Craven, Manchester, had a common characteristic in that they had 'served five years time as an apprentice mechanical engineer'. Consequently, Floud argues that successful entrepreneurship was related to the fact that managers acquired 'technical expertise and training', and this was related to the importance of innovation in the machine tool trade. Successful firms depended upon a flow of new ideas, new markets or sub-innovations in the form of adaptations to existing machines.[24]

The market environment conducive to the American 'invasion' of the 1890s was also prescribed by the short-run phenomena of the bicycle boom, but whether this represented a genuine long-run breakthrough remained an open question. Certainly, for Herbert Austin, the Americans had made only short-term gains, and he warned them against a belief that their 'product is ousting the home made article'. British makers were working at full capacity, 'three to six months behind in their contracts', but as Austin concluded, 'the present demand is a temporary one'. Further, while American makers might have been more adept at supplying the British market than domestic producers, they were not above rapprochement. A London agent importing machine tools in 1899 referred to delays in delivery, and of 'the unsatisfactory conditions of some American machine tools'. He asserted that previously it had been the exception for a British importer to receive a consignment of badly finished goods from the U.S., but he regretted to say 'that lately a very good deal of that shipped has been badly finished', and had been 'utterly rejected by buyers'. Although the agent

---

[22] Zeitlin, 'Labour Strategies', p. 25. For a discussion on the performance of British engineering, see Saul, S. B., 'The Engineering Industry', in D. H. Aldcroft (ed.), *British Industry and Foreign Competition, 1870-1914* (London, Allen and Unwin, 1968); S. B. Saul, 'The Market and the Development of the Mechanical Engineering Industries in Britain, 1860-1914', *Economic History Review*, Vol. 20 (1967).

[23] *American Machinist*, 14 July 1898, pp. 524-5.

[24] Floud, *British Machine Tool Industry*, pp. 47-8.

acknowledged the general superiority of American machines to their British equivalents, he feared that the Americans were 'in danger of losing their reputation'. A key factor in breaking the resistance of British users to American imports had been the ability of the Americans to execute prompt delivery of superior finished machine tools. However, according to the London agent delays in contracted delivery time of between 6 to 9 months, and the 'strategy of sending over inferior articles' from America, did 'more damage ... in one month ... than could be repaired in 12'.[25]

Over-extended the American machine tool industry may have been in the British market, but more damning was the alleged 'economic gap' between machine tool makers in the two countries, a function, as we have seen, of the alleged reluctance of the British maker to specialise. British makers tended to build a wide range of different machine tools, while the Americans focused on the high volume output of a small range. Even a progressive firm, such as Alfred Herbert of Coventry, whose market reputation had been strengthened by the accolades it received in the trade press for its technical capabilities, rejected a strategy of concentrating production on a narrow range of machine tools. Its founder, Alfred Herbert, recounting his early days in the business, stated that:

> It has often been suggested to me that we should have done better if we had specialised more intensively on a limited range of machines. There is no doubt much force in this contention; but in the early days I doubt very much whether there was scope for a growing business, which confined itself to the production of one or two machines. Rightly, or wrongly, I was attracted by the idea of covering a fairly wide field.[26]

Alfred's business experience suggests that the distinction made by contemporaries between American and British practices may be too sharply drawn, and Floud has pointed out that there are different forms of specialisation. A maker might manufacture a wide range of machines, or 'a small number of types', or machines which were dedicated for use by specialised customers 'with particular technical requirements', and often situated in 'a particular geographical location'. The relationship between makers and users in Britain was different from that of the U.S.A., and according to Floud the British tended to design their machine tools to meet the requirements of the user who had a particular product specification to meet. Once the machine tool was installed, there would be little need for the user to modify it or adapt it. In contrast, the American system encouraged the maker 'to produce a range of machine tools, designed to perform particular operations, but not specifically designed to meet the specific needs of any one user'. Considerable contemporary discussion occurred concerning the relative merits of the two systems, but Floud maintains that the evidence available provides no clear indication of the greater efficiency of one system over the other. Acknowledging that the Americans probably produced higher volume output per

---

[25] *American Machinist*, 14 September 1899, p. 874.
[26] Cited in Floud, *British Machine Tool Industry*, p. 53.

machine than did the British, Floud, nevertheless remains unconvinced that the resulting difference in unit costs were that significant. He speculates that the two systems may have been on a convergent path, with British makers beginning 'to specialise in fewer tools, and the American manufacturers to make more specialised tools'.[27]

Firms specialised along a customer and regional path, and four regional centres of machine tool production can be located in Britain, each specialising in different types of machine tools. Manchester, particularly Broadheath, was associated with the needs of textile machinery makers. In the Midlands, firms producing a large range of machines of the type required for repetition work evolved, suitable for small arms, bicycle and motor manufacture. The Glasgow region tended to concentrate on the heavier types of tools associated with shipbuilding and marine engineering, whereas in the Halifax-Leeds region, including Keighley, Huddersfield, Sowerby Bridge, local machine tools were generally regarded as 'being simpler in design' than their competitors across the Pennines. The pattern of specialisation in Britain took on a different form to that of the U.S.A., where there was a concentration on the 'manufacture of a restricted range'. American makers worked to a 'plan, to which all industries in this country tend', and this confined 'their energies and skills to implements of one kind, and in some cases to a few sizes of all kinds'.[28]

What was evident, however, was the enormous capacity that the American machine tool industry was developing, and this raised the importance of the British and continental markets as outlets to sustain the enlarged supply emanating from American shops. 'The gravest problem' confronting the American machine tool trade in 1900, was 'how to get the returns for its productiveness'. For example, in the machine tool centre of Cincinnati output had expanded by an estimated 40 to 75 per cent between 1898 and 1900, and not surprisingly the industrial markets of Britain and Europe were crucially important in keeping American machine shops at 'full' capacity.[29] It is too simplistic, therefore, to interpret the American 'invasion' of the British market as the outcome of specialist machine tool firms in the U.S. sweeping aside outmoded and generalist British makers. In part, the 'invasion' was driven by the needs of American producers for markets, and the fact that the mature British market offered rich opportunities. The significant question

---

[27] Ibid., pp. 57-9, 61.

[28] Ibid., pp. 52-5; R. Lloyd-Jones and M. J. Lewis, 'Technological Pathways, Mode of Development, and the British National Innovation System: Examples from British industry, 1880-1914', in L. Tissote and B. Veyrassat (eds), *Technological Trajectories, Markets, Institutions. Industrialised Countries Nineteenth and Twentieth Centuries* (Bern, Peter Lang, 2001), p. 149; R. Lloyd-Jones and M. J. Lewis, 'Business Networks, Social Habits, and the Evolution of a Regional Industrial Cluster: Coventry 1880-1930s', in J. F. Wilson and A. Popp (eds), *Industrial Clusters and Regional Business Network in England, 1750-1990* (Aldershot, Ashgate, 2003), p. 233; A. J. Arnold, 'Innovation, Deskilling and Profitability in the British Machine Tool Industry: Alfred Herbert, 1887-1927', *Journal of Industrial History*, Vol. 1, No. 2 (1999); *American Machinist*, 17 April 1899, p. 351, 27 April 1899, p. 353.

[29] *American Machinist*, 10 April 1900, p. 340.

in the study of the evolution of the British machine tool industry is how did it respond to the entrepreneurial and technological challenge of the U.S.A.?

Declinism: Institutional Constraints and Path Dependency

Of all the debates in British economic history, that of the alleged relative decline of the British economy between 1870 and 1914 is perhaps the most enduring.[30] The debate stretches back to the period itself, an editorial in *The American Machinist* of 1901 enquiring 'What is the matter with British industry?' Despite the fact that there was no 'agreement' on the question, a list of deficiencies familiar to the modern economic historian was rolled out. These included a lack of adequate technical education, the resistance of trade unions to changes in technology and work practices, conservative entrepreneurs wedded to existing forms of business organisation, and a general unwillingness to adopt new methods or to be receptive to new ways of doing things. At the same time, the journal was obliged to point out that 'there is that contingent that contends that there is nothing whatever the matter with Great Britain's industries'.[31] In a modern interpretation, Elbaum and Lazonick have claimed that it was institutional rigidities and constraints that held back British industry, and consequently the root cause of the alleged decline could not be the quality of British entrepreneurship. The institutional constraints that are highlighted include industrial relations and technical education, enterprise and market organisation, and finance and international trade.[32] Informing this approach is the notion of path dependency, based on the assumption that contemporary entrepreneurs were constrained in their business behaviour by an 'institutional legacy' associated with an 'atomistic nineteenth century organisation'.[33] This raises the probability that there exist important diversities 'in the organisation of capitalist economies and the institutionally mediated paths of national economic development'.[34] That is, national economies may well experience more or less distinct national innovation systems, and consequently their responses to 'common

---

[30] The literature is extensive, but see D. C. Coleman and C. Macleod, 'Attitudes to New Techniques: British Businessmen 1800-1950', *Economic History Review*, Vol. 24, No. 4 (1986); B. Elbaum and W. Lazonick (eds), *The Decline of the British Economy* (Oxford, Oxford University Press, 1986); Dormois and Dintenfass (eds), *The British Industrial Decline*; S. Pollard, *Britain's Prime and Britain's Decline: The British Economy 1870-1914* (London, Edward Arnold, 1989).

[31] *American Machinist*, 27 July 1901, p. 770.

[32] B. W. Elbaum and W. Lazonick, 'An Institutional Perspective on British Decline', in Elbaum and Lazonick (eds), *Decline of the British Economy*, p. 2.

[33] E. Abe, 'The Technological Strategy of a Leading Iron and Steel Firm: Bolkow Vaughn & Co. Ltd.: Late Victorian Industrialists Did Fail', *Business History*, Vol. 38, No. 1 (1996), p. 47.

[34] J. Zysman, 'How Institutions Create Historically Rooted Trajectories of Growth?', *Industrial and Corporate Change*, Vol. 3 (1994); Lloyd-Jones and Lewis, 'Technological Pathways', p. 118.

or related changes thrown up by the course of world technological development, such as the second industrial revolution', may well differ significantly.[35]

Empirical evidence in support of the diversity in technological response may be gleaned from *The American Machinist*, which was well aware of the importance of machine tools to the industrial advances associated with the second industrial revolution.[36] In 1900 *The American Machinist*, referring to an article in the *Engineer*, observed that the British trade journal initially responded positively to the American machine tool 'invasion' of the British market, and was somewhat critical of British machine tool practices. But the *Engineer* quickly indulged in 'backsliding' and articulated the view that 'Nothing that came from without the British Isles was of much account in its eyes'. According to the *Engineer*, the domestic machine tool industry, and indeed British engineering in general, produced work of the highest quality, and the established reputation of its firms meant that 'The best of everything is still made in England and those who want the best must come to us to supply their wants'. The *Engineer* accepted that some of 'our old works, our largest and most famous ... are antiquated in arrangement and design', but contended that so would 'hundreds of American works' be so in '50 years hence'. What, the *Engineer* speculated, should future American entre-preneurs do when they were faced by a new wave of technological change? Should they, for example, 'utterly cast out the ways of their fathers and grand fathers [and] will they be able to stamp out tradition?'[37] 'No' was the answer; the Americans would most probably do what the British were doing at the turn of the nineteenth century and make the best use of the means they had at hand. 'They would modify and renew just as our manufacturers do now, but with caution and discretion ... not with immediate haste ... which marks some of their movement today. That restless stirring for the foremost place will be a nightmare of the past'.[38]

In this scenario, the historical pathway of American industrial development would evolve institutional habits that would constrain its own capacity to adapt to future technological and competitive challenges. *The American Machinist*, however, was not convinced, and contended that the interpretation placed on the issue by the *Engineer* was a 'factual misconception of the conditions under which American methods have been developed'. Thus, the British tended to 'keep the old machinery turning over as long as it would be made to do the work'. In comparison, American methods were to scrap machines as soon as a newer one could be innovated that produced a 'sufficient increase of product to pay the required interest on the investment'. The difference in technical practice was put down to differences in the environment of the two countries, and the *Engineer*

---

[35] Lloyd-Jones and Lewis, 'Technological Pathways', pp. 128-9. See also C. Freeman, 'The National Innovation System in Historical Perspective', *Cambridge Journal of Economics*, Vol. 19 (1995).

[36] See J. P. Hull, 'From Rostow to Chandler to You: How Revolutionary was the Second Industrial Revolution?', *Journal of European Economic History*, Vol. 25, No. 1 (1996), pp. 192-7.

[37] *American Machinist*, 6 October 1900, p. 895.

[38] Ibid.

itself mentioned that simply 'transplanting' American methods and technology to Britain 'could lead to no good results'.[39] This controversy in 1900 anticipates the observations of Rosenberg that 'today's technical possibilities are dependent upon yesterday's actions in the quality of factor endowments'.[40]

Concepts such as path dependency and national innovation systems carry considerable explanatory power in the study of the process of technological change, but there is also a need for caution.[41] Transplanting technology between British and American firms did occur during the second industrial revolution, and it did lead to some positive business results in key industries such as machine tools. At the broad industry level it is reasonable to suppose that British institutional attitudes to technological change were path dependent, but at the level of the individual firm there were a number of examples of good practice, not unrelated to American influence, that helped to establish a viable British machine tool industry by the eve of the First World War. The next section explores some of the business and technological responses of British machine tool firms to the competitive challenge they confronted in the two decades before 1914.

British Machine Tool Firms and American Practice

The surge of American imports to Britain and the continent from the second half of the 1890s has been explained on the one hand by American foresight in meeting the needs of users who had failed to acquire the machine tools they required from indigenous supplies. On the other hand, the American's 'inventive genius' enabled them to develop a range of products which could not be constructed abroad. While the Americans expected that Britain and Western Europe would react to their challenge and develop their own machine tool capabilities, they still took for granted that their machine makers would retain a technological lead. Indeed, American technological knowledge of machine tool production and design 'was not exported with the tools' that they produced, and the 'inventive facility' was retained in the U.S. This did not mean, however, that British firms were technically moribund, or were reduced to simple imitators of American designs and methods.[42]

Floud's analysis of the trade directories suggests that there were approximately 350 to 400 firms producing machine tools in Britain in the early 1900s, and this number probably fell to around 250 by 1910-13 (Table 2.5). The figures are problematic because of the difficulties associated with disentangling those firms who were specialist machine tool producers from those who produced machine tools as part of a range of engineering products, the latter typified by

---

[39] Ibid.

[40] N. Rosenberg, *Exploring the Black Box: Technology, Economics and History* (Cambridge, Cambridge University Press, 1994), p. 10.

[41] For recent work in this area see R. Nelson, *The Sources of Economic Growth* (Harvard, Harvard University Press, 1996); D. Archibugi, J. Howells and J. Michie (eds), *Innovation Policy in a Global Economy* (Cambridge, Cambridge University Press, 1999).

[42] *American Machinist*, 1 December 1900, p. 1,076.

Greenwood & Batley of Leeds, the main case study employed by Floud.[43] Nevertheless, Floud's estimates are a useful benchmark and lead us to a key question. How many of the firms identified by Floud may be described as leading or entrepreneurial firms who adopted an innovatory strategy to meet the American competitive challenge? This in itself proves a major challenge, because as Floud observes, 'the evidence concerning the operation of individual firms comes primarily from the large and successful firms',[44] while, as Schumpeter informs us, the innovative firms associated with periods of rapid change were inevitably new and initially small enterprises.[45] Surviving business records of firms in the British industry, such as Alfred Herbert, Webster & Bennett, J. Butler & Co, and Greenwood & Batley do provide some useful insight into their evolution, but are too limited and fragmentary to make a case for a cluster of innovative firms at the beginning of the twentieth century. It is possible, however, to record those British firms which were reported to have introduced new products or sub-innovatory improvements, and new plant or extensions incorporating modern design and work practices. These were reported in *The American Machinist*, a trade journal not particularly receptive to British machine tool practices, but which fastidiously surveyed machine tool design in its pages. The survey enables the identification of a core of firms that were at, or close to, the cutting edge of machine tool design in the first decade of the twentieth century.

Taking the year 1903, and accepting the number of firms in the industry as 315 in 1900, Table 2.2 shows the number of firms recorded in *The American Machinist*, and also differentiates firms by the number of times they were reported in the journal. In total, 75 firms were recorded at least once, while 25 firms (Table 2.3) were recorded 3 or more times. Table 2.3 should be considered with caution, as there were no doubt variations between the regional correspondents in their recordings of the activities of firms, and there is, for example, a suspicion that the Birmingham correspondent was less adept at recording firms than in other districts, or at least recording firms in Coventry. The latter was a rapidly emerging machine tool centre at the end of the nineteenth century, boosted initially by the cycle boom of the mid-1890s, but apart from Alfred Herbert the only other Coventry machine tool firm recorded was that of Webster & Bennett. Nevertheless, the data does indicate a core of firms that were innovatory in 1903, and these range from a minimum of 25 to an upper limit of 70. Thus we can assume that nearly one in five British machine tool firms were sufficiently innovative and enterprising to draw the attention of *The American Machinist* at the beginning of the century. It would seem that foreign competition had stimulated British manufacturers, both machine tool makers and users, and there was at the beginning of the twentieth century both a 'steady demand for English made machine tools', in particular for lathes, planers, shapers and milling machines, and significant advances made in workshop

---

[43] Floud, *British Machine Tool Industry*, p. 32.
[44] Ibid.
[45] J. A. Schumpeter, *Capitalism, Socialism and Democracy* (London, Routledge, 1994), chs. 7-8.

practices. In addition, new developments in tool steel provided a technological and business stimulus to British machine tool makers. Prior to the main breakthrough in high speed steel in 1900, the main production of high quality tool steel was provided by 'Mushet steel', produced by Samuel Osborn of Sheffield and 'other varieties of steel-hardening tool steel [that] held sway in the engineering workshops around the world'. This form of tool steel perpetuated a 'rule of thumb' approach as 'each mechanic was allowed to have his tools forged and ground individually, with no regard whatever to the earning power of machine tools'.[46]

Table 2.2
British Machine Tool Firms Recorded in *The American Machinist*, 1903

Times Reporting	No. of Firms	Total No. of Firms	% of Total
1	71	315	22.5
2	46	315	14.6
3+	25	315	7.9

Source: *The American Machinist* for 1903.

Developments in high speed steel, attributed to the Americans Frederick William Taylor and Maunsel White in 1899 ended the rule of thumb approach, but it was in Sheffield where the new alloys were rapidly exploited and diffused. In 1901 Seebohm & Dieckstahl of Sheffield became the first British company to produce high speed steel, and this firm was rapidly followed by Thomas Firth, Edgar Allen, Cocker Bros., John Brown & Co., Jones & Colver, Samuel Osborne, Vickers, Son & Maxim and Joseph Beardshaw & Co. The technical requirements of specialist steel production introduced a more scientific approach to steel manufacture, and its cutting power opened up new opportunities for British machine tool makers.[47] By 1905 British makers were sending high speed twist drill and other cutting tools all over the world.[48] The technical interdependence between high speed steel manufacturers and their users, the machine tool makers, was emphasised by H. Spear, the London agent of Joseph Beardshaw. In the 1890s the company had promoted the sale of its specialist 'Profile Steel' for machine tools, and in 1900 Spear informed the management that recent developments in high speed steel were receiving the attention of machine makers. The success of the steel business, Spear argued, now depended upon the 'recommendation' of

---

[46] *American Machinist*, 10 October 1903, p. 754E.

[47] G. Tweedale, *Steel City. Entrepreneurship, Strategy and Technology in Sheffield, 1743-1993* (Oxford, Clarendon Press, 1995), pp. 113-16; G. Tweedale, *Sheffield Steel and America: A Century of Commercial and Technological Interdependence, 1830-1930* (Cambridge, Cambridge University Press, 1987), pp. 34, 65; *American Machinist*, 27 February 1904, p. 117E.

[48] M. J. Lewis, 'The Growth and Development of Sheffield's Industrial Structure, 1880-1930', unpublished Ph.D., Sheffield Hallam University (1990), p. 148.

machine makers such as Alfred Herbert 'of your tool steel to the users of their machine tools'. The advent of automatic machine tools had given a new priority for steel manufacturers to develop specialist materials to meet the requirements of users.[49]

Table 2.3
List of Machine Tool Firms Recorded 3+ Times for 1903 by Region

Firm	Recordings	Location
		Yorkshire Region:
Maud & Turner	4	Halifax
C. Redman & Sons	5	Halifax
William Asquith & Co.	4	Halifax
Carter & Wright	3	Halifax
George Swift	5	Halifax
Ward, Haggis & Smith	3	Keighley
David Brown & Sons	4	Huddersfield
John Dickinson & Co.	3	Keighley
Darling & Sellers	3	Halifax
James Butler	3	Halifax
		Midland Region:
James Archdale & Co.	4	Birmingham
Taylor & Challen Ltd.	4	Birmingham
Charles Taylor	4	Birmingham
Tangye Tool & Electric Co.	4	Birmingham
E. G. Wrigley & Co.	3	Birmingham
Alfred Herbert Ltd.	3	Coventry
		Manchester Region:
Kendal & Gent	4	Manchester
Hulse & Co.	5	Salford
Hetherington & Co.	5	Manchester
George Richards & Co.	3	Broadheath
		Glasgow Region:
Louden Bros.	7	Johnstone
Jonathan Lang & Co.	7	Johnstone
Whyte & Waddell	5	Johnstone
Thomas Shanks & Co.	3	Johnstone

Source: *The American Machinist* for 1903.

High speed steel offered new design opportunities to British makers. American makers tended to build less robust machine tools than the British, 'who have perhaps always been more accustomed to heavy drives and course cuts'.

---

[49] Sheffield City Archives, MD7091 (5), Records of Joseph Beardshaw & Co., Minute Book of H. Spear, 28 December 1894, 20 July 1900.

Specialist steels, however, offered the potential for British makers to bring standards in line with the American 'demand for lathes to take cuts 1 inch deep by 1/8 inch wide and at cutting speeds from 130 to 150 feet a minute so as to utilise the capabilities of the new tool steel'. British lathe manufacturers were not slow to seize the opportunity. In 1903 Joshua Buckton & Co. of Leeds completed the production of several 12 inch lathes specially designed for high speed cutting, utilising 'the full capabilities of the new tool steels in the way of heavy traverses and deep cutting'. Manufacturers of planing machines were also quick off the mark. The small Halifax firm of Cornelius Redman & Sons, founded 1871, began experimental work on new planing machines utilising high speed steel. A visitor to their works observed that operating under high speed the performance of the machines 'under this heavy duty was remarkable', and the potential increase in production had not been reached 'even with the new high grade steels'. By early 1903 Redman's were offering for sale large stocks of a variety of new and different types of machines, 'all ... designed to work the high speed steels'. Quick to realise the potential demand from users, Redman's embarked upon an ambitious extension programme during 1903 'to facilitate ... a greater output by systematic methods'. Their production programme was now geared to manufacture machines in 'groups', enabling the stocking of large quantities of standardised components. Expansion and standardisation was aimed at enabling the firm to double its output, but with 'no intention of increasing the variety of machine tools they manufacture'. The management of the firm had great 'confidence in their policy' and recognised the need to specialise in the manufacture of planing, drilling and shaping machines, as well as lathes.[50]

Within the Yorkshire region there was 'a healthy rivalry' between makers in the main machine tool centres of Halifax, Keighley and Leeds who were introducing 'specially designed lathes for working with the high speed cutting steels'.[51] Another enterprising Halifax firm, James Butler & Co., had developed in 1902 a heavy lathe specially designed for high speed cutting, and by October 1903 had just finished the production of four 'newly designed 12 inch centre high speed lathes [of] exceptional power and strength'. The firm was also manufacturing a larger 18 inch centre high speed lathe which it was supplying under government contract to Natal, as well as wheel lathes for a number of Indian state railways. By 1904 Butler's was producing for the Natal government gap, surfacing and boring lathes with electrically driven drives.[52] A pioneer of radial drilling machines, William Asquith of Halifax, had in 1902 introduced high speed cutting steels. In another Yorkshire centre of engineering, Keighley, five firms in 1903 were utilising high speed steel in their production designs. Darling and Sellers were marketing several new patented lathes and gear cutting machines 'embodying all the latest improvements'. John Dickinson & Co. was producing high speed cutting lathes. Ward Haggas & Smith were about to place on the market a new lathe specially designed for high

[50] *American Machinist*, 2 May 1902, p. 253E; 7 February 1903, p. 68E; 29 August 1903, p. 631E; 17 October 1903, p. 772E; 5 December 1903, p. 910E.

[51] *American Machinist*, 12 July 1902, p. 429E.

[52] *American Machinist*, 17 October 1903, p. 772E; 16 January 1904, p. 1,026E.

cutting steels for the motor car industry, a decision which had involved a doubling of its plant size since 1901, and Dean, Smith & Grace had introduced high speed tools utilising the knowledge of their new tool room manager, C. Caton, appointed from Birmingham.[53] In the Manchester region Hulse & Co. had gained a reputation for their patented twin screw shifting lathes, and were in 1903 introducing new designs 'for high speed cutting', which was to use electrical power for driving. Hulse specialised in heavy machine tools, and manufactured the 'Snowden' patented turning, drilling and screwing machine that was in high demand from government dockyards and shipbuilding and marine engineering works. An important centre of machine tool making in the Manchester region was Broadheath, and here George Richards & Co., a firm which was to build a long-term reputation for its products, was producing a range of machine tools, including boring and turning mills, planing, radial drilling, slotting and key cutting machines, their latest models designed to be applied with high speed steels. Their new machines were apparently well received, the company having 18 orders on its books in September 1903.[54]

A paper presented by Percy Vernon, of Alfred Herbert, to the Manchester Association of Engineers, outlined the potential of the new tool steels. Vernon emphasised that the greatly increased cutting power and speeds of the new tool steels, would inevitably place the onus on makers and users to experiment with new machine tool designs. Using the example of the large engineering firm of Armstrong-Whitworth, which was trialling high-speed tool steel, he urged the need for both makers and users to recognise its implications for production engineering.[55] Vernon, of course, was a manager of the leading firm in the Midlands, Herbert's, and this region was host to a number of progressive machine tool producers. In 1902 Herbert's exhibited its improved vertical drilling machine at a trade fair in Wolverhampton, designed to enable specialised high speed work, and targeted at the increasing demand for such machines from the motor-vehicle industry of the Midlands. In Birmingham, Charles Taylor marketed a new capstan lathe for light working on steel and brass tubes in 1903, delivering lower costs compared to ordinary lathes. Further claims of improved productivity through faster cutting speeds were made by James Archdale of Birmingham who patented a new screw thread milling machine designed for cutting internal and external screw threads in boiler tubes.[56]

In the Glasgow district of Scotland, 'Fast cutting tool steel' came into wider use in the early twentieth century, convincing machine makers who had delayed its application 'that the new steel had become a necessary accessory for up-to-date machine tools'. This trend was not lost on Loudon Bros. of Johnstone who in May 1903 were redesigning 'a number of their new lathes for the use of the new high speed cutting steel which is fast coming into adoption in Scottish machine tool

---

[53] *American Machinist*, 10 May 1902, p. 253E; 7 June 1902, p. 339E; 4 April 1903, p. 213E; E. Grierson, *A Little Farm Well Tilled* (Keighley, Dean, Smith & Grace, 1955), pp. 42-3.

[54] *American Machinist*, 5 September 1903, p. 651E; 19 September 1903, p. 694E.

[55] *American Machinist*, 5 December 1903, p. 911E.

[56] *American Machinist*, 21 March 1903, pp. 173E, 178E.

works'. Similarly John Lang & Son of Johnstone were also active in placing new lathes on the market in 1903, which were widely reported in the trade press.[57]

In the four main producing districts there was evidence of new design innovation in response to the need to exploit the opportunities opened up by the increasing supply of high speed tool steel. This, in turn, triggered off 'keen competition among the tool builders', and led a number of firms to extend and modernise their plant (Table 2.4). In its review of the British machine tool trade for 1903, *The American Machinist* claimed that the main advances for the year were the increasing use of high speed steel, particularly by the leading makers, the diffusion of electrically driven machine tools, and the 'large number of firms who have enlarged or built new works for the more economical production of machine tools'.[58] A core of British machine tool firms that deployed their organisational and technical capabilities to respond positively to the competitive and technological challenges at the beginning of the twentieth century can be identified. However, as Floud argues, the diffusion of new machine tools, using high speed steel and electrically driven motors in Britain was 'a very gradual process ... largely because of the inertia of many potential customers', and the competitive challenge that indigenous firms faced from American makers, not least because they placed a high value on the British market.[59] Certainly, American makers did not forego the opportunity to exploit their foothold in the British market. For example, the importing firm of Charles Churchill stocked the latest designs of American machine tools in 1904, their salesroom fully equipped to demonstrate 'any machine tool in actual working operation'. Included in its 'latest American novelties' was the Kinsey Burt bench filing machine, allowing mechanical filing'.[60]

Table 2.4
Machine Tool Firms Reporting Extension and Modernisation of Plant, 1902-3

Firm	Location
David Brown	Keighley
E. A. Wrigley	Birmingham
Smith, Barker & Wilson	Halifax
Tangye	Birmingham
Smith & Coventry	Manchester
James Butler & Co.	Halifax
Craven Bros.	Manchester
William Asquith	Halifax
Alfred Herbert	Coventry
Greenwood & Batley	Leeds

Source: *The American Machinist*, 1902-3.

---

[57] *American Machinist*, 4 April 1903, p. 212E; 2 May 1903, p. 293E.
[58] *American Machinist*, 16 January 1904, p. 1,026E.
[59] Floud, *British Machine Tool Industry*, p. 25.
[60] *American Machinist*, 23 January 1904, p. 16E.

Nevertheless, British makers responded to competitive pressures by forms of collaboration at the intra and inter regional levels, and reduced the cost of knowledge acquisition and transfer by inserting themselves into a set of business networks. The most dynamic example of this can be found in the rapidly growing Midland industrial region, associated with newly emerging machine tool entrepreneurs and typified by the activities of Alfred Herbert, a seed corn firm in the industry.[61]

Alfred Herbert and Regional Business Networks

The empirical investigation of business networks present formidable problems, not least because they are often informal in character and tend to transcend simple economic transactions between firms.[62] Accepting this caveat, it is nevertheless possible to show that in expanding machine tool centres in the Midlands, such as Coventry, there evolved from the 1880s a cluster of interconnected industries, characterised by a common set of production technologies.[63] Within this cluster important seed corn firms such as Herbert's emerged, tapping into the growing demand by the engineering industry for machine tools. As Table 2.5 shows, the 1890s was clearly associated with a major growth of machine tool firms in the Midlands, and their rising contribution to the industry's business structure.

Table 2.5
Data on the British Machine Tool Industry, 1870-1913

	No. Firms	No. in Midlands	Output of Leading Firms (£)	Output Excluding Herbert's (£)	% Herbert's
1870	131	12	32,238	-	
1890	228	22	227,481	219,532	3.5
1900	315	53	497,648	379,994	25.7
1913	250	64	1,219,878	693, 925	42.1

Source: Floud, *British Machine Tool Industry*, pp. 33, 36-7, 41.

In manufacturing centres such as Coventry, a set of interrelated business firms emerged that embraced bicycle manufacture, engineering component manufacture, motor vehicle production, and machine tools. At the centre of these

---

[61] The following section is based on Lloyd-Jones and Lewis, 'Business Networks'.

[62] See J. F. Wilson and A. Popp, 'Districts, Networks and Clusters in England: An Introduction'; M. Casson, 'An Economic Approach to Regional Business Networks', both in Wilson and Popp (eds), *Industrial Clusters*.

[63] See D. Thoms and T. Donnelly, 'Coventry's Industrial Economy, 1880-1980', in B. Lancaster and T. Mason (eds), *Life and Labour in a Twentieth Century City: The Experience of Coventry* (Coventry, Cryfield Press, n.d.), pp. 11-56.

activities was Herbert's, whose early development and its rise to prominence in the industry, owed much to the expanding bicycle trade. Founded in 1887, the company began by producing a range of components and machine tools for the Coventry bicycle trade, as well as machinery for the ribbon trade.[64] Bicycle production stimulated machine tools in Coventry, and Herbert's, 'among others, took its share in the designing and building of machines particularly suitable for the bicycle trade'.[65] The company's early association with the bicycle industry set a technological pathway for future product development, as Herbert's diversified into supplying firms in general engineering, as well as manufacturers in the emerging Coventry motor vehicle industry. In 1914 Herbert's was one of 17 firms in Coventry, 'generally of somewhat greater size than firms in other areas and specialising in support for the local cycle, motor and small arms trades'.[66] The output of the British machine tool industry increased significantly between 1890 and 1913, and central to this expansion was Herbert's which accounted for 42.1 per cent of output of leading firms on the eve of the war (Table 2.5).

The founder of the company, Alfred Edward Herbert (1866-1957), symbolised the new men in the machine tool trade. A common characteristic of machine tool entrepreneurs was that they had served formal apprenticeships with firms engaged in mechanical engineering, facilitating 'a stream of new ideas, new machine tools, or modifications to old tools'. In-house training was a prerequisite to success, and in 1880 Alfred was apprenticed to the engineering business of Joseph Jessop and Sons, Leicester. This enabled him to secure the post of works manager at the Coventry boiler making firm of Cole & Matthews in 1887, and in partnership with William S. Hubbard they purchased the firm, having been provided with £2,000 each from their fathers. Assistance was also provided by Alfred's brother, William, who owned the Premiere Cycle Co. of Coventry. William facilitated the purchase of Cole & Matthews by offering the owner an 'alternative source of income' as a sales manager for Premiere in Germany. The new business of Herbert & Hubbard acquired its initial reputation by manufacturing weldless bicycle tubes, using a French patent secured by William Herbert. The profits earned 'from the tube agency business were ploughed back into machine tool manufacture', and 'also laid the foundations of the agency side of the business', which later focused on the marketing of other firm's machine tools, both British and foreign. Pursuing a strategy of profusion, manufacturing a wide range of specialist machine tools for the expanding Coventry cycle trade, success was ensured by guaranteed orders from the Premiere Cycle Co.[67]

---

[64] J. Lane, 'Herbert, Sir Alfred Edward', in D. J. Jeremy (ed.), *Dictionary of Business Biography* (London, Butterworth, 1984), pp. 174-5.

[65] *Machine Tool Review*, Vol. 18, 1930, p. 58.

[66] Floud, *British Machine Tool Industry*, p. 38.

[67] Ibid., pp. 43, 46-8; J. McG. Davies, 'A Twentieth Century Paternalist. Alfred Herbert and the Skilled Coventry Workmen', in Lancaster and Mason (eds), *Life and Labour*, pp. 102-3; Lane, 'Herbert', p. 174; Lloyd-Jones and Lewis, *Raleigh*, p. 22; D. Thoms and T. Donnelly, *The Motor Car Industry in Coventry Since the 1890s* (London, Croom Helm, 1985), p. 22.

In 1887 Herbert's was a small firm, employing just 12. During the period 1888 to 1896 total sales were modest, peaking in 1891 at £29,000 (Table 2.6). Net profits were also modest (Table 2.7), but in 1894 Alfred became the sole owner, converting the company to limited liability with a capital of £25,000, and trading under the name of Alfred Herbert Ltd. From 1896 to 1907, the company experienced a rapid phase of growth, total sales rising steadily, with the exception of 1901, to a peak of £324,000. Sales fell sharply in the short slump after 1907, but then recovered rapidly to 1914 (Table 2.6). The expansion of sales matched general trends in the machine tool industry, the pattern reflected in trade peaks in 1890-1, 1900, 1907, and 1913, and troughs in 1894, 1902, and 1909. In its early business evolution, Herbert's was a highly profitable concern (Table 2.7), net profits rising rapidly from 1896 to 1907, and despite a sharp fall in 1908 and 1909 accelerating to £100,000 in 1914. The business success of the enterprise was also reflected in a high return of profit to sales, averaging 21 per cent between 1896 and 1907, and 15.4 per cent between 1908 and 1914. A key indicator of business success, the rate of profits to shareholder interest, showed exceptionally high returns between 1896 and 1907, averaging 23 per cent, and despite the downturn in 1908-9, returns averaged 14 per cent to 1914.[68] As Arnold concludes, 'profitability was very high relative to the available benchmark returns' for industrial companies.[69] Expansion was rapid after 1896, the company employing 500 by the end of the bicycle boom in 1897, 930 in 1903, and 2,000 by 1914. By the latter date Herbert's had grown to be the largest machine tool maker in Europe.[70] Expansion was sustained by re-investing profits; before 1914 only in two years, 1890 and 1898, was loan capital used, and this was soon repaid. As a family business, Herbert's 'was able to grow substantially ... without the need for substantial amounts of outside capital'.[71] In 1908 Alfred converted the company to a private limited, and in 1911 he assumed the title of 'Governing Director', ably supported on the board by his brother William, who was a major shareholder.[72]

The firm was a classic example of the personal capitalist form of ownership and control. Over time, shareholding was widened to include managers and senior employees, but family control remained dominant, and Alfred's initial holding of 71 per cent of the equity capital never fell below 65 per cent, and members of the Herbert family held at least 88 per cent of the total voting shares. 'Contrary' to the view of Chandler, that personally managed firms were short-term in their strategic direction, paying high dividends to family members rather than re-investing in future growth, Herbert's provides an example of a firm where business success meant that profits were sufficient to maintain further expansion.[73] From its

---

[68] Arnold, 'Innovation', pp. 56-7, 61-3.

[69] Ibid., p. 61.

[70] Ibid., pp. 57, 61.

[71] Ibid., p. 57.

[72] Coventry Archive, 926/1/4/1-3, Alfred Herbert Ltd., Minute Books of the Departmental Board of Directors, 1911-41, 14 July 1911; 586/11, General Minute Book, 1894-1950, 24 August 1911, 'Agreements Appointing Departmental Directors'.

[73] Arnold, 'Innovation', pp. 56, 59.

origins, internal finance was the main instrument of future growth, and this
principle, determined by the personal views of its founder, remained a key feature
of the company's long business history.[74]

Table 2.6
Alfred Herbert Sales: Own Manufacture and Factored Machine Tools (£000),
1888-1914

	Factored	Own	Total	% Factored
1888	0.0	2.5	2.5	0.0
1889	3.6	4.4	8.0	45.0
1890	12.9	7.7	20.6	62.6
1891	19.4	9.6	29.0	66.9
1892	14.1	8.7	22.8	61.8
1893	5.4	9.7	15.1	35.8
1894	3.3	14.0	17.3	19.1
1895	3.5	18.0	21.5	16.3
1896	7.5	41.3	48.8	15.4
1897	4.0	62.6	66.6	6.0
1898	1.0	86.2	87.2	1.1
1899	0.0	99.2	99.2	0.0
1900	27	91	118	22.9
1901	26	91	117	22.2
1902	29	113	141	20.6
1903	23	131	153	15.0
1904	21	142	163	12.9
1905	35	183	217	16.1
1906	52	198	250	20.8
1907	92	232	324	28.4
1908	47	142	189	24.9
1909	68	165	233	29.2
1910	82	250	332	24.7
1911	148	281	429	34.5
1912	224	295	519	43.2
1913	220	306	526	41.8
1914	270	325	595	45.4

Source: Arnold, 'Innovation', pp. 60-61.

[74] For a discussion of personal capitalism see Chandler, *Scale and Scope*, pp. 235-
94; R. A. Church, 'The Limitations of the Personal Capitalism Paradigm', *Business History
Review*, Vol. 64 (1990); R. A. Church, 'The Family Firm in Industrial Capitalism:
International Perspectives on Hypothesis and History', *Business History*, Vol. 35, No. 4,
Special Issue on Family Capitalism, (1993); P. L. Payne, 'Family Business in Britain: An
Historical and Analytical Survey', in A. Okochi and S. Yasuoka (eds), *Family Business in
the Era of Industrial Growth* (Tokyo, University of Tokyo Press 1984); R. Lloyd-Jones and
M. J. Lewis, 'British Industrial Capitalism During the Second Industrial Revolution: A Neo-
Schumpeterian Approach', *Journal of Industrial History*, Vol. 1, No. 1 (1998), pp. 72-82.

Table 2.7
Profitability at Alfred Herbert Ltd., 1888-1914

	Net Profits (£000)	Net Profit: Total Sales (%)	Net Profits: Shareholders Interest (%)[a]
1888	-0.1	-4.0	-2.8
1889	1.0	12.5	21.7
1890	2.4	11.7	63.2
1891	5.7	19.7	61.3
1892	2.9	12.7	24.4
1893	2.0	13.2	14.8
1894	2.8	16.2	15.7
1895	2.9	13.5	13.6
1896	14.3	29.3	41.7
1897	13.8	20.7	31.0
1898	13.6	15.6	22.1
1899	21.3	21.5	24.3
1900	31	26.2	25.5
1901	20	17.4	14.7
1902	22	15.6	14.4
1903	34	22.4	19.3
1904	31	19.3	15.9
1905	41	18.7	19.3
1906	56	22.3	22.4
1907	76	23.4	25.1
1908	20	10.6	6.5
1909	21	9.0	6.5
1910	55	16.6	15.1
1911	79	18.4	18.7
1912	99	19.1	19.9
1913	90	17.1	15.9
1914	100	16.8	15.6

Source: Arnold, 'Innovation', pp. 60-61.
Notes: a. Shareholders' interest = total value of shares and reserves. Arnold, 'Innovation', p. 61.

Central to the commercial success of the Herbert organisation was the building of networks of trust, both warranted (behaving in a trustworthy way) and mutual (reciprocal), linked to Casson's notion of 'reputation'.[75] In turn, trust and reputation are linked to those of personal capitalism and the quality of the product. These notions are closely associated with Herbert's, Alfred himself recognising that 'the ideals of the tool maker [were] to lead – to make others follow – to make a reputation'. He added that 'This may mean more money or perhaps not, but in any case leading is better than following, if more difficult'.[76] Such a forthright business philosophy placed Herbert's as a progressive firm in the machine tool industry, a fact which needs to be kept in mind when assessing the criticisms of contemporaries, such as Charles Churchill, that British makers were conservative, and in particular were reluctant to innovate American machine tool designs. Herbert's rise to predominance in the industry was based upon establishing a reputation for using American machine tools, and the company was well aware of 'the value' of developing a 'factored business ... and maintaining an effective selling organisation'. As Arnold points out, from its foundation the company 'sold on imported American machine tools and their own (particularly capstan) lathes, which made use both of new steels and of American practices'. In 1894, Herbert's was 'a firm of engineers, machine tool makers', and they had exclusive agency agreements in Europe for the sale of American machines produced by Lodge and Davis. Factored sales complimented their own manufacture, and in the early days of the business factoring mainly consisted of selling French weldless steel tubing. As shown in Table 2.6 factored sales fell sharply after 1892, but from 1900, and especially in the years leading to the war they expanded rapidly as new agencies were opened, especially with American makers. In 1914, factored machines represented 45.4 per cent of total sales, providing an important income stream to support 'the company's own manufacturing operations'. Moreover, factored goods required lower capital; the machines were often purchased on credit, and did not necessitate a heavy investment in fixed plant.[77] Factoring also equated to the principals of international specialisation, allowing free imports, especially of American machines, to the benefit of technological advancement in British engineering industry. In 1918, John Milburn, an American who had joined Herbert's in 1897, reflected on the success of the company since the 1890s. The Herbert reputation, he claimed, was built on its responsibility to supply British engineering with a wide range of machines 'for the full equipment of workshops, from both Herbert and factored machines'.[78]

The American influence in Herbert's factoring business clearly had an impact on technological developments at the company. The technological pathway followed 'American lines', but Herbert's were not simply imitators, using their own skilled engineers 'to better adapt them to the British market'. In 1897 Alfred was instrumental in recruiting an American, Oscar Harmer, who was well

---

[75] M. Casson, 'Regional Business Networks: An Economic Perspective', Paper presented to the International Conference on Business History and Theory, Glasgow, 24 July 1999, p. 2.

[76] *Machine Tool Review*, Vol. 14, 1926, p. 1.

[77] Arnold, 'Innovation', pp. 55, 63-4.

[78] Herbert, Departmental Board, 23 September 1918.

connected both with American machine tool makers and British engineering firms, and was a close friend of Charles Churchill. Harmer recruited another American, Percy Vernon as general manager, as well as John Milburn from Rhode Island. Harmer's knowledge of American methods enabled Herbert's to perfect new designs, allowing the company to diversify when the bicycle boom collapsed in 1897, and to rapidly build for itself a high reputation as an innovator of high quality machines, with a clear American design influence, especially capstan and automatic turret lathes. Harmer reflected that: 'Just as I joined the firm the cycle boom collapsed, and it was necessary to find fresh outlets for our products. I went out to engineering works, got samples, quoted them for machines and tools for their production, gave schedules of operations, and times in which we guaranteed to do the work'.[79] Herbert's, however, did not simply imitate, and remained alert to meeting the needs of customers in British, Empire and foreign markets. At the Paris Exposition of 1900, it was observed that Herbert machines were 'constructed on American lines, and are yet not American machines nor blind copies of them, but included features thought by the builders to better adapt them to the British market'.[80]

Herbert's were not alone in their adaptation of American designs. W. H. Ward of Birmingham exhibited at Paris in 1900 machines 'designed to do the same class of work as is being done by modern tool manufacturers in the U.S.A.'. The management were 'students and admirers of American machine tool practice', but also insistent that their machines were not 'exact replicas', many of the features of American machine tools being 'too light to stand up well to the conditions prevailing in British workshops'. Smith & Coventry of Manchester exhibited at Paris their vertical spindle machine, influenced by American designs and used more extensively in British workshops than American models, but which had been developed from their own drawings.[81] In 1901 Charles Churchill obtained exclusive agency rights for Potter and Johnson and Gridley automatics, on condition they manufactured the necessary tools for these machines. This led in 1906 to the formation of the Churchill Machine Tool Co, the engineering arm of the concern, and by 1910, they were building a variety of grinders influenced by their long association with the American makers Browne & Sharpe.[82] These examples demonstrate how innovative British machine tool firms tailored their product designs to meet a variety of user specific needs, which was a common feature of the business strategies of British engineering producers in general.[83]

---

[79] Coventry Archive, 1270/4/1, Oscar Harmer for the Alfred Herbert Testimonial, 22 July 1917.

[80] *American Machinist*, 4 August 1900, p. 682E.

[81] *American Machinist*, 4 August 1900, pp. 682-3E; 1 September 1900, p. 785E.

[82] 'Charles Churchill 1865-1965', *Machine Shop and Engineering Manufacture*, March 1965, p. 110.

[83] See A. Reed, 'Employers' Strategy and Craft Production, The British Shipbuilding Industry, 1870-1950', in S. Tolliday and J. Zeitlin (eds), *The Power to Manage? Employers and Industrial Relations in Comparative Historical Perspective* (London, Routledge, 1991), p. 35.

Further, British machine tool firms responded to competitive pressures by forms of collaboration at the intra and inter regional levels, and reduced the cost of knowledge acquisition and transfer by inserting themselves into a set of business networks.

This is clearly demonstrated by the example of Herbert's. In 1897 Harmer persuaded Alfred to establish a network of U.K. sale branches as well as associate sales companies in France, Italy, Argentina, Australia, and India. Herbert's foreign agencies were used extensively by local firms, such as Webster & Bennett, who could gain external economies by association with the Herbert organisation and the accumulated knowledge of foreign markets and technological requirements. The activities of Webster & Bennett and their links with Herbert's is worthy of some attention. Webster & Bennett, founded 1887, employed 70 workers in the 1890s. It established a reputation first for its vertical boring and turning mills for the bicycle trade, and then by developing a duplex vertical boring mill for the motor industry. In 1906, the company was incorporated as a private limited company with Thomas Webster and Edward Bennett confirmed as the two directors and joint managing directors. Between 1906 and 1911, the company embarked upon an ambitious expansion programme, which involved the development of a wide range of products. Webster & Bennett developed the business through a long and fruitful relationship with Herbert's, and with a number of other Coventry firms which had originally started as bicycle makers but had then diversified into motor vehicle production, such as Singer, Hilman, Humber, Riley, and Swift. For example, a key factor in the expansion of sales in 1904 was the company's horizontal profile milling machine, specially designed for the motor trade. Inter-firm transactions evolved with local machine makers, notably Herbert's, and in 1906 the Webster & Bennett workshops included 'several Herbert machine tools which are doing good work in the production of component parts for the simple and duplex type mills'. [84]

The firm's relationship with Herbert's became embedded in strong business linkages, and this was typified by the use of the Herbert's factoring services to sell Webster & Bennett milling machines abroad. For example, in September 1901 the company sold a vertical profile miller to Herbert's for export to Japan, and further sales were recorded in November and December. Between 1910 and 1914, Webster & Bennett sold, in total, machines to the value of £4,725 to the Herbert's factoring department for export to Japan, Italy, and France. In addition, they also sold machines directly to Herbert's, valued at £3,265. Numerous machine tool accessories were also sold to Herbert's, including marking-out tables, tool holders, chucks, and saws, as well as supplies of foundry castings. The business connections of Webster & Bennett were not simply confined to Herbert's. During 1910 to 1911 the firm purchased radial drills from Kendall & Gent, planing machines from Cornelius Redman, Halifax, grinding machines from Charles Churchill, Manchester, and chuck lathes from Pollack & McNab,

[84] Coventry Archive, 1050/1/3, Typed History of the Company; 1050/1/1, Webster & Bennett, Minutes of Board of Directors, 11 May, 12, 26 June, 27 August, 5, 12 November 1906; 20 March, 28 June 1907; 10 February 1908; 26 March 1909; 10 March, 6 June 1910; 2 January, 6 March 1911; 1050/56/1, Press Cuttings for Webster & Bennett.

Manchester. In 1913 the Board sanctioned negotiations for the purchase of additional equipment at an estimated cost of £1,600 to be spent principally on boring, grinding and planing machines, and a high speed lathe. An examination of the Webster and Bennett sales register shows extensive trading with other engineering and machine tool firms both inside and outside the region, including Birmingham Small Arms (BSA), Brook Tool Manufacturing Co., James Archdale, Associated British Machine Tool Makers, all of Birmingham; Brett Patent Lifts, Coventry, William Beardmore, Glasgow, and William Asquith, Halifax.[85]

Inserting itself into a set of market networks was one thing, but Webster & Bennett also developed inter-regional collaboration. In 1906 the Board was approached by George Richards & Co. of Broadheath, a highly innovative firm which was researching the application of high speed cutting steel to machine tool design. The proposal made by Richards was to sell Webster & Bennett boring, simple and duplex mills, machines that they did not build themselves. In exchange, Richards would supply milling machines of a type not built by Webster & Bennett. Initially, the proposal was rejected, and it was not until 1914 that an exchange programme was finally agreed. This allowed both firms in their respective markets to offer a wider range, and greater volume of machine tools, than their limited size and capital base would normally have facilitated, and consequently they could maintain independence as personally managed firms and still meet growing customer needs. Indeed, the companies retained their market identity by each selling the exchanged machines 'as own manufacture'.[86] Collaboration of this type suggests that the notion of personal capitalism is not simply reducible to the individualistic actions of businessmen, or the perceptions of high levels of market competition, but rather firms could defend and nurture their core values by collaborating over a set of ancillary capabilities. This process was also facilitated by the widespread practice of sub-contracting, an activity pursued by Herbert's who saw it as a means of supporting flexible production. For example, in 1913 the company sub-contracted their designs for standard lathes to Brown and Ward of Birmingham, allowing Herbert's to fully utilise its own plant for an increased output of turret lathes.[87]

Herbert's role as a lead firm within the Midland region also had much to do with the dominant personality of Alfred himself. The business advance of the firm was consolidated by Alfred's own reputation, both among his own workers and managers and with other firms regionally, nationally, and internationally. Alfred cultivated the 'Herbert spirit', believing that his business was 'considerably more than a mere machine for earning profit', and Herbert's had 'won a reputation in every corner of the world where machine tools are used, for sound design, good

[85] *Cycle and Motor Cycle Trader*, 4 November 1904; Webster & Bennett, Minutes, 11 May 1906; 7 March, 6 June 1910; 6 March 1911; 5 May 1913; 1050/9/1, Webster & Bennett, Sales Register.
[86] Webster & Bennett, Minutes, 15 October 1906; 18 March 1914.
[87] Herbert, Departmental Board, 9 January 1913.

workmanship and honest dealing'.[88] Under his leadership, the firm did develop a high business reputation for the technical quality of its products and its extensive marketing service, and it rapidly became Britain's premiere machine tool firm. According to John Milburn, the key to competitive success was experimentation in design. Learning by doing led to 'an accumulation of knowledge to enable us to build really good machines for the purposes involved'.[89] In the early stages of the company's history, this was not an insular strategy, the management being well aware of the need to cultivate its networks with other local firms, learn from American practice, and disseminate good practice to the rest of the trade by exhibiting at national and international exhibitions its own and factored lines of machine tools. In many ways, Herbert's symbolised the British response to the American challenge, a leading firm amongst a cluster of innovative machine tool firms in Britain by the early twentieth century. Yet a greater challenge was to face the industry, as the clouds of war loomed in 1914.

---

[88] *Alfred Herbert News*, Vol. 1, No 5 (1926), pp. 1-2. See also McG. Davis, 'Twentieth Century Paternalist', pp. 100, 112-14.

[89] Herbert, Departmental Board, 9 September 1918.

CHAPTER THREE

'A War of Machinery': The British Machine Tool Industry, 1914-18

'Artillery was the great Leveller' [Private T. Jacobs, 1st Yorkshire Regiment].

'Do you realise this is a war of machinery? A war between the British and French workmen on the one hand and German workmen on the other.' [David Lloyd-George, the 'Shell Wizard'].[1]

Introduction

The Great War was fought with weapons of increasing destructive power, although the full capabilities of modern technology were never realised as the great armies of Europe fought to a standstill in the trenches of the Western and Eastern fronts.[2] Yet, as Lloyd-George was well aware, the capability of the British military to sustain total warfare demanded the full utilisation of the nation's industrial potential; it was a 'war of machinery'. The war placed enormous pressures on British engineering, and created heavy demands for machine tools in an industry that was of 'key' importance for the production of munitions.[3] During the first year of the War the industry faced a number of constraints that limited its productive capacity. In particular, there were acute shortages of skilled workers as the war drained the labour force, and these problems were compounded in the first year of the conflict by deteriorating industrial relations. The problem of labour recruitment signified the initial response by government to the crisis of war, with ministers endorsing a policy of 'business as usual'.[4] During 1915, the government faced a growing military and political crisis, accompanied by adverse publicity surrounding the alleged shortages of shells to the Western front. In this environment supplies of machine tools became of vital importance, and led to an increasing intervention in the affairs of the industry. The response of the government, through the creation of the Ministry of Munitions will be examined,

---

[1] Jacobs cited in J. Keegan, *The First World War* (London, Hutchinson, 1999), p. 427; I. F. Marcosson, War Correspondent of *Saturday Evening Post*, recounting a conversation with Lloyd-George in 1915, *The American Machinist*, 17 May 1918, p. 960.

[2] Keegan, *First World War*, pp. 22-3.

[3] *History of the Ministry of Munitions*, Vol. 8 (London, H.M.S.O., 1921-2), p. 36.

[4] D. French, 'The Rise and Fall of Business as Usual', in K. Burke (ed.), *War and the State. The Transformation of British Government, 1914-1919* (London, Allen and Unwin, 1982), pp. 7-31.

as will the relationships with businessmen within the industry. A key issue that will be examined is the effects of the war on stimulating increasing modernisation in the industry,[5] and the response of makers to the demands of total war.

'Business as Usual'

The prevailing consensus in government and business circles in August 1914 was that the war would be a short one, and this optimism was replicated in German strategic planning, which assumed nine months as the upper limit to the conflict. British planning also faced delays as debates arose between 'navalists' who advocated the use of naval power to blockade Germany, and 'continentalists' who advocated a full military commitment. This hesitant approach symbolised the fact that Britain had prepared no systematic plan for the economic and industrial pursuit of a continental war, nor, when hostilities broke out, did it instigate planning. It should be recognised, however, that Lord Kitchener had been predicting a three year war since 1909, and at his first Cabinet meeting as Secretary of State for War he repeated his prediction. Nevertheless, by the winter of 1914, when trench warfare was a reality, the government had no definite plans to supply 'the right kind of ammunition'.[6] These views do not simply rest on hindsight, as shown by an American perspective on the conflict in March 1915:

> it is beyond doubt that the chief secret in the present position of the war, a fairly open secret, is that in a material sense the enemies of Great Britain and her allies were prepared at the outset, while the allies themselves may possibly be criticised on the grounds of want of preparation.[7]

Nevertheless, such a statement requires qualification. Although Germany had planned and prepared for war over a long period, its ability to sustain a war of attrition was to prove 'inadequate in the extreme'.[8]

---

[5] For an account of the debate on modernisation see B. W. E. Alford, 'Lost Opportunity: British Business and Businessmen During the First World War', in N. McKendrick and R. B. Outhwaite (eds.), *Business Life and Public Policy: Essays in Honour of D. C. Coleman* (Cambridge, Cambridge University Press, 1986), p. 207.

[6] T. Wilson, *The Myriad Faces of War: Britain and the Great War, 1914-18* (Cambridge, Polity Press, 1986), p. 215; S. J. Hurwitz, *State Intervention in Great Britain: A Study of Economic Control and Social Response, 1914-1919* (N.Y., Columbia University Press, 1949), p. 62; M. Howard, *The First World War* (Oxford, Oxford University Press, 2002), p. 63; G. Hardach, *The First World War* (London, Allan Lane, 1973), p. 56; French, 'Business as Usual', p. 7; Keegan, *First World War*, pp. 37-40; P. J. Cain and A. G. Hopkins, *British Imperialism 1688-2000* (Harlow, Longman, 2001), pp. 394-5; H. Strachan, *The First World War, Volume 1, To Arms* (Oxford, Oxford University Press, 2001), pp. 1,005-6.

[7] *The American Machinist*, 6 March 1915, p. 27E.

[8] Hardach, *First World War*, p. 55.

In 1914, Winston Churchill still believed that the nation could maintain 'business as usual'. Indeed, in the early phase the state played a minimal role in the regulation of business, confining its actions to military recruitment, financial borrowing, direction of foreign trade and exchanges, the maintenance of food and raw material imports, and direct control over the railways.[9] Government intervention was prescribed, and the economic orthodoxy of 'business as usual' was summed up by Walter Runciman, President of the Board of Trade, in February 1915: 'the greatest contribution the government could make was to reassure the business community that there would be no state interference'.[10] Government controls over industry, of course, were often 'little realised by the general public',[11] but in terms of the direct co-ordination of private industrial enterprise the British state lacked a cohesive strategy in the early years of the war. What were the effects of this on a key strategic sector such as machine tools, and why did this industry become so important to the war effort?

As Lloyd-George claimed, 'The war made unprecedented and insatiable demands upon ... industrial capacity. The utmost possible production was required ... to supply our needs'. This was the outcome of a growing war of attrition. The failed German assault at the first Battle of Ypres, October to November 1914, marked 'the end of mobile war on the Western Front'. By the end of 1914 a continuous maze of trenches stretched for 475 miles from the Swiss border to the North Sea, and was to remain largely unchanged for the duration of the war. Trenches were the physical outcome 'of offence and counter offensive', and the defence of the line required vast supplies of rifles, machine guns, and ammunition. Above all, the strategy of trench warfare required powerful artillery batteries using large volumes of high explosive shells in support of advancing troops. Shortages of artillery on all sides now intensified the stalemate. By the end of 1914 British batteries were rationed to firing six rounds per day, and by early 1915 the Germans, enclosed in a defensive system of perfected trenches, lacked the supplies of shells necessary to deploy infantry against 'well defended trenches'. Kitchener wrote to Sir John French, the Commander in Chief of the British Expeditionary Force, in October 1914. 'The supply of ammunition gives me great anxiety. Do you think we are keeping munitions back. All we can gather is being sent, but at present rate of expenditure we are certain before long to run short, and then to produce more than a small daily allowance per gun will be impossible'. In the ensuing stalemate, which witnessed the upgrade of trench systems, the demand for munitions increased enormously.[12] To produce them in the quantities required

---

[9] L. Hannah, *The Rise of the Corporate* Economy (London, Methuen, 1983), p. 27; S. Pollard, *The Development of the British Economy, 1914-1980* (London, Edward Arnold, 1983), pp. 19-20.

[10] Cited in Hurwitz, *State Intervention*, p. 65.

[11] French, 'Business as Usual', p. 8, who is critical of the notion that government simply assumed a non-interventionist strategy from the outset.

[12] D. Lloyd-George, *War Memoirs of David Lloyd-George*, Vol. II (London, Odhams Press, 1936), p. 1,144; Howard, *First World War*, pp. 40, 62; Wilson, *The Myriad Faces*, p. 102; Keegan, *First World War*, pp. 109-10, 134-5, 147, 191-3; Kitchener, cited in

necessitated an unprecedented increase in the deployment of machine tools in British engineering industry.

From the outset, the question of labour supply taxed the minds of politicians, militarists, and businessmen. War required a vast mobilisation, and consequently an organised system of allocation between competing military and industrial needs. In the first year of the war, the allocation of manpower neither pleased the generals nor the captains of industry. Despite the rhetoric of 'business as usual', the government took immediate action, through its powers to control foreign trade, to shift production from export to domestic markets, which reflected the demands of the War Office for increased supply. As a result, opportunities that had opened up for machine tool makers to supply Russian and Scandinavian markets, a consequence of the loss of German trade, were foregone. 'Business as usual', but in a modified form, and the government showed it would use its prescribed powers to indirectly influence domestic industry. Paradoxically, in the early weeks of the war, before War Office orders accelerated, industrialists anticipated the disruption to normal commerce, and this led to cancelled contracts and the discharge of workers. Within a short period, however, manufacturers in the machine tool districts 'were bewailing the lack of men who they had discharged, or who had discharged themselves, and had gone into the army and navy'. The government reaction to this problem was to place firms on lists that defined them as 'off-limit' to military recruiters. In the Midlands, for example, 50 firms were initially declared 'off-limit', but this had been reduced to just seven by March 1915. This was partly related to confusion over sub-contracting, a procedure which was widespread in the machine tool industry. Sub-contractors were initially included in the lists, but were subsequently removed. A key factor, however, was the competing demand from the military. As demand increased and labour shortages manifested themselves, there were loud complaints that lathes and automatic machines 'could not be produced fast enough to meet the requirements of the munitions manufacturers'.[13] The labour supply problem rested with the War Office, where Kitchener was well aware that uncoordinated recruitment was counter productive, but recruitment officers continued to take skilled mechanics involved in vital war work.[14]

Given the importance of the machine tool industry to the war effort, one may take some sympathy with the view of *The American Machinist*, who hypothesised that it should have the 'lowest ratio of losses' from men who had joined the armed forces. Its comprehensive survey of the industry, however, revealed some 'remarkable' results.[15] The survey included specialist machine tool firms, as well as some allied firms who produced machine tools as part of a wider

R. J. Q. Adams, *Arms and the Wizard: Lloyd-George at the Ministry of Munitions, 1915-16* (London, Cassell, 1978), p. 15.

[13] R. H. Brayers and E. Sandford, *Birmingham and the Great War, 1914-1919* (Birmingham, Cornish Bros., 1921), p. 112; *American Machinist*, 6 March 1915, p. 29E.

[14] C. Wrigley, 'The Ministry of Munitions, an Innovating Department', in Burk (ed.), *War and the State*, p. 36.

[15] *American Machinist*, 13 March 1915, p. 32E.

range of engineering products. Table 3.1 shows 114 firms who reported their percentage losses of employment. The vast majority of firms, totalling 74.6 per cent, lost between 10 and 29 per cent of their labour force, and more firms reported losses of 30+ per cent than those reporting losses of less than 10 per cent. The largest number of firms, 50 in total, reported losses between 10 and 19 per cent. Well established and innovative firms such as James Butler, Halifax, Morton & Weaver, Coventry, recorded losses of 15 per cent, and Cunliffe & Croom, Manchester, and Louden Bros. of Glasgow lost a staggering one-quarter of their workforce. There were marked differences, of course, in the experiences of firms. For example, J. Buckton & Co. of Leeds reported a loss of 30 per cent, while H. Broadbent Ltd. of Sowerby Bridge lost a mere two per cent. Table 3.2 shows the results from the main machine tool producing centres, and illustrates some interesting regional trends. While it would appear that Glaswegians and Mancunians were more inclined to take the 'colours', than the men from Birmingham or Halifax, the average loss to these important centres of machine tool production of 17 per cent of their workforce meant an inevitable loss of their productive potential.

Table 3.1
Machine Tool Firms Reporting Percentages of Workers Lost to Armed Forces, First Six Months of War

Range of % Loss	No. of Firms	% of Total Firms
1-9	13	11.4
10-19	50	43.9
10-29	35	30.7
30+	16	14.0
Total	114	100.0

Source: Compiled from *The American Machinist*, 13 March 1915, pp. 32-4E.

Table 3.2
Average Loss of Workforce in the Main Machine Tool Manufacturing Centres, First Six Months of War

Machine Tool Centre	No. of Firms Reporting	% Loss
Manchester	20	19.5
Birmingham	12	13.8
Halifax	9	12.0
Johnstone (Glasgow)	7	20.4
Keighley	7	16.6
Coventry	4	21.5
Total	59	17.3

Source: Compiled from *The American Machinist*, 13 March 1915, pp. 32-4E.

Early 1915 witnessed 'boom' conditions in engineering for work 'even remotely connected with war requirements', but in the machine tool firms of Manchester 'the shortage of skilled and semi-skilled labour was as marked as ever'. This was replicated in Yorkshire, where leading makers in Keighley were concentrating production efforts on lathes for shell turning. Thus, Dean, Smith & Grace were full-out producing mainly standard and high speed lathes, J. Spencer & Co. were working overtime on turning lathes, Darling & Sellers had heavy orders for lathes and milling machines, and Ward, Haggis & Smith were exceptionally busy on shell turning lathes for the War Office. All these firms reported acute labour shortages and the loss of valuable orders because delivery targets could not be met. Neither were Scottish makers exempt from these problems, firms in Johnstone losing 20 per cent of their workforce during the first six months of the war.[16]

The juxtaposition of heavy and urgent demand with the loss of skilled and semi-skilled labour could manifest itself in inter-firm conflict. For example, the scarcity of skilled workers became a particular problem for small firms who faced the difficulty of retaining skilled workers against the higher wages offered by larger concerns. Indeed, for some firms working overtime became an 'imperative', not because they needed to increase output, but to enhance earnings to provide an 'inducement' for labour 'to remain with the firm'.[17] High labour mobility was recognised by the Ministry of Munitions, established under Lloyd-George in May 1915, as one of the 'big problems' facing industry and it was observed that 'good pay and conditions [were] a winner in holding labour'.[18] In the long-run, of course, the concentration of workers and plant in larger units may allow increased technical and economic efficiency, particularly in the context of a high and sustained level of demand which can absorb high volume output. But the war could not wait for the long-run, as the offensive against German trenches in 1915 needed all the munitions that the home front could deliver. Indeed, in the short-run inter-firm competition for scarce resources could prove disruptive in the absence of appropriate regulatory mechanisms by the authorities.

Further, the belief that the war would be of short duration, a view articulated in the machine tool industry as late as January 1915, inhibited the expansion of capacity. For example, in Birmingham machine tool production lagged behind new orders, and users were 'pressing urgently' for tools to enable them to fulfil government contracts. There still remained a belief, however, in the 'possibility of an early termination to the conflict', and this influenced investment decisions. Business psychology in relation to the war dictated that investment in new plant for the future was 'highly speculative', and consequently there was an active market in second hand machines that were adapted for war purposes. Second hand tools were quickly 'snapped up', but the key demand was for special lathes for turning shells. This placed pressure on managers to increase output, but short-

---

[16] Reports of local correspondents for *American Machinist*, 30 January 1915, p. 2E; 7 February 1915, p. 7E.

[17] *American Machinist*, 6 February 1915, p. 12E.

[18] Wrigley, 'Ministry of Munitions', p. 50.

term capacity constraints on existing plant, compounded by increases in the cost of production, frustrated expansion plans. In unregulated markets makers faced increased charges for fuel, raw materials, transport, and, with labour in short supply, rising wage costs. For example, in February 1915 between 15,000 and 20,000 workers in the engineering and allied trades of Birmingham received a wage advance, a reluctant recognition by employers of the need to retain scarce labour resources.[19]

A tight labour market increased the power of unions, and manufacturers had to tread carefully in their industrial relations strategies, although this had mixed outcomes. Shortages of labour had not been 'appreciably relieved' after six to seven months of war, and thus 'systematic overtime' and night work was a common practice. To reduce the potential for conflict, management were prepared to make concessions on the wage front. For example, in February 1915 the Midland's Employers Federation and the Engineering Employers Federation granted a wage increase to semi-skilled workers and labourers in the engineering trades, and in the important machine tool centre of Coventry there was a three year deal struck with the unions that guaranteed an increase of 2s 6d per week on time rates and an equivalent addition to piece rates. Labour shortages meant that a 'good workman realises his value', and manufacturers found it 'a very delicate matter to avoid causes of offence'. In the Midlands employers were adept an ensuring the minimum of industrial conflict, but this was not the case on the Clyde where serious disruption occurred. At the end of February 1915 over 10,000 engineers were on strike in Glasgow against union advice and, in the district of Johnstone, machine tool output was severely restricted. At John Lang & Co., and other firms there was a full-blown strike over the refusal to work overtime. Within two weeks tensions had eased as manufacturers and workers confronted the question of long hours. It is little wonder that industrial relations came under pressure, with a 90 hour week being a common experience for workers, and reports of men working 132 hours per week. Nevertheless, labour shortages meant that intensive working continued, and in March Lang & Co. were reporting '800 men going night and day on special government work'.[20]

Labour shortages and industrial relations problems, as constraints on capacity expansion there may have been, but machine makers did make positive moves in 1915 to expand the output for the high and sustained demand for shell-turning lathes and standard machine tools, which, in addition to lathes, included drills, presses and milling machines. In particular, makers attempted to design machines to meet the demands of users for larger volume production. In early 1915 Birmingham makers were reported to be expanding 'productive capacity ... methodically and ceaselessly', and foregoing non-war work. In March the Birmingham firm of Charles Taylor & Co. was operating 'every department' at full capacity 'with no sign of abatement'. They were also expanding their plant to

---

[19] *American Machinist*, 15 January 1915, pp. 16-17E; 20 February 1915, p. 17E.

[20] *American Machinist*, 30 January 1915, p. 7E; 6 February 1915, pp. 12-13E; 20 February 1915, p. 18E; 27 February 1915, p. 23E; 6 March 1915, p. 29E; 9 March 1915, p. 34E; 13 March 1915, p. 46E.

increase the manufacture of chucks, which were in short supply with the curtailment of supplies from Germany. Similarly, in Halifax, a number of firms, including H. Holmes and George Swift & Co. were making 'considerable extensions to their plant'. In 1915 the demand for lathes was so strong that firms from other sectors of engineering entered the trade. For example, the Bolton Engineering Co., a branch of the textile machine maker Dobson & Barlow, began manufacturing lathes for munitions work, and a number of Bolton textile machine firms converted plant to war needs. The demands of war placed enormous pressure on machine tool firms to switch their lines to produce machines appropriate for munitions work. Thus, G. A. Harvey Ltd., Glasgow, was, in March 1915, still producing heavy machine tools for the Indian and colonial markets, but they were now confronted with 'new urgent orders for standard machine tools from government contractors'. While working at full capacity, machine tool firms did not forego the opportunity to innovate new lines. James Butler & Co, Halifax, were operating overtime and day and night shifts to produce 'reciprocating machine tools', such as shell-turning lathes and bar cutting machines. The company was also introducing 'special lathes ... designed for turning and boring torpedo tubes'. J. Holroyd & Co. were busy producing small milling machines for the manufacture of rifle components, but had also introduced new special lathes for munitions work. These included 'heavy shell nose forming lathes, 4 1/2" capacity shell-cutting off lathes and copy forming lathes for rifle stocks'. In March and April alone, *The American Machinist* reported the introduction of new designs, and/or, improvements or adaptations of existing designs by 17 machine tool firms. These included leading makers such as Alfred Herbert and Webster & Bennett, Coventry, Scott Bros, W. Asquith Ltd., and James Butler, Halifax, George Richards & Co., Craven Bros., Churchill Machine Tool Co., and Cunliffe & Croom, Manchester, and E. A. Wrigley and Tangye of Birmingham.[21]

Productive efficiency was also augmented by the increasing use of electric power, and the application of electric motors to drive machine tools. James Archdale & Co., Birmingham, one of Britain's most innovative makers, announced in July 1915 the near completion of its electrification plant. The installation was undertaken when the plant was operating 'at high pressure', and caused serious disruption, but the firm was confident that 'production will be greatly facilitated', and additional production space made available by the removal of the existing boilers and stacks. The increased space was to be utilised for the use of high speed planers and automatic machine tools for turning operations, all fitted with electric drives. A number of other firms, such as B. R. Rowland & Co. and G. Swift, Halifax, and John Lang & Son, Johnstone, also reported the application of electric motors to their machine tool range. Improvement innovations, directly affecting key munitions industries, were also evident. In December 1915, J. Hamilton & Son, Salford, introduced a new lathe by which 'shells could be turned on the outside at one operation'. This reduced machining costs and 'had the advantage in

---

[21] *American Machinist*, 15 January 1915, pp. 6-7E; 20 February 1915, p. 17E; 13 March 1915, p. 34E; 27 March 1915, p. 45E; 17 April 1915, p. 76E; 26 April 1915, p. 81E.

solving the problems as to whether one man shall be confined to a single lathe or shall look after more than one when on continuous work of this description'.[22]

Despite firms innovating and investing in capacity expansion, severe constraints continued to inhibit output. In addition to labour shortages there were the problems of component and capital equipment supply and the logistics of altering plant to meet the unprecedented demands of war. Component and machinery supply was a key issue. For example, in April 1915, Buck & Hickman had arranged production to meet the 'incessant' demand for automatic screw and gear cutting machines, and precision grinders, but vital machinery was held-up in Liverpool docks due to a labour dispute. The management of Alfred Herbert, a major producer of ancillary tools, reported that its 'Coventry chucks' were in short supply, and despite existing high prices of chucks sold to the trade it was not 'opportune' to sell lower because of the uncertainty over future wage rises. The logistical problems of expanding output were demonstrated at Jones & Shipman, Leicester. In April 1915 the company recruited 100 additional workers, but now they complained about 'the crowded state of their shops'. Rapid expansion along one product line, could also create problems for the supply of other products. For example, D. Mitchell & Co. of Keighley reported a high demand for their radial drills, 'but, owing to the big call for lathes, they are much behind with deliveries'. The demand by users was for a variety of special machine tools, because of the variegated needs of munitions manufacture itself, and this placed enormous pressures on makers. Thus, Colonel Oliver C. Armstrong, the Chairman of Greenwood & Batley of Leeds, a general engineering firm with a major reputation as a machine tool manufacturer, informed Lloyd-George at a meeting in October 1915 that his company's efforts in manufacturing cartridge cases and bullets for a French government contract required the company to buy a range of specialist machine tools. The French bullet was 'entirely different to the English bullet, necessitating the manufacture of machine tools' not made by his own company. Consequently, the company was contracting to 50 different suppliers for a variety of machine tools and ancillary components. Companies now had to co-ordinate a range of different product needs. For example, Jones & Shipman opened a new specially designed factory in 1915 to produce 'Jumbo' drilling machines for large shells, but also had to deploy resources to manufacture 'lighter types' for producing fuses and small components.[23]

---

[22] *American Machinist*, 5 June 1915, p. 113E; 19 June 1915, p. 126E; 24 July 1915, p. 136E; *Archdale Machine Tools 1868-1948* (Birmingham, James Archdale Ltd., 1948), p. 21; *Engineer*, 11 February 1916, p. 136.

[23] *American Machinist*, 24 April 1915, p. 81E; 15 May 1915, p. 98E; Coventry Archive, Alfred Herbert, 926/1/4/1-3, Minute Books of Departmental Board of Directors, 1911-41, 7 January 1915; West Yorkshire Archive Service (WYAS), Leeds, Records of Greenwood & Batley Ltd., Box 53, Director's Minute Books, 1888-1925, 26 October 1915, Minutes of Proceedings between the Ministry of Munitions and the Company; H. Miller, *Tools that Built a Business. The Story of A. A. Jones & Shipman Ltd.* (London, Hutchinson Benham, 1972), p. 22.

Logistical problems were related both to constraints faced by management, and to structural problems within the organisation itself. Greenwood & Batley, for example, remained cautious about expanding capacity, and in September 1914 decided that 'under prevailing conditions, capital commitments should as far as possible be restricted to the necessity of fulfilment of immediately remunerative contracts'. By November 1914, however, Armstrong, reported on the company's pre-occupation with War Office directives to expand capacity to meet the French government contract to deliver one million cartridges and bullets per week. In this situation, the management had to make fine judgements about the appropriation of capital resources between machine tool production and general munitions work. Given constraints on plant it was felt 'unadvisable to occupy valuable floor space' for the increased manufacture of lathes. Repeating the belief of manufacturers in a short war, Armstrong concluded that increasing lathe output would create 'a glut on the market after the war'. Labour issues also frustrated the ability of management to increase output of its full range of engineering products. To increase the supply of labour large numbers of 'trainee girls' were employed as early as October 1914 to work in the Cartridge factory, with the aim to release skilled men for machine tool and other engineering work. The company found, however, that many of them left to go to local clothing factories who were employed on government contracts, despite the company offering day wages to encourage them to stay. In early 1915 the company reported the completion of expanded workshop capacity but noted 'acute' shortages of trained workers, and the fact that they were negotiating with the War Office to secure Belgian labour to meet output targets.[24]

The function of management is to make key decisions about the allocation of the resources of the organisation, but the external demands of war placed increasing pressures on management. Given the diversity of engineering products produced by Greenwood & Batley, the management had considered a holding company structure in 1913, but rejected it on the grounds that there would be a loss of financial control. This was not reconsidered with the outbreak of war, but faced with the need to expand output, management did recognise the need to adopt more centralised control over the diverse departments. In September 1914 two board members, Thomas Greenwood and A. G. Hopper, were appointed 'Managing Directors of Departments'. Each controlled eight departments, Greenwood alone being in charge of the heavy and light machine tools, gauges, milling, cartridge, and screw departments, as well as the iron foundry and pattern makers shop. Beneath these directors were departmental managers for each of the 16 departments. In such a structure, it is little wonder than managerial friction arose. In November 1914 a long debate ensued in which Greenwood pleaded for more resources for the manufacture of lathes, which was contested by Hopper and finally rejected by Armstrong. Departmental structures of this kind required co-operation between departmental managers, but in March 1915 both Greenwood and Hopper reported inter-departmental conflict 'nullifying the anticipated co-operation which

---

[24] Greenwood & Batley, Minute Book, 8 September, 20 October, 12 November 1914, 14 February 1915.

had been relied upon to bring the output ... up to the full manufacturing potential'.[25]

Organisational problems also arose at Alfred Herbert. Inundated with orders at the outbreak of war, and 'in view of the difficulty of obtaining machines of our own make', the works manager, John Milburn, announced that he was re-organising the present plant to 'balance' production between different types of machine tools, and was preparing to expand the Edgwick factory 'if necessary'. By January 1915 the expansion of the factory had become a necessity, not to increase the output of finished machines but to expand capacity for tool production, which was presently inadequate at their tool department situated at the Red Lane Works in Coventry. Red Lane produced cutting tools, drill chucks, gear pumps, and oil pipe fittings, vital ancillary components for the expansion of the company's own machine tools. The pressure on this department was intensified because of the organisational form of the company and the division between manufacturing and factoring. Herbert's was not only Britain's leading manufacturer of machine tools, but also the largest factoring company, and its tool department supplied components not only to its Edgwick factory but to makers who supplied machines for the company to sell through its factoring division. Increasing demand on the tool room, and an inability to co-ordinate the operations of its manufacturing and factoring divisions, placed enormous pressure on the company to expand the output of its own machines. The problems of tool production were further compounded by shortages of skilled tool room workers. Such was the problem of meeting orders that they made the decision to sub-contact discontinued lines to other firms, using Herbert patterns and drawings, and sell them through their factoring department.[26]

The more general problems of the machine tool industry by June of 1915 were summed up by the Birmingham correspondent of *The American Machinist*. While 'makers ... were working their hardest', the volume of demand remained 'out of all proportion to supply', resulting in 'a big balance of unexecuted orders'. This was put down to a lack of organisation in machine tool supply, the 'mobilisation of local industry' having not met the urgent demand for key machine tools:

> This is retarding the reorganisation of our industrial resources. Without disparaging the tremendous amount of work which has been accomplished in increasing industrial capacity, it has to be recognised that munitions are being produced in many cases under uneconomical conditions owing to inadequate plant and labour and lack of cohesion. This is the penalty of the unorganised condition of our Midland industries ... Sub-division of manufactures among a large number of small employers has not made for progress.[27]

---

[25] Greenwood & Batley, Minute Book, 30 and 31 December 1913; 8 September; 12 November 1914; 4 March 1915.

[26] Herbert, Departmental Board, 8 October 1914; 7 January 1915.

[27] *American Machinist*, 12 June 1915, p. 119E.

The problems faced by machine tool producers was in supplying the needs of a vast range of potential users, many of whom were operating on a small scale, a problem which was to continue throughout the war.[28] But this was also a serious condemnation of the lack of government planning to co-ordinate production, which is made more poignant by the fact that it was made a month after the establishment of the Ministry of Munitions under Lloyd-George. As Ferguson claims, the initial amateur approach to the war, supported by 'business as usual', was not simply swept away in May 1915 by the creation of the Ministry under the 'Welsh Wizard'.[29] The Ministry, however, did represent the forces of change, and it was itself born out of crisis. The political crisis of 1915, which marked the collapse of the Liberal Government and the formation of the War Coalition under Asquith was set against the 'shell crisis' so forcefully pushed by the Northcliffe Press. The military advantages of the allies, Lloyd-George made clear, lay in what he considered to be their superior capability in industrial production, but at the same time he acknowledged that there had been a 'failure' of supply resulting from the inability to 'adequately mobilise' manufacturing resources. In a memorandum to Cabinet in February 1915, he hit the point home: 'All the engineering works of the country ought to be turned to the production of war material'.[30] This became an overwhelming priority as Britain prepared for the great offensive on the Somme in 1916.

'Shells More Shells': The Western Front and the Machine Tool Industry

The Ministry of Munitions assumed control over strategic firms, and created Munitions Areas and District Munitions Boards of management, to co-ordinate a programme to increase the output of munitions for the armed forces. Several hundred engineering firms participated, under 'direction' from the Ministry, and the inclusion of machine tool makers was given a high priority. Ministerial controls were immediately welcomed by the Machine Tool and Engineering Trade Association (MTEA), whose chairman, Alfred Herbert, wrote to Kitchener and Lloyd-George in March 1915. Recognising the 'enormous' demand for machine tools, and the need for regulation of the industry, Alfred guaranteed full support to schemes for the control of factories through powers vested in the government under the March Defence of the Realm Act. This was followed by calls for the Ministry to extend its powers, especially in the area of labour co-ordination. In June the MTEA passed a resolution urging Lloyd-George to extend the powers of the Ministry, which already had authority to take over munitions factories, to include the expansion of the industrial labour force. Recognising the 'urgent need' to increase the supply of machine tools, the Association supported recommendations incorporated in the Munitions of War Bill, which was eventually passed in early July. These included exemption for its members from military

---

[28] See N. Ferguson, *The Pity of War* (London, Penguin, 1999), pp. 256, 259, 262.

[29] Ibid., p. 255.

[30] Cited in Adams, *Arms and the Wizard*, p. 21.

recruitment, the blocking of enlistment for skilled workers through the issue of exemption 'badges', and the return of trained mechanics from the armed forces.[31] At the top level, however, frustration continued over the individualistic approach of the War Office. In October 1915, Lloyd-George replied to a request from Greenwood & Batley to assist in providing more trained men: 'This is a demand which comes from every munitions firm in the Kingdom. They want highly skilled turners and I cannot get them out'.[32]

War demands intensified from the summer of 1915, and consequently women were increasingly assimilated into industrial employment.[33] The proportion of women employed in the industrial workforce rose from between 26 to 30 per cent on the eve of war to between 36 and 37 per cent by the end of the conflict, a significant increase but not matching the 55 per cent achieved in Germany by 1918.[34] Women were mainly employed directly on munitions work, but in that bastion of skilled labour, the machine tool shop, there was an increasing use of female labour to make good the shortfall of workers lost to the armed forces. This did not come, however, without resistance by employers. As *The Engineer* commented, the 'wholesale eulogia ... showered upon female workers in the manufacture of munitions are ... somewhat overdone'.[35] Given this prejudice, the Ministry of Munitions had to cajole employers to expand the female workforce. A report of September 1916 from the Machine Tool Department (MTD) of the Ministry of Munitions to Dr. Christopher Addison, the deputy to Lloyd-George at the Ministry, acknowledged that by the middle of 1915 there was a clear recognition of 'the necessity of dilution of labour in the manufacture of machine tools', but the implementation of the policy had taken place 'in the face of very great difficulty to introduce women labour'.[36]

In the autumn of 1915, for example, John Lang & Son, Johnstone, were at full capacity on standard lathes for munitions work, and were requested by the District Munitions Committee to introduce female workers. Initially 50 women were engaged on 'light machines', but by January 1916, with the workshops still operating night and day, only 20 women were employed 'satisfactorily' compared to 1,000 men. Problems of training women in machining operations persuaded management to adopt a gradual approach, which did not satisfy government officials. In February the new government commissioner on the dilution of labour

---

[31] Machine Tool Trade Association, Machine Tools and Engineering Association (hereafter MTEA), Minute Book, 16 March, 30 June 1915; Pollard, *Development*, p. 21.

[32] Greenwood & Batley, Minute Book, 26 October 1915.

[33] For accounts of the role of women in the industrial workforce see J. Horne, *Labour at War: France and Britain, 1914-18* (Oxford, Oxford University Press, 1991); C. Dewy, 'Military Recruitment and the British Labour Force During the First World War', *Historical Journal* (1984); S. H. Hogg, 'The Employment of Women in Great Britain, 1891-1921, unpublished D. Phil., University of Oxford, 1961; Wilson, *Myriad Faces*, Ch. 64; Ferguson, *Pity*, pp. 267-70

[34] Ferguson, *Pity*, p. 268.

[35] *Engineer*, 19 November 1915, p. 489.

[36] Bodleian Library, University of Oxford, Addison MSS, D2/1/c43, Report on the Utilisation of Labour in the Machine Tool Trade, 8 September 1916.

visited the works, and directed management to increase female employment.[37] Attempts by management to impose the ministerial directive, however, met with stern labour resistance, the resulting strike at Lang's in February 1916 being described by Addison as 'illegal'. Attempts to 'prevent picketing' met with some success in enabling a small number of women to enter the works, and the seriousness of the dispute was reflected by the fact that the London executive of the Amalgamated Society of Engineers (ASE) travelled to Glasgow in an attempt to persuade the men back. The strike was still prolonged for one week, Addison remaining less than impressed with the efforts of the ASE who were 'not in control of the rank and file'.[38] Nevertheless, the Ministry's efforts did achieve some positive outcomes, and by April 1916 Lang's were employing 60 'girls' on manufacturing lathes.[39]

In other districts the assimilation of women seems to have attracted less resistance than in Scotland. By November 1915, in the Midlands, female employment had doubled within three months, in Yorkshire women were 'being extensively employed in many machine tools shops' by December, and a similar absorption was taking place in the Manchester district.[40] By October 1915, female employment was common in munitions factories, but it was seen as a key 'innovation' in the machine tool trade, a fact later recognised by the Ministry of Munitions in 1917.[41] In the autumn of 1915 the MTD reported that 22 firms had arranged to employ women, and its director, Alfred Herbert, declared that it was 'proving most satisfactory'. Nevertheless, the Department had to cajole firms to increase the speed of dilution, and trade circulars were issued in October, November 1915, and in January 1916 urging an increased intake of women workers.[42]

Women performed a number of tasks in the workshops. For example, at the Halifax firm of Smith, Barker & Wilson, 14 women out of a total of 204 workers were 'adapting themselves to their new surroundings', being employed on drilling, lathe work, rack-cutting, tool grinding, and the inspection of finished parts. This was a crucial part of the company's strategy of augmenting its labour force to produce large machine batches to meet government contracts. At the Broadheath firm of W. H. Kearns & Co. women released men for work on more skilled operations during the night shifts for the production of boring and facing machines. Such was the demands to increase output that firms employed women on special work, and at Clay & Atkinson of Bradford their new female employees were engaged in milling, drilling, tapping, and final assembly work. Many firms introduced short training programmes for women, and when the Birmingham firm

---

[37] *American Machinist*, 15 September 1915, p. 38E; 8 January 1916, p. 121E; 5 February 1916, p. 12E.

[38] Addison MSS, C43/d2, Diary of Christopher Addison, 2, 3, 8 February 1916.

[39] *American Machinist*, 1 April 1916, p. 59E.

[40] *American Machinist*, 20 November 1915, p. 81E; 18 December 1915, p. 104E.

[41] *Engineer*, 15 October 1915, p. 376; *Ministry of Munitions Journal*, No. 13, December 1917, p. 5.

[42] *History of Ministry of Munitions*, Vol. 8, p. 68.

of Brown and Ward opened a new workshop gallery in May 1916, it contained a special area for the training of women on lathes and drills with the objective of distributing them 'throughout the machine shops'.[43]

Alfred Herbert as director of the MTD ensured that his own firm led the way in female employment. As early as July 1915 he introduced 'girls' to operate centre lathes for work on manufacturing capstan lathes, and the firm's management entered negotiations with some of their male employees to assist in the training of female workers. Dilution at Herbert's caused alarm at the Coventry branch of the ASE, who demanded that the same rates should be paid to the women as to the men. Recognition of the role of women in the workplace was a slow process. A conference between the Coventry branch of the ASE and the Coventry district Engineering Employers' Association in the Autumn of 1915 found no common ground, the union recommending not 'to countenance in any way the introduction of female labour' in workshops manufacturing machine tools. Herbert's and other local employers simply delayed their response to the request of the ASE for a formal meeting to discuss the issue, and led by Herbert's continued to employ female workers in the fitting shops. In the face of mounting 'pressure from the employers and the Ministry of Munitions the ASE 'appeared impotent'.[44] The example set by Herbert's was important, because the MTD acknowledged that it had faced 'very great difficulty' over the introduction of female labour, but from early 1916 the actions of the MTD did seem to be taking effect.[45] During 1916, the proportion of female workers employed in making machine tools increased sharply (Table 3.3), approximately 3,172 being employed by September. By the end of the war women contributed nearly one-quarter of the industry's workforce, a remarkable achievement in an industry considered to be one of the bastions of skilled male labour.

Table 3.3
Female Employment in Machine Tool Trade (% of total)

January 1916	2.5
September 1916	9.0
January 1917	10.7
September 1918	24.4

Source: *History of Ministry of Munitions*, p. 68.

The use of female labour was a positive response by makers to meet the need for increased supplies of munitions. The 'shell crisis', of May 1915, could not be repeated, and this was the task of the Minister for Munitions, Lloyd-George, and

---

[43] *American Machinist*, 6 November 1915, p. 70E; 18 November 1915, pp. 70E, 81E; 26 February 1916, p. 31E; 13 May 1916, p. 93E.

[44] McG. Davies, 'A Twentieth Century Paternalist', p. 105.

[45] Addison MSS, D2/1/c43, Report on the Utilisation of Labour in the Machine Tool Trade, 8 September 1916.

the organising capabilities of his Ministry. Increased munitions supply was premised on two main principles. First, increased shell output required a 'rapid multiplication of machine tools'.[46] Second, in a 'war of machines' industry would have to adapt to the changing military demands of the frontline. The need to break the deadlock of trench warfare influenced the type of military hardware and components demanded. Consequently, the demands of the frontline introduced 'an element of uncertainty into the contracts given for the manufacture of artillery, shells, fuses, for changes in demand from the front necessitated changes in type ordered'.[47] In 1915-16 the belief of the allies on the Western front was that artillery using high explosive shells, tactically directed as a 'creeping barrage' in support of advancing troops, would break the stalemate.[48] By the middle of 1915 there was an enormous demand for projectiles, and most of the 'leading engineering workshops' were concentrating efforts on the manufacture of shells and other munitions. As Table 3.4 shows, there was a corresponding substantial increase in the delivery of shells to the BEF in the year and a half to June 1916.

Table 3.4
Shell Deliveries, January 1915 to January 1916

	Jan.-June 1915	July-Dec. 1915	Jan.-June 1916
Number of Shells (millions)	2.28	5.38	13.99
Tonnage (thousands)	36.46	90.08	248.67

% Increase:	Jan.-June 1915-July-Dec. 1915	July-Dec. 1915-Jan.-June 1916	Jan. 1915-June 1916
Number of Shells	136.2	160.1	514.3
Tonnage	147.1	176.1	582.0

Source: R. Q. J. Adams, *Arms and the Wizard*, pp. 243-4.

As Kitchener and the War Cabinet prepared to unleash the 'new army' of volunteer troops on the Western Front, which finally led to the devastating Battle of the Somme, machine tool makers were 'striving to the utmost of their capacity to provide the tools which are necessary for increasing the output of ammunition'.[49] Aggregate output for machine tools is not available, but sales data for Britain's largest maker, Herbert, shows a substantial increase. Sales of the company's own machines rose from £595,000 in 1914 to £1,320,000 in 1915 and

---

[46] *American Machinist*, 15 May 1915, p. 98E.
[47] G. D. Feldman, *Army, Industry and Labour in Germany, 1914-18* (Princeton, Princeton University Press, 1966), p. 55.
[48] Keegan, *First World War*, pp. 313-21, who also shows the limitations of this strategy.
[49] *Engineer*, 11 June 1915, p. 572.

£2,372,000 by 1916. Production of ancillary tools also expanded during the war, Birmingham Small Arms (BSA), for example, doubling its sales of drills, chucks, cutters and gauges, from £21,245 in 1915 to £42,676 by 1916. Vital war machinery was increasingly specially made for both the War Office and large engineering firms. Thus, during 1915 the Butler Machine Tool Co. of Halifax made large sales of special planers to Woolwich Arsenal, as well as a variety of special shell-turning lathes to Armstrong-Whitworth and Vickers, the latter at low prices which were un-remunerative.[50] Under pressure from the Ministry of Munitions after May 1915, machine makers attempted to tailor production to the requirements of munitions, especially for shell-turning lathes. At Keighley nearly every maker had incorporated the production of shell-turning lathes in their output portfolio, and at Leeds firms were working at 'high pressure' on government lathe contracts, a number of makers having converted to lathe production for the first time. C. Redman & Sons, Halifax, a specialist lathe maker, was operating a 71 and 1/2 hour week manufacturing large batches of shell turning-lathes for Woolwich, and for government contractors such as Armstrong-Whitworth, John Brown & Co., and Thomas Firth. In the Manchester district, the pressure of demand for lathes led to extensive sub-contracting, a number of textile machinery firms being employed 'to swell the output'. Specialist demands also increased for drills and planers, a need met by Coventry firms such as Morton & Weaver, Webster & Bennett, and the Selson Engineering Co., who were operating 70 hour weeks in early 1916. The demands of war exposed a weakness in the industry's product base. For example, Jones & Shipman was operating a 141 hour week supplying drilling machines for different sizes of shells. The company also installed plant for the manufacture of scroll chucks, copied from American designs, a machine component in short supply having been imported from Germany before the war. Gaps in the market were also evident in centre drilling machines, previously imported from the U.S.A., but now restricted by the German blockade.[51]

The task facing the machine tool industry may be gauged by the fact that a turret lathe could produce on average 20 three inch shells per working day, yet at the Battle of Neuve Chapelle in March 1915 the British fired as many shells in a few days as they had done during the entire Boar War.[52] This battle was 'an isolated attempt on a small front', fought 'with inadequate resources',[53] but it fuelled demands for increased volumes of munitions in the spring and summer of 1915. For example, James Keith, a member of the Institute of Mechanical Engineers, in a letter to *The Engineer* headed 'Shells, More Shells', asserted that engineering firms were at full capacity, and machine tool makers were faced with

---

[50] Arnold, 'Innovation', p. 60; Coventry Archive, Records of BSA, 594/1/1/2/2, BSA Meetings File, 9 October 1918; WYAS, Halifax Central Library, Butler Machine Tool Co., ASQ 1/1, Accounts for Year Ending 31 December 1915.

[51] *American Machinist*, 15 May 1916, p. 33E; 11 September 1916, pp. 70E. 76E; 6 November 1916, p. 99E; 11 December 1916, p. 127E; Miller, *Tools That Built a Business*, p. 22.

[52] *Engineer*, 14 June 1915, p. 572.

[53] C. L. Hart, *History of the First World War* (London, Papermac, 1977), p. 141.

'far more orders than they can possibly comply with, maybe for weeks or months to come'. He went on to propose a strategy of high volume production with the existing machine tool stock. Advocating that it was not feasible to wait until new machine tools, especially shell-turning lathes, were ordered, and more importantly delivered, Keith called for a rapid increase in shell output, and warned that the only way the country could achieve parity with Germany was 'by turning on all our engineering shops and foundries available to make all kinds of shells with the tools they have got'.[54]

Pressure to increase munitions production led to lengthening delivery times for machine tools, but the views of productionists such as Keith did not appreciate the problems this entailed for machine tool users who had been pressed to increase munitions supply. The production engineer, H. P. Walley, observing shell-making practices in small engineering shops, claimed that 'there are hundreds of firms with unsuitable plant engaged in the manufacture of shells'. Users were applying machine tools designed for other purposes, or employing those that were in need of urgent repair. Obsolete machinery militated both against the manufacture of munitions in quantities, and more importantly against the quality of the final product. *The Engineer* also registered concern, claiming that many engineering firms had been forced to adapt existing machines to meet the demands of the front, 'chiefly on account of the expense of producing new tools, and the delay which would necessarily be entailed in obtaining them'. Not convinced by these arguments, *The American Machinist* defended users, claiming that special machine tools were not required for every process involved in shell production, and added the rider that 'shrapnel shells could be produced with ordinary equipment'.[55] This, of course, prejudged the historical view of the Battle of the Somme of 1916, where out of the 1.79 million shells fired in the prelude to the offensive, 'about one million were shrapnel'. At this stage, the inability of machine tool firms to supply specialist machines in quantities, limited the production of high explosive shells. This was to prove disastrous on the Somme, where shrapnel shells made little impact against troops entrenched in deep earthworks. Shrapnel shells were designed to cut barbed wire, but they were not manufactured with great precision or finished with great accuracy, nor did British artillery have the capability to pin-point targets accurately. A lethal combination of the wrong type of shell, and a high proportion of duds, left British and Empire troops dangerously exposed on the Somme.[56]

Any assessment of the role of engineering and the machine tool industry in the War needs to consider crucial issues about the quality of output. Shell cases

---

[54] *Engineer*, 25 June 1915, p. 625.

[55] H. P. Walley, 'Shell-making in the Small Shop', *American Machinist*, 15 January 1916; *Engineer*, 11 June 1915, p. 572; *American Machinist*, 1 May 1915, p. 85E. For the issue of the trade off between quantity and quality in shell production, see Strachan, *The First World War, Vol. 1*, p. 1,086.

[56] Wilson, *Myriad Faces*, p. 320; Howard, *First World War*, pp. 78-9; Keegan, *First World War*, pp. 313-4. In the first day of the battle 21,000 British and Imperial troops were dead or missing.

made from high tensile steel were extremely difficult to machine and required a high degree of finish and accuracy. The fact that between one-quarter and one-third of the shells fired on the Somme were duds is testimony to the specific technical deficiencies of British engineering, and its machine tool equipment in 1916. Jones & Shipman found, for example, that munitions producers were desperately short of gauges for the accurate fitting of components, and there were large outstanding orders for the firm's grinders, 'remodelled to an improved standard of precision'. The priority given to the production of shrapnel shells also suggested to the Ministry of Munitions that British engineers had little knowledge of the machining processes involved in the manufacture of high explosive shells. For example, the directors of Herbert's noted with concern in November 1916 that there was a deficiency of information between users and makers on the technical specifications of high precision machine tools for volume output. The company's technical capabilities included a pool of knowledge which could provide 'a good deal of useful information', but the directors acknowledged that this was not matched by users of their machines, nor was there a 'department' established 'to collect and make use of it'.[57]

Despite the fact that there was no talk of a shell crisis after May 1915, the mobilisation of industry owed as much to expediency as to co-ordinated planning. For example, the National Shell Factories, first proposed in Leeds in May 1915, demonstrated the problems. By June 17 factories had been approved, and by the end of the year 30 were under the control of Ministry of Munitions Local Management Boards. Their initial operations were 'frequently handicapped by poor equipment', and the Boards were forced to utilise local machine tools which could be readily supplied, but which were 'often ill-adapted to the purpose to which it was put'. During 1915-16 frequent complaints were made about the use of 'faulty or worn equipment, efficiency having been in the first instance sacrificed to speed'.[58] Given the demands of war in 1915-16 'speed' was, indeed, of the essence. This is understandable on the part of politicians, military commanders, and producers who faced the reality of the human and economic costs of stalemate on the Western Front. Nevertheless, the pressure exerted to increase munitions output may, in the context of the technical capabilities of the British Army, have paradoxically sacrificed the real needs of the front to the necessity for 'speed'.

There is a case to be made for this in the experience of Greenwood & Batley with government officials. As a general engineer and machine tool maker this firm was caught in the government drive to increase the manufacture of ammunition. In June 1915 the management received an urgent demand from the War Office to increase the output of bullets to the French army to 8 million per week. Given the 'National Emergency', they would do everything possible to comply. However, they noted that their plant was short of high precision machine tools for cutting and shaping bullet caps, and warned that this would worsen with

---

[57] *Engineer*, 11 June 1915, p. 572; Miller, *Tools That Built a Business*, p. 22; *History of Ministry of Munitions*, Vol. 8, p. 73; Herbert, Departmental Board, 27 November 1916.

[58] *History of the Ministry of Munitions*, Vol. 8, pp. 66, 73.

increased output, leading to quality issues which would 'incur undue risks'. The inability of the firm to supply went down badly at the Ministry of Munitions, and in October Lloyd-George took the management to task. Defending his Company Armstrong claimed that they were constrained by skilled labour shortages, deficiencies in the availability of specialist machine tools, and the need to apply 'the commercial test'. By the latter he meant that experimentation in design, material usage, and machining operations were key factors in maintaining quality. For example, Armstrong referred to faulty metal supplied from the U.S.A. and problems of utilising the existing machine tool stock for designing to French specifications, which had shown up in tests a number of duds. Lloyd-George, however, was not for whinging. His reply was simple: 'absurd' ... You undertook to deliver at the end of April and you have delivered nothing'. A direct threat followed: the Ministry would take over the business and 'direct it from here'. Armstrong again pleaded that experimentation work was vital, but Lloyd-George had no desire to compromise: 'it is no use telling me that it is an insuperable difficulty ... if you had really tackled it you would not be in this position at the present moment'. Playing the patriotic card, he concluded that a shortage of small arms ammunition 'is very serious, especially if there is a great German attack in the West'. With the approach of the Battle of the Somme, the Ministry heaped further pressure on the company to increase output.[59] The experience of Greenwood & Batley has to be set in a broader context, one in which the Ministry began to evolve more systematic forms of organisational control.[60]

Machine Tools and Government Control

In early July 1915 the Munitions of War Act placed the machine tool industry under broad government control. 'A remarkable feature of the British ... situation is the extraordinary influence of the state as a stabiliser of conditions', commented *The American Machinist*. By December 1915 about 2,026 engineering works were under direct government control, and this was 'applied with particular force to the machine tool industry'.[61] Earlier, in April 1915, the MTD had been established at the War Office, and in June transferred to the Ministry of Munitions. In the following month the Machine Tool Advisory Committee (MTAC) was established, which played an important role in advising the MTD on the sanctioning of orders for machine tools. The use of sanctioning formed 'the basis for the whole system of controls', the MTD itself performing a co-ordinating role acting to facilitate the process by which makers were brought into contact with end users through contractors and government departments. This division of functions was important to effective co-ordination, because if the MTD had attempted to supply directly to

---

[59] Greenwood & Batley, Minute Book, 3 July, 22, 26 Oct 1915; 8 May 1916.
[60] See Adams, *Arms and the Wizard*, Ch's. 4-5; Lloyd-George, *Memoirs*, Ch. 9; Wilson, *Myriad Faces*, Ch. 20.
[61] *American Machinist*, 1 April 1916, p. 38E.

the numerous competing demands of contractors, government departments, and the allies, 'it would have been overwhelmed'.[62]

The immediate priority for the MTD was to collate basic information on the industry, as nine months into the War there was so 'little knowledge', not even a list of machine tool makers. What was known, however, was that a national census by Factory Inspectors at the time of the Shell Crisis had indicated that only about 50 per cent of the machine tools used in engineering were deployed on government contracts. Given these circumstances, and in the light of what the authorities considered an inadequate supply of machine tools, the MTD refused to sanction orders for new machines. Rather, a register was compiled of all 'idle' machine tools, and a decision taken to transfer them to firms engaged in munitions work. This was a mere contingency, but the remit of the MTD was to plan for an increase in supply and it considered a strategy consisting of four options. First, a programme of National Machine Tool Factories, similar to the National Shell and National Projectile Factories that were being established by the Ministry of Munitions. Second, assisted contracts on the same lines as those already arranged for munitions producers. A third option available was to provide financial assistance, to enable firms to undertake extensions to plant. Finally, sub-contracting was to be actively encouraged. Although the first two options were rejected, a National Tool and Gauge Factory was established to provide ancillary tools, an area of supply that was not part of the policy remit of the MTD. Financial assistance, the third option, was accepted by the MTD, but only under the condition that it should be provided in moderation. Thus, the priority was to encourage machine makers to sub-contract to general engineering firms that had surplus capacity, and to allied industries such as textile and printing machinery. Interference between contractors and sub-contractors by the MTD was to be minimal, leaving the sphere and activity of the sub-contractor as free as possible. At first, the 'inevitable result of ... sub-contracting ... was the inferiority of many of the machine tools produced'.[63] But given that the priority was to increase machine tool output to supply munitions producers, how successful was this?

Anecdotal evidence from the trade press indicates a substantial investment in new plant and extensions by machine makers. For example by December 1916, in the Halifax district, 'Every week sees the completion of additions to works and extension to plant', and in the Manchester region makers 'big and little, are laying down more new plant to increase output of war material'. The general impression was that British makers had invested in 'enormous installations of new and additional machine tool plants for munitions purposes'.[64] This view is supported by accounting evidence from Herbert's, where investments in fixed assets increased by £91,400 between 1914-19, compared to £23,500 between 1908 and 1914.[65] Table 3.5 provides data on the number of machine tools sanctioned by the MTD,

---

[62] *History of the Ministry of Munitions*, Vol. 8, p. 46.

[63] Ibid., pp. 46-9; *American Machinist*, 10 June 1916, p. 116E.

[64] *American Machinist*, 16 December 1916 p. 139E; *Engineer*, 15 December 1916, p. 540.

[65] Arnold, 'Innovation', p. 58.

and although incomplete provides a proxy in the absence of aggregate output data.[66] In 1916 the demand for additional machinery, especially to equip the newly established National Shell and Projectile Factories, was heavy, and the small increase in 1918 is attributed to a decrease in American imports, which necessitated a compensating increase in domestic output. The MTD anticipated an upward trend of sanctions from July 1918, to be delivered in 1919, indicating a 'much increased programme of British manufacture in the last few months of the conflict. The official account concluded:

> Broadly speaking the deliveries of 1918 compared more nearly with the sanctions of 1917 than of 1918, and insofar as any conclusion can be drawn from such rough data, the balance of supply and demand appears to have been very fairly attained in 1918, considering the increasing scarcity of labour and the general difficulty attending the supply of all munitions.[67]

Table 3.5
Average Monthly Value of Machine Tool Orders Sanctioned by the MTD (£ million), 1916-18

Last 7 Months, 1916	1.12
9 Months, 1917[a]	1.06
10 Months, Jan.-Oct. 1918	1.10

Source: *History of Ministry of Munitions*, Vol. 8, p. 58.
Notes: a. for January-June, and October-December.

Table 3.6
Employment in Machine Tool Industry, 1916-18

Jan. 1916	42,269
Jan. 1917	36,401
Jan. 1918	29,000
Nov. 1918	27,000

Source: *History of the Ministry of Munitions*, Vol. 8, p. 69.

---

[66] Data for orders delivered is a more reliable proxy, but these only exist for 1918 and are not comparable.

[67] *History of Ministry of Munitions*, Vol. 8, pp. 58-9.

Table 3.7
Proxy Value of Output Per Worker in Machine Tools, 1916-18

	Average No. Employed	Monthly Value of Sanctions (£ million)	Value of Sanctions per Worker (£)
Jan. 1916-Jan. 1917	39,335	1.12	28.45
Jan. 1917-Jan. 1918	32,700	1.06	32.43
Jan. 1918-Nov. 1918	28,000	1.10	39.40

For all its limitations, the evidence suggests no more than a satisfactory performance by the industry, but this may underestimate its actual contribution to the munitions industries. During 1915 and early 1916 the Ministry of Munitions adopted a 'favoured industry' approach towards machine tools, and this was expressed in terms of the use of skilled labour. The assumption was that as the demand for machine tools slackened, so the industry could release some of its skilled labour to other prioritised trades, but the pressure of demand remained high between 1916 and 1918, as naval and aircraft production demand increased and American supplies were reduced when she entered the war. The Ministry nevertheless insisted on the release of skilled workers from the industry, and as shown in Table 3.6 there was a downward trend in employment between 1916 and 1918, the total number employed falling by 36.1 per cent over the period. Consequently, if we consider the value of output per worker, a different interpretation of performance emerges. Table 3.7 uses sanctions as a proxy for output, and while the industry lost over one-third of its workforce, the value of orders sanctioned per worker rose by 38.5 per cent. This result was achieved in the context of continued demand pressures, and it suggests that makers made economical use of their effective labour by the deployment of more efficient methods of production.

Improvement took a variety of forms, but of particular importance were increased specialisation and a greater focus on the production of single-purpose tools. In April 1916, *The American Machinist* commented on the enormous increase in the output of machine tools for home consumption. It explained this trend in terms of the revised outlook of makers who had shifted from the manufacture of a wide range of machines to specialise in the manufacture of 'one or two types, in which they have advantageously introduced more modern methods of manufacture'. Herbert's, who employed 3,000 workers in 1918, approximately 11 per cent of the industry's total workforce, expanded output by reducing the range of machines produced and concentrating on fewer types. The increased focus on specialisation meant that by 1918, the scale of output was four times its pre-war level,[68] and references to a revolution in machine tool production were common.[69] At the MTD officials were quick to assert their role in facilitating change. Condemning the lack of organisation and the conservatism of managers in the industry during the early stages, the MTD

---

[68] *American Machinist*, 1 April 1916, p. 38E; *Engineer*, 5 April 1918, p. 289.
[69] See *American Machinist*, 24 June 1916, p. 126E.

formed teams of inspectors, who made regular visits to machine firms, and were seen as 'one of the most valued parts of its work'. Inspectors were important in providing advice on 'speeding up output', introducing new production processes and methods, cutting out waste and duplication, utilising more standardised components, and crucially in encouraging firms to accept greater standardisation and to concentrate their production on a more limited number of machine lines. In 1918, when American supplies of machine tools were diverted to support that country's war economy, greater specialisation was the key factor insisted upon by the MTD.[70]

Accompanying increased specialisation was a growing trend towards the manufacture of single-purpose machine tools. Components deemed unnecessary for the selected functions were stripped out and the machines considerably simplified. For example, capstan lathes were built for single-purposes, designed to perform one job, and 'turned out in their thousands ... have made it possible for practically untrained labour to do first class work'.[71] In November 1916 Oscar Harmer and John Millburn, of Alfred Herbert, reported that their Edgwick factory in Coventry was producing a variety of machines by 'repetition', and they were planning to extend this to lathes, radial drills and chucks. By December, Thomas Woof, a Herbert director, referred to the company producing capstan and turret lathes built in larger batches, which had been simplified by the standardisation of ancillary parts.[72] At one of Britain's largest engineering and munitions producers, BSA, the management invested £1.2 million in additional plant and extensions between 1914 and 1918, to manufacture a range of munitions, including the Lewis machine gun, rifles and shells. BSA was also a major producer of small tools, including twist drills, cutters, and gauges, but also diversified during the war to design and manufacture special-purpose machine tools, which were supplied to its own engineering departments, government factories and other munitions firms for the production of 'standardised products'. Receiving financial assistance from the Ministry of Munitions of £385,000, the company expanded its Sparkbrook factory in Birmingham to create a 'super tool department'. Sir Hallewell Rogers, the chairman, later reflected that special purpose machines had evolved from 'the very wide and diverse experience which the increased demands of the Munitions Department had forced upon us'. Designing machine tools for munitions was an education in 'mass production ... planned to make the smallest range of products but on the largest possible scale'. To facilitate this, they established an 'expert consulting branch' to advise on the application of machine tools to specialised jobs, technical problems in production, and the design of plant to enable 'the most scientific method of carrying it out and to supply the means by which the method could be made operative'.[73] This reflected a general view by 1917 that 'many old, wasteful and inefficient methods had gone for ever', and that the principles of large-scale

---

[70] *History of the Ministry of Munitions*, Vol. 8, p. 66; *Ministry of Munitions Journal*, No. 12, November 1917, p. 366.

[71] *American Machinist*, 19 August 1916, p. 17E; *Engineer*, 7 January 1916, p. 14.

[72] Herbert, Departmental Board, 27 November, 4 December 1916.

[73] 594/1/1/2/3-4, BSA Meetings Files, October 1919, October 1920.

production were 'receiving widespread recognition in the machine tool trade'.[74]

Given these examples, the future would appear to lie in the formation of large-scale groups of specialised but interrelated manufacture. For machine tool makers this future apparently arrived in February 1917 with the formation of Associated British Machine Tool Makers Ltd (ABMTM). Established with a capital of £100 million, the 10 founder members, all firms with established reputations as innovators of high quality machines, agreed to avoid duplication by specialising in the production of a narrow range of machines, shown in Table 3.8. A centralised selling agency for the ABMTM was established in London, and subsidiary trading companies formed in Italy, France and Belgium. A main objective of the Association was to 'speed the selling and use of British machine tools, especially in the colonies and foreign countries'. In essence, ABMTM was a combined selling organisation, and while it did promote a degree of specialisation, members were insistent on retaining their own individuality, and ownership and control remained firmly embedded in the constituent firms.[75] ABMTM had all the appearances of a classic British compromise, which acknowledged the importance of specialisation and the advantages of pooled marketing and selling, and yet remained committed to personal ownership that kept the management of production, design, and finance firmly under the control of individual firms. Indeed, there are a number of reservations about how far the achievements of the machine tool industry was premised upon more efficient methods of production, and the effective utilisation of the firm's organisational and human capabilities.

Table 3.8
Founder Members of the ABMTM Ltd. and their Specialities, 1917

Firm	Location	Speciality
James Archdale Ltd.	Birmingham	Light radial drills and certain sizes of milling machines
William Asquith Ltd.	Halifax	Mainly heavy radial and vertical drills
James Butler & Co.	Halifax	Light slotters, light planers and shapers
Churchill Machine Tool Co.	Manchester	Grinding machines
Kendall & Gent	Manchester	Plano-mills
G. Richards & Co.	Manchester	Boring mills
Smith & Coventry Ltd.	Manchester	Plain and universal millers, high speed planers, gear cutting machines
J. Lang & Sons	Johnstone	Lathes of light patterns
J. Shanks & Co.	Johnstone	Heavy lathes, planers and slotters

Source: *The Engineer*, 6 April 1917, p. 316; *American Machinist*, 7 June 1917, p. 840.

---

[74] *American Machinist*, 7 April 1917, p. 101E.
[75] *American Machinist*, 7 April 1917, p. 95E.

Modernisation and War: The British Machine Tool Industry

Leslie Hannah views the First World War as 'a watershed in business and economic development', and in engineering there was a growing movement towards mass production, standardisation, and de-skilling. Indeed, for contemporaries there was much talk of a 'New Industrial Revolution'.[76] For machine tools, however, this view of modernisation, based on the full diffusion of large-scale production methods, needs to be examined more closely. Despite government intervention and the movement of firms to increased standardisation and specialisation, the diffusion of large-scale production technologies still had a long way to go. This is supported by the fact that even in 1917 the machine tool industry was 'taxed to the utmost', makers operating plant night and day, and thus utilising existing plant more extensively to meet demand. Nevertheless, deliveries of new machines were 'long delayed'. By September 1917 potential customers were waiting between 12 to 14 weeks for standard machines. Indeed, from December 1916 the Ministry of Munitions, through its Clearing House, had placed heavy pressure on users to restrict their demand for vital machine tools.[77] Partly, these deficiencies can be explained by the problems firms encountered in co-ordinating production to meet larger volume output but, at the same time, meet the variegated demands of machine tool users during the war.

During the last year of the war BSA was working night and day on the manufacture of munitions. Sir Hallewell Rogers was in no doubt about the lessons of war. 'Parallel to a training in mass production' he claimed 'we got an education in flexibility and adaptiveness'.[78] Coordinating a strategy of increased volume output, with flexibility in meeting user needs was no easy task, as shown by the example of Herbert's. Despite the movement of the firm to the manufacture of more standardised lines, Herbert's was inundated by demands for a variety of different machine lines. In December 1916, Joseph Pickin reviewed the company's manufacturing and selling programme. The company was operating a flexible batch production programme, arranging 'from time to time its manufacturing portfolio to produce machines 'in advance of the original promise'. Such flexibility, inevitably caused 'delay' and increased 'expense', as producing in advance of orders meant that they had to stop batches when partially completed, or alter erected machines to meet customer requirements. Accepting this critical review, the Board declared that the existing manufacturing system did not 'permit the most economical methods of manufacture to be followed', resulting in rising costs and high prices to users. Consequently, it was decided to use a flexible selling policy and strictly adhere to a fixed manufacturing programme. As the management concluded, 'selling methods, which may always be made much more elastic than shop systems, should be arranged'. This meant, of course, that the firm would have to produce stock in anticipation of user demand, but this was

---

[76] Hannah, *Rise of the Corporate Economy*, pp. 27-9.

[77] *Ministry of Munitions Journal*, No. 1, December 1916, p. 3; No. 5, April 1917, p. 156; *American Machinist*, 1 September 1917, p. 17E.

[78] BSA Meeting File, Ordinary, October 1919.

considered an acceptable risk as the investment would 'sooner or later ... be realised as profit'.[79]

But the demands of war were not suitable to more rigid systems of manufacture. For example, such was the vagaries of demand in 1917 that Pickin argued for the need to expand their line of machine tools to include batches of automatic turning machines for stock, which were in large demand. Alfred Herbert himself was well aware of the way that the demands of war militated against the move towards standardised output, when he directed the Board in 1918 to continue to manufacture 'Big Boring Machines', which should be built 'as occasion demanded'. To cover the market they were to be manufactured in four distinct types: single, vertical, horizontal, and combined spindles. During 1917, the continuation of flexible batch production techniques was conditioned by the demands of users, but it had repercussions for the coordination of integrated production within the factory. Limited tool room space continued to be a key problem, as did inadequate supplies of castings from the company's foundry, and shortages of supplies from outside contractors. This led Alfred Herbert in early 1918 to report that their present manufacturing systems were facing severe 'bottlenecks', delays in delivery being unacceptable. By August 1918, Pickin was reporting a 'general loss of goodwill', and compounding their problems was the continuation of a severe drain of skilled tool room labour to the armed forces. The cost of this to the war effort was summed up by a letter to Sir Arthur Duckham at the War Office, the directors warning of the severe delay this caused to aircraft production.[80]

Britain's largest producer, Herbert's, is testimony to the partial development of mass production systems in the machine tool industry, but also exemplifies the strategies of large firms in bridging the gap between supply and demand through systems of sub-contracting, a method which was promoted by the Ministry of Munitions. Sub-contracting for Herbert's was a means not only to increase output, but also to expand the range of machine tools offered to users. Management's manufacturing programme was to reduce the number of lines produced in its own factories, so tailoring output to existing constraints, and to expand the range of machines in high demand through sub-contracting. For example, during 1917 and 1918 Herbert's sub-contracted to a number of engineering firms to manufacture a range of machines which were in large demand, but the firm lacked the capacity to manufacture themselves. Sub-contracting was crucial in enabling the firm to expand its machine tool lines, but also brought with it the costs of transacting in the market. In early 1917 there were numerous complaints from French and Italian importers about the production efficiency of sub-contracted machines bearing the Herbert name. Extensive sub-contracting also meant a loss of control by the company over machine specifications, a crucial factor in the demands of the Ministry of Munitions for a flexible approach to production. Thus, Oscar Harmer referred to stoppages in production, and delays in delivery, caused by the diversion by the Ministry of

[79] Herbert, Departmental Board, 11 December 1916.
[80] Herbert, Departmental Board, 19 March, 2 July 1917; 14·January, 26 Aug 1918.

machines from the customer that originally ordered them to others. Sub-contractors on these machines refused to make alterations necessitated by the Ministry's instructions, and so the cost of adaptation fell on Herbert's who had to divert their works capacity from their own manufacturing programme.[81]

. Sub-contracting brought with it problems of quality control, but was based as much on business expediency than the patriotic actions of manufacturers during the war. For example, Herbert's negotiated with Chance Bros. of Birmingham at the end of 1917 for the manufacture of the Herbert 'Nos. 6, 9 and 12 Horizontal Milling Machines', and the 'No. 6 Universal Milling Machine'. Chance Bros. declined, as they were not prepared to invest in equipping a new factory, but the terms of the deal indicated the perception of the Herbert management concerning the future commercial value of sub-contracting to their business. Chance Bros. were to 'build for us and no one else'. Indeed, by 1917, the Herbert's management were already planning its post-war manufacturing programme, and sub-contracting formed a platform for an extension of its machine range. Far from patriotic cooperation, machine makers constructed business networks with commercial advantages to the forefront of negotiations. In April 1917 contact was made with Tangye, Birmingham, to build exclusively for Herbert's medium and heavy machine tools, either with designs supplied by Herbert's or if satisfactory designs provided by Tangye. Negotiations, however, dragged on, both companies looking after their own interests. It was not until November that a deal was struck, the managing director of Tangye, Seeley, forcing through a guarantee in the contract of orders valued at £75,000 per annum. By July 1918 Tangye was also supplying radial drills to Herbert's, which were in large demand by munitions factories, and which Herbert's hoped to exploit the market for after the end of the war.[82]

Sub-contracting is suggestive of the deficiencies of firms in the mass production of machine tools, and this is further supported by the huge surge of American imports during the war, which also affected the design capabilities of British makers. Table 3.9 clearly demonstrates the heavy British reliance on foreign supplies, and America was practically 'our sole source of ... supply', as shown in Table 3.10.[83] Total British imports of machine tools were 14 times higher during the war than the immediate pre-war years, and American imports formed the vast bulk of this increase. These imports were largely destined for munitions work, imports of machine tools being tightly regulated by Board of Trade licences, which were only granted for 'special undertakings' to enforce 'a limitation of projects'.[84] This trend was compounded by a fall in machine tool exports (Table 3.9) in 1915, as resources switched towards domestic demand to meet war time requirements. Consequently, the balance of trade in machine tools swung heavily into deficit, but remarkably, after 1915, exports rose rapidly, boosted by the

---

[81] Herbert, Departmental Board, 8 January, 19 February 1917.

[82] Herbert, Departmental Board, 30 April, 20 August, 3, 17 September, 26 November 1917; 4 January, 22 July 1918

[83] *History of Ministry of Munitions*, Vol. 8, p. 39.

[84] *Ministry of Munitions Journal*, No. 1, December 1916, p. 24.

demands by Britain's allies for increased industrial capacity, and the willingness of the British authorities to share the burden of meeting their requirements. The average value of war-time exports was nearly twice the level of the pre-war period, and during the peak export year, 1917, the largest three recipient countries, France, Russia and Italy took 88 per cent of all exports (Table 3.11). This suggests that war time changes in production, working practices and design carried with them a number of positive features. It is plausible to describe Britain as the 'workshop of the allies',[85] partly a consequence of French and Italian dependence on Germany for their supplies before the war. Out of a French import bill of $10 million for machine tools in 1913, France paid approximately $3 million to Germany. In the same year, Germany supplied two-thirds of Italian machine tool imports.[86] To fill the allied gap the British sacrificed some domestic supplies, although meeting home needs remained a priority. In these circumstances, the British, as well as her allies became reliant on American imports. In July 1915 the American market for machines had 'been ransacked', even second hand lathes being in short supply, and by December machine tool agents in the U.S. 'were busy ordering wherever they possibly could'. Not discounting the contribution of American imports to the British cause, it was nevertheless in supplying France where America made a decisive impact, and by doing so eased the pressure on British makers. The 'industrial resources of France stood in sore need of assistance', and in the first year of the war French imports rose at twice the rate of the British. By 1916 'Thousands of American lathes' as well as screw machines, millers and grinders, were allowing the French to produce 'thousands of projectiles daily'. Such was the demand that American makers faced severe problems in meeting it with increased output.[87]

The inflow of American technology to Britain, of course, was facilitated by existing marketing networks. As was shown in Chapter 2, British makers such as Alfred Herbert were networked with American makers before the war, adapting imported technology to the needs of domestic manufacturers. This was reinforced by specialist American machine importers, who expanded their business extensively during the war. One of Britain's leading import firms was Burton, Griffiths & Co. of London, which had established a high reputation through its agencies with American machine makers. During the war they were highly successful in promoting sales for various agencies they held 'on a scale unheard of', and their competitive capabilities were based on staff who were 'trained in selling American lines' such as Landis, Gisholt, Ingersoll, and Milwaukee.[88] In July 1917, the company was converted from a private to a public limited company, and for E. M. Griffiths, the chairman, the injection of new capital was crucial to the company's plans to expand the American business both during and after the war. In

---

[85] *Engineer*, 6 August 1915, p. 135.

[86] *American Machinist*, July-December 1916, p. 62.

[87] *Engineer*, 2 July 1915, p. 11; 7 January 1916, p. 2; *The American Machinist*, 11 March 1916, p. 41E, January-June 1916, pp. 393, 694.

[88] 594/1/1/3/58, BSA Board Minutes, 30 November 1928, Report on Burton, Griffiths, and BSA Tools Ltd.

May 1918 Griffiths proudly reported to shareholders record sales of £881,000, the formation of a subsidiary trading company in New York, and the opening of offices in Manchester, Birmingham and Leeds for the promotion of American machines.[89]

Table 3.9
British Imports, Exports, and the Balance of Trade in Machine Tools, 1908-19

	Imports (£000)	Imports, Value Per Ton (£)	Exports (000)	Trade Balance (£000)[a]
1908	116	118	416	+300
1909	81	129	768	+687
1910	82	144	714	+632
1911	214	118	759	+545
1912	283	103	935	+652
1913	361	94	1,013	+652
1914	427	88	1,020	+593
1915	2,128	103	779	-1,349
1916	2,912	132	1,117	-1,795
1917	2,655	167	2,112	-543
1918	3,858	199	1,280	-2,578
1919	3,962	232	2,286	-1,670
Averages:				
1908-14	223	113	804	+580
1915-19	3,103	167	1,515	-1,588

Source: *American Machinist*, July-December 1922, pp. 804-5.
Notes: a. exports-imports

The lessons of American imports were not lost on Herbert's, who were large factorers of machine tools, both for British makers and most importantly for American machine firms.[90] As shown in Table 3.12, the proportion of sales accounted for by factored goods accelerated during the war, reaching a peak of nearly 70 per cent of all sales in 1918. Large importers such as Herbert's were crucial to developing a market network in Britain for American machine tools, and enabled this company to maintain a wide range of products, especially single-purpose machines. For example, in 1917 the management referred to the manufacture of automatic multiple spindle machines by American makers, and noted that they 'could not make anything to compete for some considerable time',

---

[89] Coventry Archive, 926/12/1/1, Burton, Griffiths & Co., General Minute Book, 3 July 1917; 24 May 1918.
[90] Arnold, 'Innovation', pp. 61-2.

Table 3.10
British Imports of Machine Tools by Place of Origin, 1914-20 (values £000)

	1914	1915	1916	1917	1918	1919	1920
Sweden	0	0	0	0	0	0	58
Germany	31	0	0	0	0	2	119
Netherlands	0	0	0	0	0	0	21
Belgium	0	0	0	0	0	0	8
Denmark	0	0	0	0	0	0	60
France	3	4	8	8	3	15	49
Switzerland	0	0	0	0	0	0	25
U.S.A.	377	2,099	2,849	2,616	3,772	3,861	2,576
British Possessions	3	12	22	8	40	16	23
Other	13	14	32	22	43	69	81
Total	427	2,128	2,912	2,655	3,858	3,962	3,020
% Of U.S.A. to Total	88.3	98.6	97.8	98.5	97.8	97.5	85.3

Source: *American Machinist*, July-December 1922, p. 805.

and consequently were in the market to act as agents for U.S. producers. In October 1917 the company had accumulated stocks of American machine tools to the value of £329,000, and Pickin reported that 'we should face the loss of business in order to decrease our commitments in America ... for machines and small tools'. This decision followed a prohibition by America on the export of machinery for stock, and forced the Herbert board to consider increasing the output of their own manufactured vertical mills, universal grinders, and tool and cutter grinders. To achieve this, however, they were desperately short of additional plant, and consequently wrote to Alfred Herbert as Director General of Machine tools pleading for Ministry permission to install additional machinery.[91] Nevertheless, the company's reliance on American design influence caused unease amongst members of the board, and raised questions about the technical and competitive capabilities of British makers after the war.

The influence of American designs at Herbert's during the war was important to the technological trajectory of the company. For example, James Archdale Ltd. of Birmingham was also a firm with a high reputation for utilising American designs, and in late 1916 Herbert's employed a leading Archdale designer in their Factoring Department to design a range of radial drills on American lines. Nevertheless, in September 1918 Pickin drew to the attention of management the need for 'concentrated energy' to develop 'original designs'.

---

[91] Herbert, Departmental Board, 15, 29 October, 26 November 1917.

Table 3.11
Percentage of Total British Machine Tool Exports to Main European Allies, 1914-18

	1914	1915	1916	1917	1918
France	9.1	24.8	32.5	40.1	54.1
Italy	5.4	6.3	10.4	9.8	21.3
Russia	26.8	35.0	33.8	38.1	0.0

Source: Compiled from *The American Machinist*, July-December 1922, p. 805.

Reflecting on the company's design policy he concluded that that 'there are none of any striking originality'. The war, according to Pickin, had not brought radical design innovation, and there is evidence to suggest that the pressure of the authorities to increase output militated against experimentation with new designs. For example, in 1917 directives from the Ministry of Munitions to increase supply led to the conversion of the Herbert 'experimental department' to tool room use, and proposals to the Ministry in February 1918 to reconvert it fell on deaf ears, the officials refusing to allow the appropriation of skilled production workers for experimental work.[92] This, as we shall see in the next chapter, caused problems for the company in organising its post-war production programme.

Table 3.12
Alfred Herbert Ltd.: Sales, 1913-19 (000)

	Factored Machines	Own Manufacture	Total	% Factored to Total
1913	220	306	526	41.8
1914	270	325	595	45.4
1915	703	617	1320	53.3
1916	1333	1039	2372	56.2
1917	1871	1032	2903	64.4
1918	2155	933	3088	69.8
1919	1456	712	2168	67.2

Source: Arnold, 'Innovation', p. 60.

The machine tool industry during the Great War was closely monitored by the Ministry, and was perhaps the most controlled of all industries. But control meant less the creation of a new industry than the stimulus and re-modelling of an established one which strived to meet the abnormal demands of war. Extensive use was made of sub-contracting, which limited the trend towards increased specialisation, and the state-directed objective of raising output meant that there

[92] Herbert, Departmental Board, 11 December 1916; 25 Feb, 9 September 1918.

was a reduced effort on developing new designs. In addition, the heavy reliance on American machine tools, especially of special types, was promoted by firms such as Herbert's who used their factoring business to facilitate the growing deployment of advanced American designs. At the same time, the industry had made a valiant effort to increase output. By the end of hostilities, its labour force was about one-quarter female, and it had shown itself to be adaptable to the diverse demands of the war. It was in this situation that machine makers began to think about reconstruction to meet the needs of the post-war world, one in which technological progress would be a key factor in business success. Within two years of the end of the conflict, of course, the British economy entered a severe slump, and it is to the issues of reconstruction and the response to the depression that the next chapter turns.

CHAPTER FOUR

Meeting the Challenge: Alfred Herbert and the British Machine Tool Industry, 1918-34

'Talk to any business man for fifteen minutes and if you are not convinced that his particular business is the hardest one in which to make a living it isn't his fault. When it comes to the machine tool builder he can tell you a tale of woe that beggars description.'[1]

Introduction

In the immediate post-war years, the international machine tool industry experienced a sharp, but short boom. Frank A. Scott, the Vice President of one of America's largest machine makers, Warner & Swasey of Cleveland, Ohio, observed that during the War, output and investment had risen to unprecedented levels and high profits had enticed new firms into the industry. The insatiable 'demand for the production of weapons' could not be satisfied, despite a considerably enlarged capacity, and following the Armistice there was a fresh wave of world orders for machine tools as industry reconverted back to peacetime conditions. The boom broke in the middle of 1920, and this was evident on both sides of the Atlantic, Scott observing that the 'unprecedented demand' for machine tools in the re-equipment phase after the war was 'satisfied', the industry sinking into the greatest depression that it had ever experienced.[2] Unlike American makers, however, who faced a sharp but short recession, the British machine tool industry faced an intense and prolonged economic depression. Declining export markets, depressed and uncertain domestic demand, falling prices, lowered profit expectations, and rising foreign competition all added to the 'tales of woe'.

Gauging the long-run output performance of the British industry, given the 'paucity of data', is difficult, but estimates in Table 4.1 indicate that the volume of output was 37 per cent lower by 1924 compared to 1913, and values were down by 20 per cent. The value of output fell further in 1925, 'and it is unlikely that 1926 proved very much better'. Output moved upwards vigorously in the two years preceding the crash of 1929, but apart from this brief revival, the output performance of the industry over the 1920s was weak. As Aldcroft observes, 'for

---

[1] *American Machinist*, 12 January 1924, p. 1.
[2] *American Machinist*, 10 January 1922, pp. 73-5.

much of the 1920's the home market for machine tools remained fairly depressed despite the growth in demand for the industry's products from the motor manufacturers'. A general fall in demand for machine tools followed the post-war boom, a trend intensified by the government disposal scheme that 'released at bargain prices' some 70,000 machines by the end of 1922. In the longer-term, the demand for machine tools was adversely affected by the depression in core industries, in particular shipbuilding, 'which offset the increase in demand from the motor industry'. The consequence was that machine tool capacity contracted in the first half of the 1920s as a response to the general malaise of Britain's heavy industry.[3]

Table 4.1
Output of Machine Tools in the U.K., 1907-35

	Volume (Tons)	Value ($ million)
1907	78,000	2.936
1913	-	4.00*
1924	49,000	3.65
1925	-	3.20*
1929	-	6.00*
1930	35,000	4.96
1934	40,962	4.83
1935	53,450	6.74

Source: Aldcroft, 'The Performance of the British Machine-Tool Industry', p. 282.
Notes: * are estimates.

The shock of the early 1920s had severe repercussions for Britain's machine tool firms, and later the world economic crash of 1929 rebounded hard on an industry suffering low and uncertain demand in the 1920s. Output crashed, and by 1933 was 48.2 per cent lower than the peak year of 1929. It was not until 1935 that output surpassed that of 1929, and then only marginally, and as we shall see in the next chapter demand for machine tools rose rapidly in the government's re-armament drive leading up to the Second World War. Depressed domestic demand, however, characterised the business experience of the industry in the 1920s and early 1930s. By 1922, for example, shortages of orders in the Midlands resulted in only 25 per cent of the industry's potential capacity being utilised. Overcapacity was a function of the sharp fall in demand experienced in the engineering industry, in particular from the heavy goods sector and, albeit temporarily, from automobile manufacturers. 'Abnormal conditions' confronted the industry, makers abandoned stock building in anticipation of an upturn, but their confidence was shattered by the unpredictability of future demand.[4] As 'the servant of general engineering', the

---

[3] D. H. Aldcroft, 'The Performance of the British Machine-Tool Industry in the Interwar Years', *Business History Review*, Vol. 40, No. 3 (1966), pp. 281-5.
[4] *American Machinist*, 4 March 1922, pp. 177-8E.

machine tool industry confronted the full blast of the depression.[5] Aldcroft concludes that 'machine tool firms were operating under very difficult conditions', but he also considers that the industry is open to three serious allegations concerning its performance in the interwar years. First, makers failed to anticipate demand during the post-war boom, later during the revival of trade from the mid-1920s to 1929, and again in the recovery stage from 1932. Second, Britain continued to rely on imports of 'gap' machines constituting mainly special-purpose machines not produced domestically, but also in periods of rising activity imports of general-purpose machines. In particular, British makers lacked the capacity to meet upturns in economic activity, and were competitively weak in manufacturing special-purpose machines in growing demand by industries such as automobiles that were introducing continuous production techniques. Third, and 'most serious' was the condemnation of the industry's competitive performance in export markets relative to the Americans and Germans. British makers lost ground in export markets, and this raised questions about the technical competency of the industry.[6] This chapter will examine these allegations by a general survey of the industry, and by focusing upon the company that Aldcroft symbolises as the most progressive firm, Alfred Herbert.[7] This company failed to take a lead role in generating policies to create inter-firm co-operation at the industrial level, symbolic of an industry composed mainly of small-scale individualistic producers, and consistent with Chandler's notion of the retention of personal capitalism in British manufacturing industry.[8] As a starting point, we explore the performance of the industry in the post-war boom, which highlights a number of constraints facing the industry.

Facing the Post-War World, 1918-20

Machine tools were central to the re-equipment and re-conversion of British industry to peace production. E. M. Griffiths, the chairman of Burton, Griffiths, had no doubt that an adequate supply of machine tools was central to the future efficiency of British manufacturing industry, enabling 'this country to produce the utmost possible maximum not only to restore worn out plant but in order to do a big export trade'.[9] The fundamental question in 1918, however, was 'how prepared' machine makers were for a 'buying movement when it set in?'[10] Even before the war ended, there were doubts about the capacity of machine makers to meet anticipated demand. Thus, in October 1918 Percy Vernon, a Herbert's director, informed the board that customers 'were anxious to place orders to pursue their regular business as soon as possible', and in November the technical director, Oscar Harmer, reported that the company had received orders for the

---

[5] *American Machinist*, 15 January 1921, p. 193E.

[6] Aldcroft, 'The Performance of the British Machine Tool Industry', pp. 282-7.

[7] Ibid., pp. 286, 291.

[8] See Chandler, *Scale and Scope*, pp. 235-94.

[9] 926/12/1/1, Burton, Griffiths & Co., General Minute Book, 24 May 1918.

[10] *American Machinist*, 20 November 1918, p. 308.

month valued at £40,000, the bulk of them 'for post-war business'. Rising demand opened a window of opportunity for progressive firms to capture the market, but as Vernon conceded, customers were already 'anticipating problems of obtaining machines after the war'.[11]

Capacity constraints were evident before the war ended, and undermined product planning in a buoyant post-war market. Joseph Pickin reported on the post-war planning strategy, in which the directors intended to return to the pre-1914 policy of manufacturing a wide range of machines. A diverse product range would enable the company to hold stock to supply the varied demands of customers, but forward planning was constrained by limited tool room capacity to sufficiently enable 'experimentation' and the concentration of 'energy and attention to the development of machines of original design'. Commenting on the company's potential product lines, and reflecting on past developments, Pickin observed that 'there are none of any striking originality ... we have usually been content to develop existing types of machines and have never seemed, either by accident or design, to have dropped on anything that might be called a distinctive type of machine'. Reinforcing his point, he cited American machines built by Jones & Lamson, Fisholt, Fellows, Lumsden, and Pratt & Whitney, all incorporating original designs ensuring high performance and precision, and well respected by customers. Given the competition, Pickin 'wondered whether we had not been too much concerned with perfecting existing methods to the exclusion and search for possible better methods'. Responding to these allegations, Vernon defended the reputation of the company, claiming that 'new' machine designs were incorporated into the company's universal milling and gear hobbing machines, manufacturing lathes, automatic screw machine, and radial drills and turret lathes. Design capability was sufficient to supply machines that were 'quite original in many ways', but Vernon was forced to concede that capacity shortages had delayed commercial application, restricting the company's ambitions to meet future demand. For example, the machine shops had been unable to convert engineering drawings into prototypes for manufacture because of limited capacity, and this 'did not ... stimulate design', which was 'a disappointing and discouraging fact'. The technical capability to design was in advance of the 'capacity to manufacture', and although a few 'experimental' machines had been built, 'the works cannot tackle them'.[12]

Limited capacity reflected the cautious investment strategy of management. The Herbert works' director, John Milburn, commenting upon the effects of capacity shortages on the company's design programme, noted that there was a commitment to a low risk strategy. Investment, to expand capacity, was only forthcoming 'when the demand was established and we were absolutely crowded out'. Milburn communicated his concerns over the 'reluctance to extend ... manufacture' to Sir Alfred Herbert:[13]

---

[11] 926/1/4/1-3, Alfred Herbert Ltd., Minute Books of the Departmental Board of Directors, 1911-41, 17 October, 25 November 1918.

[12] Herbert, Departmental Board, 25 February, 9 September 1918.

[13] He was knighted during the war for his services at the Ministry of Munitions.

He had ... called his attention to the fact that lots of processes and methods might come to light if only we had sufficient tool room capacity to try experiments ... and Sir Alfred had agreed with him. In fact, at present we are bound down by the smallness of our tool room capacity to produce only bare necessities ... if we did more the results would be an accumulation of knowledge to enable us to build really good machines for the purposes involved.

Despite the acceptance by Sir Alfred of the link between capacity and design capability, caution remained paramount, and following Sir Alfred's advice Vernon informed the board that there was no certainty that new machines 'built in quantities' could find a large and profitable market after the war. 'A number of machines might be tackled', Vernon claimed, 'and only one make good'. Caution reflected uncertain market information on the types of machines demanded by customers after the war, but, as Vernon stressed, 'the main obstacle' to initiating a programme based on a wide range of new designs was related to capacity limitations hindering the building 'of a proper experimental shop'. Consequently, Vernon proposed that the company should concentrate manufacturing capabilities on a small select range of machines, with proven market potential, such as the Herbert Automatic Turning Machine, which had the potential to 'knock out' of the market American competitors such as Potter & Johnson. Supporting this alternative strategy, Harmer recommended a delay in the development of new product lines, and the board generally concluded that it was 'impracticable to do anything in the way of manufacturing new machines'.[14]

Inadequate market information, combined with insufficient capacity, delayed the formulation of a coherent manufacturing plan, a fact that manifested itself in the differing views of the directors concerning the scope of the post-war programme. Contrary to Vernon, Pickin, for example, called for the manufacture of a wide range of machines, expanding their lines beyond the traditional turret lathes into universal milling machines, which were in demand by the motor trade. Universal millers also complimented the company's vertical milling machines, a product that had gained a market reputation during the war. Harmer took an opposite view. Observing that 'The hardest thing to decide was what we should manufacture', he advised Sir Alfred that the company should devote its 'energies' to the manufacture of turret lathes, and continue the building of vertical millers rather than develop the new universal types. In Harmer's judgement, the company had already committed investment to designing existing lines, justifying the specialisation 'in all sizes of capstan lathes, turret lathes, combination turret lathes, bar lathes and automatic turning machines'. Specialisation, according to Harmer, would enable the company to build machines in large batches, placing their standardised lines in an 'impregnable position' in the market, and 'keep ... our works fully employed, even if they were extended'. Producing large batches of general-purpose standardised machines was clearly Harmer's vision for future business success:

---

[14] Herbert, Departmental Board, 9 September 1918.

it would pay us better to do a few types well with sufficient sizes, rather than to make too many types in inadequate quantities, and he thought that we could cut out everyone else on turret machinery if we went for it properly and manufactured, in such quantities, as would enable us to cut down prices. We should find that if we confined ourselves to turret machines we should have a very heavy business ... and if they were to make milling machines they should confine them to vertical types.

A priority towards large batch production was also given by John Milburn, who contended that orders for universal millers were small, coming in 'ones or twos'. Although Milburn supported Harmer's position, he nevertheless raised major concerns about the process of planning, arguing that the first priority should be to decide on the investment policy in additional capacity, rather than the type of machines built. As he informed the board:

the most important thing to decide first of all, was the volume of machines per annum we would take as our object, and then find out if the works had the necessary capacity for such output, and if not make the works large enough. The question of exactly what types and numbers of machines the programme would consist of could be thrashed out later on.

For the executive board, investment in capacity expansion was the primary consideration'. Large batch production methods would ensure economies of scale, a lesson that had been important to learn during the First World War.[15] Nevertheless, there were clearly different messages emanating from the Herbert board over the future direction of the company.

Sir Alfred's response was not to set a clear strategic direction for the company. Rather, he opted for a policy of contingency, informing his directors in October 1918 that 'the best position the company could be in at the end of the war would be to have as few commitments as possible and the maximum amount of money in the bank to be ready to jump off in any direction'. In justifying this decision to defer a programme of capacity expansion, he referred to uncertainty over future demand, but also the limited market information available to executive management. In a letter to Pickin, Sir Alfred urged the board to 'get out and about during the transition' to tout for business, but as Pickin observed 'What we wanted was simple records of observed facts of technical and commercial interest'. By November 1918, the company's sales representatives were actively engaged in acquiring customer information on their future requirements, but as Pickin noted, heavy engineering firms and automobile producers were uncertain in their future investment strategy. Market uncertainty led to a cautious approach to investment, leading to major problems in meeting customer demand. As the directors conceded in May 1919, their intention to build large stocks of standard machines in advance of customer orders had been frustrated 'because at present the capacity of our works is not sufficient to meet demand'. Decisions to extend capacity, as demand rose in 1919, came piecemeal. In January 1919, a sanction to extend the workshops

---

[15] Herbert, Departmental Board, 23 September 1918.

of the company's Edgwick Road factory in Coventry was authorised, and later in May to extend foundry capacity to eradicate bottlenecks in the supply of castings.[16] Additional capacity, however, did not come on stream until the middle of 1920, and the company continued to experience problems in meeting rising consumer demand.[17]

Britain's largest maker, Herbert's, may be held culpable in failing to meet rising demand in the post-war boom, and consequently this confirms Aldcroft's first criticism of the industry. Uncertain markets, however, constrained managerial decision-making in the industry, and adding to this confusion was the un-coordinated actions of government. Machine makers, caught unprepared by the sudden military collapse of Germany, now faced a withdrawal of government contracts. During the war, for example, the Sparkbrook factory of Birmingham Small Arms (BSA) had been fully engaged in manufacturing small tools for their own manufacture of guns, cycles, motor cycles and cars, as well as supplying outside firms. The company had also developed a range of special-purpose machine tools for standardised mass production. The signing of the Armistice in November 1918, as the company's chairman Sir Hallewell Rogers acknowledged, brought a sudden slackening of government orders for machine tools, which finally ceased in January 1919, and this delayed the formulation of planning for post-war production.[18] In May 1918, the MTEA had complained that the industry was 'not properly informed on key issues by the Ministry' of Munitions, and in October the Selson Engineering Co. condemned the cancellation of government contracts. Prompted by complaints from Burton, Griffiths & Co., an MTEA circular in November attacked the government for creating 'extraordinary uncertainty', but in that month, the Ministry, in consultation with its Machine Tool Advisory Committee, immediately cancelled all existing war contracts. The Ministry rejected a phased programme of reducing contracts, but at the same time, it placated the industry by removing government wartime controls. Sir Alfred Herbert was in no doubt of the wisdom of a return to business as usual when he informed the Ministry that the MTEA was unanimous in its desire 'for the immediate removal of war restrictions'. His words resonated with Winston Churchill, who in December 1918 thanked the industry for 'expediting the output of the necessary munitions of war', while announcing the removal of restrictions on machine tools and the restoration of trade permits.[19] The return to the spirit of free enterprise was widely applauded by the industry, but the un-phased withdrawal of contracts was condemned, Oscar Harmer of Herbert's complaining in January 1919 of the

---

[16] Herbert, Departmental Board, 28 October, 25 November 1918; 27 January, 26 May, 8 December 1919.

[17] *American Machinist*, 10 July 1920, p. 78E.

[18] Coventry Archive, 594/1/1/2/3, BSA Meetings File, Ordinary Meeting, October 1919.

[19] MTEA, Minute Book, 1 May, 30 October, 13 November, 5 December 1918.

consequent financial losses incurred, especially on sub-contracted business, which the company was forced to honour.[20]

The sudden withdrawal of the industry's largest customer in 1918 added to the confusion in post-war industrial planning at Herbert's. During the war there was a 'spectacular growth in the firm's sales',[21] achieved by specialisation on a limited range of machines in high demand.[22] Specialisation by machine type 'was actively encouraged' under the auspices of the Machine Tool Department of the Ministry of Munitions, actively enforced in October 1917 by a prohibition on the design of new machines without departmental sanction.[23] As Controller General of Machine Tools at the Department Sir Alfred had reluctantly endorsed the prohibition, in the interests of the war, but as he informed his directors in late 1917, this would necessitate the deferral of planning for post-war manufacture.[24] The limitation of new design concepts in machine building, emphasised in the boardroom in 1918, reflected the constraints on machine firms to plan forward as the war closed. It also forced management to re-evaluate its strategy of providing a wide range of machine tools to customers and to focus on standard lines. Indeed, the finalisation of the manufacturing programme, decided upon in March 1919, demonstrated the limited range of the company's products. The head works at the Butts, Coventry, was to concentrate on building the No. 4 Capstan Lathe, No's. 1 and 9 Combination Turret Lathes, and No's. 11 to 14 Hexagon Turret Lathes. Another factory, at Edgwick Road, concentrated on the No. 20 Combination Turret Lathe, the No. 5 Automatic Turning Lathe, and the No's. 16 and 22 Horizontal Millers, together with the No. 8 Vertical Miller. Arriving at this concentrated programme, the board considered the need to produce machines in quantities and at competitive prices under prevailing capacity constraints.[25] With a restricted manufacturing programme, three factors became paramount in the process of strategic decision-making. Firstly, the company would have to increase sub-contracting, a minimum requirement in the circumstances to enable the supply of a wider range of machine tools. Second, the company would have to co-ordinate its manufacturing programme with its factoring business, again to ensure the fulfilment of customer needs. Finally, given rising domestic demand and limited capacity, supply would have to be directed to the home market and exports sacrificed.

Herbert's dependence on sub-contracting continued after the war. For example, Tangye & Co. of Birmingham manufactured radial drills utilising Herbert technical drawings, Chance Bros. manufactured a variety of Herbert horizontal milling machines, and the Coventry Gauge & Tool Co. produced a range of machines. Sub-contracting enabled Herbert's to facilitate 'flexible production', widening its product range to customers, while at the same time 'easing the

---

[20] Herbert, Departmental Board, 27 January 1919.
[21] Arnold, 'Innovation', p. 63.
[22] Herbert, Departmental Board, 9 September 1918.
[23] Aldcroft, 'The Performance of the British Machine-Tool Industry', p. 290.
[24] Herbert, Departmental Board, 1 October 1917.
[25] Herbert, Departmental Board, 24 March 1919.

pressure' on its own limited 'production capacity' which could concentrate on turret lathes and vertical millers. In 1918 alone, Herbert's sub-contracted to six firms for the manufacture of vertical and horizontal millers. Sub-contracting, of course, increased transaction costs, the company having to carefully monitor and co-ordinate the supply and quality of machines. Consequently, continued problems in supplying orders by Tangye led to the dissolution of this agreement in 1920.[26] The management were well aware that they did not have 'complete control' over the manufacturing programme, 'having to place orders for machines of our own design with the various sub-contractors'. As a result, the board considered acquiring one of the firms it sub-contracted to, Webster and Bennett of Coventry, effecting 'a more permanent and satisfactory' arrangement. Cautious about committing investment funds the Herbert directors discounted the acquisition, maintaining their commitment to sub-contracting, which offered flexibility and lowered their exposure in a market characterised by a cyclical pattern of ordering.[27]

While sub-contracting was an important function of the business, it was factoring which enabled the company to widen the scope of its manufacturing range. From its early beginnings, Herbert's manufactured 'their own, high quality tools', but also sold machines made at both home and abroad on a 'factored basis alongside their own tools'. Factored sales contributed to total sales, supplementing 'the company's own manufacturing operation'. Unlike the manufacture of machine tools, which required investment in expensive capital equipment and entailed 'a far higher wage cost element', factored machines could be purchased often by credit, had lower capital costs, and the business could be conducted with a small specialist sales force.[28] Total sales of Herbert's own machines fell significantly in 1919 as government orders ceased, although by 1920 sales had risen to £837,000. The company's factored sales also showed a marked downturn in 1918, as war demand fell, but rose again by 1920. Indeed, the factored sales remained the mainstay of the company's operations, accounting for 68.2 per cent of total sales in 1920 (see Table 4.2). Factoring was a means to expand both the type and range of machine tools offered to customers, and was crucial given the limitations of manufacturing capacity. It nevertheless raised serious problems of co-ordination between the factored department and Herbert machine tool operations. As Pickin argued, this was a 'big subject because our [own] manufacturing programme is not quite as settled as it might be', and delays in finalising the company's post-war manufacturing programme obstructed decisions on agency agreements for factored machines. For example, the board agreed that they could profitably sell small capstan lathes, 'but it would not do ... to arrange for someone to build them if we decided to make them ourselves'. Complex decisions of opportunity cost underpinned planning procedures at the company, and in business terms the management had to ensure that it could meet customer demand, but at the same time to produce or factor sufficient numbers of machines to ensure cost

---

[26] Herbert, Departmental Board, 28 September, 25 November 1918; 22 January, 27 April 1920.

[27] Herbert, Departmental Board, 10 November 1919.

[28] Arnold, 'Innovation', pp. 63-4.

effectiveness. As Vernon made clear, their present manufacturing programme was 'much larger' than the capacity of the works, and this created a tension in the structure of the organisation between manufacturing and factoring. Management perceived factoring and manufacturing as complementary functions of a unitary business organisation, but as Vernon pointed out, these activities needed to be systematically co-ordinated. Advancing a counterfactual Vernon argued that by 'imagining that our Factored business was a separate concern and acted as agents for our manufactures, we should be able to stipulate that no agency should be held for manufactures competing with our own'. Consequently, the factored department 'would be entitled to stipulate that we must undertake to fill its requirements and this went to indicate that we must not manufacture any articles unless we are prepared to do so on a proper scale'. In essence, if the board decided to manufacture on a larger scale a more limited range of machines, then this required them to plan the manufacturing programme in conjuncture with the acquisition of factored agencies, thus avoiding competition and duplication with their own product range.[29]

A finalised programme for factoring, however, was itself constrained by delays in deciding the company's own manufacturing programme, and thus agency agreements came piecemeal. In January 1919, for example, Herbert's established a sole agency to sell American Norton grinders in the European market, Norton transferring its business from Charles Churchill & Co. At the Birmingham Engineering Exhibition in 1919, Herbert's displayed from three stalls. The first, exhibited machines of their own make, the second factored machines, and the third chucks, dies and factored small tools. The factored stall contained a predominance of machines made by American manufacturers, including a Norton grinding machine, a Fellows gear shaper, and a Landis bolt screwer. Herbert's also acted as sole selling agents for a number of British makers, including planers built by Cornelius Redman & Sons of Halifax through the Herbert associate sales companies in France, Belgium, Italy, and India. The expansion of factoring, however, continued to cause problems of co-ordination. As D. M. Gimson, the director responsible for factored sales, informed Sir Alfred in July 1920, there was a considerable 'overlapping' of factored machines with those of their own make, as well as sub-contracted machines, and the information flows between the two sides of the business were not sufficiently robust to effect a co-ordinated strategy.[30] Despite the view taken by the board that manufacturing and factoring represented complimentary functions, in reality they operated as separate activities, the key rational behind factoring being to widen the range of products sold by the

---

[29] Herbert, Departmental Board, 23 September 1918.
[30] Ibid. and Herbert, Departmental Board, 14 January, 8 September 1919; 13 July 1920; WYAS, Halifax Central Library, CR2-CR4, Churchill-Redman, Director's Minute Books, 1919-60, 2 May 1919.

company. At the company, there seemed to be a mismatch between what management desired and what was actually possible.[31]

Herbert factored machines found sales largely in the domestic market, which accounted for 94 per cent of the company's factored sales in 1920 (see Table 4.3). The continued use of factoring by British machine makers, especially of American machines after the war accounts for the high importation of machine tools. This relates to Aldcroft's second complaint against the industry that it failed to match output with demand. The value of imports into the British market rose from £2.13 million in 1915 to £3.86 million in 1918, £3.97 million in 1919, and was still at £3.02 million in 1920 (see Tables 3.10 and 4.9). In 1920, 85.4 per cent of all imports still originated from the U.S.A., with the second largest exporter to Britain, Germany, accounting for just 3.9 per cent.[32] To accommodate domestic demand, British makers and merchant firms imported foreign machines. For example, in October 1919 a moulders' strike at Herbert's seriously reduced output and Sir Alfred sanctioned the placement of sub-contracted work with Belgium and French makers, taking advantage of favourable rates of exchange, and also imported factored machines from American makers.[33] Despite high importation, Britain's trade balance in machine tools moved in a positive direction, a deficit of £2.58 million in 1918 being converted to a surplus of £341,000 by 1920, the result of a robust export performance in 1919 and 1920 (see Tables 4.7 and 4.8). In December 1919, the Machine Tool Trade Association (MTTA), constituted in April 1919 to replace the MTEA as a specialist organisation representing the industry, celebrated the fact that British makers, concentrating their efforts on empire markets, had made a valuable contribution to national prosperity through a drive for exports. At the same time, the MTTA observed that imports remained high, a consequence of insufficient domestic supply, especially of special-purpose machines for the re-equipment of British industry. From this perspective, the MTTA rejected calls for import controls on machine tools, considering that imports were vital to fill gaps in the market.[34] In the post-war boom, firms expanded exports leaving imports to fill the gap. Dean, Smith & Grace of Keighley, for example, in the buoyant international market geared its output towards Germany, South Africa, Spain, Australasia, Holland, France, Norway, Switzerland, and Belgium. Jones & Shipman, Leicester, immediately resumed sales after the war in their principle markets in New Zealand and Canada.[35] Britain's post-war export drive is a reminder of the continued vitality of the industry. In 1920, the U.K. accounted for 24.6 per cent of world exports, only superseded by the U.S.A. with 49.0 per cent, and above Germany at 20.9 per cent. British exports found

---

[31] For a discussion on the issue of this mismatch in organisations see P. M. Senge, 'The Leaders' New Work: Building Learning Organisations', in H. Mintzburg, J. B. Quinn and S. Ghoshal (eds), *The Strategy Process* (Hemel Hempstead, Prentice Hall, 1995), p. 45.

[32] *American Machinist*, 1921, p. 805.

[33] Herbert, Departmental Board, 1919-42, 27 October 1919.

[34] MTTA, Director's Minute Books, 3 December 1919.

[35] Grierson, *A Little Farm Well Tilled*, p. 51; Miller, *Tools that Built a Business*, p. 28.

expanding markets in the empire, which accounted for 44.0 per cent of total exports in 1920, compared to 32.7 per cent for Western Europe. British machine tool exports to the U.S.A. in 1920, however, were only £18,413, 0.6 per cent of the total exported.[36]

Despite an impressive export record by the British machine tool industry generally, especially in empire markets, the export performance of Herbert's was weak, suggesting that capacity constraints led the company to orientate its output to meet demand in the domestic market. Domestic sales remained central to the company's sales initiative after the war, accounting for 99 per cent of sales for Herbert machines in 1918 and 94 per cent in 1920, although factored sales showed a higher percentage for export (see Table 4.3). As Vernon reported in January 1919, there was a large demand for the Herbert 1" Capstan Lathe, equipped with automatic feed, in European markets, and according to market information the only other competitor in the field was the American firm of Pratt & Whitney who were at present not making them in sufficient quantities to export. The decision to manufacture for export was delayed, the company having insufficient capacity to extend its manufacturing programme, and unable to find suitable sub-contractors who could build the machines to Herbert technical standards. In February, Pickin visited the Herbert associate companies in France and Italy. The foreign managers were disappointed that Herbert's could not supply capstan lathes from stock, and on a more general level, they complained that they 'cannot get more machines of our manufacture'. Capacity constraints pushed the board into directing supply to the building of machines for domestic stock, and in January 1920 the directors, noting that exports accounted for only a small proportion of total sales, recommended the need to raise foreign sales by keeping larger stocks in overseas depots. It is also reasonable to suggest that the Herbert directors curtailed investment in marketing to the overseas companies, the board recognising in October 1919 that they were facing stiff competition in the French market from competitors who were pushing machines through advertisement programmes, which highlighted their 'distinct' features.[37]

The post-war boom was a difficult period for British machine makers. Adding to the problem of capacity constraints were shortages of skilled labour, and escalating wages that reduced competitive advantage. Low levels of co-operative action compounded these problems, and the rapid ending of war controls opened the industry to the full force of the market. As the demand for machine tools rose, labour shortages, which had been acute during the war, remained a persistent problem. Oscar Harmer referred to serious shortages of draughtsmen and gauge makers in late 1918, and in January 1919 John Milburn observed that 'demobilisation was proceeding very slowly'.[38] Indeed, the MTEA condemned the Ministry of Labour for the 'slow' demobilisation of the armed forces, and for its

---

[36] *American Machinist*, 1921, p. 805.

[37] Herbert, Departmental Board, 14 January, 24 February, 27 October 1919; 7 January 1920.

[38] Herbert, Departmental Board, 9 December 1918; 14 January 1919.

impact on constraining output.[39] In a tight labour market, shortages placed pressure on wages and in turn inflated prices. As early as November 1918 Oscar Harmer, welcoming the abolition of price and output controls by the Ministry of Munitions, nevertheless warned that the company had to be alive to the effects of the buoyant demand on wages and prices.[40]

The sudden removal of regulation had repercussions for the price competitiveness of the industry. For example, Redman & Sons typified the cost-push inflation of the immediate post-war era. By March 1919, the company had orders totalling £38,000 for its lathes and planers, the directors reporting on the problems of meeting output targets due to shortages of skilled labour. In an attempt to recruit labour, wages were increased leading to a rise in the price of both lathes and planers of 5 per cent in April, followed by a further increase of 5 per cent and 10 per cent during July. An additional 5 per cent increase in prices followed in November, a result of a wage rise to engineers, and it is little wonder that management reflected on a year of spiralling inflation leading to intense pressures on maintaining sales.[41] Cost pressures were not peculiar to firms such as Redman's in the Yorkshire district. For example, in the Midlands, Sir Hallewell Rogers at BSA complained vociferously over the increasing costs of labour and raw materials in 1919 and in 1920 Shipman & Jones of Leicester noted that wages had risen steadily since the end of the war and had outpaced the rise in prices.[42]

Faced with a wage-price spiral, attempts at formulating a common price policy through the actions of a trade association proved difficult to implement given the individualistic and regionally dispersed nature of firms in the industry. In August 1918, for example, G. & A. Harvey, Glasgow, recommended to the MTEA the creation of a uniform price system tied to a common sales clause in contracts enabling 'payment on account' for all members of the Association. On rejecting the recommendation, the MTEA Council alluded to the wide regional variations in trade conditions, and the fact that Scottish makers were concentrated on the manufacture of heavy machinery for heavy capital goods industry, which was not compatible with the type of demand in the Midlands. Initiatives for uniform pricing persisted, Ransome & Co., Newark-on-Trent, petitioning the MTEA in December for their introduction on an industry-wide basis. The persistence of price disparities between regions and between firms in the same region continued to provide an excuse for the Association to avoid compelling common action on prices. Wage-bargaining structures in the industry further hindered a process of collective action. Employer-union negotiations were conducted under the guidance of the Engineering Employers Federation (EEF), and consequently wage bargaining was conditioned by factors pertaining to general engineering. For example, in September 1918 a number of machine tool firms complained over the need to raise

---

[39] MTEA, Minute Book, 1916-19, 5 December 1918.

[40] Herbert, Departmental Board, 25 November 1918.

[41] Churchill-Redman, Director's Minute Book, 25 March, 14 July, 11 November 1919.

[42] BSA Meetings File, Ordinary Meeting, October 1919; Miller, *Tools that Built a Business*, p. 46.

prices given general increases in engineering wages, but they were quickly rebutted by the MTEA who reminded them that 'all matters on labour should be dealt with by the EEF'. Regulation of industry codes of practice were consequently difficult to instigate, but, on the promptings of one of Britain's leading machine makers, William Asquith of Halifax, a voluntary system of 'optional' uniform price clauses on contracts was sanctioned by the MTEA in January 1919. Contract prices were to be based on a 1s per week rise or fall in wages and material costs and a pro rata one per cent change in the contract price.[43] Voluntary codes, however, proved problematic in an industry where individualism remained paramount, the MTEA, and its successor the MTTA, standing aloof from direct involvement in regulating prices and wages.[44] Voluntarism was consequently the principle guiding the MTTA, its uniform price clauses in contracts of February 1920 being recommended, but not mandatory. Without direct regulation, however, machine tool firms pursued their own individual course, defending their position in the market by discounts and special deals with customers.[45]

Price inflation during the post-war boom undermined the competitive position of firms, both in domestic and export markets. In the case of Herbert's, a competitive dilemma faced the executive management. In November 1918 Sir Alfred informed Gimson that the removal of government price controls made it appropriate to raise prices, and for 'guidance' cited the mark-up on costs for the Herbert No. 4 Capstan Lathe, which now stood at 27.5 per cent compared to an average of 35 to 43 per cent before the war. Rectifying a falling rate of profit on sales during the war was clearly prominent in management thinking, and as Vernon pointed out, the prices of Herbert machines had been kept down, while 'those of our competitors had been increasing, because they had always worked on a smaller margin than us'. Before the war, he claimed, 'we got more for our machines than our competitors whose prices had now risen to almost the level of our own'. Added to the upward price trend was the need to compensate for increases in wages, a fact which persuaded Sir Alfred to sanction a 20 per cent increase in list prices from December, raising the mark-up for profits to 37 per cent. As Alfred concluded, given uncertainty over competitive pricing policy, and faced with wage pressures, they would have to 'see how the market went'. An assessment of costs in February 1919 showed an escalation in wages and material charges, leading to a further hike of 15 per cent in list prices, the decision taken to offer discounts of 2.5 per cent to maintain orders from 'established customers'. Rising coal prices in July saw prices rise by 5 per cent, followed by a further 5 per cent increase in November to cover increased wages to engineers. In January 1920, the board observed that the sequence of price rises had seriously undermined sales potential, in particular export sales affected by cheaper American and German competitors.[46] For

[43] MTEA, Minute Book, 28 August, 11 September, 5 December 1918; 22 January 1919.

[44] See Lloyd-Jones and Lewis, 'Business Networks', pp. 229-50.

[45] MTTA, Director's Minute Book, 1919-25, 25 February 1920.

[46] Herbert, Departmental Board, 25 November, 9 December 1918; 10 February, 28 July 1919; 22 January 1920.

example, T. Woof, a Herbert director, noted sales resistance to the company's No 2 Hexagon Turret Lathe in the U.S.A. because of high prices and prohibitive tariffs compared to equivalent American lathes built by Jones & Lamson and Gisholt & Co. Indeed, the management had considered building them in the U.S.A., but discounted this after consideration of the capital investment cost required so soon after the war.[47] Herbert grinding machines, manufactured under sub-contract also faced intense price competition from cheaper equivalents built by the Churchill Machine Tool Co, Broadheath, Manchester, a manufacturing subsidiary of Charles Churchill & Co since 1906,[48] and from the Norton Co. of the U.S.A. Options to build Norton machines under licence at Coventry were considered by the Herbert board, but rejected, the management realising that they lacked the capacity to absorb increased output, and that American designs could not be adapted to their own manufacturing procedures. This decision reinforced the reliance on sub-contracting, and in March 1919 the Herbert designed No. 4 Tool and Cutter Grinder was sub-contracted to the engineering concern of Wadkin, Mills & Co. Sub-contracting, in the inflationary post-war environment, was a precarious activity, and by July 1919 the board was complaining of the high mark-up on costs charged for sub-contracting by Wadkin of 33.3 per cent, compared to controlled charges during the war of 10 per cent, leaving little room for profits from Herbert sales.[49]

The experience of Britain's largest machine tool firm in the immediate post-war period both lends support to Aldcroft's general observation concerning the industry, and indicates the constraints that this sector faced. It also demonstrates the market networking within the industry through the large Herbert factoring and sub-contracting operations. However, the performance of the firm was a mixed one. Indecision over the post-war manufacturing programme led to delays in building up capacity, and, in turn, this complicated decisions on the company's factoring operations. Factoring too, showed the continuing importance of imports, especially of American origin, to British engineering, and foreign competition was to hit hard as Britain's machine makers fell into the trough of depression in the 1920s.

Meeting the Challenge: The Industry in Depression

As Table 4.2 indicates, in 1920 total sales of Herbert machines were valued at £2,634,000, but by 1921 this had fallen to £958,000, a drop of 63.6 per cent. Total sales fell further between 1921 and 1923, and then recovered slowly to 1927. Even by the latter date, total sales were still 44.2 per cent below the post-war peak of 1920. Both sides of the Herbert business felt the full blast of the depression. On the one hand, sales of their own machines fell by a dramatic 66.1 per cent between 1920 and 1923, but then slowly recovered to 1927. On the other hand, factored

---

[47] Herbert, Departmental Board, 24 February 1919.
[48] For this company see Jeremy, 'Gabriel, John Beresford Stuart', p. 456.
[49] Herbert, Departmental Board, 14 January, 10, 24 March, 23 June 1919.

machines, accounting for the largest share of total sales, crashed during the downturn in general economic activity, falling by 73 per cent between 1920 and 1923. Despite recovering thereafter, they were still only 55.6 per cent of the level of 1920 in 1927 (Table 4.2). The main cause of falling sales was the severity of the downturn in domestic demand. For example between 1920 and 1921, Herbert sales of their own machines in the domestic market fell by 72 per cent, and despite a slow and uncertain recovery to 1927 domestic sales were still 16.4 per cent below the level of 1920 (Table 4.3). Export sales of the Herbert make, accounting for only 6 per cent of all sales in 1920, also fell sharply in 1921, although briefly they formed a larger proportion of the smaller total sales. Exports, reflecting low demand in foreign markets, remained flat, accounting for only 1.9 per cent of the total sales of their own machines in 1927. Factored sales to foreign markets also showed a marked downturn in the 1920s, although in 1921 and 1922 they compensated for the severe reduction in home demand, accounting on average in those two years for 34.2 per cent of total factored sales.

Table 4.2
Alfred Herbert Sales of Own and Factored Machine Tools (£000), 1918-35

	Factored Machines[c]	Own Manufacture	Total	% Factored to Total
1918	2,155	933	3088	69.8
1919	1,456	712	2168	67,2
1920	1,797	837	2634	68.2
1921	707	251	958	73.8
1922	506	272	778	65.0
1923	485	284	769	63.1
1924	560	444	1004	53.8
1925	696	525	1221	57.0
1926	726	553	1279	56.8
1927	798	671	1469	54.3
1928				
1929[a]	539	1274	1813	29.7
1930[b]	725	1410	2135	33.9
1931	328	629	957	34.3
1932	287	661	948	30.3
1933	228	603	831	27.4
1934	393	920	1313	29.9
1935	564	1151	1715	32.8

Source: Arnold, 'Innovation', pp. 60-1; Coventry Archive, 926/1/5/32-49, Alfred Herbert Ltd., Annual Accounts and Schedules, 1918-35.
Notes: a. for 17 months to March; b. for 19 months to October; c. factored sales include machine tools and small tools.

Sales rose significantly during the 17 months to March 1929 and again during the 19 months to October 1930, before the company felt the full impact of the world economic downturn. Total sales of their own machines crashed between 1930 and 1933, factored sales moving downwards earlier in 1929. (Table 4.2), reflecting a general lack of confidence by the company's customers in future capital investment. Sales in both domestic and foreign markets (Table 4.3) moved sharply downwards from 1930 to 1933, and then recovered rapidly to 1935. Overall, during the 1920s and early 1930s, the company's experience was typical of firms in the British machine tool industry, which faced the adverse market environment of this period. Falling sales reduced profitability, which in turn affected investment. Net profits at Herbert's (Table 4.4), fell sharply from 1920 to 1923, recovered strongly in 1925, but declined again over the next two years. From his survey of the company accounts, Arnold concludes that over the period 1888 to 1927 the company was a highly profitable concern, profits allowing a considerable expansion of operations over the period. Re-invested profit was the key engine of growth, but as Arnold notes, the 1920s saw a sharp downturn in profitability. The ratio of net profits to sales in Table 4.4 averaged 8 per cent between 1915 and 1919, and 8.8 per cent between 1920 and 1927, the figures distorted by the high rates of returns to sales in 1923 and 1925. A return on sales of 8.8 per cent, however, was well below the average for the period 1888 to 1927 of 13.8 per cent. A 'key indicator of business success', the ratio of net profits to shareholders' funds, declined from an average of 17.4 per cent between 1915 and 1919 to 6.6 per cent between 1920 and 1927, representing 'a poor return for the risks involved'. Dividends, although well below the returns of the war years, continued to be paid until 1931.[50]

Falling returns from profits delayed investment, in an industry where re-invested profits were the key financial resource for expansion. The British machine tool industry 'has not to any great extent in the past appealed for its capital to the ordinary public', and few firms issued financial reports to the press.[51] Reflecting this personal capitalist ethos, Sir Alfred informed the AGM of Barclay's Bank in 1930 that 'the most valuable kind of capital that could be held in any business was the capital that business had been able to save for itself by care, economy, and a conservative policy in dealing with its accounts'.[52] His observation reflected general trends in British manufacturing industry during the inter-war years. Internal funds, as John Wilson notes, 'continued to act as the major contrib-utor to capital formation, and business savings still accounted for approximately eighty per cent of total industrial investment in the inter-war era'.[53] Profitability at Herbert's again fell sharply between 1931 and 1932, the company paying no dividend, before a vigorous recovery set in between 1933 and 1935. Falling profitability was typical of firms in the industry generally, and for small firms, accounting for the bulk of producers, it brought with it severe financial problems.

---

[50] Arnold, 'Innovation', pp. 59-62.

[51] *American* Machinist, 2 December 1922, p. 91E.

[52] *American Machinist*, 25 January 1930, p. 287E

[53] Wilson, *British Business History*, p. 183.

Table 4.3
Alfred Herbert: Home and Foreign Sales, 1918-35

	Own				Factored[c]			
	Home (000)	Home (%)	Foreign (000)	Foreign (%)	Home (000)	Home (%)	Foreign (000)	Foreign (%)
1918	924	99.0	19	1.0	1765	81.9	390	8.1
1919	693	97.3	19	2.7	1040	71.4	416	18.6
1920	787	94.0	50	6.0	1538	85.6	259	14.4
1921	223	88.8	28	11.2	481	68.0	226	32.0
1922	245	90.1	27	9.9	322	63.6	184	36.4
1923	267	94.0	17	6.0	393	81.0	92	19.0
1924	422	95.0	22	5.0	464	82.8	96	17.2
1925	512	97.5	13	2.5	615	88.3	81	11.7
1926	541	74.5	12	15.5	652	89.8	74	10.2
1927	658	82.4	13	17.6	725	90.1	73	9.9
1928								
1929[a]	1238	97.2	36	2.8	502	93.1	37	6.9
1930[b]	1374	97.4	36	2.6	666	91.9	59	8.1
1931	616	97.9	13	2.1	306	93.3	22	6.7
1932	606	91.7	55	8.3	269	93.7	18	6.3
1933	519	86.1	84	13.9	204	89.5	24	10.5
1934	846	91.9	74	8.1	318	80.9	75	19.1
1935	1090	94.7	61	5.3	467	82.8	97	17.2

Source: 926/1/5/32-49, Alfred Herbert Ltd., Annual Accounts and Schedules, 1918-35.
Notes: a. for 17 months to March; b. for 19 months to October; c. factored sales include machine tools and small tools.

To some extent Herbert's, through its accumulated capital reserves, could weather the storm better than smaller makers. For example, Arthur Chamberlain, the managing director of the Churchill Machine Tool Co., reflecting on the past 10 years of business in 1933, considered it a period 'fraught with anxiety', characterised by volatile demand, and presently 'trade all over the world continues to be bad'. During the 1920s, the company experienced rising liquidity problems and increasing indebtedness to Barclay's Bank. In a frank admission to shareholders, he concluded that 'It has taken 10 years to re-establish the company on a sound footing' by repaying loans and removing the burden of 'heavy initial charges'. Chamberlain, however, could offer no comfort to shareholders, and he reminded them that 'it would be very wrong to take any risk with the company's finance by undue eagerness to pay the arrears of dividends'. The company incurred losses in 1922-3, which seriously depleted its reserves for re-investment, and although the losses fell in 1924, the company moving back to surplus by 1925 (Table 4.5), it remained in a precarious financial situation. Chamberlain's report to the board in 1924 showed a 67 per cent increase in sales for 1923 over 1922, but as Chamberlain reminded his fellow directors, there had been a significant depreciation in the value of plant and stock, and the company had been forced to dispose of surplus capital assets to reduce overheads as capacity utilisation fell. Increasing demand from the motor trade in 1925, to which the company supplied grinding machines for gears, led to a decision to replace a small amount of outdated equipment. But as Chamberlain concluded, the depression had seen a severe cut in capacity and a lack of investment in modernising production facilities, and the market remained 'too uncertain to make it profitable' for a major re-investment programme. It was not until 1928 that the company sanctioned a scheme for capital re-investment, a decision taken to meet rising orders from the motor trade, as well as exploiting demand from the Soviet Union for British machine tools. Indeed, the latter was crucial to the company's rising profits in 1932, following a drastic reduction of profitability during 1931.[54]

Financial hardship typified the experience of firms in this era. Jones & Shipman, a personally managed firm, 'lived from hand to mouth' in the 1920s, 'paying its bills as it received payment for each job delivered'.[55] Redman & Sons also experienced deep financial distress in the 1920s. Employing about 30 in 1920, the company specialised in lathes and planers, and in January 1919 one-third of the business was acquired by Charles Churchill & Co.[56] Despite fresh capital from Churchill's, as Table 4.5 indicates, Redman made losses in 5 years between 1924 and 1934 and, with the exception of 1929-30, profits were severely depleted. The Butler Machine Tool Co., Halifax, also faced considerable pressures on profits in the 1920s. Although the company sustained its profits in the early 1930s, a result of its extensive export business to the Soviet Union, they crashed in 1933. General engineering firms engaged in the machine tool market, such as Greenwood & Batley, also felt the full blast of the depression, its profits stagnating in the 1920s (Table 4.5).

As Aldcroft observes, the industry faced severe constraints in the 1920s, given its heavy dependence upon sectors of the economy that were declining, or on industries such as automobiles which were prone to sharp fluctuations in the level of demand.[57] In June 1920, for example, Herbert's had large orders from the shipbuilding and railway sectors, but Sir Alfred was already forecasting a downturn of demand, cautioning that 'Care should be used when placing contracts so that we should not accumulate stock, and so lock up capital'. By July, faced with falling orders, the company was preparing for retrenchment, revising downwards its manufacturing and sub-contracting programmes to reduce output by

---

[54] Coventry Archive, 926/17/1/2, Churchill Machine Tool Co., Minute Book of Board and General Meetings, 1924-39, 9 April 1924; 26 November 1925; 28 January 1928; 27 October 1932; 30 March 1933.

[55] Miller, *Tools that Built a Business*, p. 31.

[56] 'Charles Churchill 1865 to 1965', in *Machine Shop and Engineering Manufacture* (March 1965), p. 111; Jeremy, 'Gabriel, John Beresford Stuart', p. 456; Redman, Director's Minute Book, 4 February 1919.

[57] Aldcroft, 'The Performance of the British Machine-Tool Industry', p. 286.

Table 4.4
Profitability at Alfred Herbert Ltd., 1915-35

	Net Profits (£000)	Net Profit: Total Sales (%)	Net Profits: Shareholders Interest (%)[a]	Ordinary Share Dividend (%)
1915	149	11.3	20.0	50
1916	222	9.4	24.2	50
1917	114	3.9	11.5	50
1918	143	4.6	13.2	60
1919	230	10.6	18.2	6
1920	-48.0	-1.8	-4.1	3
1921	-33	-3.4	-3.0	3
1922	-21	-2.7	-2.0	3
1923	140	18.2	12.0	5
1924	146	14.5	11.6	5
1925	263	21.5	17.8	5
1926	179	14.0	11.3	5
1927	151	10.3	9.0	7
1928				
1929	319[b]	17.6		15
1930	295[c]	13.8		7.5
1931	-38	-4.0		0
1932	28	2.9		0
1933	153	18.4		17.5
1934	217	16.5		35
1935	243	14.1		40

Source: Arnold, 'Innovation', pp. 60-1; 926/1/5/42-49, Alfred Herbert, Annual Accounts and Schedules, 1928-35; 586/11; Alfred Herbert General Minute Book, 1894-1950.
Notes: a. Shareholders interest = total value of shares and reserves. Arnold, 'Innovation', p. 61. b. for 17 months ending March 1929. c. for 19 months ending October 1930. d. Preference dividends were fixed at 5% 1915-25, and 6% 1926-35.

Table 4.5
Profits for Four Machine Tool Companies in the Inter-War Years (£000)

	Churchill Machine Tool	Redman	Greenwood & Batley	Butler
1918			93.0	
1919			46.6	
1920			60.0	
1921			23.4	
1922	-24.1		50.4	
1923	-32.1		24.1	
1924	-9.2	-5.6	30.2	
1925	3.4	0.4	30.7	
1926	8.0	1.3	28.6	
1927	11.3	-1.0	30.2	
1928	18.4	0.6	30.5	
1929	24.2	3.8	28.4	21.6
1930	20.1	5.2	39.3	24.3
1931	6.5	0.4	24.5	30.2
1932	27.3	-0.6	19.2	15.6
1933	28.6	-1.8	32.9	-6.8
1934	28.9	-0.6	38.5	12.0
1935	51.4	2.3	45.1	23.2
1936	66.7	3.8	46.3	31.1
1937	78.3	5.4	64.3	
1938	118.8	13.9	139.3	

Sources: Extracted from Yearly Financial Statements in Churchill Machine Tool Co., Minute Books, 1924-39; CR8, Churchill-Redman, Director's Reports and Statements of Accounts, 1919-38; ASQ33, Correspondence File of Butler Machine Tool Co., 1936-8; Box 47, Annual Reports and Accounts of Greenwood & Batley, 1889-1971.

20 per cent. Despite attempts to bolster orders through extending hire purchase to customers, a risky business given the 'locking up of capital', orders continued to fall, forcing the board by November to lay off productive workers.[58] By March 1921, reports from regional branch offices were despondent. Heavy industry in Scotland and the North East was severely depressed, and the automobile industry in the Midlands had drastically reduced orders.[59] Export markets proved equally disappointing. In 1921 Pickin urged a drive for exports, targeting markets in France, Belgium, China, Japan and South Africa, but sales remained low, the company's prices being uncompetitive, and the board reluctant to sacrifice profit margins. Despite cuts in prices and profit margins in 1921, combined with discounts of 25 per cent to customers and extended credit facilities, export sales

[58] Herbert, Departmental Board, 8 June, 15, 28 July, 23 November 1920.
[59] Herbert, Departmental Board, 8 March 1921.

remained disappointing.[60] A consequence of depressed demand was falling prices and profit margins, evident in the company's factored business, where machine makers were offering open consignment for deliveries and extended credit terms, and Herbert's selling on the machines to the trade at discounts of 10 to 20 per cent in 1921.[61]

During 1922 and 1923, in a vain attempt to buck the market, the management of the company offered substantial price discounts on both their factored and their own machines. For example, following major discussions at the board in late 1922 Sir Alfred sanctioned reductions in the mark-up of profits on lathes from 33.3 to 25 per cent, with discounts of 20 per cent offered to established customers. Price cuts on milling machines of 10 per cent followed in May 1923, and by August it had been established as a 'general principal' to accept a lower rate of profit on sales, offering special discounts to customers in an attempt to match price cuts by competitors. In 1923, an analysis of the order books by Milburn concluded that orders were holding up, but were still insufficient to ensure full employment, reductions in prices offering the only hope for a substantial improvement of orders. However, even by 1925 the company was circulating lists of 'surplus machines' to their foreign customers at specially reduced prices and allowing their associate sales companies and dedicated agents discounts of 10 per cent.[62]

Herbert's actions in cutting prices symbolised the desperation of makers confronted with the enormity of the depression, but also showed the failure of collaboration in the industry to regulate prices. In April 1920, a number of firms complained of the existence of cut-throat competition, and proposed to the MTTA that they act to enforce uniform price clauses in contracts. These firms included Judson, Jackson & Co., Midgley & Sutcliffe, Charles Taylor (Birmingham) Ltd., G. & H. Harvey, and the prominent name of Alfred Herbert Ltd. In the debate that followed, Sir Alfred, the President of the MTTA, supported calls for price regulation, but also noted that in times of economic adversity it was likely that individualism would prevail. Consequently, the Association decided to reaffirm its position that uniform pricing 'was impossible to adopt' due to 'varying conditions in the trade'.[63] The pricing policy at Herbert's was testimony to this individualism, and the industry, given no lead by its largest firm, was to pursue a policy that resulted in a downward price spiral. By 1924 'cut-throat competition' had created instability in ordering, resulting in customers delaying plant replacement in anticipation of further falls in prices.[64] In 1925, the MTTA attempted to set conditions of tender for the industry, a decision that was not well received by members of the Association. Consequently, and as an alternative to enforced regulation, a general communication was circulated urging makers 'to refrain from

---

[60] Herbert, Departmental Board, 10 May, 23 August 1921; 28 March, 9 May 1922.

[61] Herbert, Departmental Board, 11 January 1922.

[62] Herbert, Departmental Board, 17 October, 28 November 1922; 9 May, 21 August 1923; 2 September 1925.

[63] MTTA, Director's Minute Book, 14 April 1920.

[64] *American Machinist*, 26 April 1924, pp. 61-2E.

the cutting down of prices'.[65] Price competition led to wide variations in prices for similar machines, and, from a business perspective, it was irrational to sell stocks below their replacement values. However, 'with the volume of trade low' and in an industry where 'rigid price regulation has been shown to be almost impossible in times of very keen competition', machine makers were desperate to get orders even if they returned only a low percentage of the on-costs. There was a certain logic in this, given that wages and material costs had fallen during the downturn, but it still remained 'commercially unsound' because overhead charges had not fallen to the same extent'.[66] At Herbert's, the board was well aware of the problem of reducing overheads as output and sales fell, through a vigorous policy of cutting administrative staff to control the costs of what they termed 'non-productive workers'. In late 1920, a reduction of staff' in the company's small tool and factored departments was sanctioned, matching the cost of 'non-productive labour' to the reduction of 'shop labour'. As the directors pointed out, this was not easy to achieve, given the need to cut capacity and 'productive labour'. Nevertheless, by early 1921, the company's orders and sales departments were working on short-time, and 74 staff had been discharged from the works office. In January 1923, Sir Alfred sent a letter to Gimson, reminding his director of the imperative that they cut overhead costs by monitoring in their monthly reviews the level of administrative staff required for the lower production of the factory.[67]

At the same time, the firm was at the centre of attempts to control wage costs in the industry. As the *American Machinist* observed in 1921, the prevailing rate of wages was 'incompatible with labour conditions abroad unless substantial countervailing advantages can be devised'. Employers generally believed that 'labour shall bear its share in pulling the situation round – if prices are to be stabilised the wage bill must decline along with our production costs'.[68] Manufacturer's perceptions of high wages were associated with the cost of the inflationary boom following the war, a point made by the MTTA in a petition to the House of Commons, endorsed by the Association's President Sir Alfred Herbert, in 1920. Continued rises 'in wages which have been granted in the engineering trade ... has caused a serious injury to the prospect of the trade, and which has begun and will continue to produce unemployment on an increasing scale'. The consequent increase in prices resulted in falling orders in the home market, and with high prices and unfavourable exchange rates in continental markets a natural decline in exports. Government policies associated with the taxation of profits through the wartime excess profit tax, the raising of bank rates through a policy of 'dear money', all combined with rising wage costs to produce a 'disastrous' situation for 'capital and ... labour alike'. In summing up its position

[65] MTTA, Annual Report for 1925, p. 4.

[66] *American Machinist*, 20 September 1922, p. 33E.

[67] Herbert, Departmental Board, 8 June, 13, 28 July, 15 September, 6 October, 9, 23 November 1920; 8 February 1921; 9 January 1923.

[68] Lloyd-Jones and Lewis, 'Business Networks', p. 246.

on labour, the MTTA concluded that 'it would be far better to force a strike rather than to consent to any further increase whatever'.[69]

Belligerency towards organised labour was evident from 1920, the MTTA fighting its corner under the general umbrella of the EEF. In 1920, following a resolution by Sir Alfred, the MTTA abandoned its separate wage review agreement with the Allied Engineering Union (AEU), its future wage negotiations delegated to the EEF. As Sir Alfred argued, the economics of wages and prices in the machine tool industry, which represented 'a branch of engineering industry', were linked to demand factors pertaining to general engineering, and consequently it made sense to concentrate action in a larger negotiating body.[70] Through the medium of the EEF, Herbert's played a lead role in instigating 'wage cuts locally and nationally during the trade depression in the early 1920s'. In an attempt to protect jobs in the autumn of 1920 the AEU proposed reducing overtime and implementing a two-shift system. The employers' immediate reaction was conciliatory, publicly declaring a willingness to negotiate, but in December John Milburn, the Herbert general manager and a member of the Negotiating Committee of the EEF, gained support from the Coventry and District Engineering Employers Association for a resolution to reduce wages.[71] Conciliation was no longer an option, as emphasised by Sir Hallewell Rogers, the chair of BSA, during the engineering lock-out of 1922: 'extremists in some of the Labour Unions have still the power to hamstring industry by insistence upon conditions that make profitable industry impossible'.[72] Such an aggressive stance was pursued by Herbert's and other Coventry firms, who were 'in the vanguard' of the employer's movement. Milburn, for example, urged the Coventry Association that they should seize the opportunity to force through 'a wage reduction'. The eventual victory for the employers led to a 25 per cent reduction in wages, Milburn and Colonel Cole of Humber, the two Coventry representatives on the National Negotiating Committee of the EEF, being warmly thanked for devoting 'a large amount of time and energy' to the cause of Coventry's industrial employers. Herbert's had a reputation as a progressive employer of labour, deploying polices of industrial welfarism to provide social amenities for its workforce, and cultivating the 'Herbert Spirit' through an emphasis upon rewarding 'long service and loyalty' from its highly skilled workers. In contrast, it took a hard line on the wage question, and even when trade revived in 1925 the company's 'Black Book' outlawed 'union or strike activists', a common policy adopted by the EEF.[73]

While Herbert's seemed to project a lead role on wage policy for the industry, it did so as part of a general movement in the Midland's engineering industry to combat the power of labour. Indeed, the MTTA publicly maintained a

[69] MTTA, Director's Minute Book, 10 June 1920.
[70] Ibid.
[71] McG. Davies, 'Twentieth Century Paternalist', pp. 108-9.
[72] 594/1/1/2, BSA Meeting File, Ordinary Meeting, October 1922.
[73] Mc G. Davies, 'Twentieth Century Paternalist', pp. 98, 108-9; 113-14; Arnold, 'Innovation', pp. 56, 70 n. 55; A. J. McIvor, 'Employers Organisations and Strike Breaking in Britain, 1880-1914', *International Review of Social History*, Vol. 29 (1984), pp. 20-23.

non-interventionist line during the lock out of 1922. It 'would not be proper to ... take part in wage questions', announced the MTTA, 'the prospects of revival were now such that the evil of abnormal price cutting would shortly cure itself, and it remained 'contrary to the principles of the Association to interfere in labour matters or to attempt to fix prices'.[74] Nevertheless, machine makers in the Midlands took advantage of the lead taken by Herbert's, in combination with larger engineering firms, to force home an assault on labour, an offensive given added weight by two key factors. First, the changes during the war had increased the proportion of semi-skilled to skilled workers in machine tool firms, because of the simplification of machine operations, and this had reduced the power of the union's traditional support. Second, with the industry facing exceptionally low orders in 1922, the lock out was an opportunity to force home the case for reduced wages, albeit under the shelter of the EEF.[75] The question of lower wages was not necessarily welcomed by smaller makers in the industry, who faced competition from larger firms in the engineering industry when signs of trade revival appeared in 1924. For example, in 1924 a modest rise in economic activity brought forth complaints from machine makers that their labour costs were rising because of the higher wages being paid by automobile manufacturers for skilled workers, a consequence of the fact that automobiles were 'sheltered' under the war-time Mackenna duties, which were extended by the Safeguarding of Industries Act of 1921.[76] Machine makers, however, remained divided on the wage question. In 1920, the MTTA had delivered its verdict on the dangers of wage inflation in guarded terms. 'This Association', it claimed, 'represents a branch of engineering industry the productions of which, up to a certain point, are in greater demand when wages are high than when they are low, but it is firmly convinced that the level now attained has already passed the critical point'.[77] With signs of a sustained revival in 1925, however, a minority of firms in the industry projected the view that they should concede to the demands of operatives for a wage rate more proportionate to that prevailing in other sectors of engineering, as a positive step towards stimulating the introduction of labour-saving machinery in general engineering. This section of the machine trade 'looks to reconstruction as the best thing calculated to advance its own prospects'. A more widely accepted position, however, was that increased wages would aggravate the 'evil of high production costs', and thus postpone the chances of a recovery in demand.[78]

By the mid-1920s, the fundamental questions facing the machine tool industry were to what extent there would be a sustained recovery in economic activity and how prepared were makers to meet an expected upturn in demand? These questions also raised the matter of imported machine tools, especially special-purpose machines, and consequently brought into focus the technical

---

[74] MTTA, Director's Minute Book, 14 September, 18 October 1922.

[75] *American Machinist*, 18 March 1922, pp. 33-4E; 1 April 1922, pp. 49-50E; 21 May 1922, pp. 99-100E.

[76] *American Machinist*, 20 December 1924, p. 171E.

[77] MTTA, Director's Minute Book, 10 June 1920.

[78] *American Machinist*, 31 January 1925, pp. 213-4E.

capabilities of firms within the industry compared to their American and German competitors. In June 1924, John Milburn reported on an anticipated revival of demand, which brought forth a cautious response from Sir Alfred. The uncertainty of future demand, he claimed, required 'caution as regards the volume of work we are putting into the shop', his company concentrating on a limited range of machines in which there was a firm demand. Nevertheless, by August Oscar Harmer was warning that in the face of the company's curtailment of capacity, and with genuine signs of a revival of trade, there was a need to increase output 'so as to overtake the present excess of orders over deliveries'. Indeed, a year later the company had received increasing orders from Morris Motors, and noted the problems of ensuring adequate delivery times. By 1928, Sir Alfred was complaining about the 'congestion in the works', and the problems of taking on any new orders 'of a special nature'. Indeed, by 1929 Herbert's were back to negotiating sub-contract arrangements to meet supply, confirming agreements, for example, with the Selson Engineering Co. of London to build Herbert Horizontal Milling Machines under Herbert drawings.[79]

In the case of Herbert's, Aldcroft's criticism that there was a failure to anticipate the upturn of demand from the mid-1920s is defendable, in particular given the unpredictability of that demand after 1924. As Milburn noted in 1924, in response to Sir Alfred's request for caution, there was instability associated with the revival of demand in the automobile industry.[80] A projected recovery in the automobile industry was raised as early as September 1922, car makers publishing extension programmes to plant. However, the *American Machinist* added a note of caution, observing that if automobile expansion did not materialise this would have serious repercussions for machine makers. This, indeed, proved a false dawn, and by 1923 automobile manufacturers and large engineering concerns were doing much to bring equipment up-to-date, but the volume of demand was still greatly below capacity, and these concerns, for which the machine industry 'depend', were conserving their 'resources'. The automobile industry was prone to short-term fluctuations in trade, and it was a case of 'hand to mouth times'. By 1924, although car makers in the Midlands had substantially increased production, 'Machinists are getting no more business than they expected from the motor car firms, and their expectations were not pitched very high'.[81] A survey of trade in the Midlands concluded that:

> The advance made has depended too much on the automobile industry to be stable. That industry has become under normal conditions the mainstay of the machine tool trade in the district. It was the boldest buyer in the pre-war days and its post-war reconstruction was carried out on correspondingly lavish lines. There is firm faith in its future, in spite of present anxieties. But machinists ... do not

---

[79] Herbert, Departmental Board, 26 August 1924; 8 September 1925; 15 August 1928; 9 January 1929.

[80] Herbert, Departmental Board, 22 July 1924.

[81] *American Machinist*, 23 September 1922, pp. 31-2E; 24 March 1923, pp. 37-38E; 9 June 1923, pp. 101-2E; 21 July 1923, p. 140E; 1 March 1924, pp. 11-12E.

care to feel that all their eggs are in one basket, a basket too that has proved somewhat rickety at times.[82]

Dependency on the domestic market, and in particular the automobile industry for recovery, created an unpredictable business environment. In September 1924, for example, optimism that car manufacturers would expand orders was dented, the industry in a 'temporary malaise' over the short-term cancellation of the McKenna duties. Despite hopes that car manufacturers would reach full output by the end of the year, as the new seasons models came on stream, large-scale re-equipment did not materialise, most firms having 'more plant than they know what to do with'. By late 1924, 'pessimism' had given way to a renewed 'faith in the future of the machine tool industry', a slow expansion of demand encouraging machine makers that the 'worst effects of the post-war slump are now past'. Nevertheless, machine makers delayed long-term 'plans' for the expansion of capacity and employment, the demand for machines 'still subject to frequent intermissions'.[83] Instability in ordering by the car industry edged machine makers to caution. As the directors of Herbert's complained in 1928, despite rising demand from car manufacturers, notably from the Morris Motor Co., there was still considerable uncertainty over future ordering trends, creating 'doubts' over Herbert's future investment in its manufacturing programme.[84] *The American Machinist* observed that short-term fluctuations in ordering 'was not conducive to enterprise or to economy of working' for machine makers. Firms with extensive connections with the automobile industry, such as Herbert's, Asquith, and Archdale, found that the extension of output in the car industry to meet the new season turned out to be disappointing. By the late 1920s, home demand was largely coming from the automobile industry and ancillary trades, providing the machine tool industry in the Midlands with more business than all others combined. In late 1929, there were serious bottlenecks in supply, in particular shortages of grinding and milling machines, and automatic and capstan lathes, buyers 'impatient about the delays in delivery'. Intense pressure on machine tool capacity now combined with severe shortages of skilled workers, a fact which was particularly evident in the expanding Midlands.[85]

Increasing dependency on the domestic car industry, combined with a growth in demand from the electricity industry, reflected the recovery of these industries after 1924, but theses two sectors did not represent a general upturn in demand. There was a 'stubborn depression' in Britain's heavy industries, few machine makers in 1927 were 'under pressure of consumptive demand' from this sector. 'A new trade', a reference to a broad expansion of demand, had not materialised, hopes blown away by inflated estimates of the pace of recovery

---

[82] *American Machinist*, 12 July 1924, p. 143E.

[83] *American Machinist*, 3 May 1924, p. 73E; 27 September 1924, pp. 75-6; 11 October 1924, pp. 91-2E; 8 November 1924, pp. 123-4E.

[84] Herbert, Departmental Board, 11 July 1928.

[85] *American Machinist*, 3 December 1927, p. 209E; 17 December 1927, pp. 235-6E; 24 August 1929, pp. 25-6E; 21 September 1929, pp. 69-70E.

following the General Strike of 1926.[86] By late 1928 there were few signs of 'a trade movement such as will penetrate with fresh vigour the whole cosmos of ... industrial life'. Consequently, there was a diverse experience amongst firms in the machine tool industry. Firms concentrating on the automobile sector were at the 'mercy' of fluctuations of demand, with manufacturers cutting investment in slack periods, and then bunching it when activity increased. In contrast, firms which sold to a wider market were, in the short-run, under intense pressure to produce, 'notwithstanding the variability of demand generally'.[87] In 1927, for example, order books at Herbert's were rising rapidly, the company selling automatic lathes to the automobile and electrical industry, and finding a market for its No. 20 Turret Lathe from the shipbuilding and railway sectors. Recovery, however, even for firms with an extended market, remained illusionary, with vast differences between potential and actual demand.[88]

Table 4.6
Exports of Machine Tools, 1918-34

	Exports (£ million)	Exports (000 Tons))	Value per ton (£)
1918	1.28		
1919	2.29		
1920	3.36		
1921	2.89		
1922	1.53	12.2	126
1923	1.51	14.1	107
1924	1.36	12.0	114
1925	1.56	14.3	109
1926	1.53	13.7	112
1927	1.61	14.5	111
1928	1.77	14.5	122
1929	2.15	16.2	133
1930	1.86	13.9	133
1931	2.06	14.6	141
1932	3.14	23.8	132
1933	1.27	8.9	142
1934	1.62	12.3	132

Source: 'British Overseas Trading in Machine Tools', annual, in *The American Machinist*.

Adding to the problems of the industry was a disappointing export performance (Table 4.6). Export values fell sharply from 1920, remaining flat until 1929, although value per ton rose sharply in 1928, reflecting rising prices in foreign markets. In 1927, however, exports were not of a sufficient scale to aid the

---

[86] *American Machinist*, 13 August 1927, p. 19E; 8 October 1927, p. 103E.
[87] *American Machinist*, 3 November 1928, pp. 190-1E.
[88] *American Machinist*, 3 December 1927, p. 209E.

stabilisation of economic activity, and European markets were yielding fewer orders, the main demand arising in Empire markets.[89] During the inter-war years, the destination of British exports varied widely. Over the 1920s, Britain's largest markets continued to be in Empire areas, although European markets, especially in France did expand (Table 4.7). Just prior to the introduction of imperial preference in 1932, Empire trade had fallen to 9 per cent of total export values, the U.S.S.R. temporarily becoming Britain's largest foreign customer, accounting for 81.2 per cent of the value of British exports, and providing a short-term boost to British machine makers.[90]

Table 4.7
Distribution of British Machine Tool Exports by Value, 1921-29 (%)

	1921	1929
British India	27.08	16.36
British Africa	4.86	6.30
Australia	12.36	4.82
New Zealand	1.02	2.02
Canada	0.03	2.39
Other British Countries	8.22	8.82
Total to Empire	53.57	40.71
U.S.S.R. (for 1921 in other)		4.60
Japan	10.45	3.22
France	7.46	12.73
Belgium	6.51	2.99
Other Foreign Countries	22.01	35.75

Source: PEP, 'The Machine Tool Industry', p. 189.

Faced with difficult domestic trading conditions in the 1920s, the industry found little relief from its export performance. Britain's share of world machine tool exports (Table 4.8) fell sharply between 1923 and 1929, and by the latter date was lower than 1913 with America and Germany dominating international markets.[91] Further, imports increased as economic activity picked-up after 1924, and the balance of trade in machine tools steadily dwindled to 1930 (Table 4.9). This suggests that the British industry could not meet the upturn in domestic demand, and also raises questions about the technical performance of the industry, in particular its inability to produce 'gap' machines, of a specialist type,

---

[89] *American Machinist*, 13 August 1927, p. 19E; 8 October 1927, p. 104E; 3 December 1927, p. 209E; 17 December 1927, pp. 235-6E; 3 November 1928, pp. 190-1E.
[90] Political and Economic Planning (PEP), Report on 'The Machine Tool Industry', in *Planning*, Vol. 15, No. 292 (1948), p. 188; Aldcroft, 'The Performance of the British Machine Tool Industry', p.283; 'British Overseas Trading in Machine Tools', in *American Machinist*, 21 January 1928, p. 281E; 26 January 1935, p. 807E.
[91] Aldcroft, 'The Performance of the British Machine Tool Industry', p. 283

supplied by American and German producers. As the Balfour Committee concluded in 1928, in machine tools Germany had 'regained her pre-eminence as an exporting country ... sending abroad roughly three times the value of British exports ... while in the U.S.A. exports were rather more than twice the British values'.[92] The next section examines how the British machine tool industry met this growing challenge.

Table 4.8
Shares of International Machine Tool Exports, 1913-29 (%)

	U.K.	Germany	U.S.A.
1913	11.5	45.5	37.6
1923	19.7	32.9	37.3
1929	10.2	42.2	39.6

Source: Aldcroft, 'The Performance of the British Machine Tool Industry', p. 248.

Table 4.9
Imports, Re-Exports, and the Balance of Trade in Machine Tools, 1918-34

	Imports (£ million)	Imports (Tons 000)	Value per ton (£)	Re-Exports (£ million)	Retained Imports (£ million)	Balance of Trade[a] (£ million)
1918	3.86	19.4	199			-2.58
1919	3.97	17.1	232			-1.68
1920	3.02	13.3	228			-0.34
1921	0.61					2.28
1922	0.42			0.04	0.39	1.14
1923	0.50	3.8	131	0.05	0.45	1.05
1924	0.55	3.4	165	0.06	0.49	0.87
1925	0.73	4.9	149	0.04	0.68	0.88
1926	0.93	7.9	117	0.04	0.88	0.65
1927	1.18	7.7	154	0.04	1.14	0.47
1928	1.40	8.8	160	0.05	1.35	0.42
1929	1.95	11.1	176	0.07	1.88	0.27
1930	1.71	10.9	156	0.05	1.66	0.19
1931	1.61	10.8	149	0.06	1.55	0.51
1932	0.95	4.4	216	0.03	0.92	2.22
1933	0.85	3.3	253	0.04	0.81	0.45
1934	1.42	6.6	216	0.05	1.37	0.25

Source: 'British Overseas Trading in Machine Tools', Annual, in *The American Machinist*.
Note: a. Balance of Trade = imports-exports (Table 4.7) to 1921, and retained imports-exports (Table 4.7) from 1922.

---

[92] Balfour Committee on Trade and Industry, reported in *American Machinist*, 12 May 1928, pp. 167-8E.

Meeting the Challenge: Technology and Market Demand

In 1922, Frank A. Scott predicted that both makers and users would have to accept that innovation and enterprise would 'be the ruling force' determining business success in the highly competitive post-war world.[93] British makers were alive to this technological challenge at the Olympia Machine Tool Exhibition of 1920, organised by the MTTA, yet complaints of technological conservatism abounded. Few machines exhibited demonstrated 'innovation or spectacular breakthrough', rather there were examples of practical improvements 'in detail, in design, and in workmanship'. Incremental improvement symbolised British technological innovation, but this did not mean that makers were technologically moribund. Examples of technical ingenuity included the radial drills of William Asquith, Halifax, following an 'entirely new design', and rival drills built by Herbert's own engineering force, designed without belts and shafts, enabled centralised control and ease of operations. Favourable reviews were also forthcoming for the Churchill Machine Tool Co., the Selson Machine Tool Co., and Wards of Birmingham.[94]

'On the strictly technical side', Aldcroft argues, British makers during the inter-war years 'compared favourably with their closest competitors', and made considerable advances in both the design and operational efficiency of machines. Makers 'adapted' machines to allow 'faster speeds and greater stresses', continuous feeds 'to keep the machines supplied with work, whilst control mechanisms had to be rearranged or relocated to ensure safe and easy operation'.[95] British lathe design, for example, had been completely 'overhauled', makers introducing a series of 'minor improvements' such as stronger beds, higher stress load on carriages, headstocks and tailstocks, and continuous feed mechanisms.[96] Ahead of the field in 1924 was the Herbert No. 4 Capstan Lathe, which had 'undergone constant design improvements, including a two-speed special head, traversing saddle, and hand feed to capstan slide.[97] In 1925, the company launched its new No. 5 Auto Lathe that was fully automatic and incorporated several new features.[98] Makers concentrating on the automobile industry, such as James Archdale, launched in 1926 their 8 and 12 spindle drills for Morris Motors, meeting the needs for increased workload and durability.[99] At the Olympia Exhibition of 1928, key improvements in design included the extended use of electric drives, and the application of hydraulics to the driving and feeds of machines increased the cutting speed and prolonged the life of the tool compared to mechanically operated machines. Electric drives, designed as integrated units to the machine tool, became more rapidly diffused in the 1920s, a feature of the grinding machines displayed by Jones & Shipman at the British Industries Fair in

---

[93] *American Machinist*, June 1920, pp. 73-5.

[94] *American Machinist*, 4 September 1920, pp. 1-9E.

[95] Aldcroft, 'The Performance of the British Machine Tool Industry', p. 288.

[96] *American Machinist*, 1923, p. 245.

[97] Herbert, Departmental Board, 13 November 1923; 25 June 1924.

[98] *Engineer*, 9 October 1925, p. 384.

[99] *American Machinist*, 20 March 1926, p. 23E.

1932.[100] By the late 1920s and early 1930s, British makers were also using tungsten carbide to replace high speed steel, a 'revolutionary development' increasing cutting speeds from 75 to 80 feet per minute to 500 to 1,000 feet, and encouraging further design improvements to accommodate higher cutting speeds. According to Aldcroft, 'Most of the major firms as well as many smaller ones seem to have adopted these technical improvements fairly rapidly'.[101]

If the industry adapted adequately to key improvement innovations in the 1920s, there is still a need to consider the type of machines the industry produced, whether it met the changing demands from the engineering industry for labour-saving machinery, and whether the industry itself adopted the most efficient methods of production and marketing? The adaptability of British makers to meet the demand of engineering for volume output was recognised by Carl F. Dietz, Vice President of one of America's leading machine makers, the Norton Grinding Machine Co. 'English makers', he claimed, 'will try to meet the demand of her growing mass production industries, especially the automobile development'. Dietz showed no American complacency, but expectations of a British challenge to America's lead in semi-automatic and automatic machinery proved premature. S. Houghton, a British engineer, observed that British engineering was resistant to mass production techniques, and consequently only one British machine maker, A. Butterworth, Rochdale, had 'any reputation' in building high quality automatics.[102] British makers were thus reliant upon 'the manufacturing policy of those making the demand', in contrast to American makers who built machines in larger quantities exploiting the more extensive market for automatic labour-saving machinery to produce standardised components.[103]

In September 1922, *The American Machinist* assessed future demand conditions in the British automobile industry, observing that manufacturers were concentrating efforts on smaller cars requiring special-purpose machines to reduce manufacturing costs. Consequently, it predicted not to expect a high demand by motor manufacturers for general-purpose machines, the industry being fully equipped during the reconstruction phase following the war. The launching of new car models in November confirmed this, car manufacturers estimating a 20 to 25 per cent increase in turnover for the forthcoming year, and registering the fact that they were turning to the import of American special-purpose machines, which had 'no counterpart' in Britain. Car manufacturers focused investment planning not on major extensions or renewals to plant, having 'more standard tools than they know what to do with', but on the introduction of 'specials', especially for gear cutting, to effect economies in manufacture. Prominent suppliers of gear cutting machines to the British market were Gleason, Rochester, New York, and Browne and Sharpe

---

[100] *American Machinist*, 8 September 1928, p. 49E; Miller, *Tools that Built a Business*, p. 40.

[101] Aldcroft, 'The Performance of the British Machine Tool Industry, p. 288.

[102] *American Machinist*, 11 September 1920, p. 75E; 2 October 1920, p. 74E.

[103] *American Machinist*, 2 October 1920, p. 88E; 1922, p. 781.

of Providence, Rhode Island.[104] British makers faced 'a narrow demand' in 1923 and 1924, engineering concerns directing their order patterns to specials to economise on production costs, and 'so far as standard types are concerned the times are not propitious for the sinking of capital in new models'. In the Midlands, for example, replacement investment on 'obsolete general-purpose machines' remained low, the bulk of orders going to 'special-purpose machines which promise direct economies in production costs'. In particular, manufacturers of light cars were aware that competitive success depended upon cost effective machinery to produce higher turnover with finer profit margins, and there was 'no room for lax organisation or inefficient equipment'.[105] By 1927, there was an increasing demand for 'automatic and semi-automatic labour saving specialities', engineering firms in the Midlands sending representatives to the Cleveland Exhibition to view 'the progress' of American machine tool makers. British automobile manufacturers, for example, recognising the need to augment their productive capacity, were calling for labour-saving machinery to cut costs and meet increased competition. The response of the British industry to these trends was disappointing. New machines designed to meet changing production practices were too slow coming on the market to meet the demand, and consequently 'The business has gone to Americans, along with a good deal more for special-purpose tools'.[106]

Automobiles, which were central to the debate on the technical proficiency of the British machine tool industry, did not typify Britain's engineering sector. As early as 1917, the Board of Trade Committee on the Engineering Trades had remarked on the small-scale structure of British engineering firms, and the 'multiplicity of articles' produced by each. A Survey of the Metal Trades in 1928 reinforced this view, noting that engineering firms were not of an optimum size to utilise efficiently high performance machines. There were clearly constraints operating for machine makers, shaping the pattern of demand for more traditional machine tool products. Nevertheless, the survey did observe that there had been substantial changes since the early 1920s, notably in the rise of employment in motor vehicles, cycles, aircraft manufacture, and electrical engineering. Employment in these sectors increased by 26.9 per cent, 1923-7, compared to a rise of just 3.2 per cent for general engineering, and the growth of larger-scale enterprise in these sectors brought changes in both machining techniques and the skills of the workforce. These changes were a product of 'the demand for inter-changeability in the finished product and the development of machining processes', which in turn led to an 'intensification of specialities with machine operations partly substituting for skilled fitters'. Skill was not eradicated, the need for accuracy in machining necessitating 'skilled control', but the proportion of skilled workers in the engineering trades fell from

---

[104] *American Machinist*, 23 September 1922, pp. 31-2E; 18 November 1922, p. 83E.

[105] *American Machinist*, 9 June 1923, pp. 101-2E; 28 June 1924, p. 130E 11 October 1924, pp. 91-2E.

[106] *American Machinist*, 13 August 1927, p. 19E; 10 September 1927, p. 56E; 17 December 1927, pp. 235-6E.

50 per cent in 1921 to 40 per cent in 1926, corresponding to a rise from 30 to 45 per cent in semi-skilled labour. Unskilled workers fell from 20 to 15 per cent, the rising proportion of semi-skilled largely employed as machine tool operatives.[107]

Given these trends, and in the face of uncertain markets, labour-saving machine tools took precedence in the minds of Britain's automobile manufacturers. From the 1890s, the motor industry had been a growing consumer of machine tools, and it placed great pressure on the maker 'to improve and develop his design'. As Herbert's informed the trade in 1926, the high grade cutting steel used by the automobile industry, combined with the need for increased output, led to considerable alterations in design. The introduction of ancillary motors, which eradicated complex pulleys and gears, made it possible to use standard units, inclusive of powered work heads, to build-up a special-purpose machine designed to perform a number of operations either simultaneously or in succession.[108] Boring machines represented a classic example of specialisation. Estimates of machine costs for boring cylinders by two British engineers, G. E. Bailey and Thomas Smith, in 1927 showed that to perform the same amount of work using a standard pit lathe took 150 hours compared to 100 for a 'modern' vertical boring machine. Overhead charges for the lathe were £18 15s, which combined with labour costs of £8 18s. 2d. gave a total cost of £27 13s. 2d. In comparison, overhead charges for the boring machine were £22 10s, the extra charge accounted for by depreciation, while labour costs were lower at £5 18 s 19d, giving a slightly higher total cost of £28 8s 9d. However, the boring machine performed 'the work ... in two-thirds of the time, thus increasing the shop capacity', reducing work in progress, economising in investment, and decreasing supervision.[109] Special multiple boring machines, not adaptable to other engineering industries, but capable of boring 8 to 12 engine cylinders simultaneously, were a major innovation for car manufacturers. Other significant developments included specialised multiple drilling machines, fitted with three or four heads and each operating 20 to 30 drills simultaneously. Specialised milling operations on cams, which operate the valves of the engine, also found employment, grinding machines completing the finished component. Perhaps the most important application was the gear grinding machine, the most advanced development by the early 1930s in enabling high production at cheap cost. The machine allowed for degrees 'of inter-changeability which is so absolutely necessary if mass production ... methods are to be successful'. Further, the introduction of ancillary motors, that eradicated complex pulleys and gears, made it possible to use standard units, inclusive of powered work heads, to build-up a special-purpose machine designed to perform a number of operations either simultaneously or successively'. These specialised machines

---

[107] *Committee on Industry and Trade: Survey of Metal Trades* (London, HMSO, 1928), pp. 146, 149-52.
[108] L. T. C. Rolt, *A Short History of Machine Tools* (Cambridge, Mass., MIT Press, 1965), pp. 192, 196; *American Machinist*, 28 November 1926, p. 280E.
[109] *American Machinist*, 25 February 1927, p. 48E.

contrasted with general-purpose turret, capstan and automatic lathes that 'were more suitable to the general market'.[110]

Increasing demand for high performance machines in automobile manufacture opened up debates concerning the level of 'Enterprise' in British machine making. F. P. Terry, a Belfast engineer, claimed in 1923, that British makers had failed to profit from the experiences of the War, and did not provide the improved machines demanded by the engineering industries. In response, Pickin, of Herbert's, referred to the Olympia Exhibition of 1920, which had witnessed significant improvements in British design, and since that date a number of labour-saving machine tools, which had been formerly imported from the U.S.A., were now manufactured in Britain. Nevertheless, criticisms of the technical capabilities of the industry continued, and in 1927, C. R. F. Engelbach, Works Director at Austin Motors, informed the Institute of Production Engineers, in front of their President Sir Alfred Herbert, that Britain was 'backward' in providing modern machinery for automobile manufacture. Austin, he claimed, would acquire 50 per cent of its new plant from abroad, as certain types of machines were not available at home, and he further condemned British makers who, unlike their foreign competitors, would not provide machine 'guarantees' on productivity performance. Acknowledging that British makers were making up the leeway, Engelbach concluded that they did not specialise sufficiently to provide the necessary 'service' required by the automobile industry.[111]

Sir Alfred Herbert answered Engelbach's critique in 1928. Accepting that orders were higher than at any time since 1920, Sir Alfred acknowledged that makers were still unable to meet demand, despite extensive overtime. In particular, he identified a rising demand for 'ingenious' labour-saving machinery, which he saw as a prerequisite for the competitive success of British industry. His platitudes, however, were not accepted by Sir Herbert Austin, who in a speech to the Institute of Production Engineers, presided over by Sir Alfred, observed that where special machines are needed 'the manufacturer is mostly called upon to make them himself', or to import from abroad. British makers, he alleged, anticipating Aldcroft's later criticism of the industry, failed to predict demand 'in advance of manufacture'. Unlike the practice of American makers, there was no close interaction with users to determine the production requirements of the machine 'in advance' of design, British machine tool firms 'following on the heels of manufacture'. 'Trial and error', as Austin claimed, symbolised the method of R&D in the British machine tool industry. This led to delays in fully incorporating electric motors into machine design, the failure to perfect hydraulic control, and the slow introduction of vertical millers, an alternative to the horizontal type, which saved on space allowing machines to be organised for continuous line production.[112] Supporting Austin's allegations was the fact that imports were high between 1925 and 1931 (Table 4.9). Such was the demand for foreign machines in

---

[110] Rolt, *A Short History*, p. 206; *Engineer*, 23 September 1932, pp. 302-3; 7 October 1932, pp. 348-50; *American Machinist*, 28 November 1926, p. 280E.

[111] *American Machinist*, 8 October 1927, p. 104E.

[112] *American Machinist*, 22 September 1928, pp. 95-6E.

1929 that American machine makers, and German suppliers of high-grade tools, were unable to keep pace. The 'absorptive capacity' of automobiles, especially for special-purpose machines, coupled with the expansion of electrical engineering gave an impulse to increasing imports.[113] Herbert C. Armitage, a member of the Institute of Mechanical Engineers, observed in 1930 that British makers failed to perceive a demand for special machine tools, concentrating instead on a wide range of general-purpose types.[114]

The 'automotive' production systems installed at the Coventry Engine Branch of Morris Motors in 1927, demonstrated the 'absorptive power' of the car industry for special-purpose machines. Designed for an output of 1,500 units, the engine factory consisted of two assembly lines, one utilising special machines and the other mainly of standard lines 'adapted for special operations' by Morris engineers. Morris engineers designed their own special machines, as well as utilising vertical milling machines supplied by American makers. The only evidence of British ingenuity, were the specially designed radial drills for repetitive work by James Archdale and William Asquith, two companies that built almost exclusively for the motor trade.[115] In 1931, F. G. Woolard, the managing director at the Morris Cowley works, and an exponent of flow production methods,[116] acknowledged that British makers had responded to the demand for higher productivity machines, but observed that American makers still dominated for special types. In particular, American suppliers such as Fellows, Heald, and Landis supplied extensively to the British car industry, constantly up-dating designs to meet the demand for higher productivity. For example, in 1927 the Heald Sizematic, a machine that incorporated electrical control, hydraulic feed and automatic accuracy gauges, superseded the Heald Internal Grinder. Costing £1,100, compared to £500 for the Internal Grinder, the Sizematic guaranteed a 300 per cent increase in output.[117] It is little wonder that at the 1928 Machine Tool Exhibition at Olympia, far more American machines were exhibited than in 1924, a warning that British makers 'would ... be well advised to study what their rivals overseas are doing'.[118]

While British makers could point to examples of incremental improvements in design by the late 1920s, the condemnation of machine users over the failure to compete in higher productivity, and especially specialist machines, raised serious doubts about the competitive response of the industry. The American Machinist in 1927, provided a list of machines which were either neglected or insufficiently developed in Britain, including crank-turning lathes, crankpin grinders, multiple borers, honing machines, manufacturing internal grinders, automatic milling machines, drum-type milling machines, hydraulically-actuated

[113] American Machinist, 9 March 1929, pp. 60-1E.

[114] American Machinist, 22 March 1930, p. 98E.

[115] American Machinist, June 1927, pp. 359-62; 27 February 1927, p. 38E.

[116] See R. Church, 'Deconstructing Nuffield: The Evolution of Managerial Culture in the British Motor Industry', Economic History Review, Vol. 49, No. 3 (1996), pp. 569-71.

[117] American Machinist, 10 January 1931, p. 282E.

[118] American Machinist, 1 September 1928, pp. 31-2E.

cylindrical grinders, and machines for cutting spur, bevel and spiral gears in quantities. In 1932, the MTTA reported that there were 37 categories of machine tools imported. These represented types that makers could not manufacture domestically, and were vital 'gaps' in the British supply.[119] At the 1928 Olympia Exhibition, of the 657 machines displayed by British firms 132 were imported. Prominent machine merchants such as Burton, Griffiths & Co., Buck and Hickman, and G. H. Alexander, displayed a variety of imported American automatics, but prominent amongst the exhibitors was Alfred Herbert, which displayed 46 imported machines (Table 4.10).

At an industry level, importation during the 1920s was acceptable as part of the industry's commitment to free trade and international specialisation, although the strength of this obligation did depend upon the prevailing economic climate. For example, faced with adverse trading conditions in 1923, the members of the MTTA voted 79 to 12 in favour of the application of import duties to the industry. After a lengthy debate, led by Sir Alfred Herbert, it was decided by the MTTA Council that no further action should be taken, protection considered as detrimental to the interests of merchants and factorers of foreign machines. Following a report by Sir Alfred on the rising trend in imports, protection again became an issue in 1925, the MTTA concluding that import penetration was not sufficiently large enough to justify further representations to the Board of Trade on the inclusion of machine tools under safeguarding.[120] By 1928, the management of BSA reported that the MTTA were 'definitely opposed to any serious thought of safeguarding', the Association acknowledging that it needed to serve the interests of both importers and manufacturers.[121] The advent of the serious depression of the early 1930s was a catalyst for change, the industry now recognising that foreign competition was having serious effects on the performance of the industry. A questionnaire sent by the Federation of British Industry to 109 firms in the MTTA brought forth a positive response in favour of protection. Of the 62 firms who responded, 9, employing 1,000, were in favour of maintaining free trade, while 53, employing 17,143, wanted some form of protection.[122] The imposition of a general tariff of 20 per cent ad valorem on all machine tools in November 1931 was welcomed by the Association, as was the proviso that the Import Duties Advisory Committee (IDAC), on which the MTTA was represented, could sanction the free importation of 'specialised machinery which it is still necessary to import'. Sir George May, chairman of the IDAC, informed the MTTA in 1933 that the Committee, under advice from the MTTA, would give favourable treatment to gap machines which were vital to the efficiency of British manufacturing industry.[123]

---

[119] *American Machinist*, 8 October 1927, pp. 93-4E; Aldcroft, 'The Performance of the British Machine Tool Industry', p. 283.

[120] MTTA, Annual Report for 1923, p. 8; Annual Report for 1925, p. 6.

[121] 594/1/1/3/58, BSA Board Minutes, 30 November 1928, Report on Burton, Griffiths & Co. and BSA Tools.

[122] *Engineer*, 3 April 1931, p. 363.

[123] MTTA, Annual Report for 1932, pp. 8-10, and Annual General Meeting, 1933, p. 10.

Gap machines were indeed important to British manufacturing industry, a fact made clear by Sir Herbert Austin in a speech to the MTTA in 1933. He condemned British makers for surrendering the field in special machine tools to American and German producers. In reply, Sir Alfred argued that given the limited market for these machines, it was rational to import, and he further condemned the conservative attitude of users to high productivity machinery.[124] On this point, users were not devoid of blame. For example, in 1924, makers claimed that there was a general reluctance amongst engineering concerns to modernise production methods. 'The main stumbling block', it was argued, was 'the inaccessibility of works officials who are able to appreciate the value of a new idea in practical working and who at the same time have the authority to lay out the money to give it effect'. This suggested a business culture in British engineering that militated against new technology. Top-level executives were divorced from the process of production planning, machine tool buyers on behalf of the company lacked the technical knowledge to gauge the economic advantages of new machines, and managers and foremen were suspicious of issues which involved more than a 'technical' consideration of the production problem. Machine makers, it was claimed, 'often find that amour ropre [self-esteem] is the ruling factor. They can never get an intelligent hearing in some works, they complain'.[125] By 1930, 'a quantity complex' influenced 'the minds of makers, salesmen and users, militating against a quicker realisation of the value of automatic machinery'. Sales personnel were reluctant to push automatic lathes, especially if they competed with capstans, 'agreeing that the automatic is not the machine for the job'. Production engineers were sceptical of the initial investment costs and set-up time, oblivious to the potential cost-saving advantages of advanced machine tools.[126] As Brown argues, workshop practices in British engineering was based on a 'culture of mechanical engineering', responding to 'inchoate beliefs about design', and avoiding 'American-style production engineering' with its emphasis upon 'cost calculation'.[127]

Low-level interaction characterised relations between users and makers, based on self-interest, and in the environment of the 1920s, with reductions in profits and reserve capital, it was difficult to get across the cost-saving advantages of modern machinery.[128] In 1927, British makers charged automobile manufacturers with a failure to encourage new machine designs by their conservative response to new technology, and responded critically to suggestions that they should be 'copyists' of American designs.[129] T. S. Catmur, a director of Burton, Griffiths, developed these arguments further, placing an emphasis upon the relative size of the British market, which limited the capabilities of machine

---

[124] MTTA, Annual General Meeting, 1933, pp. 2-3.
[125] *American Machinist*, 15 March 1924, pp. 31-2E.
[126] *American Machinist*, 15 February 1930, p. 20E.
[127] Brown, 'Design Plans', pp. 223, 226.
[128] *American Machinist*, 26 July 1924, p. 155E; 8 November 1924, pp. 123-4E.
[129] *American Machinist*, 22 October 1927, p. 126E.

Table 4.10
Machine Tool Exhibition 1928: Firms Displaying Imported Machines

	Total Machines Shown	No. Imported
G. H. Alexander Machines Ltd.	7	7
Blundstone Engineering Service Ltd.	7	5
Buck & Hickman Ltd.	18	18
Burton, Griffith & Co. Ltd.	16	11
Churchill Machine Tool Co.	36	30
Crossley & Co.	7	5
George Hatch Ltd.	35	8
Alfred Herbert Ltd.	120	46
A. A. Jones & Shipman Ltd.	18	2

Source: *The American Machinist*, 29 September 1928, p. 117E.

makers to supply in large quantities special-purpose machines. For example, America produced in 1926 four million cars, compared to 160,000 in Britain, enabling U.S. makers to specialise on certain types of machines to supply a large market. In this sense, as Catmur argued, rising American imports into the British market in 1926 were beneficial to domestic engineering, being 'unlike any other import' and enabling users to utilise cost effective machinery. Consequently, British engineering industry was aided by machine tool merchants such as Burton Griffiths, as well as by machine makers such as Alfred Herbert who factored foreign machine tools. Such business relations, Catmur claimed, provided 'mutual advantage', enabling British engineering to import high productivity machines, which could not be economically produced by domestic makers because of the limited market, and providing American makers with expanded export markets. International specialisation determined that Britain would concentrate on standard general-purpose machines, allowing America to manufacture specials.[130] As *The American Machinist* conceded in 1930, it was logical for British makers to concentrate on standard machines 'for which the demand is readier', and British makers have no 'extended experience' of building specials and 'consequently they could not compete on price with overseas makers'.[131] From this perspective, the failure of British makers to develop specialist high performance machines was constrained by the market environment conditioned by British manufacturing firms. At the same time, the machine tool industry faced a technological trajectory that was set within the context of viewing technology as an evolutionary process, forcing firms to adapt to competitive forces rather than to lead.

This was consistent with an industry which was highly individualistic, and where there was no institutional development for collaborative action. A culture of secrecy infused throughout the industry, and although makers could complain that

---

[130] *American Machinist*, 12 November 1927, p. 164E.
[131] *American Machinist*, 22 March 1930, pp. 91-2E.

users were conservative in their approach to the introduction of modern equipment, makers were reluctant to disseminate information to the trade. For example, in 1918, the Department of Scientific and Industrial Research invited the MTTA to form a research association for machine tools. The committee appointed to consider the issue rejected the invite, justifying this by pointing out that research conducted by the industry was the prerogative of 'individualistic' firms, and consequently the initiative would not receive support from MTTA members.[132] In 1922 *The American Machinist* welcomed the fact that 24 research associations had been granted licences from the Board of Trade, and hoped that this represented a 'movement in the industrial world away from pure competition towards ... emulative competition'.[133] This was a false dawn as far as the machine tool industry was concerned, and in the 1920s, the debates on the merits of rationalisation and amalgamation further emphasised the individual attitude of firms. In 1925, for example, the engineer S. C. Sumner condemned the lack of co-operation in the industry. With the exception of Associated British Machine Tool Makers Ltd., a sales organisation formed in 1917, there was no centralised marketing in the industry to co-ordinate the activities of large numbers of small producers, and larger firms operated individually, organising marketing through their own domestic branch offices or overseas sales companies. Thus, the engineer W. George extolled the virtues of the German machine tool industry in 1929, where formal amalgamations existed for joint marketing, the pooling of technological knowledge, and the standardisation of machine tool lines. Such collaborative action in Britain, he claimed, was unfeasible because of the problems of reconciling 'the conflicting thoughts that exist in groups of employers [and] the many personal jealousies and fears in individuals who are essentially in competition with each other'. As the depression struck in 1930, *The American Machinist* was unequivocal in its view that 'Although rationalisation is put forward as a probable part solution of the trading position, many engineers adhere to the individualistic feature which has characterised British production up to the present'.[134] The behaviour of machine tool firms would appear to confirm Chandler's criticism that the persistence of personal capitalism in Britain held back innovative development and instilled a culture of conservatism.[135]

Individualism determined the technological frontiers of the industry, firms evolving machine tool design internally with little formal interaction. The evolution of technology was more adaptive than pioneering, knowledge acquired through recourse to constant experimentation. Sir Alfred Herbert summed up this pattern of technological development in 1918. Responding to the proposal for the formation of a research association, he observed that 'jealousy and secrecy do of necessity exist and ... most companies would prefer to solve their own problems

---

[132] MTEA, Minute Book, 3 October, 13 November 1918; *Report of the Committee of the Privy Council for Scientific and Industrial Research for 1917-1918* (cd. 9144).
[133] *American Machinist*, 16 September 1922, p. 26E.
[134] *American Machinist*, 8 January 1925, p. 2E; 20 April 1929, pp. 124-5E; 24 May 1930, p. 219E.
[135] Chandler, *Scale and Scope*, pp. 339-40.

themselves rather than to submit same to an Institution'. The direction of his own company on R&D, he claimed, was to develop precision machines, through constant experimentation, the company controlling the process rather than submitting to a research association.[136] As Chandler points out, 'at Alfred Herbert Ltd., Britain's premier maker of machine tools, Sir Alfred ... remained chairman and sole governing director' throughout the inter-war years'.[137] To examine the evolution of technology in the industry, the final section will focus on the experience of two of Britain's leading firms, Herbert's and BSA.

The Machine Tool Firm and Technological Evolution

In 1919, Sir Hallewell Rogers inferred that the war did have some positive impact on technological change. He informed BSA shareholders that 'With the reversion to peace conditions we find a continuously increasing desire on the part of engineers and manufacturing concerns to take advantage of our unique experience in the design and manufacture of special machinery and tools, for the production of their standardised products'. Premised on a strategy of meeting the need of large-scale production in engineering the management restructured the company's machinery and small tool division in 1919 by creating BSA Tools (BSAT), a subsidiary of the new BSA holding company. Adding to the company's machine tool capabilities, BSA also acquired Burton, Griffiths in 1919, a company with extensive agencies with American makers. Machine tools, Rogers claimed, now constituted 'a large business' and both subsidiaries were to be operated as 'more or less separate concerns, having separate detailed management'.[138] An ambitious policy was set to expand the market for BSAT in the early 1920s, based both on the development of its established small tool business, and on the design and manufacture of special equipment and fixtures for engineering. Special machine production had evolved during the war, when diverse demands had created the need for flexibility in meeting the engineering problems of customers. Thus, Rogers perceived BSAT as an 'expert consulting branch', always 'ready to examine the operation ... to lay out the most scientific method of carrying it out, and to supply the means by which the method could be made operative'. In the early 1920s, BSAT developed special machine tools in conjuncture with Daimler, the BSA car subsidiary, providing a platform for converting them into standard lines of high performance machine tools for sale to general engineering.[139]

The concentration on specials, however, caused serious problems in the early 1920s. Depression forced BSAT to delay the development of more standard designs, confining their programme to the building of special types, 'frequently ...

---

[136] Herbert, Departmental Board, 28 October 1918.

[137] Chandler, *Scale and Scope*, p. 340. See also J. Quail, 'The Proprietorial Theory of the Firm and its Consequences', *Journal of Industrial History*, Vol. 3, No. 1 (2000), pp. 1-28.

[138] 594/1/1/2/3, BSA Meeting File, Ordinary Meeting, October 1919.

[139] 594/1/1/2/5, BSA Meeting File, Ordinary Meeting, October 1922.

of a very special character ... to help fill the shops'. By 1924, 'this class of business was too precarious', the shops either working full time at high pressure for short periods of the year, or at other times they were devoid of orders, reduced to introducing economies 'in order to make ends meet'. Moreover, during slack periods workers responded by 'adjusting their effort accordingly and inefficiency resulted'. Nevertheless, in 1921 the company experimented with its first major commercial line, a centreless grinding machine built in two sizes, and the first of its kind in the U.K. Utilising patents purchased from the Cincinnati Grinding Co., BSAT launched the machine at the Olympia Exhibition of 1924, but delays occurred in its commercial application, technical deficiencies necessitating a complete re-design in 1925. At the same time, the company evolved its specialist 4-spindle grinder, a machine originally designed for Daimler to reduce that company's dependency on American imports.[140] With a limited and uncertain market for specials, from 1924 BSAT attempted to standardise its range. The aim was 'to develop from a nebulous group of all kinds of special machinery a line of machines which would tend to command a more even demand upon the factory organisation'. BSAT employed 566 workers and 124 staff in 1925 and by the Olympia Exhibition of 1928 the company, for the first time, could regard themselves 'as serious people in the machine tool business, with lines of ... machines suitable for various classes of engineering industry'. F. V. Turrell, managing director of BSAT, summarised the company's production strategy: 'to increase demand for machines they are making, up-date design and manufacture and evolve new types of machines and sizes, or modify types they already manage'.[141]

The process of technical evolution at BSAT was to move from specialised machines, with a low market potential, to standardised lines that the company could build in larger batches. In 1925, for example, BSAT designed special lathes for Daimler, in anticipation that they 'may develop into quite a useful line for us'. In the same year, improvements to their centreless grinding machines, manufactured in batches of 6 and 12, provided increased adaptability for users, and offered a standard line to engineering. Again, in 1926, the company received special orders from Armstrong-Siddeley for machines to manufacture aero-engine components, and built a variety of other special machines. Standardising the product in the market, however, was no easy task. As the management noted, 'In certain cases, whilst the machines were effective for their purpose, trade conditions were against their development' into more standard lines, but in anticipation of a revival of trade the company continued to build batches of special centreless grinding machines, multi-spindle drilling machines, and automatic turning and chucking lathes. Celebrating their concentration on special machining, the management noted that 'with the possible exception of the Multi-spindle Drilling

---

[140] 594/1/1/3/1-78, BSA Board Minutes, 3/3, 29 February 1924, Memorandum on BSA Tools and Burton, Griffiths; 3/10, 31 October 1924; 3/58, 30 November 1928, Report on Burton, Griffiths & Co. and BSA Tools.
[141] BSA Board, 3/58, 30 November 1928, Report on Burton, Griffiths & Co. and BSA Tools.

Machines, no firm in this country has made a serious attempt to manufacture them, as they have been mainly imported from abroad'. The aim, however, remained to produce in larger batches standard machines providing 'a more staple line of production instead of having to rely upon promiscuous orders for special plant'. This was frustrated by capacity constraints, which delayed the building of stocks of standard lines, the management noting that they were facing competition from American suppliers 'who are better equipped for this work'. Nevertheless, in 1926 the BSA parent board sanctioned a £5,000 capital expansion programme for the development of standard machines.[142]

Developing machine tool technology at BSAT followed an evolutionary learning curve, the company designing specials, which were then converted to standard lines following an assessment of the machine's commercial potential and its technical feasibility. Initial market signs showed promise, the company receiving orders from the Nakashima Trading Co. of Tokyo who were co-operating with the Bristol Aeroplane Co. to manufacture components. Armstrong-Siddeley also placed orders for grinding machines, and BSAT supplied special machinery to the International Standard Electric Co. By 1927, BSAT was building centreless grinders for stock to meet future orders for speedy delivery, with 90 BSA standard machines in progress and a number of specials to 'customers' designs'. In 1927, a large order from International Standard Electric for specials amounted to £14,000 and there were several 'repeat orders' for grinders. The quality of their machines, and their adaptability, was clearly important to customers, the company beating a French firm to an order for £3,000 'for specials' for the General Electric Co., not on price but because of the ability to meet technical specifications. In 1928, BSAT launched its new high-speed automatic lathe as a standard machine. Despite BSAT achieving some notable contracts, there still remained the problem of uncertain market demand. For example, the demand for both specials and standard lines fluctuated wildly in 1928. In June, orders for new lines of specials fell, the company losing orders from International Standard Electric, the business going to German makers who offered 'very much lower prices'. Sales of standard lines also fell flat, the management observing that 'Unfortunately the general attitude of British buyers is very critical of British machines, and ... they will tolerate defects with imported machines with small comment'. During 1929, there was a surge of orders for both specials and standards, with the former representing a large share of total orders. Rising demand from the automobile and electrical industries fuelled orders for specials, leading to the inevitable problem of capacity constraints. Production of specials added to the capacity burden, increasing the time of manufacture due to the need for testing, and delaying the delivery of standard lines, which resulted in cancelled orders. As the management commented, new designs 'frequently' require 'a number of modifications ... at the last moment which caused the delay'.[143]

---

[142] BSA Board, 3/17, 26 June 1925; 3/20, 25 September 1925; 3/25, 26 February 1926; 3/27, 4 June 1926, Memorandum on Machinery Section of BSA Tools.

[143] BSA Board, 3/32, 24 September 1926; 3/37, 28 February 1927; 3/38, 23 March 1927; 3/39, 22 April 1927; 3/40, 27 May 1927; 3/47, 22 November-27 December 1927;

During the depression, orders for standard machines fell sharply, customers searching for special high productivity machines.[144] Percy Martin, the Managing Director of the BSA parent board, informed shareholders in September 1930 that it had been a 'particularly disappointing' year for BSAT. 'It is fortunate that we have still been able to retain our goodwill with the firms for whom we make special machines, as the orders we have received from this source have been very useful'. In that year, orders for standard machines totalled just £8,439 compared to £45,441 for specials.[145] Special lines were bolstered by orders from car makers for centreless grinders and small simple-operation multi-tool lathes, 'designed to meet the peculiar requirements of the British automobile industry'.[146] BSAT clearly did adapt to the increasing demand for special machine tools, building a range of them for conversion to standard lines, but as Martin pointed out the growth of sales had not met expectations since 1924, and did not justify the capital outlays involved.[147] Uncertain markets tended to depress sales, but there was also limited marketing capability at BSAT related to structural flaws in the BSA machine tool organisation.

In 1919, the BSA machine tool division utilised the sales and marketing capabilities of Burton, Griffiths, which offered 'a ... well-respected selling organisation, apart from its profit earning capability', and during the war had been highly successful in promoting sales under American agencies. The initial strategy was to rationalise sales in one company, Burton, Griffiths acting 'as sole agents or distributors for all the products of BSA Tools', including small tools and machine tools, and BSAT operating as 'purely a manufacturing firm without any selling organisation'. At the same time, Burton, Griffiths would continue to factor imported machine tools 'which would ... run parallel to the Special Machine businesses of BSA Tools'. Integrating the factoring of American machine tools, with the development of the specialities of BSAT, the management envisaged, would enable them to offer to customers a wide range of machine types. By 1924, this organisational arrangement had not delivered an integrated and co-ordinated sales strategy, an internal report concluding that there was no evidence of an 'intensive sales effort or economy of working'. The result was 'two self-contained companies whose operations for all practical purposes were those of two companies acting independently'. The report recommended that the BSAT head office take responsibility for enquiries for special machine tools, Burton, Griffiths continuing to act to promote BSAT standard machines and as sales agents of BSAT small tools, a reorganisation that BSA implemented in 1926. Co-ordination problems continued, and a report by Turrell in 1928 claimed that both subsidiaries were still 'separate organisations', each selling their own lines of machine tools and small tools, and there were clear contradictions in the sales strategy. The

---

3/48, 20 January 1928; 3/52, 1 June 1928; 3/56, 27 September 1928; 3/59, 4 January 1929; 3/66, 26 July 1929; 3/69, 29 November 1929.
[144] BSA Board, 3/71, 31 January 1930; 3/74, 25 April 1930; 3/77, 18 July 1930.
[145] BSA Board, 3/78, 26 September 1930.
[146] *American Machinist*, 13 December 1930, p. 241E.
[147] BSA Board, 3/78, 26 September 1930.

strategy of Burton, Griffiths was to maintain a certain number of representative lines, mainly American, and 'promote sales of them to the greatest extent'. Thus, the company's reputation depended on satisfying their 'most lucrative' American agencies by 'The judicious carrying of stocks to meet the needs of the home market and the maintenance of good service between themselves as agents and their customers in order to maintain the maximum possible turnover'. In 1927, Burton, Griffiths purchased machine tools valued at £173,767, and small tools valued at £147,593, with 78 per cent of total purchases, consisting mainly of machine tools, emanating from the U.S.A., while only 22 per cent were ordered from European and English suppliers. As the 1928 report observed, Burton, Griffiths sales personnel were experienced in selling American lines, in which there was only a small amount of effort needed to promote these machines compared to the 'considerable effort required to introduce, what to some extent were, new types of machines manufactured by a hitherto unknown firm [BSAT] in the business'. The types of machines developed by BSAT, especially of a specialist type, was itself open to criticism, the company expanding its manufacturing programme without close 'co-operation with the sales department'.[148]

To confront these organisational defects, the report recommended extending the agencies of Burton, Griffiths to include German machine tool firms, thus reducing the dependency on American lines that competed with BSAT, an integrated sales office in Birmingham, the strengthening of the BSAT sales force, and the appointment of a joint sales manager to co-ordinate the activities of both subsidiaries. In 1930, the BSA parent board redesigned the BSAT factory on modern lines, and at the same time erected a joint showroom at Birmingham, projecting the image of a 'combined organisation'. Attempts to create agencies with German firms resulted in frustration, the depression militating against collaboration, and during 1930, Martin visited the American agencies of Burton, Griffiths to negotiate closer co-operation and possible manufacture under patents at Birmingham.[149] American influence at the company was clearly important by 1930, but during the 1920s Burton, Griffiths acted in direct competition with the products of BSAT, and the problem of marketing was central to the slow development in the sale of BSAT standardised machines. Adapting to these problems, and with the introduction of import duties in 1931, Burton, Griffiths became sole agents in the UK for Potter & Johnson automatic lathes, and, at the same time, BSAT manufactured these machines under licence. In 1932, Burton, Griffiths also established sole agencies in the UK for Norton semi-automatic

---

[148] BSA Board, 3/3, 29 February 1924, Memorandum on BSA Tools and Burton, Griffiths; 3/27, 4 June 1926, Memorandum on Machinery Section of BSA Tools; 3/46, 25 November 1927; 3/58, 30 November 1928, Report on Burton, Griffiths & Co. and BSA Tools.
[149] BSA Board, 3/58, 30 November 1928, Report on Burton, Griffiths & Co. and BSA Tools; 3/78, 26 September 1930.

grinders, and automatic cylindrical grinders made by the Arter Grinding Machine Co. of Worcester, Massachusetts.[150]

Closer interaction with foreign makers by BSA was indicative of a general trend to more formal business relations, and was representative of the fact that British firms tended to follow rather than lead in the process of technological change. In 1931, for example, the Selson Engineering Co. joined with the Naxos Union of Frankfurt to launch a joint venture in Britain, the Selson Grinding Co., to distribute in the British Empire Naxos precision grinding machines. Selson also acquired rights as sole agents in Britain for the Cleveland Automatic Machine Co.[151] In 1929 Charles Churchill & Co. announced its sole agency agreement in the UK for the new Cincinnati horizontal milling machine with hydraulic feed, 'one of the most striking examples of machine tool practice'.[152] John Gabriel, the assistant managing director of Charles Churchill since 1920, reacted to the slump of 1931 and the imposition of tariffs that followed by turning the company's attention to manufacture at home, which took time to effect. Consequently, when Gabriel became sole managing director in 1932 he began negotiating with a number of American suppliers for licences, including the Cone Co. of Windsor, Vermont; Goss & de Leeuw of New Britain, Connecticut; The Cleveland Hobbing Machinery Co.; and Jones & Lamson of Springfield, Vermont. From the last company, he secured rights to the Fay lathe, an automatic noted for its versatility and suitable for mass production and easy operation.[153] From 1930 Gabriel had been influential, together with Arthur Chamberlain, the chairman of both Charles Churchill and the company's manufacturing subsidiary, the Churchill Machine Tool Co., in technical collaboration with the Cincinnati Milling Machine Co. to 'keep abreast of progress' in the market for precision grinders. By October 1931, Cincinnati engineers were investigating the manufacturing systems at the Churchill Machine Tool Co., and in July 1933 an English subsidiary of the Cincinnati Co., with Gabriel as chair, was launched. Operating under a manufacturing royalty of 10 per cent, the subsidiary engaged with the Churchill Machine Tool Co. in joint development work on precision grinders.[154] In 1934, differences on the Charles Churchill board led to the resignation of Chamberlain, who took over the Churchill Machine Tool Co. At the same time, Gabriel acquired for Charles Churchill the full control of Redman & Co., which was renamed Churchill-Redman, and became engaged in manufacturing under licence American machine tools.[155]

The involvement of British makers with foreign companies raises issues concerning the lead role taken by British firms in the advancement of technology, especially in automatic machine tools suitable for mass production industries

---

[150] *Engineer*, 8 January 1932, p. 57; 23 September 1932, pp. 302-3; 7 October 1932, pp. 348-50.

[151] *Engineer*, 27 February 1931, p. 251; 10 April 1931, p. 417.

[152] *American Machinist*, 21 September 1929, p. 70E.

[153] Jeremy, 'Gabriel, John Beresford Stuart', pp. 456-7.

[154] Churchill Machine Tool Co., Minute Book of Board, 26 February 1930; 29 October 1931; 27 July 1933.

[155] Jeremy, 'Gabriel, John Beresford Stuart', pp. 456-7.

during the inter-war years. Technological development was evolutionary, aided in the British case by transfers of knowledge from American makers. A classic example of the evolution of technology was that of the leading British firm of Herbert's. In 1921, the company based its design strategy on the principle that no new machine, embodying improvements, should be put in hand in batches until an experimental machine had been made. Monitoring this strategy, the board sanctioned new models based on costing, competitive pricing, and market feasibility. A system of manufacturing, determined by constant experimentation, however, as noted by Pickin, led to high production costs, the company's engineers paying insufficient 'attention to economy in design and construction', leading to the building of 'expensive' machines.[156] It is a reminder, as Mintzberg has commented, that 'strategy is less a rational plan arrived at in the abstract ... as an emergent phenomenon', and as business organisations attempt to 'craft strategy ... they continually learn about shifting business conditions and balance what is desirable and what is possible'.[157]

Faced with low demand, new designs were desirable, and seen as crucial to the recovery of sales. In 1922, however, Sir Alfred considered that experimentation undermined the commercial logic of their policy. 'In the present state of affairs', he claimed, 'we shall not be able to get a sufficient amount of work into our shops unless we are much more active in getting new lines on the market'. The 'practice of building experimentally', he concluded, meant that 'At present, when we get a new design we are so long in getting it on the market that much valuable time is lost'. Experimentation was deeply embedded in the engineering culture of the company, ensuring that machines met user specifications and were reliable, but given depressed demand it was not 'the soundest' policy, and the fundamental problem was low capacity utilisation and rising overheads. In this situation, the company was 'losing so much money every day because our shop is so badly occupied that it will pay us to take risks in order to get our works more fully employed'. While not denying that experimentation was central to the company's market reputation, Sir Alfred advocated that they 'take more risks and put batches into the works more boldly'. To implement this, 'new designs should avoid risky elements whenever the desired result can be attained by well tried methods'. Accepting his criticisms, and shifting the balance from what the company desired to what was possible, the board immediately discontinued experimental work on the new No. 28 Vertical Miller and the No. 19 Hexagon Turret Lathe, both machines to be immediately built in batches. By 1923, depressed demand had reinforced the company's batch production strategy, the directors constructing a programme to provide more work for the shops, including 12 each of the Herbert No. 16 universal milling machine, Universal Grinder, Broaching Machine, and Ball Bearing Radial Drills. However, the board deferred a decision to launch the No. 19 Hexagon Turret Lathe until its market potential could be realised following further experimentation to improve design.[158]

---

[156] Herbert, Departmental Board, 28 June, 12 July, 23 August 1921.

[157] H. Mintzberg cited in Senge, 'The Leaders' New Work', p. 45.

[158] Herbert, Departmental Board, 24 January 1922; 24 April 1923.

The No. 19 illustrates the incremental and 'evolutionary process of machine tool design' at the company. When it was finally launched in 1926, it had evolved through a series of stages as the result of direct experience, the product starting life as the No 4 Hexagon Turret, designed before the war, and 'since been developed and re-designed to such an extent that it is virtually a new machine'. Improved performance was the least striking feature of the machine; rather its design concentrated on increasing its effective life and improving the safety of operation and convenience and ease of control. Similarly, the company's capstan lathe of 1927, redesigned with new features, was a 'remarkable testimony to the merits of the original design', based on the Herbert No. 4 Capstan Lathe of 1895. The development of combination turret lathes followed a similar trajectory, the company launching in 1930 its tenth model, and 'while it is undoubtedly a lineal descendent of the various patterns of combination turret lathes made by the firm [it] can justly be said to be new in design'. There were no new movements, nor fitments, but there was increasing 'novelty' with enhanced accuracy of component construction, and the machine design incorporated new tungsten carbide cutting metals. New cutting alloys required increased rigidity in machine tool design, enabling the employment of the machine at maximum efficiency. In 1931, the new Herbert milling machine incorporated a strengthened frame, push button control, and hydraulic operation, which was increasingly the standard practice.[159]

Herbert typified the process of machine tool design in many British firms. The improved combination turret lathe built by Dean, Smith & Grace in 1926, was an 'evolutionary' design incorporating time saving features.[160] At the Olympia show of 1928 machines displayed by Herbert's, James Archdale, Charles Taylor, the Churchill Machine Tool Co., the Butler Machine Tool Co., and Thomas Ryder & Sons, were all based on earlier models, but including improvements to durability, control, and speed of tool setting.[161] Surveying the exhibition, *The Engineer* believed that this was evidence of major changes in British machine tool design, representing a move from machines influenced by 'traditions handed down by pattern makers and fitters' to engineers who had studied the manufacturing problems involved with machine tool operations, leading to 'modifications of old designs', as good as anything produced abroad. The machine tool, the journal argued, is no longer the 'servant' of the engineering shop, 'it is now the master'; the maker tells the user how to perform the job, rather than the user proscribing the machine tool.[162] Nevertheless, the business reality was that a process of evolutionary design obstructed the commercial development of machine tools, a factor well recognised by the management of Herbert's. A weak link between research, represented by constant experimentation in incremental design improvements, and the marketing of machines, remained a problem, and continued to adversely affect sales, with Herbert's selling at prices above its competitors. In

---

[159] *Engineer*, 18 June 1926, pp. 42-4; 18 November 1927, pp. 84-6; 28 November 1930, pp. 603-4; 20 March 1931, p. 325.

[160] *Engineer*, 23 July 1926, pp. 96-7.

[161] *Engineer*, 7 September 1928, Supplement, pp. i-xvi.

[162] *Engineer*, 21 September 1928, pp. 319-20.

November 1923, Vernon referred to the company's No. 4 Capstan Lathe which had undergone constant improvements, but now required that design be 'stabilised', enabling the machine to be manufactured 'more economically and so reduce the selling price'. By June 1924, the lathe design had been finalised, allowing the machine shops to build them more regularly for stock. Low capacity utilisation, however, continued to be a major problem, and can be explained, in part, by the vagaries of the market. In late 1925, for example, uncertain demand meant that batch production was often suspended, and machines not always finished in their programmed sequence, resulting in rising costs and lost orders, with the firm unable to guarantee delivery dates to customers from stock.[163]

From a technical perspective, Herbert's were an adaptive rather than a pioneering company, a feature reflected in both the company's own manufacturing programme and in its factoring operations. In July 1923, Pickin drew the board's attention to new developments by other machine makers, notably the combined boring and turning mill of Webster & Bennett, and the commercial success in the British market of gear shapers built by the American Fellows Gear Shaper Co. Reacting to these developments, the board arranged to factor Webster & Bennett machines under agency agreements to avoid 'conflicts' with Herbert built boring and turning mills, and arranged to act as sole agents for Fellows gear machines in Britain. Also in 1923, the company established factoring arrangements with George Richards & Co., Broadheath, Manchester, selling that company's patent thread milling machines, although rejecting a manufacturing agreement due to 'the congested state of our designing department'. The company also opened negotiations with Fellows to factor their machine in the British market, an American connection that they followed up in 1924 by licensing to manufacture Norton Grinding Machines at Edgwick under a 7.5 per cent royalty. Herbert's displayed all the characteristics of a follower company, in technical design. In 1925, for example, Pickin commented on the 6 and 12 spindle ball bearing drilling machines built by Archdale for the Cowley engine factory of Morris Motors, designed to a heavier construction than Herbert machines and selling at £10 per spindle less. Aware of Archdale's competitive advantage, Pickin noted the necessity of adopting the heavier construction design of the Archdale machine, which was a key selling point to motor manufacturers. The failure to build on Archdale lines had repercussions, the Archdale machines underselling Herbert equivalents in 1926, forcing the Herbert board to sell unsold batches of radial drills in a general auction at knock down prices. Similarly, in 1925, the board raised questions about the market potential of the Herbert milling machine. Despite the company's efforts to market the machine as a new design, with an improved pyramid form of column, sales remained disappointing, the Herbert machine facing stiff competition from the higher productivity models sold by the Cincinnati Milling Co. Consequently, Herbert's eventually re-designed

---

[163] Herbert, Departmental Board, 13 November 1923; 25 June 1924; 8 December 1925.

milling machines to Cincinnati patterns, as well as introducing multiple tool kits to their turret lathes, following designs by Lodge & Shipley of the U.S.A.[164]

Networks with American companies, of course, had been established through the involvement of Herbert's in extensive factoring operations. Factoring provided a technical learning curve for the company as well as shaping the programme of manufacture within the company itself. In March 1924, for example, Sir Alfred instructed the board to 'carefully consider the situation arising out of the impossibility of selling ... machines imported from America at their present prices', including grinding machines, boring and turning mills, and automatic screw machines. This followed a general fall in factored sales in 1922 and 1923 (Table 4.2), the depression curtailing the demand for American imports in large quantities. At the same time, Herbert's had developed a re-conditioning business for the sale of second-hand factored machines, which temporarily displaced factored products. Consequently, the board considered resuming the building of automatic screw machines, 'the real problem being the possibility or otherwise, of designing and building grinding machines ourselves'. After consideration, the board decided that their present capacity and technical capability to design and manufacture grinders was not sufficient to enable them to manufacture, but that they could resume the building of automatic screw machines if they terminated their Agency agreement with the Cleveland Co. The agreement with the Cleveland Co. was terminated, Herbert's resuming its own manufacture of screw machines, the company now faced with the dilemma that it had to ensure that design was 'stabilised' and the machine could be manufactured at competitive prices. The board also decided to resume the building of milling machines, adopting the practice of two American companies, Cincinnati and Kearney & Trecker, to design special tool outfits supplied with their own milling machines. The development of tool outfits complimented their expanding activities in the market for small tools, with Herbert's manufacturing the 'Coventry Die and Chuck', as well as selling factored tapers, dies and dieheads under an agency agreement with Landis.[165]

As trade revived from the mid-1920's, Herbert's faced increasing pressure both to expand its output and reduce costs, as well as developing machines suitable for larger-scale production in engineering. Thus, in 1926, the board decided to concentrate production at an extended factory at Edgwick, transferring plant from its main machining centre at the Butts. Concentration at Edgwick alleviated congestion at the Butts as business expanded, and eradicated transport problems between the two works. Edgwick was designed for integrated production, and incorporated two foundries, a machine shop, power house and offices, an experimental laboratory, and a separate building known as the 'Factory' for the manufacture of Coventry dieheads, chucks, milling cutters, and ball bearing drilling machines. Production facilities at Edgwick were calculated to turn out 3,000 sets of small tools per week, facilitating bulk ordering, and the machine tool

---

[164] Herbert, Departmental Board, 24 July 1923; 14 October, 11 November 1924; 8 September, 27 October 1925; 23 June, 14 September 1926.

[165] Herbert, Departmental Board, 11 March, 8 April, 25 June, 29 December 1924; 13 March 1925.

programme was constructed to design and build machines on large batch production systems, ensuring output of 'a similar type'. To achieve increased capacity the company doubled the size of the Edgwick machine shop, which became one of the largest of its kind. Edgwick covered an area of seven acres under one roof, and the number of machines employed had risen from 544, before the alterations to 898 when it opened in October 1927. Arranged for flow production, the machine shop incorporated electric battery trucks connecting the bays, and the machinery was either single pulley or electrically driven, with few countershafts in evidence. In 1927, Edgwick employed 3,000 workers, and by the end of 1928, it was busy satisfying orders for turret and auto lathes and the firm's high power milling machines, both horizontal and vertical.[166]

Increased capacity allowed the company to develop a range of new automatic machines, including a universal cutter grinder and automatic drilling machines, targeted at the automobile and electrical engineering industries, alongside their more traditional lathes. In this respect, the company made a positive response to the challenges facing the British machine tool industry. With enlarged production facilities, it could develop high performance machines, initially developed as specialist products, and then stabilise the design to manufacture in larger batches, as users became accustomed with the machines. In 1928, Sir Alfred sanctioned the recommendation of the board to simplify the programme of manufacture, moving to an increasing standardisation of machine lines. By early 1929, the company had also extended its agencies for factored machines, 'pushing ... new lines' of American and continental make. The production programme in 1930 focused on building standard lines, supplemented by factored machines, and targeting towards the demand for labour-saving equipment for high output. In 1930, the company was offering customers high performance automatic chucking lathes, and new drilling machines for quantity production, both machines designed to meet the demand for labour-saving equipment. At the same time, the company offered an extended range of specialised fixtures, 'to suit the requirement of users', and announced that it would discontinue any contracts for specialist machines.[167]

Standard lines, the hallmark of the Herbert product range, complemented the general pattern of output in the British machine tool industry. The industry concentrated its output on standard machines in which it could guarantee markets, and limited its desire to develop specialist machine tools. At Herbert's the concentration on standard lines reflected a desire to build larger batches at reduced costs, but it also reflected the fact that the company could not design special-purpose machines at competitive prices. In February 1929, for example, Sir Alfred referred to the building of special-purpose machine tools as 'stunt jobs', which should be avoided when the machine shops were 'so busy'.[168] By 1929, the

---

[166] *Engineer*, 7 September 1927, pp. 248-51; *American Machinist*, 8 October 1927, p. 104E; 6 October 1928, p. 139E.

[167] Herbert, Departmental Board, 11 July, 9 October 1928; 5 January, 13 February 1929; 15 April 1930; *American Machinist*, 5 January 1929, p. 301E; 11 October 1930, p. 109E; 10 January 1931, p. 282E.

[168] Herbert, Departmental Board, 13 February 1929.

company's ability to quote for special machines was restricted by the fact that their 'prices are not competitive', in some cases double that of their competitors, leading to a loss of 'goodwill'. As Sir Alfred concluded, the concentration on increasing the output of standardised machines absorbed existing capacity, and 'we cannot produce specials in large enough quantities'.[169] Within the constraints of the market and its own internal capacity, Herbert's focused on what was possible, which meant that Britain's premiere machine tool producer forewent the production of special-purpose machine tools and relied on its factoring business to supply mainly American made machines.

As shown in Table 4.2, Herbert's sales of its own manufactured machines increased substantially between 1927 and 1930. Facilitating this expansion of sales was the company's increasing emphasis upon providing an engineering service to users, a function of the business that recognised the necessity of persuading customers of the advantages of up dating their plant with labour-saving machinery. The expansion of the service function, however, required a reconsideration of the disclosure of technical information to customers by the company, and an abandonment of a secretive attitude. Indeed, as the board recognised in 1923, the refusal to release technical data deprived customers of important networks of information, and the company's service compared poorly to that offered by German makers.[170] This self-criticism applied equally to the British machine tool industry, the engineer W. Groocock claiming in 1929 that 'There are firms in England today who are being passed for orders simply because their service is distinctly bad ... to that of foreign competitors'.[171]

Herbert's, however, did make a positive response. By 1926, the directors had conceded that they were not pushing the cost saving advantages of their high performance machines, and despite introducing a hiring scheme to induce purchase, their travellers lacked the technical information to persuade engineers to replace obsolete equipment. This also reflected the technical capabilities of the company's sales personnel and the difficulty in recruiting and training them. An inadequate technical service limited the company's ability to promote their machine tool lines. For example, in 1927 the directors reported on sales resistance to their new universal cutter grinder, and automatic lathes. A clear problem was price competition, but as Sir Alfred argued, price was not the only consideration. Customers, he urged, needed persuading that the machines could deliver enhanced productivity. As Vernon acknowledged, the company's marketing service was insufficient, and he called for a renewed 'endeavour to convert customers from turret lathes to auto lathes, as in the past we converted them from the engine lathe to the turret lathe'. By 1929, the company had revamped its service function, and this became fundamental to the management's longer-term vision for business

---

[169] Herbert, Departmental Board, 11 June 1929.

[170] Herbert, Departmental Board, 13 December 1921; 13 March, 12 June 1923.

[171] *American Machinist*, 13 April 1929, p. 112E. A number of observers criticised the failure of the industry to adequately disseminate technical knowledge, either amongst machine tool firms or to their customers. *The American Machinist*, 12 May 1923, p. 77E; 26 May 1923, p. 90E.

success. Outlining the scheme, Pickin claimed that 'when we know that a machinist is in the market for machine tools both the Alfred Herbert and Factored Sales Departments should be advised so that they collaborate and offer the most complete and efficient plant'. Reinforcing the point, Sir Alfred urged that they ascertain 'from customers their exact technical requirements', the Herbert technical sales staff being equipped to provide information on tool layouts and production times. The engineering advantages of the machines were to be the key selling point in the company's sales drive, facilitated by a part exchange scheme to install new machines. Consequently, the board instructed the sales branches to report on the suitability of Herbert and factored machines to meet the needs of customers for a complete plant layout, a policy designed to add to business turnover. By 1930, full technical information was provided to domestic sales branches, detailing production comparisons with competing machines, and overseas associate companies were supplied with comprehensive engineering drawings. Complementing this was the company's new demonstration department, opened in Coventry in 1930, providing a focal point for the dissemination of technical information to users, as well as a site for the training of sales personnel.[172] In 1933 J. C. Blair, who replaced Milburn, and C. W. Clark joined the board, both new directors commissioned to expand the engineering service of the company.[173]

The increasing emphasis upon engineering servicing was vital to the company as economic conditions deteriorated in 1930. In September 1929 there were already worrying signs that production was moving ahead of sales, and by April 1930 there were falling orders for capstan lathes. A 'serious falling off in trade' occurred in the middle of 1930, leading to reductions in prices, and the familiar recurrence of cut-throat competition.[174] As sales fell in the early 1930's, the company reduced its lines of both factored and own makes, and curtailed investment in new machines. A. H. Lloyd, the Herbert design director who had replaced Vernon in 1928, noted that a priority was to re-design existing machines 'to bring them up to date'. This required an adequate service provision, while at the same time it reinforced the engineering tradition of constant experimentation. For example, Lloyd informed the board in October 1930 that it was not advisable to build additional small batches of combination turret lathes and milling machines until they had been tested, and technical information supplied to sales branches.[175] Thus, the management continued with extensive testing programmes, designed to develop increased efficiency in cutting operations through the application of tungsten carbide to a range of machines.[176] In the midst of the depression, the company's manufacturing programme was concentrated on improvements to existing models, and this reinforced the commitment to factoring. In April 1931,

---

[172] Herbert, Departmental Board, 7 December 1926; 4 January, 1 February 1927; 10 September, 11 June, 12 November 1929; 17 June, 9 July, 11 September 1930.

[173] Herbert, Departmental Board, 14 June, 22 November 1933.

[174] Herbert, Departmental Board, 10 September 1929; 15 April, 17 June, 9 July 1930.

[175] Herbert, Departmental Board, 9 July, 14 October 1930.

[176] *American Machinist*, 9 May 1931, pp. 199-200E; 12 December 1931, p. 205E.

for example, the company discontinued its manufacture of milling machines, facing severe price competition from Asquith and Archdale, the directors concentrating efforts on selling factored millers supplied by Kitchen & Wade of Halifax, while at the same time redesigning their own drilling machines 'to bring up to date'. The Factored Department also sought new foreign agencies, a decision which later conflicted with the introduction of protection.[177]

The general tariff of November 1931, as the management noted, opened up the potential for the development of gap machines to substitute for foreign imports. In the face of low demand, however, the management reaffirmed its decision to curtail the development of new machines. 'The general opinion' of the board was 'that rather than undertake new lines we should put the whole of our energies to the development of our present lines, making them as good and complete as possible'. Consequently, the company re-designed its automatic lathes, with larger chucks and less complex operating procedures, to compete with the American Johnson & Potter designs. Deliberations by the IDAC in July 1932 to allow the entry of essential machine tools, free, or at a reduced duty, encouraged an optimistic outlook by Herbert's concerning the expansion of factored sales. As the directors argued, given the reduction of output during the downturn, when demand revived the company would have low capacity which could be supplemented by factored machines.[178] By late 1932, with more buoyant trade, importers and factorers were praising the IDAC. The boost given to domestic manufacturing industry by protection stimulated the demand for machine tools. British makers, however, caught by 'the sudden increase', had insufficient capacity to meet demand, especially for special types, which were provided from outside under the guidance of the IDAC.[179] Indeed, in April 1934, Sir Alfred could report that the bulk of the company's orders emanated from three main sources, the motor trade, Japan and Russia, but there were also signs of a general improvement in trade, with 'orders ... coming in from other sources'. By June, he was urging the necessity of increasing output, reducing the amount of special work undertaken, and avoiding short guarantees of delivery to customers.[180] At the end of 1934, there was intense pressure on British makers to produce, overtime was common, and delivery dates lengthening.[181] As we shall see in the next chapter, this raised a new challenge for the British machine industry, a challenge that intensified with the growing demands of rearmament.

---

[177] Herbert, Departmental Board, 14 April 1931.

[178] Herbert, Departmental Board, 10 November 1931; 12 July 1932.

[179] *Machinist*, 17 December 1932, pp. 577-8E. In 1932 *The American Machinist* was re-titled *The Machinist*.

[180] Herbert, Departmental Board, 11 April, 14 June 1934.

[181] *Machinist*, 29 December 1934, p. 753E.

CHAPTER FIVE

A Call to Arms: The British Machine Tool Industry, 1935-40

'The present situation was abnormal and it would be better if conditions were more normal' [Sir Alfred Herbert, 1936].[1]

Introduction

The First World War had elevated the industry to a key position in the economy, but its experience during the inter-war years had been a troubled one. As Sir Thomas Inskip, Minister for the Co-ordination of Defence, observed in 1938, 'the machine tool industry had for some time been languishing'.[2] As the clouds of war darkened in the late 1930s machine tools were again elevated to prominence as a strategic war industry. Politicians, militarists, and industrialists, would have agreed with the German assessment that 'a shortage of machine tools in time of war is equivalent to a shortage of munitions and guns'.[3] How effectively did the British machine tool industry respond to the demands of rearmament, what was the role of the state in the industry's affairs, and how prepared was the industry to enter the conflict in 1939? In 1936, Sir Alfred Herbert informed shareholders that he wished for a return to normality, but this would have to wait, as the period between 1935 and 1940 placed heavy and changing pressures on British machine makers.

Discussion on rearmament began in 1934, but it was not until the turn of 1935-6 that policy began in earnest. Thereafter, 'the history of rearmament and military production is one of continuing mounting requirements, of an ever-widening scale of munitions ... and a progressively growing output of war stores'.[4] In this situation, as shown in Table 5.1, there was a marked shift in the distribution of machine tool output from export to the home market. Given the rearmament programme, this would seem a logical trend, but the figures in Table 5.1 are open to interpretation. The figures for 1937 and 1938 were based on a survey carried out by the MTTA, and according to Gourvish the reliability of the data came in for

---

[1] 586/11, Alfred Herbert Ltd, General Minute Book, 1894-1950, 10 June 1936.
[2] *Hansard, Parliamentary Debates of the House of Commons*, Vol. 341, 10 November 1938, pp. 433-8.
[3] *Machinist*, 7 October 1939, p. 445E.
[4] Postan, *British War Production*, p. 202.

severe criticism.[5] Caution is justified. Table 5.2 shows the value of total output given by Postan, together with the value of machine tool exports provided by the Board of Trade, and recorded by *The Machinist*. From this we can calculate domestic output, which rose sharply between 1935 and 1937, and accounted for 80.2 per cent of total output in the latter year, compared to just 19.8 per cent for exports. However, in 1938 the rate of growth of output for the domestic market decelerated, and the share of exports to total output increased to 32.2 per cent, far higher than the 22 per cent recorded by the MTTA in Table 5.1, and at a same level as that for 1935. The foreign trade sector remained important to the machine tool industry, despite the demands of rearmament, and this was a key issue in the formulation of a planned programme of supply negotiated between the government and the industry, which also included the demand for imported machines.

Table 5.1
Distribution of Gross Output Value of Machine Tools by Home and Export Markets, 1934-38, Provided by the MTTA (%)

	Home	Export
1934	67	33
1935	67	33
1937	80	20
1938	78	22

Source: Gourvish, 'Mechanical Engineering', p. 140.

Table 5.2
Shares of Total Output of Machine Tools to Export and Domestic Markets, 1930-38

	Total Output (£ million)	Domestic (£ million)	% Domestic	Export (£ million)	% Export
1930	5.0	3.1	62.0	1.9	38.0
1935	6.7	4.4	65.7	2.3	34.3
1937	11.1	8.9	80.2	2.2	19.8
1938	14.0	9.5	67.8	4.5	32.2

Source: Postan, *War Production*, p. 202; *The Machinist*, 4 February 1939, p. 701E.

At the annual dinner of the MTTA in 1937, Sir Thomas Inskip warmly thanked the industry for its assistance in supporting rearmament by accepting a 'deficiency' policy, which recognised the need for imported machines to close the

---

[5] T. R. Gourvish, 'Mechanical Engineering', in N. K. Buxton and D. H. Aldcroft (eds), *British Industry Between the Wars: Instability and Industrial Development, 1919-39* (London, Scolar Press, 1979), p. 141.

gap between demand and supply. Keeping up the public persona of mutual co-operation, the Association's President, Sir William Lang, reciprocated Inskip's overtures.[6] Nevertheless, the whole question of imports was a matter of political diplomacy between politicians and manufacturers, as they linked it directly to the maintenance of normality through the encouragement of exports. This implied that makers had to make complex decisions about co-ordinating output between the competing needs of domestic and foreign markets.

The Co-ordination of Output for the Defence Programme

At two key meetings, chaired by Inskip in July and October 1936, the main item on the agenda was imports. Despite public remarks by Inskip that the MTTA was fully behind a 'deficiency' policy, he was well aware that for his policies to gain full support from the industry the government would have to make concessions. Lang, who endorsed the position of the MTTA on the need to allow imports, raised the issue of concessions. He insisted that 'they were not anxious to damage their export trade in any way'. Imports of foreign machines would 'take some of the load caused by the demands of the services', but would also enable the industry to 'safeguard' exports. At present, claimed Lang, imports of machine tools were greater than exports because of rising domestic demand. Sir Alfred gave general support to Lang's arguments, but he did recognise that all makers in the industry would not support free imports. The key question for Sir Alfred was how Inskip would use the licensing powers of the IDAC, created under the Finance Act of 1932, to grant licences to regulate the level of Britain's general tariff. Recognising the need to maintain a constructive dialogue with government, Sir Alfred referred to the role of the MTTA Tariff Committee, formed in 1932 to provide advice on the granting of licences for machines imported free of duty by the IDAC. This committee, he claimed, could provide a platform to develop an importation policy that would meet the needs of both the industry and the rearmament programme. Similar to Lang, Sir Alfred's priority was 'how government demand would affect the normal export trade, and to what extent the government should place orders abroad?'[7]

General support for an interlinked import-export policy was forthcoming from the Department of Overseas Trade and the Board of Trade. Mullins, of Overseas Trade, emphasised the importance of laying down a policy for British exports, and referred to a doubling of the German and U.S. export trade in the last nine months. Expanding exports 'is what they wanted to do'. Indeed, during 1936

---

[6] MTTA, Annual Report for 1936, 12 March 1937.

[7] MTTA, Director's Minute Book, 1933-39, 5 June 1939, Statement of Setting up of Import Duties Advisory Committee and MTTA Tariff Committee, and Minutes of Meetings with Inskip, 23 July, 14 October 1936. For the introduction of protection in Britain see Pollard, *Development*, pp. 119-25; F. Capie, *Depression and Protection: Britain Between the Wars* (London, Allen & Unwin, 1983); S. Tolliday, 'Steel and Rationalisation Policies', in Elbaum and Lazonick (eds), *The Decline of the British Economy*.

the MTTA had been active in lobbying for the expansion of foreign markets, by petitioning the Department of Overseas Trade on the detrimental effects of the American-Canadian Trade Treaty, and attempting to secure favourable preferences under the Ottawa Agreement in the New Zealand and Australian markets. Support for the expansion of exports also came from Browett of the Board of Trade. Browett suggested that the industry should maintain a standard average based on a ratio of exports to output of £2.5 million to £8 million. Although Browett welcomed the proposals of the MTTA for a policy 'to keep up exports by letting in imports', he nevertheless suggested that 'starred orders', those licensed to be admitted duty free by the IDAC, should be limited to those of strategic importance, providing an incentive for British makers to fill the gap by building specialised machine tools domestically. Accepting the need for controls on imports, Sir Alfred also raised the issue of the control of exports, pointing out that they faced complex decisions concerning the balancing of government demands for rearmament and the expansion of exports in the interests of the machine tool industry. If exports expanded, he warned, 'someone else would go short'. This became all the more important, as emphasised by Lang, because the industry was facing problems in adequately supplying the rearmament programme. In his own firm, he claimed, they were 'sacrificing the export trade' to meet government orders, but the industry generally was striving to maintain the Board of Trade ratio. To achieve this they were scheduling long delivery dates, a matter which Browett thought was the crux of the whole matter and 'could not delivery dates be improved?' Machine tool firms faced difficult decisions in allocating supply, and Admiral Sir H. A. Brown, Director General of Munitions Production, observed that recent licences to import machine tools had led some makers to complain that they had sufficient manufacturing capacity available to fulfil government orders. In this event, the question arose as to whether firms having difficulty in meeting government orders should not first use vacant capacity in the home market, by sub-contracting to general engineering firms, rather than resort to imports. Concluding the meeting, Inskip proposed 'that some government orders should be made to imports in order to keep exports at current level'.[8]

The problem of prioritising output was also on the agenda in the boardrooms of machine tool firms. Following the speech by Inskip to the MTTA in 1937, Harold Butler, the chairman of the Butler Machine Tool Co., had warned that 'the present call on machines is greatly in excess of production facilities'. At the same time, he drew attention to the vital necessity of preserving export markets, and that in the push to raise output makers should not forego the opportunity to improve design.[9] The ability of firms to raise output was also constrained by a number of other factors. For example, in Birmingham in February 1937 makers were complaining loudly of insufficient fuel supplies, long delays in the delivery of iron and steel, and pressures on the transport system, all of which inhibited production schedules. The MTTA also faced complaints concerning shortages of skilled labour, attracted into alternative employment in the expanding

---

[8] MTTA, Director's Minute Book, 5 June 1939; Annual Report for 1936.
[9] MTTA, Annual Report for 1936.

engineering trades. Firms now had to appropriate resources between the needs of rearmament and the maintenance of normal business transactions. Taylor & Challen Ltd, Birmingham, reported that they were adding to plant and introducing overtime, but had to allocate output 'against existing commitments', with the 'heavy demand for ordinary industrial purposes' and increased pressure to raise production for the 'new defence programme'. This typified the experience of many Birmingham makers. James Archdale reported a 'very gradual improvement in output', and they continued to work continuous shifts with overtime for day work. Inundated by government orders for sensitive drills, a company speciality, the management had prioritised their delivery, but reported that on standard lines delivery between 6 to 12 months was the norm. Delivery of special tools was even longer, but despite these problems, which echoed the complaints of Browett at the Board of Trade, the firm remained active in export markets, supplying customers in Australia and Japan. Charles Taylor Ltd. was fully engaged on standard machine tools, and it was not feasible to quote for special types. Nevertheless, they too remained committed to fulfilling foreign orders to South Africa, Australia, New Zealand, Norway and Sweden. At H. W. Ward, the output of lathes had increased by 50 per cent with the opening of its new factory in Worcester, and similar to other lathe manufacturers they were supplying 'new factories in connection with national defence'. Yet 'national defence' had to be reconciled with the continuation of exports to Italy, France, Poland, Belgium, Scandinavia, and the Dominions, and to meet its obligations they were introducing night work.[10]

Similar intensive work systems were introduced in Coventry, where shortages of skilled labour was acute in early 1937, makers concerned that this would worsen as planned 'aircraft shadow factories' were brought into operation, a fact recognised by Inskip at a government level.[11] Established Coventry firms, such as Morton & Weaver, were still, however, conducting 'quite a fair export business' with South Africa, India, Newfoundland, China, Belgium and Holland. At the Modern Machine Tool Co. Ltd., they directed output mainly to the home market, but the firm had also completed large contracts for Italy.[12] Outside the Midlands similar trends were occurring. In Halifax, firms introduced intensive work patterns, concentrating mainly on standard lines. 'All the labour of the required skill was fully employed' and the pressure on production intensified due to 'a fair amount of export trade ... particularly with British overseas areas'. The importance of maintaining exports was 'generally recognised', makers 'allocating fairly high proportions of their output to that end'. The Butler Machine Tool Co. was supplying the Dominions, France, Belgium, Italy, Russia, South Africa, China and Japan, and Harold Butler could boast that 'the order book was never so full, nearly

---

[10] *Machinist*, 13 February 1937, p. 15E; 20 March 1937, p. 94E; MTTA, Director's Minute Book, 10 February 1937.

[11] *Machinist*, 20 March 1937, p. 95E; *Hansard*, Vol. 317, 12 November 1936, pp. 1,075-6. For aircraft shadow factories see K. Richardson, *Twentieth Century Coventry* (London, Macmillan, 1972), pp. 65-6.

[12] *Machinist*, 20 March 1937, p. 95E. See also 5 June 1937, p. 263E; 13 November 1937, p. 562E.

half of the orders being for export'. Kitchen & Wade, an important supplier of honing machines and light radials to the aircraft industry, claimed that it was doing 'much export' work, supplying 20 different countries. William Asquith had orders for 24 countries, and F. Townend & Son was supplying 14 countries. At Churchill-Redman Ltd., the managing director, A. K. McCall, reported in 1936 that the order books were 'very healthy', the works engaged for four to five months ahead. The company supplied 14 countries, 20 per cent of their exports going to Japan, and there were increasing orders from Finland and Poland for general-purpose chucking lathes. Demands were also heavy in the home market, especially for lathes for grinding propellers in the aircraft industry. Such was the pressure that the company was sub-contracting discontinued lines of lathes for India and Canada to local engineers, to enable them to fulfil orders to these markets. By August 1937, despite intensified demand for government orders, the company had 47 export and 141 domestic orders.[13]

Cultivating exports, of course, placed enormous pressure on existing capacity, and required increased investment in modernisation and expansion. This led to managerial indecision in devising investment strategies, a problem demonstrated by the example of the Churchill Machine Tool Co., Manchester specialist producers of grinders.[14] Churchill's were large contractors to the Soviet Union, as well as to the Admiralty, War Office, Air Ministry, and India Office. Anticipating rising demand, the managing director, G. S. Maginness, announced in December 1934 a capital expenditure programme of £17,000 on additional workshops, and replacement of obsolete machinery to bring production up to an average of £40,000 per month. The board sanctioned an additional sum of £1,425 in March 1935, to replace obsolete equipment, but by June the Chairman, Arthur Chamberlain, was reporting that their facilities for manufacturing new models of grinding machines were inadequate. To maintain the production average necessitated a further injection of £10,000 on replacing obsolete equipment, especially drilling machines, which had been in service for over 20 years. In sanctioning this sum, discussion also took place on increasing output beyond the £40,000 average, but further injections of investment, the board considered, was not prudent because of uncertainty over renewals of contracts to the Russian market. Prolonged negotiations by the Board of Trade for revisions to the Anglo-Russian Commercial Treaty during the second half of 1935, together with the bureaucratic system of payment, inspection, and delivery involved in Russian transactions, delayed investment by Churchill's in capacity expansion.[15]

During the period of rearmament, exports remained important to the sales strategy of British makers, a position that the MTTA and Inskip endorsed by their

---

[13] *Machinist*, 15 June 1937, pp. 263-4E; CR2-CR4, Churchill-Redman, Director's Minute Books, 1919-60, 5 January 1935; 7 May 1936; 4 August 1937.

[14] For the importance of exports to firms in the Manchester district, see *Machinist*, 15 January 1938, p. 680E.

[15] 926/17/1/2, Churchill Machine Tool Co., Minute Book of Board and General Meetings, 1924-39, 20 December 1934; 8 March, 23 May, 27 June, 1 October, 20 November 1935.

agreement to encourage imports of special machine tools to bridge the gap in domestic demand. Imports, of course, were conducive to the business of merchant firms in Britain who imported machine tools, and who had fully endorsed the acceptance of the importing policy of the defence programme.[16] It was also in the interests of Britain's largest producer, Herbert's. The firm, through its large factoring of foreign machine tools, was able to develop organisational capabilities and know how in factoring as well as production.[17] As Sir Alfred informed shareholders, the firm's prospects for 1935 were closely related to the performance of the 'factored business', and the maintenance of its extensive network of foreign agencies.[18] Table 5.3 shows that there was a trend between 1933 and 1937 towards a higher proportion of factored to total sales, and these included a significant number of imported machines. Unlike a number of machine tool firms, however, Herbert's concentrated sales on the home market (Table 5.4), although in absolute terms there was a rising trend of factored goods for export. The priority given to home sales was not simply a patriotic response by Herbert's to the demands for rearmament as the expansion of domestic demand required more sophisticated higher value machines, and Herbert's production programme reflected this. As shown in Table 5.5, the margins on their own manufactured goods was significantly higher in the domestic market compared to export markets, and prioritising home users was a rational business response. Factored sales for export do indicate slightly higher margins than those for home sale, but, supporting the claims of Arnold for the 1920s, the returns on factored machines overall were well below that for their own make.[19] Certainly, sales increased significantly from 1933 to 1937, and Britain's largest maker seems to have pursued an expansionary strategy in response to economic recovery and the rearmament programme. One should be cautious, however, in exaggerating how dynamic the company's response was. There is a need also to reassess the company's seeming disregard for exports.

Table 5.3
Alfred Herbert: Sales of Factored and Own Make of Machines, 1933-37

	Own (£ 000)	%	Factored (£000)	%	Total (£000)
1933	603	72.6	228	27.4	831
1934	920	70.1	393	29.9	1,313
1935	1,151	67.1	564	32.9	1,715
1936	1,513	67.6	726	32.4	2,239
1937	2,022	58.1	1,461	41.9	3,483

Source: 926/1/5/47-51, Alfred Herbert Ltd., Annual Accounts and Schedules, 1933-37.

---

[16] MTTA, Annual Report for 1936.
[17] For a discussion of the importance of know how and information see D. J. Teece, 'Economies of Scope and and the Scope of the Enterprise, *Journal of Economic Behaviour and Organisation*, Vol. 1 (1990), pp. 223-47.
[18] Herbert, General Minute Book, 24 May 1934.
[19] Arnold, 'Innovation', p. 64.

Abnormality was the benchmark by which Sir Alfred judged the business environment of the post-1935 period. At the 1936 AGM he announced that the 'company was very busy' but he remained anxious about the future, and they should keep 'in mind that trade would slacken as soon as demand had been met'.[20] Years of depression had installed caution into management, leading them to reject assumptions that the existing high pressure of demand was permanent. Sir Alfred, similar to many businessmen, viewed rearmament as a temporary deviation from normal business routines.[21] In reply to a speech by Walter Runciman to the MTTA in 1936, calling for co-operation on national defence, Sir Alfred had insisted that machine makers should 'institute a simple scheme of priority by which orders for machines ... for defence purposes should be given definite preference over commercial orders and over export business'. His patriotic overtures were tempered, nevertheless, by his observation that the trade was inflicted 'by a series of violent depressions and peaks which resembled the chart of a fever patient in a critical condition', and he reminded Runciman of the importance of firms maintaining links with foreign markets.[22] A year later at the company's AGM he was still singing a cautionary note. Despite a successful year 'it was essential to look ahead and avoid the dangers of a possible depression' after the completion of the defence programme. He had been informed 'that the peak of the boom period had been reached', and he was wary about sanctioning any 'unnecessary additions although the plant had been materially improved'. He was still urging caution on capacity expansion in 1938, and it was not until 1939 that he adopted a more confident approach. Three months before the outbreak of war he informed shareholders that the year had been 'extraordinary', the works operating at full capacity, and they would continue to do so as long as the 'present pressure existed'. Shareholders must have indeed been delighted. Despite a substantial drop in net profits in 1939 (Table 5.6), explained by the government control of prices which had cut margins, a 55 per cent dividend on ordinary shares was paid. Between 1933 and 1939, dividends averaged 52 per cent, compared to 12 per cent between 1930 and 1934, and 5.66 per cent during the 1920s.[23]

A cautious approach to investment had already been noted in the case of the Churchill Machine Tool Co., but this was not confined to large makers such as Churchill's and Herbert's. Small makers, for example, Arthur Scrivener of Birmingham, remained highly cautious of the future, and the company's investment policy was characterised by managerial procrastination. Scrivener's were connected through business networks to Herbert's, using the Herbert-Australian agency to sell its machines and sharing joint manufacturing patents. In the late 1930s, the firm was paying dividends between 20 and 100 per cent, and, in 1935, it urgently required additional accommodation and plant to develop a

---

[20] Herbert, General Minute Book, 10 June 1936.
[21] G. Peden, 'Arms, Government and Businessmen, 1935-45', in J. Turner (ed.), *Businessmen and Politics: Studies of Business Activity in British Politics, 1900-45* (London, Heinemann, 1984), p. 133.
[22] MTTA, Annual Report for 1935.
[23] Herbert, General Minute Book, 9 October 1937; 31 May 1938; 15 June 1939.

'rapidly expanding business'. Throughout 1937 and 1938, the management continually discussed the issue of new plant, but invariably they deferred a decision. To take one example, in September 1938, the works manager suggested the purchase of a Herbert 213 Capstan Lathe, but the decision forthcoming was that the purchase 'had not yet warranted itself'. While the management vacillated over investment policy, the board agreed a dividend of 20 per cent for the 1938 financial year, and awarded the Chairman a bonus of £534, plus an increase in salary.[24]

Table 5.4
Alfred Herbert: Home and Foreign Sales, 1933-37

	Own				Factored			
	Home (£000)	Home (%)	Foreign (£000)	Foreign (%)	Home (£000)	Home (%)	Foreign (£000)	Foreign (%)
1933	519	86.1	84	13.9	204	89.5	24	10.5
1934	846	92.0	74	8.0	317	80.9	75	19.1
1935	1,090	94.7	61	5.3	467	82.8	97	17.2
1936	1,456	96.2	57	3.8	662	91.2	64	8.8
1937	1,953	96.6	69	3.4	1,331	91.1	130	8.9

Source: Herbert, Annual Accounts and Schedules.

Table 5.5
Alfred Herbert: Gross and Net Profits as a Proportion of Sales, 1933-37 (%)

	Own Manufactures				Factored Goods			
	Gross Profit		Net Profit		Gross Profit		Net Profit	
	Home	Foreign	Home	Foreign	Home	Foreign	Home	Foreign
1933	52.6	21.4	17.9	9.5	17.6	25.0	7.4	8.3
1934	65.2	16.2	15.6	5.4	14.2	18.7	2.8	8.0
1935	65.4	18.0	12.7	4.9	17.8	20.6	6.2	8.2
1936	64.7	15.8	17.6	3.5	15.7	20.3	6.6	4.7
1937	65.5	8.7	22.0	1.4	17.4	18.5	9.4	6.9

Source: Herbert, Annual Accounts and Schedules.

What lay behind this caution was the perception of the cyclical nature of demand in the industry, a factor reinforced by the abnormal conditions of rearmament. However, for Britain's leading maker, Herbert's, there was an additional issue relating to a vision of the merits of business planning. In 1936, Sir Alfred, in reply to Runciman, had called for 'voluntary' action by individual firms

---

[24] Coventry Archive, 1140/52/1, Records of Arthur Scrivener Ltd., Minute Books, 1932-47, 4 September 1935; 22 November 1937; 17 January, 21 March, 16 May, 20 June, 17 July, 19 September 1938; 20 September 1939.

to plan manufacturing programmes to prioritise defence requirements. Dismissing regulation from the MTTA, given the individualism of member firms, he claimed that if they did not plan voluntarily then they faced the alternative of 'direct' control, which would certainly be 'imposed upon them from above, and possibly in a very drastic form'. In his own company, he claimed, planning involved the prioritisation of defence work by reducing development work on machines, and delaying the introduction of new lines, enabling the firm to concentrate on raising the output of standard lines.[25] This strategy anticipated the pattern of production during the war itself, as will be shown in the next chapter.

Table 5.6
Alfred Herbert Ltd.: Profits and Dividends, 1935-40

	Profit (£000)	Preference Dividend (%)	Ordinary Dividend (%)
1935	242.5	6	35
1936	385.0	6	40
1937	667.6	6	65
1938	633.2	6	65
1939	175.3	6	55

Source: Herbert, General Minute Book.

A debate over production planning had begun in December 1935, which highlighted the trade off between meeting government orders and designing new lines for the private market. 'Present day requirements' necessitated a discontinuation of older designs of milling machines, cutter grinders and automatic screw machines, prioritising the manufacture of more modern lines. Outlining the production and sales strategy in March 1936, Sir Alfred claimed that 'in view of the present international situation it was necessary to classify their orders and give preference to those known to be required either directly or indirectly for government purposes'. By April, the Board could report the increasing output of machines most in demand for government requirements, and, by July, they were operating at full capacity to fulfil orders for six shadow factories engaged on aircraft engines. To meet these demands, the company simplified its manufacturing programme by discontinuing obsolete lines, and by producing more standardised machines through removing selling points related to design such as tailored saddles, headstocks and feeds. Under Sir Alfred's influence, and in the abnormal climate of rearmament, planning became instrumental to the strategic direction of the company. Planning, of course, was not acceptable to all directors. For example, in June 1936 Joseph Pickin reported that competitors were incorporating 'selling points' into their designs, and urged 'the necessity of continued development of design to keep pace with modern requirements'. Sir Alfred's commercial logic,

_____

[25] MTTA, Annual Report for 1935.

however, was to urge caution, prioritising design work to avoid expensive experimentation. At the same time, in June 1937, the company announced a production policy which prioritised five new designs, four for capstan lathes, incorporating new headstocks and beds, and one for the 'No 9 Turret Lathe with new headstock'.[26]

In practice, planning at the company involved a constant re-figuration of the production and design programme, and a reconciliation of the need to increase the speed of delivery with commercial considerations. For example, in October 1937 C. W. Clark raised the issue of the industry trend towards 'manufacturing machines in styles', that is giving them a distinctive brand, and posed the question whether any 'extension or modification' of their own programme was desirable. Although the board recognised that design improvement was a commercial imperative, they nevertheless decided to maintain the existing programme, capacity constraints necessitating a priority towards building and delivering batches of established lines. Planning, in the Herbert sense, was a short-term process, involving a flexible approach to manufacturing involving batch production methods. During 1938 A. H. Lloyd and Pickin repeatedly announced changes to the current design and production programme. For example, the board discontinued the No. 18U and 35U Universal Milling Machines, and the Edgwick factory was to concentrate on developing the No. 3 Universal Milling Machine in small batches. Similarly the No. 9 Combination Turret Lathe was to be 'put in hand in small quantities and the No. 9 Junior Lathe will be brought forward as soon as an experimental machine is produced and satisfactorily tested'. In capstan lathes, the first batch of 25 No. 0 types was to be completed in October and November, and all were sold. A further 50 were to be completed in early 1939, of which 26 were already sold.[27] Batch production was conducive to a flexible approach to planning, which enabled the company to concentrate operations on fewer lines and thus increase sales to meet rising home demand. It also reflected, of course, Sir Alfred's short termism, and his cautious investment policy towards capacity expansion in what he believed to be an abnormal business environment.

The caution of businessmen, such as Sir Alfred Herbert, may of course be justified. In 1937, the pattern of demand for machine tools was indeed 'abnormal'[28] as government shadow factories came on stream. At Churchill-Redman, McCall reported in August 1937 a rush of orders in June and July for aircraft work, and at Herbert's, in July and September, Pickin observed serious delays in delivery to meet the volume of orders from aircraft shadow factories. In the first half of 1938, however, there was a slowdown in the pace of demand. By March, business was 'somewhat lower than the early months of 1937' in the machine tool industry of the Midlands, and Sir Alfred noted with concern rising stocks of machines and

[26] 926/1/4/1-3, Alfred Herbert Ltd., Minute Books of the Departmental Board of Directors, 1911-41, 11 December 1935; 10 March, 8 April, 10 June, 8 July 1936; 2 June 1937.

[27] Herbert, Departmental Board, 6 October 1937; 19 January, 3 March, 27 July 1938.

[28] *Machinist*, 19 March 1937, p. 114E.

components. The directors of the newly formed Scottish Machine Tool Corporation (SMTC), a holding company created in March 1937, reported that orders for the three months to June 1938 were 'considerably lower than the same period last year'. This 'lull' enabled British makers to shorten delivery times, which were described as 'much better all round', and standard lines were reported to be obtainable within three months. In addition, although there was a steady flow of imported machine tools in 1938, the value of machine tool imports declined from £6.2 million in 1937 to £4.5 million in 1938, a fall of 37.8 per cent.[29] The levels of imports, however, should not detract from the fact that they remained of crucial importance to the rearmament programme due to their specialised nature. Indeed, this raised deep concerns about the capabilities of the industry to meet the demands of rearmament, and the reliance on foreign imports of specialist machines in the event of war caused acute anxiety amongst businessmen and politicians alike.

At the MTTA annual dinner in 1936 Commander Sir Charles Craven, a director of a number of shipbuilding, engineering, armaments and steel firms, informed the Association that his 'group of companies had spent £1 million on machine tools since 1926, and only 25 per cent was purchased from abroad. He did not believe that the Association would 'grudge the foreign expenditure', as it was largely for special single-purpose machine tools which it did not pay the British maker to produce because the demand was limited. To demonstrate the higher technological capabilities of these machines, he quoted his dinner companion Harold Butler, who had inferred 'that he would like to go round the country with a hammer and smash up all the old machine tools – and ... make England a country fit for Englishmen to live in!' Taking a direct swipe at the industry, he added that he also hoped 'to get something a little more quickly than the home ... makers could offer'. Reinforcing the specialist nature of imports, Sir Reginald Townsend, Director of Factories, War Office, informed the Association that for the manufacture of rifles and machine guns the policy of the government was to order general-purpose machines which were 'more flexible' to changes in factory layout and to introducing new products. Crucially, however, 'for certain classes of production, such as large types of shell, a special tool might be ideal'.[30] Imports of special types became a major political issue in February 1937, when the Labour opposition attacked Runciman's policies in the Commons. Admitting that imports of machine tools had increased in volume from 54,745 tons in 1932 to 103,452 tons in 1936, and that 25 per cent of them were admitted free of duty, Runciman defended the government's position, arguing that they were of a type which were not procurable, 'for the time being', from British makers. From the Labour benches this was obviously a matter about Britain's protectionist policy, and members enquired what measures had the IDAC taken to reduce imports. In reply, Runciman

---

[29] Churchill-Redman, Director's Minute Book, 4 August 1937; Herbert, Departmental Board, 8 July, 9 September 1937; 3 March 1938; Glasgow University Archives and Business Research Centre, Records of the Scottish Machine Tool Corporation (SMTC), UGD 175/2/1/1, Minute Book 1937-42, 12 July 1938; *Machinist*, 19 March 1938, p. 114E; 4 February 1939, pp. 700-1E.
[30] MTTA, Annual Report for 1935.

referred to a recent IDAC report which had concluded that a large proportion of imported machinery 'was of a highly technical and secretive nature which could not be made' at home. Imports to serve the national interest, of course, was an accepted policy of the MTTA, but as Runciman announced to Parliament, British machine tool imports consigned from Germany had risen from 24,000 tons in 1935 to 31,900 tons in 1936, representing nearly one-third of all imports.[31]

In 1938, America supplied 57.8 per cent of total British imports, and Germany, with a value at £1.36 million accounted for 30.3 per cent. This was despite the fact that the German machine tool sector was suffering lengthy delivery times and stocks were nearing exhaustion. It was also the case that Britain imported machine tools of a higher value than they exported, the former being 12.4 per cent higher than the latter in 1938.[32] The high cost of importing machine tools was not lost on representatives of the War Office, Air Ministry and Admiralty, who gave evidence before the Select Committee on Estimates in 1938, and raised serious questions about the dependency on specialist foreign supplies.[33] In November 1938, Major James Milner, the Labour MP for Leeds South East, attacked the government's strategy for co-ordinating machine tool supply, and referred to under-capacity in British works. Supporting his case he cited Sir H. Kingsley Wood, Secretary of State for Air, that the government had placed large orders with American and German makers at prices in excess of those of domestic makers. He also referred to a combination of 20 Swiss firms, 'well equipped for repetition work', who were supplying specialist tools to aircraft factories and aero-engine manufacturers under approval from the Air Ministry, which could have been directed to British makers. Replying to these criticisms, Inskip admitted that the government had placed large orders abroad, although British machine tool output had increased. Nevertheless, he argued, it was 'a constant source of anxiety to all of us to know how these ... complex machines were to be obtained'. Defending his position, he claimed that the government had placed no orders abroad without 'the willing consent of the machine tool industry' in obtaining alterations in the tariff to facilitate imports. On this point, however, he raised serious questions about the capability of domestic makers. The IDAC, he claimed, had only sanctioned imports when it was satisfied that the date of delivery made any other course impracticable 'unless the whole of the programme was to be held up'. Foreign deliveries, especially of single-purpose machines, were essential because British makers were quoting delivery times of 50 months for them. In concluding, Inskip rejected any accusation that the departments of war had been 'dilatory' in placing orders at home.[34]

Reassurances of this type, however, did not satisfy Britain's machine tool makers. Postan refers to the fact that government contracts to machine tool makers, under the re-equipment scheme for armaments, were often for small orders,

---

[31] *Hansard*, Vol. 320, 9, 23 February 1937, pp. 191-3, 1,813-14.

[32] *Machinist*, 2 February 1939, pp. 700-1E; Paul Grodzinchi, 'Leipzig Machine Tool Exhibiton', in *Machinist*, 19 March 1938, p. 109E.

[33] MTTA, Director's Minute Book, 10 May 1939.

[34] *Hansard*, Vol. 341, 10 November 1938, pp. 362, 433.

sanctioned for short periods, and with no guarantee of future contracts. This made no 'appreciable difference to the country's industrial preparedness', as makers were reluctant to risk the expense of entering into contracts with state agencies. As late as the Autumn of 1937, the Director General of Munitions Production informed the Secretary of State for War of several examples 'of important orders which either could not be placed at all or were placed with difficulty, owing to the absence of long-term requirement'.[35] This perhaps explains the cautious approach of makers such as Herbert's to large-scale expansion, and the continuation of batch production methods, but it also raised the issue of government policy over imports, especially in relation to Germany. As early as 1935, James Archdale & Co. had complained to the MTTA about the impact of German subsidised competition on the demand for their milling machines. In response to an MTTA memorandum, the Department of Overseas Trade admitted that that there was a levy in Germany on all home sales to provide revenue for subsidising export of any class of good when a foreign contract could only be obtained with the help of a subsidy. Despite this, the MTTA had endorsed the government's import policy, but by November 1938 the German question had taken on a new significance, and had been raised by politicians in Parliament. The MTTA wrote to the Foreign Director of the Federation of British Industry on the subject of German competition and revisions to the Anglo-German Commercial Treaty. Under no circumstances, they claimed, should there be a decrease of duty on German machine tools into Britain, and that the Board of Trade should make representation to Dominion and Colonial governments not to grant concessions to German imports. In particular, the MTTA urged that the IDAC should closely monitor the extent of German subsidised competition, and they referred to the detrimental effect on British makers in 1935 of rising German imports.[36] This correspondence took place in the context of a resurgence of demand for machine tools during the last quarter of 1938, associated with 'a great burst of production' in the aircraft industry.[37] During 1939, as demand intensified, the MTTA again raised the issue of imports. In May, they tabled questions in the Commons, through the MP Ellis Smith, concerning the large numbers of specialist machine tools imported from abroad, demanding clarification of the government's policies 'to deal with the urgent need to manufacture these specialised machines and to organise the machine tool production of the country'. In this, the MTTA recommended the establishment of shadow factories for machine tools to meet the pressing need to increase the domestic supply of specialised equipment.[38] As the realities of war dawned, the state would have to take a more proactive role in business planning.

---

[35] Postan, *War Production*, p. 43.

[36] MTTA, Director's Minute Book, 9 October 1935; 9 November 1938.

[37] Postan, *War Production*, pp. 21-2; *Machinist*, 22 October 1938, p. 509E.

[38] MTTA, Director's Minute Book, 10 May 1939.

Business, State, and War Planning

Deteriorating international relations in 1939 intensified the pressure on the machine tool industry, which faced serious problems in meeting demand. Compounding this problem was the fact that exports had risen in 1938 and continued to do so in 1939. During 1939, 'both the weight and value of exports were higher than ever before'.[39] This supports Pollard's observation that although the government was much more prepared for war than it had been in 1914, 'actual preparations ... as distinct from paper planning, had been negligible', with the key exception of aircraft production. Indeed, despite a great deal of activity by September 1939 'The production of munitions was nowhere near the limits of physical capacity'.[40] In the machine tool sector, the Minister of Supply, Edward L. Burgin, announced in July the creation of an Advisory Industrial Panel, of which Sir Alfred Herbert represented the MTTA. The Ministry of Supply had also created a machine tool department, headed by Sir Stanley Rouse, Controller of Machine Tools.[41] Despite these planning initiatives, the initial practical implementation of policy was limited.

The MTTA met with the Ministry of Supply in September 1939, ten days after the declaration of war, to discuss 'mobilisation'. Maginness, Churchill Machine Tool Co., posed the key question: was there 'any great need to increase production capacity'? As he pointed out, there was a significant amount of underutilised capacity, and he referred to the fact that shadow factories were by no means in full production, and that in automobile and other factories there was idle capacity because of the drastic stop on exports. A key problem relating to effective industrial mobilisation, Maginness claimed, was the inadequate collation of information on the quantity and type of machine tools required, and the extent of existing plant utilisation.[42] Similar to the experience of the First World War, there was inadequate industrial intelligence on the utilisation and distribution of machine tools. Consequently, as Maginness suggested, it would be a mistake, until they had gathered reliable industrial information, for the Ministry of Supply to divert machines destined for export, as this would involve litigation by foreign customers. On this point, he referred to the fact that the Board of Trade was actively encouraging exports, and referred to the policy of Germany who were holding on to exports as long as possible. In his opinion, British makers should not re-direct exports until they had official authority, which, as Scaife of the Ministry of Supply pointed out lay with the Board of Trade. At this point Lang expressed surprise that the Ministry did not have full authority, 'and that other departments were still having a say', and felt that the industry was 'caught in a corner on this'. By October, the President of the MTTA, Harold Butler, could report close contact between the various committees of the Association and the Controller of Machine Tools, but in response to a letter from Rouse 'inviting' the industry to form groups

[39] PEP, Report on 'The Machine Tool Industry', p. 187.
[40] Pollard, Development, pp. 192, 194.
[41] *Hansard*, Vol. 350, 31 July 1939, p. 1,491.
[42] MTTA, Director's Minute Book, 13 September, 18 October 1939.

of firms manufacturing similar types of machines, he remained reticent. As he pointed out, the industry consisted of large numbers of individual firms, and they needed more information from them on the appropriate groups to form. 'Whatever scheme was adopted', he argued, 'it must not upset the balance of production in the various factories'.[43]

This suggests a confused state of affairs concerning practical planning for war, a problem compounded by the individualism of firms in an industry made up of a large number of small producers (Table 5.7). For example, the most contentious issue facing government planners and machine tool makers was that of the control of prices in an inflationary environment. The MTTA remained suspicious of the introduction of government price control, leaving Sir Alfred Herbert to provide a lead. At the MTTA annual dinner, in 1936, Charles Craven remarked that the Association 'did nothing to control prices'. He also thought that 'It would ... be a sorry day for this country if profits were made on such a scale that, as the chairman of a motor company said recently, manufacturers were to lie back and put on a gold watch chain and smoke a long cigar and think of nothing else than raking in profits'. Irritated by these remarks, Sir Alfred retorted that the industry was not controlled 'internally or externally, and prices were still of a highly competitive character to the benefit of the users'. The reason why the industry did not control itself, he claimed, 'was that nearly all machine-tool makers were strong individualists, who preferred the private company with its many advantages of direct control and immediate response to stimuli'.[44] As the defence programme escalated, however, the question of controls, especially of prices for government contracts became a political issue. In July 1939, this reached fever pitch in the Commons when R. C. Morrison, Labour, wondered whether the 'patriotism of machine-tool makers is beyond reproach', and another MP, Austin Hopkinson, considered that the industry had made 'terrific profits ... in the last few years out of the country'.[45] Indeed, a glance at the profit figures for Herbert's, in Table 5.6, would seem to suggest that shareholders certainly benefited from the rising demand for machine tools under the defence programme. Self-regulation, as Herbert was well aware, was no easy matter, especially as labour and material costs escalated, and the MTTA remained reluctant to intervene directly beyond mild persuasion. For example, in October 1937 Adcock & Shipley and William Asquith & Co. wrote to the MTTA enquiring whether the Association had a common policy on raising prices in the light of escalating costs of labour and raw materials. The reply was unequivocal, the MTTA had 'no standard position', and it was a matter for individual firms.[46] An examination of pricing policy at Herbert's confirms this, the company using a flexible discount policy for guaranteed sales to both government agencies and to private agents.[47] Indeed, MTTA intervention often proved ineffective. For example, in May 1936 the MTTA wrote to the trade

---

[43] MTTA, Director's Minute Book, 13 September, 18 October 1939.

[44] MTTA Annual Report for 1935.

[45] *Hansard*, Vol. 325, 31 July 1939, pp. 1,942-3.

[46] MTTA, Director's Minute Book, 13 October 1937.

[47] See Herbert, Departmental Board, 9 October 1935; 3 March 1938.

requesting that price increases should be limited to changes in the price of materials and labour, while negotiations were underway with the government on the import question, which 'was not well received' in the Halifax district. A. K. McCall, of Churchill-Redman, informed their selling agents, Charles Churchill & Co. of Birmingham, that forthwith they reserved the right in all quotations to customers to 'increase the prices at which the order is entered by an amount to cover us for any increase in cost of materials during the present period of manufacture'. Again, in May 1939, McCall reported a 5 per cent rise in all prices to cover a general 2s per week increase in adult wages.[48]

Table 5.7
Structure of the Machine Tool Industry, 1935

Average Employment	No. Firms	Total Employment	Average Employment per Firm
11-24	17	304	18
25-49	31	1118	36
50-99	28	2124	76
100-199	23	3065	133
200-299	11	2713	247
300-499	3	1221	407
500-749	3	1846	615
750+	7	8691	1242
Total	123	21082	171

Source: PEP, Report on 'The Machine Tool Industry', p. 180.

Neither the government nor the industry, however, could ignore the cost of machine tools to the defence programme. In September 1939, the MTTA reported rising prices, principally due to War Risk Insurance and ARP expenditure, in addition to increased costs of materials. Members of the Association considered that the time was opportune to increase prices, but there was divergence of opinion whether it was to be uniform action under advice from the MTTA or left to individual firms. There were two sides to the argument. On the one hand, the MTTA had never interfered with 'freedom', and it was not a 'price controlling organisation', although it admitted that the degree of individual collusion between firms was unknown. On the other hand, in July 1938 Burgin and Lord Chatfield, the new Minister for the Co-ordination of Defence, had brokered a deal with the MTTA for a voluntary discount agreement of 5 per cent on all standard products for one year on the basis of prices existing in December 1938. As the MTTA was well aware, this represented, in itself, an acceptance of a measure of price control. Recognising the constraints this placed on individual firms, in an inflationary environment, Butler informed Rouse that the industry required protective clauses

[48] Churchill-Redman, Director's Minute Book, 7 May 1936; 26 May 1939.

in future quotations. Burgin, at the Ministry of Supply, firmly rejected the industry's plea for protective clauses in October, concluding that the 5 per cent agreement was untenable, given public alarm over profiteering, and that they could not satisfy Parliament that the prices ruling in December 1938 were reasonable. To satisfy growing calls for price control at a political level, the Ministry instigated a costing system for special-purpose, non-standardised machines, which involved regulation by 'Ministerial Inspectors'. As Butler warned the MTTA, if individual firms determined prices then the government would impose extraordinary profit duty to reduce profiteering, and there had been a press campaign and statement in the House to that effect.[49]

Control of profits represented a powerful bargaining tool that the Ministry could use to force the industry to accept price controls, and this had been a contentious issue at the end of the First World War. Therefore, the MTTA preferred a voluntary code for discounting, rather than the introduction of government costing systems. In November 1939, Butler visited Sir Arthur Robinson, together with Rouse and Gordon and Norman of the War Office Contracts Board. The MTTA announced that it was prepared to extend the 5 per cent agreement on standard machines to non-standard, which impressed Robinson. Rouse, however, was unwilling to compromise, proposing to end the agreement altogether because he could not satisfy himself that the 1938 prices, on which discounting was based, were satisfactory, although both Inskip and Morrison had accepted the reliability of the price data. At a further meeting in November, Robinson informed the MTTA that after deliberation the discount agreement on standard machines would be continued, but now on a compulsory basis, and in addition he added that the government would introduce costing on non-standard machines 'as far as possible'. The introduction of costing, as Butler was well aware, would involve increased government involvement in the business affairs of individual firms. As a com-promise, he pleaded for the extension of the 5 per cent discount, which he conceded would be enforceable rather than voluntary, and would represent a 'generous gesture' on behalf of the industry. Generous gestures, however, did not placate Robinson, who was well aware that allegations of industrial profiteering had brought the industry under the public spotlight. In particular, Robinson argued that the Ministry of Supply had raised concerns that the 5 per cent discount only applied to standard machines, which allowed the industry to determine the price of specialised non-standard products. Consequently, the imposition of costing was imperative, given the importance of special machine tools to the rearmament pro-gramme, and in the light of parliamentary opposition to the retention of individual pricing policy by the industry. Robinson insisted that 'the powers of costing must not be interfered with', and informed the MTTA that all future government contracts, for non-standard machines, would be subject to costing to determine the maximum price. He concluded that 'the only way in which they could satisfy the House of Commons was by retaining their powers to cost inviolate'. Costing was reluctantly accepted by the industry, Pickin of Herbert's, for example, condemning the imposition of controls on free enterprise, and

---

[49] MTTA, Director's Minute Book, 13 September, 18 October 1939; *Hansard*, Vol. 350, 31 July 1939, pp. 1,942-3.

arguing that costing systems, devised to provide an average maximum price for non-standard machine tools, would 'penalise' the more efficient firms who produced at lower costs.[50]

Quite clearly, machine tools had become a priority sector in the debates over planning in 1939. In July, Burgin reassured the House that deliveries since December 1938 would cover the bulk of the orders needed for rearmament, and the 5 per cent reduction on standard tools would entail a large public saving. The powers for costing on non-standard machines, he argued, represented 'an extremely valuable right to the government'. By November, Burgin could proclaim that machine requirements for the war programme had been worked out, the position of supply fully surveyed, steps taken to increase output, including the installation of balancing plant, and sub-contracting systems expanded.[51] Despite optimistic overtones, by May 1940, as the nation realised the full implications of the plight of the BEF in France,[52] the British war industries were suffering from a severe shortage of machine tools.[53] As in the case of the First World War, a major problem of industrial planning was the co-ordination of labour.

As demand intensified from late 1938, firms expanded capacity to meet delivery targets, and during 1939 and 1940, the question of labour supply rose up the agenda.[54] A survey of the war experience of Coventry, conducted by Shenfield and Florence in 1944, concluded that 'The fundamental weakness of the Government's original plans was that they did not envisage the economic conditions of total war'. Consequently, in the early plans 'there was no conscription of labour or materials'.[55] As early as January 1939, Coventry machine makers were complaining of constraints on output due to shortages of skilled men, a fact which was compounded by competition for labour from automobile plants and shadow factories. Private firms could not meet the 'employment terms' offered in the shadow factories, and concern was expressed that the needs of the defence programme could 'not be met ... unless a proper supply of trainee men is available'. In the Birmingham district, delivery times were lengthening because of labour shortages, and in Manchester firms such as George Richards, Herbert Hunt & Co., Churchill Machine Tools, H. W. Kearns, and Craven Bros. reported labour shortages. Firms were frustrated in their efforts to utilise extended capacity and additional plant, and, in a tight labour market, the poaching of workers became common. Two Leicester makers, Adcock and Shipley and Jones and Shipman wrote to the MTTA in May complaining of the poaching of skilled men, which prompted the Association to complain to Sir Harold Brown, Director General

---

[50] MTTA, Director's Minute Book, 22 November 1939.

[51] *Hansard*, Vol. 350, 31 July 1939, pp. 1942-3; Vol. 352, 1 November 1939, p. 1,937

[52] See J. Keegan, *The Second World War* (London, Pimlico, 1989), p. 66.

[53] Pollard, *Development*, p. 195; Postan, *War Production*, pp. 206-7.

[54] For the problem of labour supply see Peden, 'Arms', p. 136.

[55] A. Shenfield and P. Sargant Florence, 'The Economies and Diseconomies of Industrial Concentration: The Wartime Experience of Coventry', *Review of Economic Statistics*, Vol 12, No. 1 (1944-5), p. 97.

Munitions Production, that given the 'tremendous demand for machine tools ... skilled labour was being taken away from ... firms'. Indeed, the MP James Milner, felt that it was a fundamental 'mistake' for the government to establish shadow factories in areas where labour was already fully employed.[56]

Lengthening delivery times in the first half of 1939 focused attention on the supply of labour as a constraint on the industry. In Coventry, the pull of the shadow factories and the call up for military training was compounded by the raising of the school leaving age, which a number of makers believed would considerably reduce the supply of apprentices. Between 1935 and the outbreak of war, employment in the British machine tool industry rose by 66 per cent from 21,082 to 35,000, and this may be compared to the American industry which employed 40,000 in 1938 and 80,000 in 1940.[57] Problems of labour recruitment reflected the un-coordinated nature of the defence programme, but the industry also displayed a fragmented structure, comprised of large numbers of small firms (Table 5.7). One-third of firms employed less than 50 workers in 1935, and more than half of all firms employed less than 100. Recruitment, and more importantly labour retention, would have been difficult for small producers competing in a limited labour pool with shadow factories, automobile plants, general engineering and, by 1939, the armed forces. On the other hand, the industry also had seven firms employing 750+ workers, which accounted for 41.2 per cent of the industry's labour force in 1935. The largest employer, Herbert's, voiced the opinion that not enough had been done to increase the industry's labour force in the context of heavy war demands.

In a letter to the *Times* in December 1939, Sir Alfred drew attention to labour shortages, which were inhibiting increases in munitions and machine tools. Owing to labour shortages, he asserted, less than half the machine tools installed in industry were engaged on night work. Without a radical solution to this problem, he predicted that the industry could not fully exploit any planned increase in the output of machine tools for 1940-41. Sir Alfred remained convinced that sufficient supplies of labour did exist. This was partly owing to the extensive unemployment that still persisted in some industries,[58] and partly to the fact that the country had 'thousands of men, women and young people who can be rapidly taught to perform the simple routine operations which form such a large part of present day methods of mass production'. The inability of industry to utilise effectively this pool of labour, Sir Alfred blamed on the Home Office, who restricted the employment of women and young males at night. Consequently, he called for a broad agreement between the trade unions and the government for the full application of dilution. Referring to his own experience during the First War, when he was Controller of Machine Tools, he argued that the great output of machine tools and munitions

---

[56] *Machinist*, 28 January 1939; MTTA, Director's Minute Book, 10 May 1939; *Hansard*, Vol. 341, 10 November 1938, p. 362.

[57] *Machinist*, 29 April 1939, p. 196E; 10 June 1939, p. 263E; 15 June 1939, p. 335E; 9 July 1939, p. 349E; 11 January 1941, p. 32 E.

[58] The number in the services rose from 480,000 in June 1939 to 1.85 million by March 1940, but there were still one million unemployed in April 1940. Pollard, Development, p. 195.

could not have been attained 'but for the free employment of women and all other labour which was available at night as well as by day'. He was convinced, 'that we must do the same now as we did then'.[59]

Sir Alfred returned to the issue of dilution in June 1940. He reflected that what presently governed the output of machine tools was the degree of skilled labour available, in preference to a strategy of augmenting output by a determined employment of semi-skilled labour. In what was a direct attack on his fellow manufacturers, he claimed that firms who did not implement dilution were 'completely blind to the urgency of the position and the adjective "efficient" can certainly not be applied with any justice to any organisation so lacking in vision, imagination and resources'. Sir Alfred viewed business firms as possessing a pool of resources, with managerial strategy directed towards the more effective use of the company's organisational capabilities. Accepting that many of the routines associated with what the firm actually did, the building of machine tools, could only be carried out by skilled labour, he nevertheless acknowledged that the function of management was to efficiently allocate those resources. Enhancing organisational capabilities was central to his perception of dilution, as there were innumerable jobs which could be undertaken by semi-skilled, unskilled and female labour, 'if the management of these establishments will only "go to it", obtain the labour that is available and train them in their own shops'. In this sense, the capabilities and routines of organisations are knowledge based and impact upon how firms implement production systems. Thus, for Sir Alfred the diffusion of knowledge was a managerial act, in which the creation of a more variegated work force would facilitate a more effective deployment of the firm's physical and human resources.[60]

As outlined earlier, the management at Herbert's was well aware of the need to plan and prioritise output for the war effort, and during 1939 and 1940, this took priority. In July 1939, the management had discussed policies for increasing output and implemented procedures to sub-contract work further for vertical and plain milling machines to local manufacturers. By October, the company was proposing a reconfiguration of its production programme, temporarily ceasing to make certain machines to concentrate on those of a simpler type, to enable an increase in the volume of output. To meet the production programme a large number of parts were sub-contracted from outside suppliers. A key problem, however, was shortages of skilled labour to implement night shifts, Gimson planning to overcome this by the transfer of apprentices to night work 'as soon as they were sufficiently skilled'. As the demands intensified, Sir Alfred called a special meeting in November to discuss the means of increasing output by 33 per cent. He

---

[59] Reported in *Machinist*, 16 December 1939, p. 572E.

[60] Alfred Herbert, 'Trainees and the Machine Tool Trade', in *Machinist*, 22 June 1940, p. 210E. For the issues of organisational capabilities and routines see E. Penrose, *The Theory of the Growth of the Firm* (Oxford, Basil Blackwell, 1959), p. 9; R. N. Langlois and P. L. Robinson, *Firms, Markets and Economic Change* (London, Routledge, 1995), pp. 13-17; R. R. Nelson and S. G. Winter, *An Evolutionary Theory of Economic Change* (Cambridge, Mass., Harvard University Press, 1982), pp. 14-19, 96-9.

urged upon his managers to further the development of night work and increased sub-contracting, the company already having extended the latter to include the supply of complete machines as well as components for Herbert machines. Noting that there were severe shortages of materials, especially steel and ball bearings, the departmental directors were taking steps to increase output by 25 per cent by May and 40 per cent by October 1940, and there was to be further specialisation by decreasing the types of machines built. Sub-contracting, of course, brought with it increased transaction costs. For example, there was difficulty in placing special work with sub-contractors, although there was no problem in getting products done locally. But as Lloyd put it: 'With regard to increasing production in our shops ... the bottle neck is the shortage of labour and that dilution, which would be of great help to us, is very much hampered by the Government and our agreements with the Unions'. On this point, Sir Alfred thought that the company could achieve a great deal 'by the proper training of labour, including women'. Simplifying product lines was a key factor in enabling the diffusion of routines to more unskilled labour, but this had its limitations. C. W. Clark informed the management in early 1940 that they had reached the limit of increasing production by means of reducing their product lines, but that the No. 15 Vertical Miller could be sub-contracted, and it was also agreed to 'build certain batches to a definite and simple construction'. By March 1940, the company was advertising for more women for night work, preferring those currently unemployed. On the question of labour allocation, the directors noted that 'the Government is now taking responsibility to a greater extent and the initiative in future will rest much less with us than formerly'.[61] In June 1940, Sir Alfred could claim that they had 'succeeded in building up a night shift of between 900 and 1,000 people', and was employing 500 to 600 women, 120 of whom were on night work. As a result, output had 'enormously increased'. At the same time, Sir Alfred was quick to point out that he had a great respect for skilled labour, but special circumstances called for special measures, and he urged the MTTA 'to enlighten its members'.[62]

At this stage in its evolution, Herbert's was the most important machine tool firm, and one led by a dominant individual who responded positively to the unprecedented demands of war through strategic planning. However, the general response of firms in the industry, not only on matters of labour policy, was uneven. A case in point was the SMTC, a major amalgamation between five leading Scottish machine tool makers in March 1937. Established as a holding company, with a capital of £400,000, the constituent firms were James Bennie & Sons (Govan), Louden Bros. (Johnstone), G. A. Harvey (Govan), Craig & Donald (Johnstone), and James Allen Senior (Glasgow). These long established firms enjoyed a reputation as makers of high quality machine tools, but, as war approached, they faced major problems in meeting the challenge. Four factors contributed to undermine the success of the new venture, and to inhibit its contribution to the war effort. Firstly, internal disputes at the company over the

---

[61] Herbert, Departmental Board, 5 July, 11 October, 15, 29 November 1939; 21 February, 6 March 1940.
[62] Herbert, 'Trainees'.

valuation of stock at one of its constituent companies led, within the first year of
the company's operation, to the resignation of the joint managing directors, A. D.
Clement of G. A. Harvey, and D. Sharp of Senior's, and their replacement by the
ageing Hugh Bennie.[63] Secondly, ineffective accounting practices at some of the
constituent firms presented an over-optimistic picture of the company's business
performance. For example, in November 1939 the Corporation released a press
statement asserting that

> their machine tool works were all engaged to maximum capacity, and their output
> exceeds that of any previous year in the history of the associated companies. The
> prospects for the future were excellent ... the enquiries for new machine tools at
> present time being very numerous.

This placed a gloss on the Corporation's performance that did not match the
underlying reality. In fact, at two of the member firms' output had actually fallen.
At James Bennie & Sons, output fell from £71,800 in March 1938 to £61,600 in
September, a fall of 14 per cent. In addition, output at Craig & Donnell had
'remained practically the same' over two six-month periods.[64]

Thirdly, some directors expressed alarm concerning the skewed nature of
the order books, in particular the high dependence on Russian contracts. Certainly,
this worried the chairman, Harry Grear, and the managing director, Bennie. The
latter informed the board that he was anxious that '82% of total orders in hand ...
were for Russia'. Bennie insisted that 'something needed to be done to redress
this', but quite what was not altogether made clear. Another director, Muirsmith,
worried that the Russian contract could be repudiated, leaving the Corporation with
the dilemma of selling these machines in the domestic market. As a contingency,
Bennie directed that each company in the Corporation should survey its Russian
orders, advising head office of what they could sell at home in the event of
hostilities breaking out and the Soviets cancelling orders. Grear and Bennie clearly
wished to limit the Corporation's over-exposure on the Russian market, but not all
the directors shared their anxiety. Goudie of Louden Bros., was confident that 'any
... machine tool' they produced for Russia 'would be taken up by the home
government', and he argued that future orders for Russia should be taken.[65]
Fourthly, the dispute over the Russian contract indicated the problem of
governance at the company, and it was indicative that Goudie referred to Loudon
machine tools and not to those of the Corporation. In effect, the differences over
the Russian orders reflected a basic problem facing the Corporation, that is the
tension between the need for co-ordination and central control on the one hand, and
the desire for autonomy and self-identity by the constituent firms on the other.
Responding to this tension, and concerned about its long-term implications, Grear
circulated a letter to board members in November 1940, stressing that 'steps must
be taken to secure the 'co-operation and co-ordination', which he considered was

---

[63] SMTC, Minute Book, 12 April, 11 June 1937.
[64] SMTC, Minute Book, 10 November 1938.
[65] SMTC, Minute Book, 24 January 1939.

essential if the Corporation was 'to overcome successfully the difficulties of the post-war period'. He particularly stressed the need to view 'the Corporation as a corporation and not five individual units'.[66] The inference was, of course, that the SMTC was little more than five autonomous firms, and that its capability to produce a co-ordinated production and marketing strategy was limited.

While recognising the dangers of drawing general conclusions from a single case study, the example of the SMTC does demonstrate the continued emphasis by British makers upon export markets, as well as suggesting that attempts at formal collusion to increase business efficiency, did not necessarily lead to increased output for the war effort in an industry prone to individualism. Indeed, as Table 5.2 shows, the British machine tool industry made an uneven contribution to the rearmament programme, total output rising sharply between 1935 and 1937, but then displaying a marked slow down in the rate of growth between 1937 and 1938. The data is consistent with Postan's observation that the country was still 'tooling up', and that the output of machine tools 'was for a long time unequal to the need'.[67]

There are three broad conclusions drawn from the contribution of the machine tool industry to the rearmament programme. First, the industry did significantly increase its output, expanded capacity, rationalised the number of machine tool lines built, and extended sub-contracting. There remained, however, a degree of uncertainty over the duration of the rearmament programme, and the consequent higher level of demand, and prominent leaders in the industry, such as Sir Alfred Herbert, bemoaning the disruption to normal business, pursued a cautious production strategy. Second, despite reservations on both sides, there did emerge an industry-state agreement on the policy of 'deficiency'. In practice, this meant the importation of special-purpose machines, while at the same time the industry was encouraged to maintain its export markets. British makers continued to export to a wide range of countries, including those who were to become future belligerents. In contrast, nearly one-third of Britain's total imports of machine tools emanated from Nazi Germany in 1938. The priority given to the importation of specials is also indicative of the failure of the British makers to supply adequately this type of machine within the timeframe required by the rearmament programme. Third, machine tool firms did face a number of constraints. There were clearly tensions over production planning, firms such as Herbert's delaying development work in order to meet delivery targets, while at the same time recognising the importance of prioritising the manufacture of more modern lines. Skilled labour shortages also proved difficult to overcome, shadow factories competing for scarce labour, and despite the lessons of the First World War, there continued to be a resistance to the employment of female workers. Moreover, the strong individualism embedded in the industry meant that there were major reservations, not least hostility, concerning government attempts to introduce price controls and costing systems. A number of these issues were to spill over into the war years, and the industry's role in the conflict is the subject of the next chapter.

---

[66] SMTC, Minute Book, 11 November 1940.

[67] Postan, *War Production*, p. 202.

CHAPTER SIX

The Second World War and the British Machine Tool Industry

'The ganglion nerve centre of the whole supply' [Sir Winston Churchill, 1941].[1]

Introduction

The three factors constraining war industries were raw materials, skilled labour, and machine tools.[2] Similar to the First World War, the military capability of the combatant nations during the second conflict depended upon machine tool supply, crucial equipment in the large-scale production of the munitions of modern warfare. Consequently, the industry was 'the rock on which other industries rested'.[3] How effectively did the British machine tool industry respond to the demands of war, and what assessment can be provided for its contribution to the conflict? The industry faced serious constraints in meeting the targets set for it by the needs of the government's war departments, and by the general requirements of British industry. In the early years of the war, American machine tool imports were vital to bridge the gap in British supply, notably in special-purpose machine tools.[4] The industry also faced the challenge of exporting its output, notably to the Soviet Union, a critical arena determining the eventual outcome of the war. The importance of machine tools, to Britain's wartime industrial planning, was summed up by Winston Churchill: 'Hardly any part of our common organisation of war production had been more thoroughly and precisely examined than the question of machine tools'. Adequate supplies of machine tools were central to the whole question of industrial supply, 'and no one could be engaged in munitions production for one day without feeling that they were the ganglion nerve centre of the whole supply'.[5]

---

[1] Speech to the House of Commons, cited in *Machinist*, 9 August 1941, p. 176E.

[2] Postan, *British War Production*, p. 202.

[3] M. Maiskey, Soviet Ambassador at MTTA Annual Dinner, in *Machinist*, 25 March 1939, p. 133E.

[4] For an examination of the industrial contribution of the Americans to the allied war effort, see R. Overy, *Why the Allies Won* (London, Pimlico, 1995), pp. 190-8. As Overy, p. 4, warns, despite the 'enormous' industrial capability that America brought to the allied war effort, it does not, in itself, explain the eventual outcome of the war.

[5] Speech to the House of Commons, cited in *Machinist*, 9 August 1941, p. 176E.

Machine Tool Demand and Supply

Postan's excellent work on Britain's war production allows a detailed survey of the machine tool sector.[6] Both the level and structure of demand for machine tools changed over the war. Table 6.1 shows that 1942 was a critical year, which saw the demand for machine tools from the three great purchasing departments, Ministry of Aircraft Production (MAP), Ministry of Supply, and the Admiralty, reaching a peak, and approaching an equilibrium with supply. By 1944, the general level of requirements from these three departments had fallen by 35 per cent over 1942. This was largely the result of a 50 per cent reduction in demand from MAP and a lesser fall of over one-third in the requirements of the Ministry of Supply for machine tools. Although the demands of the Admiralty increased nearly three fold between 1942 and 1944, this was insufficient to compensate for the fall-off in the other two departments. In addition to these three main departments, there were three other important sources of demand: purchasing from private firms, inter-firm purchase with machine tool firms ordering from each other, and exports. As Table 6.2 indicates, purchases from private firms and machine tool makers also peaked in 1942, while exports peaked a year later.

A major user of machine tools was the aircraft industry, but the pattern of orders did not follow a smooth upward trend (Table 6.3). Towards the end of 1941, and during 1942, the surge of orders for machine tools was a factor conditioned by the demands of the bombing campaign. For example, during 1941, Bomber Command lost 1,034 aircraft and by the end of the year 'was facing difficulty in replacing aircraft'.[7] Meeting the demands of the aircraft industry for machine tools, of a specialist nature, as will be discussed below, created problems for machine makers, but from the end of 1942 the pressure from MAP began to decline and the trend shifted towards an increased demand for general tools. This represented a switch in the pattern of demand, albeit with less intensity, emanating from the Ministry of Supply, whose requirements from 1942 onwards were for machine tools for the army. These machine tool types were significantly different from those required in the production of munitions production, largely consisting of low cost, smaller, portable workshop tools. In turn, the decision by the Admiralty in the summer of 1942 to 'force the shipbuilding industry' to substantially increase its output, called for a very different type of machine tool to that required by the army. Dissatisfaction with the shipbuilding industry by the Admiralty led to a technical inquiry, which resulted in 'an ambitious plan for a state assisted renovation of the equipment in the ship yards'. The outcome was a substantial increase in expenditure (Table 6.4) on shipyard plant and large and costly machine tools.[8] The three armed forces required different types of machine tools in different phases of the war, and collectively this affected the structure of demand facing the industry. How effective was the industry in meeting these complex requirements?

---

[6] Postan, *War Production*, pp. 201-11.

[7] Overy, *Why the Allies Won*, p. 112.

[8] Postan,. *War Production*, pp. 204-5, 210.

Table 6.1
Estimated Requirements and Actual Supply of Machine Tools to the Three Principle Supply Departments, 1941-44 (No. of Machine Tools 000)

	MAP		Ministry of Supply		Admiralty	
	Requirement	Supply	Requirement	Supply	Requirement	Supply
1941	38.6[b]	32.0[a]	27.7	29.0	6.1	4.5
1942[c]	32.9	30.6	38.0[d]	38.2	2.4[e]	5.5
1943	24.6	21.5	25.6	23.6	6.0	6.6
1944	16.4	15.8	24.2	15.5	7.0	6.0

Source: Postan, *War Production*, p. 205.
Notes: a. approximate retrospective estimate. b. figure includes some of requirement under 1942 bomber programme. c. from 1942 all estimated requirements are for first month of year, except for Ministry of Supply 1942. d. large part of Ministry of Supply requirements from 1942 onwards were machine tools for the army. e. this figure was much increased during the course of the year.

Table 6.2
Estimates of Total Requirements of Machine Tools, 1942-45 (No. of machine Tools 000)

Source of Demand	1942	1943	1944	1945
Machine Tool and Small Tool Producers	11.0	4.0	1.3	0.2
Private Purchase	30.0	20.0	25.0	25.0
Exports	5.2	17.5	10.9	6.5

Source: Postan, *War Production*, p. 486.

Table 6.3
Commitments Approved for Machine Tools and Plant in Aircraft Industry (£ million)

Production	1936-9	December 1939 - July 1941 (20 months)	September 1941 - December 1942 (16 months)
Aero-Engines	26.4	10.0	28.1
Air Frames	5.9	9.5	12.9
Propellers	0.9	1.7	6.9
Sub-Total	33.2	21.2	47.9
All Aircraft Products[a]	45.2	37.5	62.0

Source: Postan, *War Production*, p. 203.
Note: a. includes all aircraft components, equipment, instruments, armaments, fabricators.

Table 6.4
Admiralty Expenditure on Plant and Machine Tools for Naval Shipbuilding and Marine Engineering Contracts, 1940-44 (£ million)

1940	0.26
1941	0.87
1942	1.24
1943	4.00
1944	4.09

Source: Postan, *War Production*, p. 204.

Table 6.5
British Production and American Supplies of Machine Tools, 1939-44

	U.K. Production (No. Machines 000)	U.S. Supply (No. Machines 000)[b]	U.S. Imports (% of U.K. Production)
1939	37.0[a]	8.4[a]	22.6
1940	62.0	33.1	53.4
1941	80.9	32.1	39.6
1942	95.8	24.0	25.1
1943	76.2	20.6	26.9
1944	59.1	8.5	14.4

Source: Postan, *War Production*, p. 207.
Notes: a. estimated figures. b. U.S. supplies in 1939 were in tonnage. They represented 62 per cent of the total U.K. import of machine tools in 1939, 90 per cent in 1940, 95 per cent in 1941, and 99 per cent 1942-44. After 1939, Canada supplied the greater part by tonnage of the remaining imports.

Machine tool supply during the war may be categorised into three types. The general supply of machine tools, the disaggregate supply to the three main service departments, and the supply of specific types of machine tools related to the different needs of users. At the general level of supply, Postan comments favourably on the contribution of the industry, an achievement that 'was one of the great industrial successes of the war'. This he puts down to three factors. First, astute pre-war planning, particularly in terms of an adequate supply of jigs and gauges, a claim, as we will demonstrate subsequently, that is over optimistic. Second, the 'remarkable response of established machine tool firms', and finally the contribution of general engineering firms, who took in both sub-contracted work from specialist makers as well as directly supplying users. By the end of the war, approximately one-third of total machine tool production was supplied by a wide range of small and medium sized engineering firms who proved quite adept at making many different types of general-purpose machines. After America entered the war in December 1941, British makers were able to 'meet the bulk of British requirements for machine tools'. As Table 6.5 shows, dependence on American imports peaked in 1940 when they accounted for over one-half of British production, but by 1944 the situation had changed dramatically, and American supplies were largely 'confined to machine tools of certain sizes and highly specialised design'. A strategy of import substitution was also encouraged by the Controller General of Machine Tools at the Ministry of Supply. In January 1941, the Controller instructed British makers to introduce new designs to replace American ones, in particular gear cutting and specialised milling machines.[9] By the end of 1942, the supply situation appeared to be easing, and predictions for 1943 concluded that it would 'probably be easier to obtain a limited range of machine tools than in the other years'.[10] By 1944, Sir Alfred Herbert could inform shareholders that 'The grave shortage of machine tools which the country was confronted at the early stages of the war no longer exist, and there is now no longer the possibility of the progress of the war being hampered by any lack of machine tools'.[11] Indeed, it was estimated in 1945 that of the total number of machine tools installed in British factories and shipyards since the war began 73 per cent were manufactured in Britain, and, of the remainder, 14.5 per cent were purchased for cash from the U.S.A., and 12.5 per cent provided under lend-lease.[12]

The contribution of Herbert's to total machine tool output was certainly significant, and reinforces its leading position within the industry. At the company's AGM in 1945, Sir Alfred could claim that the firm had supplied some 65,000 machine tools during the war, an average of 13,000 per annum. Given the shortages at the beginning of the war, and the fall off in production at the end, it is reasonable to assume that the company was supplying 16,000 to 18,000 machine tools during the peak year of 1942. Given an aggregate U.K. production of 95,800 in 1942, Herbert's contributed between 16.7-18.8 per cent of the total. The firm provided a vital supply of machine tools, but these estimates exaggerate the company's real contribution to British production because of the firm's large factored department and the use of sub-contracting. As Sir Alfred acknowledged, the company's total supply was a combination of 'goods manufactured themselves, imports from America, and machines made by sub-contractors'.[13] A tentative estimate of the firm's contribution can be made by assuming that factored sales contributed 33 per cent to total output, a figure that the company averaged for its sales of factored machines in the 1930s. Consequently, Herbert's contribution of its own make of machine tools was probably between 10,700 and 12,000 in 1942, equivalent to 11.2 to 12.5 per cent of total national production.

While Britain's largest producer made a key contribution to the war effort, and Postan is full of praise generally for the ability of the industry to supply general-purpose machine tools, he does acknowledge that there were complaints at the disaggregate level regarding machine tool delivery. For example, MAP complained about poor delivery in May and October 1942, and again in early 1943.

[9] Ibid., pp. 206-7.
[10] *Machinist*, 21 November 1942, p. 205E.
[11] Herbert, General Minute Book, 16 July 1944.
[12] *Machinist*, 27 January 1945, p. 515.
[13] Herbert, General Minute Book, 16 May 1945.

Yet, according to Postan, in the summer of 1941 the Controller General could point to a surplus of machine tools in certain MAP factories, and this was a state of affairs generally well documented in government circles at the time. It certainly came to the attention of the Minister for Aircraft Production, Lord Beaverbrook, who informed the Defence Committee for Supply that the bomber programme required 'no more machine tools' as 30,000 new machines were allocated to MAP factories in 1941. He did acknowledge, however, that 'some special-purpose tools must be provided. The flow of replenishment and renewals must be maintained [although] the main jobs are all completed, and in fact some consignment of tools remain unused and even unpacked'.[14]

MAP probably overestimated its requirements for machine tools, and retained a surplus of machinery capacity, but the devil was in the details. That is the problems manifested themselves in the third level of supply, where general and even disaggregate supply chains could disguise serious problems in the delivery of vital machine tools. Consequently, this had 'knock on effects on strategic production targets'. A case in point occurred at the end of 1942 when there were complaints from MAP over problems in the supply of large plano-millers, a machine essential for the manufacture of long-spars for airframes, and other special-purpose tools that were essential to the manufacture of aero-engines and propellers. Delay in meeting deadlines not only affected the schedules devised for major programmes of aircraft construction, but also impeded changes in aircraft models that were designated as vital to the bombing campaign. For example, in December 1942, MAP considered shifting from the production of Sterling and Wellington Bombers to the Lancaster, and this was programmed to occur at the factories of Austin, Short, and Vickers. The 'change-over' to the construction of the Lancaster, however, was only feasible to implement at one of the targeted factories, because of a short supply of 'specially designed plano-millers of large size'. In December 1942, 41 of these machines were required, 11 for existing Lancaster production, 12 for the change-over at Shorts, and 18 at Vickers. The best delivery time expected for these machines was for 12 in nine months, and then four per month thereafter.[15]

Postan's survey of the industry, and the support given to it from general engineering, presents a mixed picture. At the general and disaggregate levels the supply of general-purpose machine tools was more than satisfactory by 1942, and domestic makers rapidly compensated for the relative, and subsequently absolute decline of American supplies. Between the outbreak of war and the summer of 1944, the machine tool industry 'built as many machines as were manufactured in the proceeding 40 years'.[16] At the crucial level of special-purpose machine tool supply there remained serious deficiencies. Therefore, a surplus of general-purpose machine tools coexisted alongside the persistence of delay and extended delivery dates for specials. Consequently, at a planning level MAP and the Ministry of Supply could articulate different stories about the efficiency of supply. Postan

---

[14] Postan, *War Production*, pp. 208-9.

[15] Ibid., p. 208.

[16] *Machinist*, 19 August 1944, p. 115E.

provides a detailed analysis of the broad trends in machine tool demand and supply, as well as giving an insight on the requirements of the main users. What is missing from the account, however, is a focus on the activities and performance of machine tool firms themselves and the attitudes and strategies of those who ran them.

Machine Tool Firms at War

Machine tool firms, during the war, devised strategies that were conditioned by the constraints that they faced, and set within the context of relations with government agencies and the implementation of national industrial planning. In the crucial first two years of the war, when the industry was required to respond to the national emergency, serious constraints persisted, and relationships between the government and manufacturers was somewhat fraught. As shown in Chapter 5, a key issue of rearmament planning involved the co-ordination of labour resources, but this was incomplete by 1940, and the supply of labour continued to act as a constraint on the industry as the demands of war escalated in 1941 and 1942. P. H. Mills, the Controller General of Machine Tools, who replaced Rouse in January 1940, warned the Manufacturers Panel of the MTTA, formed to provide expert industrial advice to the Controller, in December of that year of 'the great danger' that competing industries 'would encourage severe raids on the skilled labour left to the machine tool industry'. He claimed that, so far, he had been able to counter these demands, but the issue of labour supply required a thorough reassessment. Consequently, the Ministry of Supply formed a special Labour Committee in collaboration with the Ministry of Labour, the Engineering Employers, and the Allied Employers National Federation, with the MTTA also invited by the Ministry to participate. A key finding of this committee was that the industry 'had no surplus labour and required many thousands of additional hands'. Predicting a rising demand for machine tools in the first quarter of 1941, the Labour Committee concluded that additional labour was urgently required, and the Controller was faced with excessive demands for machines 'which are so much greater than the output of the trade'. An obvious solution was dilution through the employment of more female labour. At an industry level, and similar to the First World War, the response of firms to dilution was, at best, a mixed one. In June 1941, a meeting between the Ministry of Labour and Mills led to a directive sent to the National Federation to the effect that the increasing demand for labour necessitated an increasing employment of female workers in the machine tool trade, and a minimum target of 15 per cent was set. The industry should 'pull its weight' in introducing dilution, and although the directive recognised that machine tools were not manufactured on 'mass production lines', these were not 'normal times' and it was imperative that female employment was introduced to the highest degree.[17]

---

[17] MTTA, Director's Minute Book, 18 December 1940; 10 June 1941. For an examination of women in British engineering during the war, see R. Croucher, *Engineers at War 1939-1945* (London, Merlin, 1982), Ch. 5.

Evidence to the Labour Committee suggested that the industry required an additional 15,000 female workers, but it also indicated the uneven response by makers to labour change, and emphasised marked differences in the pace of dilution. This was put down to caution by makers concerning the high cost of radical alterations to the layout of workshops necessary for dilution, and the need for government to accept the capital costs of change. Further, dilution was 'largely a matter of outlook on the part of management, and opposition in the works had to be overcome'. For example, Adcock & Shipley, Leicester, claimed that one-fifth of their employees were women, but there were problems of training female workers, the management concluding that better results were achievable if the company could have obtained boys of 14 for training. In Halifax, A. K. McCall of Churchill-Redman claimed that 17.5 per cent of its workforce were women, and noted that they hoped to expand this further by employing them on classes of work never before tried. To achieve this the company was training women under the Ministry of Labour schemes, taking eight weeks to train machine operators, fitters, scapers and inspectors. During the war, the company supplied 2,000 machines and in 1944 its workforce of 412 consisted of 50 per cent female employees. McCall also noted, however, that only three firms in Halifax were employing female workers, and they were working on pooling their resources through a local machine tool committee, under guidance from the Engineering Employers Federation, to provide information and consultation on the practicalities of dilution. Another Halifax firm, William Asquith, also supported this initiative, although the company feared that the trade unions would resist further deskilling.[18] Firms clearly adapted to the changed labour conditions, but 20 months into the war the proportion of women employed in the industry was only 1.75 per cent of the total workforce.[19]

Leading the government's campaign for dilution was Herbert's. At the company's AGM in October 1942, Sir Alfred acknowledged that during the year the company had continued to 'struggle under great disadvantages', the most prominent being the 'shortage of labour'. He also voiced concern over, what he considered, a 'lack of discipline and slackness on the behalf of labour'. That this was a reference to male workers was made clear in a speech to the Institute of Production Engineers where he condemned the ill-discipline of the 'British working man', which was compounded by the intervention of 'labour organisation'. In contrast, he referred to the 'great value of female labour', and recalled his experiences during the First World War when female workers had 'been tried and found invaluable'. During the present conflict, he asserted, the unions had failed to grasp the lessons of 1914 to 1918. While, in principle, the unions had withdrawn their resistance to dilution, they had done so reluctantly and consequently many barriers remained. In the Herbert tool rooms, there was 'an organised movement to make it difficult, if not impossible, to continue to employ women'. Male tool workers were 'refusing to give that help and assistance in the instruction of women which is necessary, and all we can do is

---

[18] MTTA, Director's Minute Book, 10 June 1941; Jeremy, 'John Beresford Stuart Gabriel', p. 457.

[19] Miller, *Tools that Built a Business*, pp. 45-6.

go through the dreadful rigmarole of Conferences and so on'. As a solution, Sir Alfred called for government assistance in removing all restrictions, 'overt or covert', that prevented the industry from reaping 'the full benefit of female labour'.[20]

Sir Alfred's inference that only trade unions and male workers were opposed to female workers was, of course, disingenuous. Engineers too had voiced their objections to female workers in the tool room. For example, the production engineer S. A. Inscoe argued in May 1941 that many skilled men had 'not been economically replaced by women for, in proportion to the money, time, supervision and wastage involved in the substitution of female labour, careful costing systems will show that, under normal conditions, male labour is more reliable and productive, and less expensive'. In the absence of the intensive need for increased production, Inscoe concluded that 'the free choice of most machine shop executives would be to severely limit the employment of women to work within the scope of their physical and mental capabilities'.[21] Such views did find support among machine makers. In April 1942 Sir Harry Greer, the chairman of the SMTC, expressed concerns that costs of production would escalate if women and trainees were taken on in greater numbers. For Greer, employing female labour raised the issue of undue interference by government in the operations of private business. Consequently, he responded negatively to the outcome of deliberations between the MTTA and the Controller General which had inferred that makers 'must employ more women and that women must be upgraded'. He deeply resented the fact 'that drastic action would be taken against any firm failing to comply with these instructions'. This reflected the management's experience in recruiting and training an adequate labour force. In August 1940, for example, the managing director, Hugh Bennie, complained that in order for the Corporation to retain labour at its Clyde Engineering Works they had to offer overtime, 'even if not needed'. Despite this, 'there had ... been a serious loss of skilled men who had been replaced by inferior labour – particularly in the Govan Works – with the result that operations took considerably longer with a definite increase of costs'. Recruitment and retention problems had resulted in the manufacturing programme becoming 'considerably disorganised'.[22]

Churchill-Redman experienced similar problems. By December 1941, the company was employing 93 women, 23 per cent of its workforce of 402, and McCall considered this had been vital in accounting for a 13 per cent increase in output over the corresponding period in 1940. A sign of dilution at the company was the fact that only 38 per cent of their machines were now under the operation of skilled men. By March 1942, however, McCall's optimistic overtures had changed. He noted that monthly output figures had remained stagnant for the last

[20] Herbert, General Minute Book, 9 October 1942; Sir Alfred Herbert, 'Address at the 21st Anniversary of the Institute of Production Engineers', in *Machinist*, 7 November 1942, p. 190E.

[21] S. A. Inscoe, 'Women and machine Work', in *Machinist*, 24 May 1941, p. 88E.

[22] Glasgow University Archives and Business Research Centre, UGD 175/2/1/1, SMTC Minute Book 1937-42, 30 August 1940; 17 April 1942.

three months, despite an increasing number of employees, and argued that this was 'due to the fact that the available supply of labour was of a standard that was gradually deteriorating'. The company now employed 412 workers of which 105, 25 per cent, were women, the highest in the district. Plans by the management for employing an extra 30-40 women were delayed, following objections by Churchill-Redman to the Ministry of Labour's prohibition on employing 'mobile female labour when labour of definite ability was essential to the machine tool industry'. By June 1942, the company had 7 months' work on the books, and McCall noted problems with the supply of labour. Competition for labour in the Halifax district was intensified by the establishment of factories by Sheffield and London companies, and from local employers who had introduced high bonus payments despite attempts at a 'collective system' of wage bargaining. Further, there was a significant loss of time due to absenteeism, which in April accounted for 9.3 per cent of the workforce.[23]

Indeed, despite Sir Alfred's public endorsement of the imperative of employing additional unskilled labour, his own company faced serious difficulties in assimilating them into the workforce. In June 1941, Sir Alfred informed the board of his concerns about the provision of adequate staff and workpeople for their horizontal boring department, which was the principal cause of delays in production. To meet targets they needed to operate the department night and day, and they were re-deploying workers from the turret and capstan lathe departments. At the same time, 'girls' were transferred to work on manufacturing sensitive drills, and 'boys and youths' moved to radial drilling machines, while the original operatives were transferred to boring drills. De-skilling involved an increasing emphasis upon labour planning within the organisation, a policy referred to by a company director, Townsend, as 'switching over'. This did not come without costs. Townsend, for example, complained in July 1941 of married women taking time off to do shopping, and gave examples of women who wanted to take Saturday out despite a reduction in salary. Such was the pressure for labour that Townsend concluded that 'if we do not allow them the time off, they will take it'.[24]

Nevertheless, dilution was a radical, if opportunistic solution to the strategic needs of a large engineering company such as Herbert's during the war. Not all manufacturers accepted the positive position taken by Sir Alfred on the employment of women, and his recognition of their lower relative pay, but the labour constraints facing the industry, blamed by makers on inadequate government planning, were part of more general complaints by the industry over the implementation of government control. In 1942, Sir Alfred complained to shareholders that the whole of 'our business was hedged round by restrictions and controls by the various government departments'. He inferred that much valuable time was wasted in providing an 'enormous' amount of 'paper work', much of which he considered unnecessary. As he informed the readers of *The Machinist*, 'the dead head of civil service influence, the numerous forms to be completed,

---

[23] Churchill-Redman, CR-3, Minute Book, 3 December 1941; 3 March, 3 June 1942.

[24] Herbert, Departmental Board, 25 June, 9 July 1941.

government book keeping [and] the difficulty of getting early decisions' stifled free enterprise. This was partly a problem related to the co-ordination of the planning system, and Sir Alfred objected to the fact that each government department had its own methods, which involved a considerable load of clerical work, tying down workers and managers. If ordinary commercial orders substituted for state contracting, he suggested, his own company could provide the turnover they were doing 'today with half the office staff'. The leading manufacturer in the industry objected to government controls infringing upon economic freedom, and warned that when the war ended it would be difficult 'to regain the old liberty'.[25] Increasing administrative routines affected not only large firms such as Herbert's, but provided an added burden in an industry comprising a large number of small makers. In the day-to-day operations of the small firm, directors often undertook a series of administrative functions, which clearly increased in volume during the war.[26]

At large producers such as Herbert's administrative issues, relating to the increased needs of planning production, became particularly acute as the company moved towards gearing operations towards the war effort from late 1940. In October 1940, for example, C. W. Clark informed the board that Machine Tool Control had requested that makers simplify their manufacturing programmes, and to contact competitors to arrange for the concentration on certain machines. Clark also noted, with some concern, that there had also been requests by the Controller for details of all orders received to enable his department to reallocate machines to targeted areas. In December, Clark reported on negotiations with Wards of Birmingham for arrangements to simplify programmes, but noted that both companies faced problems in coordinating supply because of the uncertainty of government demand. Further, Clark objected to the power of the Controller to restrict the company from accepting orders without the sanction of the Controller, a feature of policy that seriously disrupted production planning.[27] The MTTA, on behalf of the trade, questioned the effectiveness of government controls in raising output in the industry. While recognising the need to rationalise manufacturing programmes to eradicate duplication, through group agreements, the MTTA nevertheless felt that firms were facing serious problems in coordinating their programmes to meet demand. Announcing a new ordering system to ensure that orders placed for machines were in line with the defence programme, the Controller argued that an essential corollary was that Service Departments should place in his hands at least one years extent of their machine tool requirements. Although the MTTA accepted that this scheme would enable firms to plan forward with greater certainty, the Association continued to condemn the 'rigid' restrictions applied by the Controller on the pattern of ordering within the industry.[28] Indeed, the Controller's guarantee that contracting departments would ensure that they

[25] Herbert, General Minute Book, 9 October 1942; *Machinist*, 21 February 1942, p. 190E; 7 November 1942, p. 356E.
[26] *Machinist*, 24 January 1942, p. 329E.
[27] Herbert, Departmental Board, 13 October, 11 December 1940.
[28] MTTA, Director's Minute Book, 18 December 1940.

placed orders in advance was not delivered in practice. In March 1941, for example, the Herbert directors reported that since January they had accumulated stocks of factored goods to the value of £175,000 and they were constantly 'pressing the Controller to send us overriding orders to cover all the machines'. Large orders did not materialise until June, when the Controller sanctioned machine deliveries to the aircraft factories. As the management noted, the delay in guaranteeing a 'continuity' of bulk orders from the defence departments had caused lengthening delivery times to private firms, resulting in a loss of customer goodwill.[29]

Continuity in ordering was a key factor in the decision of firms to invest in long production runs, but an agreement on the continuity of production was slow to mature, and added to the uncertainty of makers in formulating strategies for investment, ordering of material supplies, and arranging machine programmes. The uncertainty surrounding government contracting was shown in December 1940 when the Controller wrote to the MTTA informing them of the possibility of orders falling off, and enquiring whether there would be a 'break' in the production of machine tools. In the ensuing discussion, E. C. Farrell, the Managing Director of BSA Tools, thought that it was probable that the Ministry of Supply would sanction advanced supplies of materials to machine makers for 15 to 18 months. Nevertheless, he was less optimistic that makers would be prepared to invest in future supplies of material without a firm commitment of orders from the Controller. T. P. Burness, of William Asquith Ltd., was less optimistic still, believing that the Ministry of Supply would restrict delivery of steel to the industry, which would inevitably lead to a break in production. Machine tool makers claimed E. H. Jones, the chairman of a machine tool merchant firm, needed to know definitely 'the extent to which they could go on manufacturing'. The concerns of makers was given an added twist by the fact that Machine Tool Control was ordering in larger quantities from the U.S.A., a fact which meant, according to representatives of Cincinnati Milling Machines, an American subsidiary in Britain, that there was no assurance that British makers would get any orders at all. Coming straight to the point, James Archdale argued that this situation was having a serious effect on the planning of output in his own company, and felt that the MTTA should get a firm commitment from the Controller 'whether they did or did not ... want machine tools'. Representing Herbert's, C. W. Clark concluded that the industry must recognise two factors, firstly that orders were falling off, and secondly there had been a considerable volume of cancelled orders. If this situation continued, he claimed, it would lead to an increasing degree of 'uncertainty'. Confirming the cancellation of orders, John Gabriel, the managing director of Charles Churchill & Co., claimed that his company was not accepting cancellations, but were 'putting them up to the Ministry'; an action that was also being pursued by Herbert's. Summing up the position of the industry, Harold Butler felt that there was 'considerable anxiety in the minds of manufacturers'. Such was the degree of anxiety caused that machine

---

[29] Herbert, Departmental Board, 9 March, 11 June 1941.

makers, including Clark and Gabriel, were perceiving the fall in orders as a signal that the war might be of short duration. On this point E. H. Jones felt that too much had been made 'about the end of war', and what really mattered was the programme which the government had set in terms of machine tool supply. Nevertheless, he felt that the industry had reached the peak of orders, and there would now be a fall whatever the duration of the war. Signifying the commercial thinking of businessmen, even in the midst of war, Jones concluded that falling orders 'would bring the position where the industry would be fighting for orders even with the end of the war not in sight'.[30]

During the first half of 1941, the MTTA negotiated an Agreement of Continuity of Production with the Ministry of Supply, implemented in June. The Agreement was to compensate the industry against possible loss by the sudden cancellation of orders, the Ministry reserving the right to break the Agreement at 24 hours notice. Even in 1941, the priorities of war were of secondary consideration to members of the MTTA, the commercial implications of government control through contracting being of paramount concern. Indeed, a representative of the Matterson Machine Tool Co. thought that members were 'losing a sense of proportion'. During war, if makers undertook to keep production going then surely 'the community had the right to expect that the special arrangements should be brought to an end as soon as possible' when the emergency had ended, 'provided' of course that 'there was indemnification against loss'. The role of the Ministry in determining supply deeply affected the commercial strategies of machine makers. As a representative of the Soag Machine Tool Co. argued, the government's refusal to commit fully to the continuity of production had serious implications for machine tool firms who had developed extensive sub-contracting with engineering firms who were not normally engaged in the manufacture of machine tools. Sub-contracting was crucial to the industry's ability to meet war targets, and start-up costs, in terms of acquiring or making jigs, gauges, and tools were high. The fact that the Ministry could cancel orders at short notice was a disincentive to invest.[31] Sub-contracting illustrated the capacity constraints facing the industry, and its expansion was vital to raising the production of finished machines, and equally important the supply of tool accessories. Sub-contracting, together with foreign supply, were key factors in sustaining the drive of the industry to increase output in the first two years of the war.

This was certainly the case at Herbert's, who faced serious problems in co-ordinating the expansion of output. A key problem in planning was to co-ordinate finished machine tool production with that of tools and accessories. The main issue identified was collaboration with customers who were slow to simplify their tool outfits, thus placing pressure on Herbert's to manufacture a range of chucks, dies, taps and other machine accessories. A Herbert director, H. Booth, explained that arrangements were in place for daily meetings between Machine Shop Planning, Factory Planning and Despatch Departments 'to keep them closely in touch with each other'. Nevertheless, Booth informed the directors that supplies

---

[30] MTTA, Director's Minute Book, 10, 18 December 1940.
[31] MTTA, Director's Minute Book, 10 June 1941.

of taps were on order from Skeffo of Gottenberg, and although steps had been taken to increase the production of dies in May 1940, in other tool accessories production had reached its limits. Enquiries for surplus tools from large engineering plants had met with limited success, only Morris Motors aiding them by returning surplus supplies of dies. To improve output they would have to look for sub-contracting. Indeed, with a 'dearth of standard tool outfits' the company decided to import standard tools from Japan, in tandem with orders for a certain number of machines. They could produce, with sub-contractors, the most popular tools, but needed various types of boring bar holders, floating reamer holders, tool slides, and box tools from Japan. To meet the insatiable demand, the company prepared 'Skeleton outfits of tools', which were 'recommended to customers', and placed orders for forgings for die bodies and shanks from the U.S.A. Imports, of course, were prone to enemy action, forcing the company to extend further its foreign supplies, for example, buying in stocks of dies from Landis in the U.S.A. By January 1941, the company had outstanding orders for dies of 145,000 sets, compared with 96,000 in September 1940, leading the management to the conclusion that they further had to increase sub-contracting.[32]

Problems in co-ordinating and planning at the Herbert factories, was complicated further by their involvement in reconditioning 'blitzed machines'. In March 1941, the company had 387 blitzed machines from Coventry, and 12 from London on its books, out of which only 68 were repaired and returned because many of the machines were waiting for replacement parts from the USA, 'which will probably mean considerable delay'. Herbert's also undertook recondition work on machines for 'special war work', for example converting 14 of their own No. 9 Combination Turret Lathes in June 1941 'under order' from the Ministry of Supply for shell work. Indeed, they dispatched 'blitzed' and reconditioned machines, of their own make, to firms all over the country, intensifying the pressure on spares and ancillary tools. Apart from its own manufacturing requirements, the company had to accommodate an extensive 'repair shop' both for users of machines, and for machine makers and machine importers. As C. W. Clark complained, this placed enormous pressure on available production capacity, and he thought that it would be more effective if British makers should, as far as possible, repair their own machines, and importers should be responsible for machines for which they acted as agents. Further, claimed Clark, the parts of scrapped machines could be used to repair other machines 'and a pool of spare parts formed accordingly'. This, of course, suggests the limitations of machine tool supply in 1941, and in August, Clark noted the remarkable fact that the company was engaged on reconditioning Herbert Combination Turret Lathes that had been in service during the First World War. During 1941, the various activities of the company was conflicting both with their ability to supply war departments and private engineering firms. In June, for example, the company was in danger of losing 'customer goodwill' because of the

---

[32] Herbert, Departmental Board, 4, 24 April, 8, 9, 22 May, 19 June, 31 July, 13 October 1940; 8 January 1941.

failure to maintain promises of delivery, and their 'record' was under scrutiny from the Controller of Machine Tools.[33]

Operating at full pressure, the company had to overcome the 'bottle-necks' which constantly occurred in their production lines. One solution was to install tighter management systems within the company, to co-ordinate overall supply. Thus, a Co-ordinating Committee was established, consisting of departmental directors and foremen, to plan the internal flow of production, and to co-ordinate vital imports of foreign parts and tools and the increasingly complex system of sub-contracting. By June 1941, the works were operating at full capacity, the management facing serious difficulties in working to the planned programme of manufacture because orders far exceeded deliveries. Consequently, the Co-ordinating Committee instigated a programme of rationalisation, with the aim 'to make only what is required'. Adopting the Committee's 'Machine Shop Plan', the management was able to implement reductions in the size of batches, 'so that as machinery is completed they could be issued to fitters without remaining for a considerable time in the finished parts store'. As the management noted, 'The development of planning in the machine shop is continuing with the object of discovering the bottlenecks and taking early steps to avoid delays'. Planning systems, however, remained inadequate, and the problems of 'bottlenecks' persisted. In August 1941, Clark referred to the 'eternal problem of getting more output and reducing the amount of work-in-progress', the latter being conditioned by the time it took for work to go through the shops. As a remedy Clark suggested making certain types of components such as headstocks and gear boxes 'in gangs or departments under one foreman; plant for all the operations on the components being available in that department'. This suggests that management did not perceive planning in a rigid way, and realised the need to adapt their manufacturing systems, but changes in the planning system itself involved considerable cost. Replying to Clark's suggestion, Sir Alfred thought that this was the 'the right move', but also realised that it would mean rearranging plant and having some machinery stationary part of the time. Consequently, changes in the system were only partial, the company applying Clark's system to their Lutterworth factory only.[34]

The key factor affecting the company was clearly the supply of tools and accessories. As Herbert put it, the solution lay in 'overcoming the tools equipment for machinery problem'. A partial solution was American imports, the company, for example, receiving 42,000 dies from Landis & Co. in April and May 1941, and in June large numbers of uni-centric chucks were supplied on an eight month contract from Pratt and Whitney to compensate for deficiencies in their own production of 'Coventry Chucks'. Imports, of course, were prone to disruption due to the war, and, in the case of imported chucks, there was considerable resistance by users who preferred Herbert designs rather than foreign imports. The company faced enormous problems in supplying spare parts for Coventry Chucks, which

---

[33] Herbert, Departmental Board, 19 March, 7, 21 May, 11, 25 June, 6 August 1941.

[34] Herbert, Departmental Board, 25 June, 20 August 1941.

affected the scale of their production, forcing the management to sub-contract for spares. In an assessment of the performance of the company, it needs to be realised that large makers such as Herbert's were not simply suppliers of finished machines, but also large makers of tools and machining equipment. It was this that placed enormous pressure on manufacturing capacity. To alleviate these problems the company sub-contracted, as well as expanding tool capacity by the creation of two new dispersal factories at Cosby and Earl Skelton, outside Coventry, which were used to meet the urgent need to relieve the pressure for box tools for machines. Nevertheless, the company remained 'handicapped by having to wait for parts of tool equipment from our sub-contractors or the small tool department, and inadequate internal systems for stock taking and ordering'. At the same time, delivery times lengthened and customers swamped the ordering departments with complaints. Consequently, the management decided to leave a margin on deliveries, quoting, for example nine months' delivery to customers on promises of six months from their own Planning Department. Summing up the position, Pickin claimed that 'the real answer to the problem was to increase our production capacity', but as Sir Alfred argued, they had reached the limit of tool equipment capacity, and were forced to sub-contract for tools as well as finished machines.[35]

Sub-contracting required careful monitoring, and the board appointed a senior engineer to provide technical and practical support to each sub-contracting firm. Herbert's also attempted to 'impress upon customers not to order unnecessary tools because of shortages'. Such was the urgency for sub-contracting, however, that, as A. H. Lloyd remarked, work was given to 'unsatisfactory sub-contractors', rather than those who were 'efficient'. The company took every measure to ensure priority to the tools in greatest demand, but effective supply by sub-contractors remained a serious concern. For example, Herbert's had to contract out for tool equipment to eight firms in order to ensure that 84 machines supplied to the New Britain Co., for the manufacture of 20 mm shells, were fully tooled. Tool supplies, however, were delayed because the sub-contractor had to adapt Herbert engineering drawings to their own workshop practices. Bar boring work, which created a serious 'bottle neck' in the production lines was also sub-contracted, six per cent of the work being undertaken by outside firms, much of it coming back to the company in a condition which did not meet production specifications. A key problem in the reliability of sub-contracted work related to government controls over prices. As Lloyd informed the directors, the fixing of prices led to low prices on sub-contracted work. His fellow director, Schofield, suggested that the company should operate a dual price system, but as Townsend informed the board for their 18 inch mill they were offering three prices, but 'if sub-contractors are not making a profit they are not going to push the work'. In July 1941, Lloyd visited a number of sub-contractors (Table 6.6) and noted that 'nobody was able to deal with the whole of the machinery themselves and delays are always because of their dependency on someone else'. Sub-contracting certainly rose in the second half of 1941, Sir Alfred reporting that deliveries increased from £62,000 in May to

---

[35] Herbert, Departmental Board, 25 June, 9 July, 6 August 1941.

£74,000 in June and £88,000 by July. Indeed, by August he could report that deliveries of finished machines, both of their own make and factored, now exceeded orders, yet still there was a persistent shortage of tools and spares, resulting in their rationing to customers, and delays in the delivery of machines.[36]

Table 6.6
Sub-contractors Visited by Herbert Management, July 1941

Firm	Machine Type
Platts of Oldham	No. 3 ND Mills
Holts of Rochdale	Type S Drills
Sagans of Halifax	No. 0 Mills
Crabtree of Leeds	No. 23V Mills and No. 33 Plain Mills
Dawson, Payne & Elliott	No. 2 Simple Mills & No. 2S Capstans
Goss Printing Press Co.	No. 3 ND Mills
Northrop Loom	OV Mills, No. 10V Mills, No. 1 Mills (hand and auto feed)
Sentinel	No. 7 & 9 Combination Turret Lathes, 6.5' Edgwick Lathes

Source: Herbert, Departmental Board, 9 July 1941.

The evaluation of Herbert's performance in the crucial first two years of the war suggests a need to modify Postan's positive account of the response of the industry. At the micro level, firms faced enormous pressures to plan output, were constrained by labour shortages, tool supplies, and the vagaries of sub-contracting and import systems. In particular, the evidence from Herbert's suggests that supplies of tools and equipment placed a serious strain on internal planning systems, and, as *The Machinist* noted as early as July 1940, 'one of the worst bottlenecks' was the inadequate supply 'of precision cutting tools, chucks, jigs, fixtures and gauges'.[37] The incentive for general engineering firms to sub-contract was also constrained by government controls on prices, and this became a major issue between machine makers and officials at the Ministry of Supply. Echoing the complaints of Sir Alfred Herbert concerning the rigidity of government controls, Sir Harry Greer, of the SMTC, complained as early as February 1940 that every government contract was subject to costing. It was not this, however, which Greer found irksome, but rather that 'the government persistently refused to specify the basis of costs or the rate of profit to be allowed'. A lack of transparency by Machine Tool Control was compounded by the fact that certain orders from private firms appeared to be at a fixed price, 'but they may subsequently be placed on behalf of the government and therefore be subject to costing'. Greer also protested that the American government provided more favourable contractual terms to their

---

[36] Herbert, Departmental Board, 7 May, 1, 11, 25 June, 9 July, 6, 20 August 1941.
[37] *Machinist*, 29 July 1940, p. 97E.

machine makers, than was the case in Britain, and this allowed them to supply machines at very high prices, receiving payment in full before delivery.[38]

Price control, and the question of government costing, had been a major issue between government and machine makers during the rearmament programme itself, and in the war it became a focal point for agitation by makers against government authority which they perceived as prohibiting the actions of individual enterprise.[39] Greer's fears that an army of Ministry of Supply cost assessors would subject the industry to constant scrutiny proved largely unfounded. In June 1940, the MTTA brokered a deal with the Ministry of Supply for a price fixing formula for standard tools, enforceable on contracts from July, based on 1935 prices plus a 22.5 per cent margin for profit above cost. Price control was designed 'to protect the nation from exploitation'. At the same time, the Ministry retained its power to cost, which in fact was compulsory on all non-standard machines contracted by government agencies. In practice, it seems likely that the Ministry did not enforce costing extensively, but rather it used it as a bargaining tool to force the industry to accept price fixing. Heading a MTTA negotiating team in late 1940, G. S. Maginness accepted price control, which he saw as a 'broad settlement avoiding the purgatory of costing'. Justifying this to the membership, he claimed that the vast majority of machine tools were standard, and therefore would not be subject to costing. The Manufacturers' Panel of the MTTA concurred 'because they knew that the majority of the industry were against the unsound system of costing – any alternative to the scheme would be to cost everything and put a percentage of profit on cost fixed by government and not to exceed 10%'. Moreover, the aim of costing, in practice, was to produce a standard across the machine tool sector, an impossible task given the relative efficiency and different cost-accounting systems of member firms. Nevertheless, costing clearly implied government intrusion into the financial affairs of the industry, and raised the spectre of controlling excess profits.[40]

In December 1940, the MTTA announced that it was the intention of the authorities to study the balance sheets and trading accounts of machine tool firms. In addition, Ministry of Supply auditors had been sending out letters demanding facilities for costing individual contracts, an action which the MTTA felt was contrary to their agreement with the Ministry. Costing created paranoia amongst machine tool makers, in January 1941. At a meeting of the MTTA, G. Hickman of Drummond Bros., felt that firms should have no fear of costing, but felt that the key question was the proportion of profit on costs, which the Ministry would allow, an issue that he believed the Association should 'fight'. Taking the matter further, James Archdale called for the MTTA to subject the powers of the Ministry to legal counsel. Fearing the worst, E. H. Jones predicted that the Ministry would squeeze profits, sanctioning no more than 10 per cent profit on the employable capital of a company, a figure which was 'ridiculous'. Quelling the fears of manufacturers, Maginness agreed that firms might well fear costing, but reminded

---

[38] SMTC, Minute Book 1937-42, 6 February 1940.

[39] See Miller, *Machines that Built a Business*, p. 46.

[40] MTTA, Director's Minute Book, 3 July 1940.

members that few firms were actually subject to it, and any alteration in the policy would not be retrospective.[41]

Cost and price issues clearly raised sensitive issues concerning the degree of regulation placed on the industry during the war. In many respects, this was a matter of legitimate business concern given the inflationary pressures placed on the economy during the conflict. Thus, Greer, responding on behalf of the SMTC to the agreement between the trade and the Ministry of Supply of June 1940, complained that the prices set were insufficient to meet the rise in costs, involving a loss to the Corporation. 'The supplies of raw materials', he complained, did not appear to be controlled in any way and the price of materials had risen considerably'. This problem of the slow implementation of controls, across industrial sectors, created inflationary pressures on costs, and this was compounded, according to Bennie, by the fact that actual wage rates had risen by 25 per cent over the 1935 benchmark used by the Ministry to calculate machine tool prices in 1940. Taking into account the introduction of intensive overtime systems to meet output targets, Bennie calculated that the real increase in wage costs to the industry since 1935 was as much as 50 per cent. In the short-run, profits were not adversely affected, and over the financial year 1940-1 profits rose by 41 per cent as turnover increased by 39 per cent. By June 1942, although Greer could report that 'relations with the officials of Control were ... cordial', he nevertheless reflected that this had not always been the case, and he complained that price controls had undermined the profit potential of the organisation. Adding to his concern was the fact that government contracts had been suddenly cancelled, and he was negotiating for a government rebate.[42] The evidence concerning firm-state relations in the critical first three years of the war suggests the need to modify Postan's positive overview of the machine tool industry. The attempt by the government to impose control, especially in the area of costing, drew a hostile response from machine tool firms, and the industry may be fairly described as a reluctant partner. Indeed, as government demand peaked in 1942, the industry was already looking ahead to a return to normality and contemplating the business environment of the post-war world, in which exports would play a vital role.

Machine Tool Exports and the Vision of the Post-War World

By 1942, the supply situation was easing, and Winston Churchill's 'ganglion nerve centre' had responded adequately to the rising demands of war industry. Nevertheless, the supply of British machine tools was of a particular type, the industry adept at the building of standard lines but making little progress in the area of special-purpose machines. Firms in South Lancashire, for example, recorded in 1942 that 'In most instances standard lines of production form practically the whole of the products, and the production of new machine tools are anything but conspicuous'. H. W. Kearns & Co., were 'engaged solely on standard

---

[41] MTTA, Director's Minute Book, 18 December 1940; 28 January 1941.

[42] SMTC, Minute Book 1937-42, 30 August 1940; 31 March 1941; 30 June 1942.

products'; E. G. Herbert & Co. 'employing all their resources on the manufacture of their standard' lines; and G Richards and Co. were 'fully engaged on standards'.[43] A similar concentration on standard lines was observable in Birmingham, Halifax, and Coventry.[44] The rationalisation of production along standard lines was itself largely shaped by the needs of war production and the application of government controls. By 1942 Machine Tool Control at the Ministry of Supply was prescribing the types of machines built, firms talking only 'tentatively of new types'. The demands of the British war effort, on the domestic industry, required standard lines, the control on special machines being 'strict and clearly defined'. Makers contemplating new designs were required to demonstrate that the machines 'have a definite purpose in war production and increase output'. Official permission was even required on modifications to existing models, and firms faced major obstacles in attempting to 'embark on new productions in addition to their current commitments'.[45] In this sense, government control reinforced the technological trajectory and path dependency of the industry towards standard lines. Reviewing technological progress in the industry during the war, a Political and Economic Planning (PEP) report of 1948 concluded that although there had been an increasing number of specialist machines utilised by British engineering during the conflict, they were not well adapted to post-war use, and the British machine tool industry had supplied vital standard lines to Britain's war industries. In technical terms, British makers continued to develop incremental improvements to machines, increasing cutting speeds and reducing the need for skilled workers to perform machining operations, rather than introducing 'fundamental changes in technique and design'. The demands of war necessitated the expansion of machines 'of proven success', curtailing 'all major development work'.[46]

While British makers concentrated on standard lines, the U.S.A. filled the gap in the market for special-purpose machines. By the summer of 1943 American machine tool production was so advanced that her war industries were 'fully tooled up for its programmes', enabling her makers to supply the British market 'even more conveniently, though subject still to lease-lend conditions'. The Catmur Machine Tool Corporation Ltd., a specialist British importer of American machines, reported that special-purpose machine tools were the most prominent items in their lists, and included a Moor Jig Grinder, Ken Norman Milling Machines, and Grand Rapid Tool and Cutter Grinders, all of which were 'meeting a good demand'. Another specialist importer, E. P. Barrows Ltd. of London, also reported that 'numerous American lines were arriving very fast', although deliveries were not sufficient to keep pace with demand.[47] During the war, Charles Churchill & Co. imported substantial numbers of American special-purpose

---

[43] *Machinist*, 25 January 1942, p. 325E.

[44] *Machinist*, 9 May 1942, p. 22; 5 September 1942, p. 139E; 20 February 1943, p. 285E.

[45] *Machinist*, 11 April 1942, p. 401E.

[46] PEP, Report on 'The Machine Tool Industry', pp. 186, 189, 191.

[47] *Machinist*, 18 September 1943, p. 138E.

machines, as well as manufacturing under licence at its subsidiary, Churchill-Redman, machines designed by the Cleveland Hobbing Co., Cone Automatic Co., and Jones & Lamson.[48] The latter company manufactured the Fay lathe, Churchill-Redman agreeing, under directions from the Ministry of Supply, to manufacture under licence three sizes of the machine in 1941.[49]

By 1943, the contribution of the British machine tool industry to the war effort had passed its peak, and *The Machinist* speculated that 'its services to the state may not again be requisitioned on the same scale'.[50] As Miller observes, 'Tooling up for war production is not a steady flow but starts as a flood and subsides to a trickle'.[51] The forced dependency of the industry on government supply was, naturally, a sensitive issue for Sir Alfred Herbert. Addressing the Wolverhampton Production Exhibition in October 1943, he was already considering the post-war prospects for the industry. While recognising that during the war the industry had to abandon their normal production programmes to meet the flood of orders, he nevertheless warned that the industry was then 'likely to find a greatly reduced demand, as the market would ... be overstocked'.[52] By October 1944, the fall in domestic orders had led the directors to accelerate 'the release of labour', which was already advancing 'at the rate of approximately 100 persons per month'.[53]

With falling demand, British output fell from a peak of 95.8 thousand machines in 1942 to 59.1 thousand in 1944 (Table 6.5), and during 1943 the majority of sub-contracting firms brought into the manufacture of machine tools during the war ceased production. As output fell, the industry contracted employment, which found alternative work in other war industries. In 1938, the number of operatives employed in the industry was 28,000, and at its peak in 1942 this had risen to 48,000, added to which were 16,000 engaged in sub-contracting work. By 1946, the number of operatives employed had fallen to 32,000.[54] The sudden reduction in government contracts could have a dramatic effect on the productive capability of firms. For example, by the end of 1943 Jones & Shipman faced the reality that shell and armament factories were fully equipped, and the Ministry of Labour redirected their employees to alternative work. At the peak of employment in 1942, the company employed 1,300; by mid-1944 this had shrunk to 680, and the management predicted an eventual workforce of 450, the number that they had employed in 1939.[55] A similar scenario was played out at Churchill-Redman, McCall reporting a 30 per cent drop in turnover for the four months to July 1944 compared to the same period in 1943, a consequence of reductions in 'shop personnel' and in hours worked. Although the company still had six to seven

---

[48] Jeremy, 'John Beresford Stuart Gabriel', p. 457.

[49] Churchill-Redman, CR3, Minute Book, 9 September 1941.

[50] *Machinist*, 25 December 1943, p. 138E.

[51] Miller, *Tools that Built a Business*, p. 53.

[52] Cited in *Machinist*, 9 October 1943, p. 155E.

[53] 926/1/1/1, Alfred Herbert, Minute Book of the Board of Directors of Alfred Herbert Ltd., 1944 to 1960, 31 October 1944.

[54] PEP, Report on 'The Machine Tool Industry', pp. 182, 184.

[55] Miller, *Tools that Built a Business*, p. 53.

months of orders on the books, sub-contracting work was discontinued under instructions from Machine Tool Control.[56]

Falling domestic demand determined that makers concentrate sales on export markets, offering future opportunities for the industry. In October 1944, Sir Alfred informed his directors that they should 'plan for the future', and emphasised the need to develop quality lines of standard machines to ensure 'an increase in the established goodwill of the company amongst its customers'. In particular, he placed the emphasis upon the development of export markets, a factor he considered in the light of the removal of German competition from international markets. Indeed, by March 1945 the company was already exporting 40 per cent of its output, Sir Alfred predicting that the end of the war would bring 'a normal and healthy competition' for exported machines. A year later, 75 per cent of the company's orders were for export markets, the company targeting foreign demand for standard lines.[57] At Jones & Shipman, the management were already considering the need to plan for post-war foreign markets in 1943, anticipating a slump in home demand, and exports were to be vital to the company's business after 1945.[58] Similarly, Churchill-Redman targeted export markets. As early as 1941, the company had orders in hand for exports worth £58,000, compared to £122,000 for the home market. The future expansion of foreign trade was restricted, however, by difficulties in obtaining export licences, which meant that output was determined by allocations from the Ministry of Supply. From 1944, as domestic demand eased, Churchill-Redman looked again to export markets. A steady fall in domestic orders between April and August 1945 was consequently offset by a corresponding rise in foreign orders. By the latter date, the company's books recorded domestic orders valued at £51,200 compared to exports of £60,600, the company selling to 14 different countries, and by December 80 per cent of the company's orders of £225,000 were destined for export. Replicating the production trends in the industry, the company was selling standard lines, reflecting McCall's policy to build a 'full range of the company's products', 'the progress of new designs' being delayed.[59] At the Butler Machine Tool Co, in 1943, the management were equally aware of the prospects offered by foreign markets in the event of the termination of hostilities, the company already negotiating with Associated British Machine Tools, of which it was a member firm, to market its standard lines after the war.[60] An ambitious strategy for post-war reconstruction was presented by the management of the SMTC. Indeed, regardless of the military crisis of 1940, the management at this stage were already considering its post-war manufacturing programme, a proposal that was frustrated by insufficient allocations of skilled

---

[56] Churchill-Redman, CR-3, Minute Book, 11 August 1944.
[57] Herbert, Board of Directors, 1944-60, 31 October 1944; 29 March 1945; 26 March 1946.
[58] Miller, *Tools that Built a Business*, pp. 54, 56.
[59] Churchill-Redman, CR3, Minute Book, 3 December 1941; 11 August 1944, 16 August, 18 December 1945.
[60] ASQ34, Butler Machine Tool Co., Minutes of Directors' Meetings, 13 August 1943.

draughtsmen. In 1943 and 1944, however, with the Corporation's business extended into supplying the Soviet Union with machine tools, the management turned their attention to its post-war strategy, which included improvements in design, an increased range of standard machine tools, and the rationalisation of its dispersed manufacturing facilities. As its joint managing director, Bennie concluded, this was essential to meet 'post-war competition in export markets'.[61]

In the 1920s and 1930s, British machine tool exports had averaged 30 per cent of total output; by 1946 this had risen to 46 per cent.[62] Planning for post-war markets placed a heavy emphasis on exports, a priority for the industry after 1945, but they also made a vital contribution to the allied war effort, the industry exporting to dominion countries and also to Russia, a critical theatre of the war. Although exports were restricted by the Ministry of Supply during the war under Board of Trade licensing, estimates of machine tool requirements for export in 1943 rose to 17,500 machines, compared to 5,200 for 1942 (Table 6.2). At the end of 1942, Jones & Shipman was already exporting 21 per cent of its output, mainly to Russia, but also to New Zealand and Australia.[63] In December 1942, firms in the Halifax district reported a moderate amount of export work, mainly concentrated on 'Russia and British areas overseas'.[64] Export values by 1945, were more than double those of 1937, largely accounted for by the 68.2 per cent of exports destined for the Soviet Union (Table 6.7).

Table 6.7
Distribution of British Machine Tool Exports by Value, 1937 and 1945

	1937 (£000)	%	1945 (£000)	%
British India	196	9.1	197	4.2
British Africa	237	11.0	256	5.4
Australia	339	15.8	235	5.0
New Zealand	34	1.6	154	3.3
Canada[a]	31	1.4	-	-
Other British Countries	192	8.9	166	3.5
USSR	214	9.9	3,225	68.2
Japan	157	7.3	-	-
France	140	6.5	170	3.6
Belgium	32	1.5	3	0.1
Other Foreign Countries	580	27.0	320	6.8
Total	2,176	100	4,726	100

Source: PEP, Report on 'The Machine Tool Industry', p. 189.
Note: a. included for 1945 under other British.

---

[61] SMTC, Minute Book 1937-42, 6 February, 11 November 1940; 20 March 1941; UGD 175/2/1/2, Minute Book, 1942-47, 17 February 1943; 4 February 1944.
[62] PEP, Report on 'The Machine Tool Industry', p. 188.
[63] Miller, *Machines that Built a Business*, p. 52.
[64] *Machinist*, 5 December 1942, p. 218E.

As was shown in Chapter 5, the SMTC was a large exporter of machine tools to the Soviet Union before the outbreak of hostilities. In 1939, 82 per cent of the Corporation's exports were destined for Russia, a large trade that was seriously affected by the German-Soviet non-aggression pact of August 1939, the Board of Trade denying the company an export licence. Following the German invasion of the Soviet Union in June 1941, the company received extensive Russian orders, totalling £482,178 in March 1943, representing 43 per cent of total sales valued at £1,041,191. On paper, this was a lucrative trade but the Corporation's business with the Soviets reflected both the constraints of dealing with the highly bureaucratic Russian planning system, and the shortcomings of the Corporation to meet delivery dates. For example, in 1943, complex Soviet procedures for payment, together with rigid inspection of machines, led to delays in delivering Russian orders, a factor which retarded the corporation's own capability to supply domestic machines, especially to the Admiralty. By April 1944, Soviet orders amounted to £2 million, Russian officials threatening that they would cancel all pending orders if the SMTC did not meet delivery targets. The Soviet action was not unwarranted, the Corporation admitting that it was stretched to the limit to meet targets, a result of shortages of skilled labour. Moreover there were claims that machines destined for Russia were of low quality, and were under investigation by an internal sub-committee. Emphasising the importance of Soviet trade to the Corporation, the sub-committee concluded that they should appoint a new director of production and inspection to oversee Russian contracts, while at the same time, and insisted upon by the Soviet officials, the SMTC replaced the managing director of the Loudon Works. The Corporation's involvement with Soviet exports was constantly fraught with difficulties, the management complaining in July and November 1944 of the constant changes in specifications for Soviet machines, but also admitting that they could not meet their requests for the quality of castings used in the building of the machines. This, in turn, related to problems of centralising and co-ordinating activities between the various works of the company, and especially in supplying quality castings from its foundries.[65]

The Soviet market, of course, was to be restricted after the war, but by the last two years of the conflict British makers were looking ahead to a post-war environment in which they would compete successfully in international markets. During the war, British makers had adequately supplied the war effort with quantities of standard general-purpose machine tools, a product range which was deemed essential to meeting competition in traditional post-war markets. As the PEP report of 1948 concluded, the aim of British makers was to return to normality and compete in its traditional product lines. The report, however, contained a note of caution. Special gap machines, 'usually of the newer types', were, 'in most cases' imported, British alternatives being delivered 'more slowly and expensively'. The demands of war had acted to reinforce the British specialisation in standard general-purpose machines, retarded innovatory developments, and locked the industry into a trajectory, which directed it towards traditional lines. The

[65] SMTC, Minute Book, 1937-42, 20 November 1939; 27 May 1940; SMTC Minute Book, 1942-7, 19 August, 19 November 1943; 3 April, 18 July, 15 November 1944.

experience of the British machine tool industry challenges the conventional wisdom that war acts as a catalyst for innovatory change, and also demonstrates that machine tool firms remained as much concerned with their own individual interests as undertaking their patriotic duty to support the war effort. As new opportunities opened in the post-war era, questions were already being posed about the capability of the industry 'to maintain a sufficient supply of efficient equipment for the home market and to retain export markets'.[66]

---

[66] PEP, Report on 'The Machine Tool Industry', p. 291.

CHAPTER SEVEN

The Changing 'Game': The British Machine Tool Industry, 1945-60

'To understand the player there is a need to specify the game that is being played.'[1]

Introduction

Understanding how industries and firms act in the economic system requires us to explore the markets, the technology, and the institutions in which they evolve.[2] Such an approach to the study of the micro economy, and its relationship to macro economic change, is central to the work of Nelson, discussed in Chapter 1, who employs the metaphor of the 'player and the game'. Business development is an evolutionary process, and 'what individual firms [the 'players'] do often matters', but their actions are also shaped by the wider environment. Accepting this, requires us to 'specify the game' in which business firms act.[3] By the late 1950s, the 'game' facing British machine tool makers had considerably changed, and there was growing concern about the productivity record and competitive performance of the industry. Although small in comparison with other sectors of engineering, machine tools were the focus for two high profile reports by Melman (1959) and Mitchell (1960), which identified the industry as vitally important to the growth of manufacturing. These reports brought the industry under the public microscope, the Department of Scientific and Industrial Research (DSIR) confirming the opinion that it was a 'key strategic' sector for 'the modernisation and expansion of British industry'.[4] In the 1960s, the industry became embroiled in the general political debates on modernisation, which involved a set of institutional reforms to promote increased productivity in British manufacturing to ensure high and stable levels of economic growth. Modernisation involved a fundamental change in the rules of the 'game', but the origins of institutional reform are located prior to 1960, and in particular in the 1950s, when there was a growing realisation that the British machine tool industry was falling behind its Western European competitors. In the

---

[1] Nelson, 'The Role of Firms in Technical Advance', p. 165.
[2] See Wilson, *British Business History*, pp. 83-4, 87-8.
[3] Nelson, 'The Role of Firms in Technical Advance', pp. 165-8.
[4] Seymour Melman, Report on the Productivity of Operations in the Machine Tool Industry in Western Europe (European Productivity Agency, 1959); Mitchell Report, p. 26; Reports from Commissioners, Vol. XX, Session 1959-60 (cmnd. 1049), DSIR, *Report of the Research Council for 1959*, pp. 16-17, 22; *National Plan* (London, HMSO, 1965), p. 104.

immediate post-war period,[5] however, a window of opportunity opened up for the British industry, with the temporary collapse of Germany as a major competitor. This opportunity was short-lived, the Korean War stimulating the continental and particularly the West German machine tool sectors. As competition intensified in the 1950s, the competitive performance of the industry came under increasing scrutiny.

From 1945 to the Korean War

In April 1945, the British Intelligence Objectives Sub-committee began its investigation, in consultation with the MTTA of Germany's machine tool capabilities. Investigators observed that with the exception of developments in gear grinding machines, and with the recognition that 50 per cent of the industry was situated in the Soviet Zone, 'Nothing uncovered ... would suggest that technical development in machine tools since the outbreak of war had been of an outstanding nature'. In addition, the 'efficiency of production' was low, there being 'a surprising lack of jigs and fixtures and automatic machines in use', German makers relying on skilled labour which had been severely curtailed by conscription. The Sub-committee recognised that the German machine tool industry still presented a 'powerful means of production', asserting that it constituted a potential future threat to world security, second only to the German steel industry. Nevertheless, there would be a curtailment of the output of the German machine tool sector for some years to come.[6] The military and industrial collapse of Germany created an optimistic outlook in the boardrooms of Britain's machine tool companies. At Alfred Herbert, the directors could optimistically predict 'that the elimination of the German Machine Tool Industry should considerably improve our position for some years to come, both on the home and the export markets'. Adding to the euphoria, Sir Alfred concluded that 'if all members of the company continue to apply themselves energetically he did not feel unduly pessimistic regarding the future'.[7] How did the British respond to this opportunity?

By 1946, British machine tool output was 45,072 machines, valued at £20.2 million, well below the peak of war production in 1942. However, compared to 1937, a year precluding the effects of re-armament, when the value of output was £12.9 million, output values were 57 per cent higher by 1946. A year later, the number of machines produced had fallen slightly to 44,734, but in value terms had increased by 25 per cent over 1946 standing at £25.25 million.[8] Rising values, of

---

[5] For a discussion of the post-war reconstruction period see Pollard, *The Development of the British Economy*, pp. 235-73; A. Cairncross, *The Years of Recovery: British Economic Policy 1945-51* (London, Methuen, 1987), Ch. 1.

[6] British Intelligence Objectives Sub-committee, Final Report No. 641, *The German Machine Tool Industry* (London, HMSO, n.d.), pp. 2, 19, 21-3.

[7] 926/1/1/1, Alfred Herbert, Minute Book of the Board of Directors, 1944-60, 26 March 1946.

[8] PEP, Report on 'The Machine Tool Industry', p. 194.

course, reflected the increased price of machines as war controls ended, and the inflationary impact of rising material prices to the machine tool industry.[9] Nevertheless, in 1947, with the German industry contained, Britain was the largest producer in Western Europe, according to estimates from the Organisation for European Economic Co-operation (OEEC) shown in Table 7.1. Machine tool output in Western Europe was only 70 per cent of its 1938 level, while in the U.K. it was 96 per cent of the 1938 benchmark.[10] By 1947, the British industry exported 41 per cent of its value of output, exports totalling £10.4 million, the bulk of them exported to India and Commonwealth markets, as well as to France. This would seem a promising performance, but the PEP Report of 1948, registered disappointment, noting that the Board of Trade had set an export target of 50 per cent of output in 1946, a figure accepted by both the Ministry of Supply and the MTTA. Acknowledging that the industry was faced with adverse international markets from 1945 to 1949, 'exports restricted by currency difficulties and by the need for potential buyers to obtain an import licence', the report also observed that 'Countries which formerly imported machine tools are increasingly tending to manufacture their own, particularly the simpler types'. Simpler types referred to the concentration of British makers on general-purpose standard lines, and the report condemned the British industry for insufficient attention to the development of more special lines.[11]

Table 7.1
European Machine Tool Output for OEEC Participating Countries, 1947

	Output ($ millions)	%
OEEC Participating Countries	140	100
Trizone[a] or Germany	-	-
U.K.	36.7	26
Italy	21.0	15
Switzerland	22.8	16
France	20.8	15

Source: Ferney, 'The European Machine Tool Trade', pp. 246-8.
Note: a. Trizone represents the military zones of Germany occupied by Britain, France, and the U.S.A.

At the same time, the PEP report referred to the industry's productivity performance, and bottlenecks in machine tool supply. An estimate of net output per worker for 1946, based on weight, indicated that it was 30 per cent below that of 1937. Accepting that weight was an unreliable measurement of productivity, given the 'changes in the nature of the machines produced', they nevertheless cited the

---

[9] Ibid., p. 183.
[10] L. A. Ferney, 'The European Machine Tool Trade – OEEC, Paris', in *Engineer*, 8 September 1950, p. 246.
[11] PEP, Report on 'The Machine Tool Industry', pp. 188-9.

opinion of manufacturers to the effect 'that productivity in 1946 was substantially below the pre-war level'.[12] Despite observed deficiencies in the German machine tool industry, the productivity record of British makers raised serious doubts about their own capabilities to meet domestic and foreign demand. Partly, the industry was constrained in its capability to improve output performance. Labour legislation reduced the working week from 47 to 44 hours, and 'there was a widespread disinclination to work overtime', effectively reducing the working week for skilled operatives to 44 hours compared to 55 during the war. At the same time, shortages of materials, notably steel, electric motors and electrical control gears, continued to adversely affect the industry and raised production costs.[13] In March 1947, Sir Alfred informed the directors of the disappointing net profits of £362,741, resulting from his decision to keep machine prices down, not wishing to add to the inflationary bias in the economy. Nevertheless, the increased cost of materials and wages now forced him to increase prices, a factor which necessitated the industry at large to recognise the need for increased productivity to meet the challenge of post-war competition.[14]

Productivity was also a major issue for the management of Churchill-Redman. In 1946, the company acquired their Scotswood, Newcastle, factory from Vickers-Armstrong, to develop their new NV Lathes, concentrating their manufacture of licensed American Fay Lathes at their Halifax works. As the management observed, raising productivity was essential given increasing wages and material costs, which had forced machine prices upwards. In December 1946, the company had received orders valued at £423,900, compared to just £73,412 in December 1945, 75 per cent of the former destined for exports. With a healthy order book, the managing director, A. K. McCall, urged the need to raise productivity. Referring to the fact that gross profits on NV Lathes were as low as 4.3 per cent, and on Fay Lathes 2.16 per cent, he complained about absenteeism, 'inconsistent work effort', and rising overhead charges. As he concluded, 'Present day cost sheets compared most unfavourably with Pre-War Cost Sheets, the On Cost now being very high, due to the fact that it must be recovered on a much smaller number of hours worked'. There were also severe shortages of skilled workers, the company having only 12 apprentices compared to 60 before the war, and shortages of materials obstructed output. The company's problems, however, were not simply reducible to external supply constraints, McCall observing that they were producing too many machine ranges, and he recognised the need to rationalise the manufacturing programme to improve cost efficiency. By late 1947, he was berating his departmental managers over the 'inefficiency in production lines' resulting in lengthening delivery times and lost orders. In 1948, the chairman, John Gabriel, urged the need to modernise plant, and noted 'inefficiencies' because of the tendency to manufacture in small batches which were uneconomic.[15]

[12] Ibid., p. 182.

[13] Ibid., pp. 182-3.

[14] Herbert, Board of Directors, 1944-60, 10 March 1947.

[15] CR3, Churchill-Redman, Director's Minute Book, 1 May 1946; CR4, 11 July, 10 December 1946; 30 May 1947; 28 October 1948.

Similar 'inefficiencies' were observed at the SMTC, further complicated by the dispersed and un-coordinated operations of its manufacturing subsidiaries. Supply constraints of both materials and skilled labour frustrated management attempts to increase delivery times to customers, but there were also internal constraints relating to the inefficiency of its Albion Works, operated by Craig and Donald. In 1947, the management sent representatives to the U.S.A. to view machine tool design and high productivity production methods, and this led to a thorough review of the productivity of the Albion operations. An internal report in June on the operations concluded that the use of standard patterns was non-existent, boring capacity was insufficient, skilled fitters and operators were in short supply, the present bonus system was ineffective in providing an inducement to raising work effort, and technical problems in the supply of castings from their foundry increased machining costs. Added to this dismal catalogue, was the fact that design capability for new machines was inadequate and costly, and that senior management was not of 'the first class'. A follow up report in October concluded that inefficiencies were also due to obsolete plant and by 1949 management were condemning the limited response of the Albion management to the directives set by the main parent board.[16]

Deficiencies in the British machine tool industry were evident in the years immediately following the war, although the industry was also constrained by external factors which placed pressure on machine tool makers to supply both rising domestic and foreign demand. Recognising the problems of increasing productivity, the MTTA established in 1948 six panels in the principal machine tool building centres 'to promote by any means possible the greater efficiency of the industry'.[17] At a national level, Sir Stafford Cripps, the Chancellor of the Exchequer, and Paul Hoffman, of the Economic Co-operation Administration in the U.S.A., established the Anglo-American Council on Productivity.[18] This was crucial given that an OEEC report of 1949 forecast a substantial rise in machine tool output in Western Europe over levels pertaining in 1947, predicting that British machine tool output would double by 1952-3. Of more concern to the British industry was the fact that it also forecast a 'spectacular comeback' by the Trizone, which became the Federal Republic of Germany in 1949, estimating that by 1952 it would produce machine tools valued at $57 million, representing 23 per cent of OEEC output, compared to Britain's production of $51.4 million, 20 per cent. According to L. A. Ferney, who reviewed the OEEC report for *The Engineer*, the predictions may have been no more than 'expressions of pious hope', based on the assumption of 'a spectacular comeback by the Trizone'.[19] However, what

---

[16] SMTC, UGD 175/2/1/2-3; Minute Books, 30 January, 20 June 1947; 14 October 1948; 23 June, 25 August 1949.

[17] *Engineer*, 20 October 1950, p. 376.

[18] Miller, *Tools that Built a Business*, p. 62. Supply side reforms initiated by the post-war labour government have not been given sufficient attention. See J. Tomlinson, 'Mr. Atlee's Supply-Side Socialism', *Economic History Review*, Vol. 46, No. 1 (1993), pp. 1-22.

[19] Ferney, 'The European Machine Tool Trade', p. 246.

observers could not have foreseen in the late 1940s was the impact of the Korean War on the British and continental, especially German, machine tool industries.

Rearmament planning placed heavy demands on the British machine tool industry, a fact noted by the directors of the SMTC, who recognised that a 'great expansion overall was being proceeded with and a very heavy defence programme was contemplated'.[20] A House of Commons Select Committee on Estimates in 1950 predicted that the domestic demand for machine tools for 1951-2 and 1952-3 was £115 million, while estimates of the full capacity output of the industry in 1950 was £40 million, just under one-third of projected demand. Rearmament required a dynamic response to raise the productive capacity of the industry, a task that would not be easy to accomplish. The Select Committee observed: 'the abnormal demand for rearmament made it impossible for the machine tool industry to function with maximum efficiency, bearing in mind the diverse and conflicting claims which already exist for machine tools'.[21] The Minister of Supply, George Strauss, recognised that a gap would exist between demand and supply and that redirecting machine tools from other users, both at home and abroad, was a short-term solution to closing the gap, as was importation. Conscious of the need, however, to maintain exports in line with government policy to aid the balance of payments, the Ministry diverted tools from domestic users, Strauss projecting that in the 18 months from the spring of 1951 this would entail a 35% reduction in deliveries to domestic users. Car manufacturers, who were planning new models for 1951-3, which required specialist machine tools and frequent re-tooling, would suffer most.[22]

J. P. Reynolds, the new chairman of the SMTC, informed his directors in March 1951 of the appointment of a Director General of Machine Tools, heralding, he warned, 'Government directives and perhaps instructions to build certain machines exclusive of our own programme'.[23] A 'system of control', involving the co-ordination of machine tool supply, was announced by Strauss in May 1951, involving the establishment of six regional panels[24] advising on methods of reducing or deferring demand. Mapped onto the existing regional efficiency panels created by the MTTA in 1948, the new panels were chaired by a machine tool maker supported by 25 'experts' selected from within the industry and from the Institute of Production Engineers. The panels were to liaise with machine buyers under the guidance of the Regional Controller of the Ministry of Supply, to determine their need for a new machine, and were empowered to grant permission for delivery. At the same time, the Ministry instructed makers to provide two months' notice of completion to the MTTA, the Regional Controller then deciding on their allocation. Given the priority for rearmament, Strauss pleaded with the engineering industry 'to exercise self denial and restraint in attempting to acquire new tools, and to accept voluntarily the setting back of orders'. The engineering

[20] SMTC, Minute Books, 27 September 1950.

[21] See *Engineer*, 1 June 1951, p. 721; *Economist*, 24 February 1951, p. 447.

[22] *Economist*, 5 May 1951, p. 1,058; 12 May 1951, p. 1,177.

[23] SMTC, Minute Books, 15 March 1951.

[24] Birmingham, Coventry, Glasgow, Halifax, London, and Manchester.

industry, Strauss made very clear, could expect 'little relief' from re-directing machine exports, as most were destined for Commonwealth and NATO countries 'for the common defence effort or for their own essential needs'.[25] Governments, for example, in the Sterling Area 'were clamouring for more capital goods in the early 1950s'.[26] Exporters to the Eastern bloc, such as the SMTC, also felt the full weight of government restrictions, machines destined to Poland being restricted by Board of Trade licensing arrangements, the products eventually being diverted to Vickers-Armstrong and the Ministry of Supply.[27]

Table 7.2
Consumption of Machine Tools, 1950-54 (£ 000)

	A	B	C	D	E
	Home Deliveries	Imports	Consumption	Imports – % of Consumption	Exports
	Manufacturers Returns	Customs-Excise	A+B	B as % of C	Manufacturers Returns
1950	40,042	4,482	44,524	10	14,564
1951	48,590	13,462	62,052	22	16,611
1952	41,669	55,890	97,559	57	20,318
1953	45,334	43,391	88,725	49	20,810
1954	47,397	13,044	60,441	21	18,198

Source: MTTA, Machine Tool Directory, 1966, (Miln and Robinson, private), p. 17.

Table 7.3
New Orders for Machine Tools and Total Output, 1950-54 (£ 000)

	Home Orders	Export Orders	Total New Orders	Actual Total Output
1950				44,904
1951				48,590
1952	39,000	19,740	58,740	61,987
1953	39,276	12,444	51,720	66,133
1954	57,870	20,991	78,861	65,595

Source: MTTA, Machine Tool Directory, 1966, p. 18.

---

[25] *Engineer*, 11 May 1951, p. 613; SMTC, Minute Books, 20 June 1951.
[26] J. Singleton, 'The British Engineering Industry and Commonwealth Development in the Early 1950s', *Journal of European Economic History*, Vol. 30, No. 2 (2001), p. 402.
[27] SMTC, Minute Books, 9 November 1950; 11 January 1951.

Table 7.2 shows that in 1952 home deliveries of machine tools fell, and remained below the 1951 level even in 1954. In contrast, exports rose between 1950 and 1953, while imports contributed over half of domestic consumption during 1952-3. As domestic users were compelled to curtail consumption, an extensive programme of importing primarily filled the gap between demand and supply. This was despite the fact that domestic production exceeded total orders during 1952-3, and output had expanded by 47 per cent over 1950 levels (Table 7.3). From the outset, the defence programme called for 35,000 extra machine tools: 8,000 from direct orders to British makers, 7-8,000 diverted from existing domestic users over an 18-month period, leaving overseas countries to supply 19-20,000. By May 1951, the Ministry of Supply had placed orders abroad for approximately 18,000 machine tools, at an estimated cost of £39.3 million, the bulk of orders placed with the U.S.A. (Table 7.4).[28] Nevertheless, during the conflict the Ministry attempted to procure 'all the machine tools of the type required that were available in Western Europe'. One-third of orders to Europe went to Germany, and together with Switzerland and Italy, these countries received a major boost from Britain's defence programme.[29] During the 1950s, continental makers mounted a serious challenge to the British industry. The new Minister of Supply, Duncan Sandys, accepted in September 1952 that the export performance of the British machine tool industry 'would have been very much higher if it had not been necessary to reserve large numbers of machines for the defence programme'.[30]

Such a scenario was already of concern to the management of the SMTC in September 1950, when they observed that West German exporters 'were very much in evidence'.[31] By 1953 West Germany[32] had secured a significantly higher share of world exports in machine tools compared to Britain, and in 1955 the Swiss established a marginal, short-term lead over the British (Table 7.5). British rearmament alone, cannot explain the advance of the Europeans in export markets, but Korea was more of a help than a hindrance to the Western Europeans compared to Britain. British defence orders 'enabled' the German machine 'industry to recover a little faster than it might otherwise have done and perhaps fostered the growing tool industry in other countries'.[33] In the early 1950s, the window of opportunity was not shut tight, but the competitive challenge had changed the nature of the 'game'. If Britain were to secure a position amongst the world's leading producer nations, then machine makers would have to be alert to new developments in machine tool production, R&D, and design.

---

[28] *Economist*, 5 May 1951, pp. 1,058-9; 12 May 1951, p. 1,117.

[29] *Engineer*, 26 September 1952, p. 401.

[30] Ibid., p. 401.

[31] SMTC, Minute Books, 27 September 1950.

[32] For a discussion on the impact of Korea and the resurgence of German industry see T. Geiger, 'Like a Phoenix from the Ashes: West Germany's Return to the European Markets 1945-58', *European Contemporary History*, Vol. 3 (1994), pp. 337-53.

[33] *Economist*, 27 September 1952, pp. 771-2.

Table 7.4
Ministry of Supply: Foreign Orders for Machine Tools, May 1951[a]

U.S.A.	6,650
Federal Republic of Germany	3,150
France	1,862
Switzerland	1,770
Italy	1,550
Belgium	1,041

Source: *Engineer*, 11 May 1951, p. 613.
Note: a. A small quantity was also ordered from Sweden and Denmark.

Table 7.5
World Share of Exports in Machine Tools (Excluding U.S.S.R., Eastern Europe and China), 1953-58 (%)

	1953	1955	1957	1958	Change
U.K.	14.6	15.8	15.3	14.2	-0.4
U.S.A.	33.5	28.3	26.9	25.7	-7.8
West Germany	23.8	26.7	30.5	31.9	+8.1
Switzerland	11.2	15.9	13.4	14.0	+2.8

Source: *Engineer*, 29 January 1960, p. 161.

Machine Tools and Productivity in the 1950s

A growing awareness of the need to raise industrial productivity, and match accelerating technological competition, especially from Western Europe, was the conditions that defined the 'game' in the 1950s. In comparison with our main European rivals, British productivity growth was less than impressive,[34] and even in the early 1950s, the Conservatives were acutely aware of the problems of relative decline.[35] According to Ben Lockspier, Secretary to the DSIR, in 1954 a great productivity campaign was in motion throughout the country, 'bringing all concerned in industry closer together for a common purpose'.[36] Machine makers

---

[34] See S. N. Broadberry, *The Productivity Race: British Manufacturing Industry in International Perspective, 1850-1990* (Cambridge, Cambridge University Press, 1997), p. 15; S. N. Broadberry and N. F. R. Crafts, 'Competition and Innovation in 1950s Britain', *Business History*, Vol. 43, No. 1 (2001), pp. 97-118; S. N. Broadberry and N. F. R. Crafts, 'British Economic Performance and Policy in the Early Post-war Years', *Business History*, Vol. 38, No. 4 (1996); N. F. R. Crafts, *Britain's Relative Economic Decline, 1870-1995* (Oxford, Oxford University Press, 1997), p. 25; Pollard, *Wasting*, p. 50.

[35] See J. Tomlinson, 'Inventing Decline', pp. 731-57.

[36] Cited in *Engineer*, 26 November 1954, p. 757.

such as John Gabriel, chairman of Charles Churchill & Co., were well aware of the future competitive challenge. In his Presidential address to the MTTA in 1950, he claimed that 'Production efficiency begins at home' with the objective of modernising machine tools to advance industrial 'efficiency'.[37] What were the sources of productivity growth that would promote increasing efficiency? Nelson identifies three key sources of productivity growth: 'technological advance, capital growth, and rising educational attainment'. The sources of growth are 'complimentary, in the sense that an increase of any one raises the marginal contribution of the others', and 'because of this, forces that lead to the augmentation of any one are likely to stimulate an increase in the others'.[38] Productivity advance in the 1950s was associated with the capabilities of the industry to exploit these sources of growth.

Table 7.6
Increase in Output, Employment and Output per Head, 1954-64 (%)

Industry	1954-60	1960-4
Machine Tools:		
Output	2.0	2.0
Employment	1.4	3.0
Output per head	0.7	-1.0
Mechanical Engineering:		
Output	2.8	4.1
Employment	1.9	0.9
Output per head	0.9	3.1
Motor Vehicles & Cycles:		
Output	8.4	4.7
Employment	3.3	1.7
Output per head	4.9	3.0

Source: *National Plan*, 1965, p. 28.

There is no clear consensus on productivity levels in the industry during the 1950s. *The Times Bulletin for Industry*, cited by *The Engineer*, estimated output per head between 1950 and 1957 at 3.6 per cent per annum, calculated from an estimated increase in the value of total output, adjusted for prices, of 50 per cent between 1950 and 1957, and an increase in the number employed in the industry of 22 per cent. Comparative to other engineering sectors the industry seemed to perform adequately, the combined growth in output per head for metals,

---

[37] Cited in *Engineer*, 20 October 1950, p. 376.
[38] Nelson, *The Sources of Economic Growth*, p. 42.

engineering and vehicles being only about one-half of that for machine tools. However, the German machine tool industry outpaced that of Britain, and this was particularly the case from the mid-1950s.[39] Later estimates, calculated for the Labour Government's National Plan of 1965, albeit over a different time-period, showed a weaker productivity performance for the industry than that given by the *Times*. In particular, productivity growth was lower than in mechanical engineering and motor vehicles between 1954 and 1960, and during 1960-64 output per head was negative (Table 7.6). Statistical inconsistencies in the official record remain. The National Plan provided alternative figures compiled from MTTA estimates of employment in the industry, which gave a positive estimate for the growth of output per head of 0.3 per cent per annum, 1960-64.[40] Productivity estimates are far from robust, but there was a marked slowing down in output per head at the end of the 1950s, and this became a matter of concern to the industry's leaders, as well as to industrial users of machine tools and to the government itself. Recalling Nelson's three sources of productivity growth, 'technological advance, educational achievement and resources, and capital growth, the British machine tool industry will now be examined in relation to these parameters.

Technological Advance in the 1950s

As early as 1952 buyers visiting the machine tool exhibitions at Olympia and Hanover could 'inspect a remarkable array of equipment from the countries now competing for his favour'. The West German machine tool industry was 'now nearly as large as the whole German industry before the war', and the technical design and quality of 'its tools are first rate, comparing with the other two leading producers, Britain and America'.[41] British makers were well aware of the challenge and that matching foreign capabilities in technical design and quality were essential to competitive success. How well did they respond to the technological challenge? A Productivity Team of 15 machine tool makers, led by R. D. G. Ryder of Thomas Ryder & Sons, Bolton, visited a number of British and American machine tool firms in 1952. Working under the direction of the Anglo-American Council on Productivity and the Economic Co-operation Administration, the Team's remit was to compare British and American production systems, and to report on the feasibility of adopting American methods to raise British productivity.[42] The report, published in 1953, concluded that there appeared to be no 'outstanding differences' between the American and British industries and in neither country was productivity as high as it reasonably should be. Machine tool

---

[39] *Engineer*, 6 June 1958, p. 866.

[40] *National Plan*, 1965, p. 95.

[41] *Economist*, 27 September 1952, p. 772.

[42] For an examination of American assistance on productivity, and the negative reaction of British managers, see N. Tiratsoo, and T. R. Gourvish, '"Making It Like in Detroit": British Managers and American Productivity Methods', *Business and Economic History*, Vol. 25, No. 1 (1996).

prices in both countries were too high, which allegedly constrained sales, and they both faced the danger of lost market share unless they raised productivity.[43] Indeed, both countries experienced falls in export shares during the 1950s (Table 7.5).

Nevertheless, despite common trends across the two countries, the Productivity Team inferred that productivity in American machine shops was on average higher in the U.S. than in the U.K., although no 'statistical means of comparing ... productivity' was available. Higher American productivity was generally perceived as primarily 'a result of wider and better application of the science of design for production', reinforced by a 'more realistic approach to accuracy and finish; ... better machinability of the steels and cast iron used; more accurate balancing of plant capacity and planned load; and better servicing of the machine operations'.[44] The management of workshop practices, and its effect on efficiency was a key factor recognised by the management of the SMTC in the early 1950s. Its Management Council, formed in 1951 to deal with 'local problems' at the Corporation's subsidiaries, reported in 1953 that the difficulties experienced in co-ordinating and balancing production of new machines across the various works was partly due to the failure to standardise design practices. There was no 'Corporation Standard' design 'on a long-term basis', and instruction manuals to users varied between the different subsidiary companies. In 1954, the Corporation established a design and development department to induce central co-ordination and control, but problems persisted, which led to delays in bringing new designs into production. As the management noted in 1955, prices of planers for the automobile industry were selling at £2,000 higher than those of their competitors. Reviewing a poor performance on deliveries due to delays in the production line in 1956, the management concluded that they should review the efficiency of the drawing office, methods of ordering components, and the whole system of progressing materials through the works. Design and production problems persisted, the management observing in 1957 that their methods for designing a new range of hydraulic machines had not produced satisfactory cost reductions, there being a lack of co-operation between the project designer, chief draughtsman and the production manager. There was a 'need for closer co-ordination between designers and the works and for leadership in design as a whole', for 'co-operation and administration to avoid duplication'. Limited design capabilities rebounded on the quality of its service to overseas customers. The Corporation's Export Sub-committee listed, amongst its complaints, a failure to provide sufficient and standardised specifications to either agents or customers, and overall there was 'no definite programme directed to concentrate on a selected range for export'.[45]

---

[43] *Productivity Team Report*, p. 46; 'Productivity Team Report on Metalworking Machine-Tools', in *Engineer*, 30 January 1953, p. 185.

[44] *Productivity Team Report*, 1953, p. 46; 'Productivity Team Report', in *Engineer*, 30 January 1953, p. 185.

[45] SMTC, Minute Books, 6 September 1951; 18 November, 16 December 1952; 17 February, 16 November 1954; 15 February, 15 March, 20 September 1955; 19 February, 25 April, 10 September, 21 November 1957.

Efficiency problems were also evident at Churchill-Redman, and again it would seem that the capabilities of firms were insufficiently co-ordinated to support technological development. In 1951, R. Mayfield, the Service Engineer of the Cleveland Hobbing Co, visited the Scotswood Division of the company, which manufactured machines for Vauxhall Motors under licence from Cleveland. Mayfield concluded that there were 'technical deficiencies in production' and confusion between designers and production engineers on the shop floor. This led to delays in production lines and a reduction in quality. In response to these allegations, McCall and Gabriel admitted that designers and production engineers 'did not get together on the problem'. In 1953, Gabriel lambasted the management, claiming that they still had no definite production policy for introducing new machines. In a series of recommendations, he gave particular attention to collaboration between the design and production departments during the design stage, the building of prototypes for customer trials, and a greater focus on planning, time study, work setting and costing.[46] Certainly, compared to European makers, lower levels of technical efficiency by British makers led to longer delivery times and delays in the dispatch of machines.[47] These examples remind us that technological change can take a variety of forms, and increases in productivity are not simply reducible to spectacular breakthroughs, but incremental changes in the production system are also an important part of the story.[48]

Aware of the need to advance Britain's technical capabilities in machine tools, the Anglo-American Council on Productivity, following discussions on the findings of the Productivity Team report of 1953, published a set of recommendations covering short, medium and long-term objectives. These ranged from suggestions to revert to war-time paint work and metal finishing for individual machine tools to a call for wholesale rationalisation leading to a significant reduction in 'the number of independent companies in the industry'. Although recognising that rationalisation would raise 'The taunt of monopoly', there was nevertheless a firm commitment to the assumed advantages of higher degrees of standardisation and concentration, providing the means to facilitate greater technical efficiency in the industry, which the absorption and amalgamation of firms would enable. Larger business units, the Council concluded, would ensure higher production efficiency and create opportunities for increased standardisation, and this in turn would provide a rising curve of technological development. Big business would also counter a business culture which created amongst machine tool firms a jealousy of their 'individuality and independence', and which tended to pay no more than 'lip service to any idea of industry-wide standardisation and rationalisation, to the great detriment of productivity and exasperation of the

---

[46] CR3, Churchill-Redman, Minute Book, 28 November 1951; 8 December 1953.

[47] *Economist*, 27 September 1952, pp. 771-2.

[48] See N. Rosenberg, *Exploring the Black Box: Technology, Economics and History* (Cambridge, Cambridge University Press, 1994), p. 15; D. C. Mowery and N. Rosenberg, *Paths of Innovation: Technological Change in Twentieth Century America* (Cambridge, Cambridge University Press, 1998), Ch. 1.

customer'.[49] In response to these recommendations, the industry went on the defensive. For example, the David Brown Machine Tool Co., Manchester, a firm with a long track-record of technical innovation, agreed with 'certain of the suggestions', but strongly rejected several criticisms of British machine tool manufacturing methods. In particular, the firm criticised the comparative methodology of the report, pointing out that makers in Britain and America faced very different markets. American makers concentrated output largely on the domestic market, exporting only 15 per cent of their production, while British makers sent abroad over one-third of their output. Consequently, British makers had to develop, design and produce their machine tools to accommodate the needs of foreign as well as domestic users.[50]

At the industrial level, the MTTA established a sub-committee to examine the Anglo-American report, considering that it contained 'conclusions and recommendations ... of a particular controversial nature'. Reporting in June 1953, the sub-committee applauded 'the dissemination of technical information contained in the productivity report to the industry', but concluded that references to inefficiency and consequently high prices for British machine tools were misleading. The MTTA, however, reserved its major offensive for an assault on the principles of rationalisation. Recommendations for a considerable reduction of the number of independent firms in the industry, it was 'strongly felt .... should not have been included tending, as it does, to suggest a certain degree of tolerance for the idea of the establishment of a monopoly'.[51] The 'Taunt of monopoly' was, in fact, the very reaction that the Council had predicted,[52] but the productivity report had clearly touched a raw nerve in an industry comprising large numbers of small producers. Indeed, the response of the MTTA, and its fears over monopoly, appear to be more to do with entrenched conservatism, aimed at bolstering the status quo, rather than genuine alarm that the industry's competitive structure was about to be substituted by monopolistic or oligopolistic business enterprise. Moreover, the sub-committee, adopting a different interpretation of rationalisation,[53] defended the industry by arguing that most firms had 'to some extent rationalised their production by specialising in a certain type of machine tool', and this was in sharp contrast to the recent history of the industry 'when most machine tool manufacturers will produce almost any kind of machine tool'. The sub-committee also rejected suggestions that firms might specialise in the production of machine tool components, while others might concentrate on the 'assembly of standard machines'. They firmly stated that recommendations for rationalisation were simply not 'possible of implementation'.[54]

---

[49] *Productivity Team Report*, 1953, pp. 46-8.

[50] *Engineer*, 26 June 1953, p. 903.

[51] *Engineer*, 26 June 1953, pp. 903-4.

[52] *Productivity Team Report*, 1953, p. 51.

[53] See Wilson, *British Business History*, pp. 141-2, for a discussion of different approaches to the idea of rationalisation.

[54] *Engineer*, 26 June 1953, pp. 903-4.

Industry-wide initiatives to co-ordinate technological development did not occur until the end of the 1950s, with the debates over modernisation and the creation of a research association for the industry. A fragmented industrial structure, bolstered by a business culture of independence, militated against rationalisation and co-operation. This was certainly the conclusion of the Mitchell Report of 1960, an impression confirmed by the MTTA who referred to large numbers of small firms who were 'handicapped when it comes to reducing costs of production, rationalising design, and marketing their products in the most efficient manner'.[55] The hostile reaction to rationalisation reflected a business structure typified by the continued survival of large numbers of small-scale independent firms. Accurate figures for the number of firms in the industry are not possible, because definitions of machine tool makers are imprecise, but estimates place the number of firms in the 1950s at 350 to 400. As a process of rationalisation and concentration did not begin to accelerate until the 1960s, we can assume that these figures provide a reasonable benchmark. From 1945 to the late 1950s, the size structure of firms remained more or less constant, with 'a small number of establishments with more than 300 employees and a large number with less than 300'. Estimates of the contribution of the five largest firms to total output for 1963 indicate a low level of concentration of just 26 per cent. Private limited companies were also common, signifying a close relationship between ownership and control. For example, even in the 20 recorded companies with an issued capital of £800,000 each, 'family holdings' were a prominent feature of governance. Large numbers of small, often family controlled firms characterised the industry and, in 1959, there were 200 firms with an average turnover of only £40,000 per annum. The industry had changed little in its structure from the 1920s.[56]

A small-scale business structure, and the persistence of family firms, was not unique to Britain in the 1950s, and some of these small British makers were recognised as highly specialist and innovative. Long established enterprises such as James Archdale, Kitchen & Wade, William Asquith, Craven Bros., James Butler, H. W. Kearns, George Richards, had accumulated technological knowledge that provided them with a high reputation in the industry. Britain could also boast the largest machine tool organisation in the world in the shape of Alfred Herbert.[57] To provide an impressionistic picture of the broad pattern of technological advancement in design in the industry in the 1950s a list was compiled of machine tool firms who were featured in *The Engineer* between 1950 and 1958 in short articles or reports on either new machines and/or ones incorporating improvements. The data does need to be treated with caution, as machine tool

---

[55] Mitchell Report, p. 21; MTTA, Council Minute Books, 1946-70, 6 October 1960, Report on British Machine Tool Exports.

[56] *Productivity Team Report*, p. 5; Mitchell Report, p. 26; Evans, 'Some Problems of Growth', pp. 46-7; Breeley and Troup, 'The Machine Tool Industry', p. 363; Broadberry and Crafts, 'Competition and Innovation', p. 3; MTTA, Machine Tool Directory, 1966, pp. 12-13.

[57] *Economist*, 23 June 1960, p. 848; 10 January 1963, p. 76; *Machine Tool Review)*, Vol. 43, 1955, p. 113; Vol. 48, 1960, p. 1; Vol. 49, 1961, p. 7.

firms often combined manufacturing with the marketing and selling of other firms' products, particularly of foreign make. They also produced machines under licence. Therefore, it was not always possible to distinguish between the different types of machine tools. Nevertheless, the data does provide a rough indicator of the technological leaders in the machine tool industry of the 1950s.

Table 7.7
Indicator of Technical Advance in the British Machine Tool Industry, 1950-58

	Number of References in *Engineer* relating to Technical Details of New or Improved Machine Tools					
	1	2	3	4	5+	10+
No. Firms	134	62	39	26	18	7

Source: *Engineer*, 1950-58.

Table 7.8
Technical Leaders in the British Machine Tool Industry in the 1950s

Firm	10+ References in *Engineer*	Location
Alfred Herbert Ltd.	22	Coventry
BSA Tools Ltd.	12	Birmingham
A. C. Wickman & Co.	11	Coventry
Rockwell Machine Tool Co.[a]	11	Wembley
Adcock & Shipley	10	Leicester
David Brown Machine Tool Co. Ltd.	10	Manchester/Huddersfield
Kitchen & Wade	10	Halifax

Note: a. Rockwell was largely a merchanting firm, and the figures do exaggerate its technical leadership.

Table 7.7 summarises the full survey, and Table 7.8 lists the most dynamic technical leaders in the industry with 10+ references. There is a case to suggest that if a firm was technically progressive then the journal should have cited it for more than one year between 1950 and 1958. As *The Engineer* was published in two volumes for each year, a firm with three references had to be cited in more than one year, and consequently three listings would appear to be a reasonable cut-off point. This would put the number of technically progressive firms at 39, accounting for 10 per cent of the industry's estimated population of 400 firms. It was possible that firms with two references could have been cited in the journal in separate years, and this was the case for 19 of the 62 firms falling into this category. According to this arbitrary categorisation, 58 firms (19+39) could be described as technically progressive as indicated by the benchmark of 3 references, and this represented approximately 14-15 per cent of the total number of firms in the industry. The small number of firms recorded 10+ times in Table 7.7 appears to confirm a survey conducted by the Noble & Lowdns Finance Co. Ltd. in 1955, which concluded 'that the bulk of technological development' in the industry 'was being carried out by a relatively few manufacturers who are willing to undertake expensive R&D work'.[58] There would seem to be a core of technically progressive firms, but there is an issue whether this was sufficient to drive the British machine tool industry forward and maintain its competitive advantage during a decade that witnessed a rapid acceleration of international competition.

Machine makers had to face the 'game' of technological advance; consequently, the 'technological frontier' in the 1950s needs to be defined, and this raises the issue of the industry's R&D performance. In terms of locating the technological frontier, *The Economist* claimed in 1952 that a key feature of 'progress' in the design of machine tools involved 'the extension of automatic control, and in particular copying systems and their application to existing ranges of machines and a more radical approach to cutting methods'.[59] In the same year, in its survey of the International Machine Tool Exhibition at Olympia, the correspondent of *The Engineer* observed that:

> Particularly noticeable is the degree to which copying methods are being adapted on a steadily widening range of machines ... Hydraulic, electrical and electronic controls are being used to an increasing extent, and these forms of control are now generally designed and built as a fundamental working part of the machine and not as special or separate units of occasional use.

The correspondent confirmed that innovations in cutting tool materials, especially the use of tungsten carbide, were an 'important factor influencing the design of the modern machine tool'. Taking a positive view of the British industry, he asserted that makers were 'keeping their designs well abreast of modern requirements and are proving capable of providing equipment equally to or better than the best made abroad'.[60]

To assess the new technological 'game' facing the industry, and in response to a Board of Trade questionnaire on 'Automation and Engineering', the MTTA established a Sub-Committee on Automation in 1956, chaired by James Archdale, and constituting three machine tool firms, William Asquith Ltd., BSA Tools Ltd., Wickman Ltd., and two electronics firms, Ferranti and British Thomson-Houston. It identified three fields of application of automation and control systems to machine tools. First, there were techniques of greater mechanisation by transfer machines or by linking machine tools in automatic production lines or by automatic handling and assembly. A leading firm in this technology was James Archdale who had introduced the first transfer machine in the U.K. in 1924, and specialised in automatic machines for component production in the automobile industry. Second, there were techniques of increasing automatic

---

[58] *Engineering*, 16 December 1955, p. 857.
[59] *Economist*, 6 December 1952, p. 1,021.
[60] *Engineer*, 12 September 1952, p 860.

control over manufacturing processes, and non-human control of individual machines. By the mid-1950s, these control systems were influenced by developments in electronic or numerical control (NC), and its application to machine tools. Numerically controlled machine tools (NCMTs) attracted the interest of a number of electronic firms, for example, Ferranti, British Thomson-Houston, and EMI, as well as traditional machine tool makers such as Alfred Herbert. Third, there were techniques in office work involving the use of electronic data processing equipment. The Sub-Committee considered the first two areas of technical development to be the most important, especially automatic control systems that involved the deployment of NC systems. By the mid-1950s, according to the Sub-Committee, the British machine tool industry was 'producing on a small scale machines embodying continuous profile control from data prepared by a computer, and also positional control by automatic coordinate settings, for example, for drilling, boring and facing'. This, it claimed, was a new development distinct from the copying process, which had become 'virtually ... standard machine tool practice, involving the use of physical models, as distinct from operations dictated from numerical information'. At this stage of development, the principal users of NCMTs were the aircraft industry, aero-engine manufacturers, and the aircraft accessories industry, and to a much smaller extent, involving single deliveries, certain sections of mechanical engineering. The present usage of NC was small, but the Sub-Committee remained positive about its potential. 'Over the next five years', it was concluded, capacity utilisation for conventional machine tools might 'be turned over to the production of automatic equipment', and it was anticipated that the demand for the application of NC to machine tools would be very large, with the potential to expand 'ten-fold' by 1961.[61]

In the mid-1950s, the industry itself was well aware of the technological frontier, and the trade press urged the industry to respond. *The Engineer* implored that unless users were prepared to depend on a large proportion of machine tools incorporating 'programme control' being imported from abroad, then the British industry would need to prioritise their design 'so that future demand can be met'. To ignore this would be sheer 'folly', as evidenced by the range of NCMT's displayed at continental and American exhibitions. *The Engineer* remained confident, however, that British makers were well aware of the technological challenge that they faced.[62] A number of British firms, such as Alfred Herbert, W. E. Sykes, William Asquith, Wickman & Co., Churchill Machine Tool Co., George Richards, and James Archdale responded by incorporating programme control into their machine tool designs, alongside their conventional product range.[63] By 1960, however, only Marwin & Co., founded in that year, concentrated solely on

[61] MTTA, Council Minute Book, 1, 28 November 1956; *Archdale Machine Tools 1868-1948* (Birmingham, James Archdale & Co., 1948); A. Astrop, *The Rise and Fall of Coventry's Machine Tool Industry* (Warwickshire, Warwickshire Industrial Archaeology Society, 2003), p. 19; *Machine Tool Review*, Vol. 43, 1955; Vol. 44, p. 8.

[62] *Engineer*, 16 December 1955, p. 858.

[63] *Engineer*, 21 August 1953, p. 420; 24 June 1954, p. 935; 22 June 1956, pp. 711-12, 715; 4 October 1957, p. 505.

NCMT's in Britain.[64] There were also a number of collaborative projects between machine makers and electronics firms to develop NC technology. For example, Webster & Bennett with the Lancashire Dynamo and Electrical Co., the Newall Engineering Group, Peterborough, with British Thomson-Houston, Coventry Gauge & Tool with the Mullard Research Laboratory, London, Craven Bros. and H. W. Kearns with British Thomson-Houston.[65] The list is not exhaustive, but what was more significant was that electronic firms also by-passed conventional machine tool firms and developed their own NC systems and machines. For example, in 1959 Ferranti introduced a system 'designed to provide simple, reliable and easily maintained equipment', and sold at a price affordable by both small and large engineering firms. The system comprised a transistor-hydraulic continuous control and a numerical control for positioning the work. Ferranti also collaborated with the Fairey Aviation Co. to develop a NCMT for the three-dimensional milling of aircraft components. Initiating an 'extensive R&D programme' to assess a variety of control systems, Fairey decided that the most suitable was the 'Ferranti Digital System', which utilised a computer 'to process the planning information'. Combining Fairey knowledge of aircraft construction engineering with Ferranti's investment in R&D on NC, led to the manufacture of a machine tool with a high degree of accuracy and effective cutting-engine that could mill aircraft components from metal slabs up to eight feet high and 25 feet long.[66]

Collaborative projects, such as this, were an embarrassment to the MTTA in 1956, who expressed the 'feeling that the ... industry had done little to help aero-engine manufacturers'. Defending its members against a lack of initiative, the Association claimed that a huge R&D programme would be required, particularly for milling, grinding and polishing machines for turbine compressor blades, but 'the ultimate demand ... would be extremely small'. High development costs, in a limited market, justified inaction, although the MTTA accepted the need for discussions with the new Director of Aircraft Production.[67] The limited market potential for NC was a view firmly entrenched in the industry by the end of the 1950s. In the early 1960s *The Machine Tool Review*, published by Alfred Herbert, commented on the application of programme controlled, tape or punch card systems, to general-purpose machines, but noted that the higher costs of these machines created a resistance on the part of users. Further, NC was appropriate to batch production systems, rather than to mass production methods, and consequently there was a limited demand from automobile and other mass production industries. While there was a recognition that demand for NC would increase, the limited scope of its application conditioned firms to continue 'the development of more orthodox machines ... since there will always be a use for them in many production schedules'.[68]

---

[64] *Engineer*, 19 February 1970, p. 47.
[65] *Engineer*, 13 January 1956, pp. 49, 52; 22 June 1956, p. 719; 29 June 1956, pp. 759, 771.
[66] *Engineer*, 9 May 1958, pp. 696-7; 28 August 1959, p. 137,
[67] MTTA, Council Minute Book, 27 September 1956.
[68] *Machine Tool Review*, Vol. 48, 1960, p. 96; Vol. 49, 1961, p. 60.

The industry's response to NC, it can be argued, displayed a short-term outlook, and this criticism was certainly levelled at the industry in the 1960s. However, in the 1950s the industry faced criticism from four interrelated directions. There were, firstly, general complaints that machine tool firms acted as agents or factorers for foreign makers, particularly for high technology machine tools actively promoted in the British market. As was shown in earlier chapters, Herbert's had a major factoring business, and a number of other machine tool firms also took an active role in pushing foreign products. For example, Charles Churchill & Co. had built a reputation as a factorer of foreign machine tools, and the concern also held manufacturing rights for American machines produced by its subsidiary Churchill-Redman. In the 1950s, the company also became agents for the Scharmann Gmbh of Rheydlt in Germany, whose boring machine incorporated programme control and full automatic positioning. Moreover, they also acted as agents for the Cleveland Hobbing Machine Co., supplying multi-spindle hobbing machines to Austin and Vauxhall, as well as acquiring manufacturing agreements for Churchill-Redman to manufacture these machines.[69] Wickman & Co. of Coventry was also heavily engaged in factoring. At the 1955 German Machine Tool Exhibition in Hanover there were a 'number of interesting applications of programme control', not least that developed by Gerb Heller Gmbh of Nuertingen, whose machine tools were handled in the U.K. by Wickman's. At Olympia in 1956 the company displayed 'over 100' machines, 'mainly' of German and American origin.[70] Factoring was a major activity of British machine tool manufacturers, as testified to by Hugh Clausen, one of Britain's leading design engineers. Speaking to the Institute of Engineering Designers in 1958, he complained that:

> Nearly all the British machine tool makers act as agents for foreign firms, and meet this country's needs for those [high technology] and many other precision machine tools, from foreign sources, evidently viewing the rake-off on the sale of foreign machines as being as well earned as the profits from the sale of a British designed and built machine.

Clausen believed that there was too little technical representation at the higher management levels, and that the British paid too little attention to creative design.[71] Such criticisms were to have significant implications for the profile of British foreign trade in machine tools, a problem that we will subsequently return to.

Factoring foreign special-purpose machine tools was symptomatic of Britain's long commitment to general-purpose machines, and this opened up a second line of criticism concerning the industry's conservative attitude towards design. The British industry appeared to follow a traditional technological

[69] *Engineer*, 30 September 1955, p. 473; CR4, Churchill-Redman, Minute Book, 17 August 1954; 6 October 1955; Jeremy, 'Gabriel, John Beresford Stuart', pp. 456-8; 'Charles Churchill 1865-1965', p. 112.
[70] *Engineer*, 23 September 1955, p. 445; 22 June 1956, p. 717.
[71] *Engineer*, 11 April 1958, p. 541.

trajectory and the majority of firms continued to concentrate on standard general-purpose machines, which substituted for a more scientific and innovative approach, rather than special-purpose machines. It was generally accepted that the industry was 'second to none in the production of a wide range of standard machines', but as *The Engineer* asked in 1955, was 'it safe to concentrate so fully on bread and butter lines, lacking the stimulus to new thought that a constant development of new lines brings with it?'[72] Clausen provided an answer to this question in 1958, when he observed that the British industry had failed to respond to the need for high inputs of scientific and engineering design, and had neglected the theoretical side of the business compared to the continent. He also asserted that the British aircraft and defence industries, the largest purchasers of special-purpose machine tools incorporating numerical programming, were 'dependent ... on foreign designed and built machine tools'. Comparative British equipment simply did not exist, and the tool rooms of most up-to-date engineering workshops, 'where real precision is needed, are mainly equipped with machines from Switzerland, America and Germany'.[73] This replicates the complaints made against the industry during the inter-war years, and reinforces the notion of a built-in path dependency associated with the production of general-purpose machine tools. There is a defence of the industry. The pattern of supply described by Clausen reflected prevailing demand conditions by domestic engineering industries, which placed constraints on the design capabilities of makers. In 1959 *The Machine Tool Review* categorised the machine tool industry into two groups: those making 'general-purpose machines which are the backbone of engineering', and could be adapted to a wide variety of uses, and those making special-purpose machines 'either to perform one type of operation or to produce one particular component'. Given the historical evolution of British engineering, with its concentration on producing a variety of non-standardised products, 'the greatest volume of demand' was for general-purpose machines, and this reflected the low number of machine makers concentrating on special types. According to the *Review*, the function of the British maker was to 'adapt' general-purpose machine tools to the requirements of domestic users, and at the same time to allow British engineers to import special-purpose machines from abroad, a long-term feature of the industry.[74]

British engineering requirements may well have distorted the pattern of demand for high technology machine tools but, by the late 1950s, the machine tool industry confronted severe criticism about its limitations in incorporating new designs and machining methods to general-purpose machines. The Economic Policy Committee of the MTTA in 1960 referred to the views of a 'major' British machine tool user that domestic makers 'were falling short by comparison with their opposite numbers abroad', both in terms of developments in special-purpose machinery and in the adoption of new designs to general-purpose machines. This was taken further in a confidential MTTA Report on British Machine Tool Exports, a wide ranging survey, which the President assured members would

[72] *Engineer*, 16 December 1955, pp. 857-8.

[73] *Engineer*, 11 April 1958, p. 541.

[74] *Machine Tool Review*, Vol. 47, 1959, p. 25.

remain unpublished. In an investigation of a number of large engineering works, there was 'a conviction based on experience that for far too high a proportion of their most modern equipment they were forced to go abroad'. In particular, German makers were far more orientated to 'meeting customer needs and modifying standard designs'.[75] Such shortcomings opened up a third line of criticism against the industry: its performance in export markets and its loss of international status.

The bulk of U.K. imports came from Germany, Switzerland, and the U.S.A., consisting of 'mainly high performance and high precision advanced types of special machine tools'. In contrast, British exports tended to be 'mainly standard' types that were shipped predominately 'to the Commonwealth and less industrial nations'. For example, by 1963 90 per cent of all British machine tool imports came from the U.S.A., West Germany, Switzerland, Italy and France, while Britain sold only 20 per cent of their exports to these markets, the bulk of British sales going to India, Australia and South Africa, representing a clear trend of exports to Commonwealth markets.[76] This export trend mirrored that of the British motor vehicle industry and that of general engineering.[77] Reliance on the Commonwealth reflected a pattern of trade stretching back to the late nineteenth century, reinforced during the 1930s by the Ottawa System, and extending after the war through the Sterling Area. Overall exports to the Commonwealth peaked in 1951 at 51 per cent, but even in the mid-1950s, the Tory Government still perceived these markets as guarantors of future prosperity. [78] For example, in 1956 the MTTA saw India as a market of future potential growth, and vital to the industry's export capabilities.[79]

A Commonwealth vision was demonstrated in government-industry dialogue over Britain's withdrawal from the Messina negotiations on the European Common Market in 1956, and the government's intent to consider negotiations for an Association with the European Six to form a free trade area. In the context of rising German competition, and the seeming inevitability of a European trading block, the industry's leaders rallied around a defence of Commonwealth markets. Representatives of the MTTA met with Leslie Robinson, Second Secretary of the

---

[75] MTTA Council Minute Book, 30 March 1960; Report on British Machine Tool Exports, 6 October 1960.

[76] Mitchell Report, p. 23; *Engineer*, 29 January 1960, p. 161; 18 November 1960, p. 840; *Economist*, 30 January 1960, p. 440; MTTA, Report on British Machine Tool Exports, 6 October 1960; G. W. Smith, 'The Challenge to Automatic Control', *Manager*, Vol. 31 (1963), p. 43.

[77] M. French, 'Public Policy and British Commercial Vehicles During the Export Drive Era, 1945-50', *Business History*, Vol. 40, No. 2 (1998), p. 2; Singleton, 'The British Engineering Industry', p. 417.

[78] D. K. Fieldhouse, 'The Metropolitan Economics of Empire', in J. M. Brown and W. Roger Louis (eds), *The Oxford History of the British Empire* (Oxford, Oxford University Press, 1999), pp. 89, 109-10; Broadberry, *Productivity Race*, pp. 94-5; F. W. S. Craig (ed.), *British General Election Manifestoes* (Chichester, Political Reference Publications, 1970), pp. 162-4.

[79] MTTA, Council Minute Book, 9 August 1956.

Board of Trade, as part of a consultation process with key industries. Reluctant to dismiss an Association out-of-hand, the MTTA nevertheless insisted upon the need to defend Commonwealth markets and retain preferences. They further warned that an immediate 'removal of import duty ... would prove disastrous'; even a staged removal 'would need careful consideration'. Dismissing these claims, Robinson, although willing to recognise the trading importance of the Commonwealth, warned that the industry should not assume that this could provide long-term alternative markets, especially as 'U.K. preferences were already under pressure and they were likely to diminish over the next few years'. Robinson dismissed the plea from the MTTA that machine tools should be allocated the status of a special case. Safeguarding he insisted would only be applied to agriculture and industries deemed vital to national security. Machine makers, however, viewed the Commonwealth as an umbrella, sheltering the industry from the full brunt of German competition. As the President of the MTTA, H. Potts, argued, 'unhampered' German competition was a danger 'both in Europe and the home market, and thus safeguarding was vital. British imports of West German machines were valued at £5 million in 1955, but this was 'a one way trade', British exports to that country being only £450,000. Accepting that high technology imports were vital to British manufacturing, Potts concluded that 'we must be careful to avoid the domination of the European market by our one real competitor, the Germans', and his associate, J. W. Kearns, predicted that German domination of the Common Market would 'mean the partial decease of the U.K. machine tool industry'.[80]

Obsessed about the superiority of German technological competence, the industry's leaders sought to maintain preferences in Commonwealth markets, despite a declining trend. For example, Britain's share of Commonwealth imports of metal working machinery fell from 62.1 per cent in 1953 to 37.3 per cent in 1959, while the German share rose from 15.2 to 41.3 per cent. Nevertheless, there remained a strong determination 'to defend their preferences', which showed 'how highly they still valued Commonwealth markets'.[81] The pull of Commonwealth markets, however, may have distorted the technological capabilities and product range of British makers, and weakened their competitive advantage in the post-war years. As the Mitchell Report concluded, the

> shrinkage of the U.K. share of the world market in machine tools [was] due mainly to over-dependence on the [Commonwealth] market ... for standardised machine tools and insufficient participation in the more rapidly expanding market for high performance and high precision special types.[82]

The MTTA Report on Exports of 1960 concurred. Observing that exports were concentrated on 'less industrially developed markets', the report referred to a 'failure in technical and design fields', and pointed out that only 10 per cent of British machine tools were of a 'precision' and 'high product' type. In its

---

[80] MTTA, Council Minute Book, 17 October 1956.
[81] Singleton, 'British Engineering', pp. 407, 417-18.
[82] Mitchell Report, p. 23.

conclusion, the report regretted the industry's 'relegation to the role of supplier of less sophisticated products'.[83] British machine tool firms were locked into a path dependent process that shaped their technological configuration.[84] As the MTTA observed in 1956, 'long continual pressure for the delivery of existing types of standard machines had made it difficult to direct resources for the design and prototype development of new machines'.[85] Design capabilities were crucial to the 'game' of technical advance in the 1950s, and the industry was found wanting. This conclusion relates to the final and most damaging criticism, which equated insufficient design capabilities with the industry's R&D record. In 1959, Professor Seymor Melman of Columbia University in the U.S.A. toured leading machine tool manufacturers in Western Europe, on behalf of the European Productivity Agency. His report asserted that British makers in particular 'were only playing at the business', and condemned the industry's low commitment to R&D, an allegation that E. W. Field, the President of the MTTA felt to be 'ill founded'.[86]

Responding to Melman, a Sub-Committee of the Machine Tool Advisory Council, under the chairmanship of Sir Steuart Mitchell, Controller of Guided Weapons and Electronics at the Royal Ordnance Factory, reported its findings in 1960 on the state of the British machine tool industry. The Mitchell Report articulated a number of complaints against the industry's performance, but it reserved its main condemnation for the industry's R&D effort. Insufficient investment in R&D, it was alleged, manifested itself in an over-concentration on general-purpose machines. In 1955, estimated expenditure on R&D in machine tools was 1.1 per cent of the industry's net output, compared to an average of 2 per cent for all manufacturing industry, with the exception of aircraft producers. According to Mitchell, a low R&D commitment meant that British makers had insufficient technical capabilities to mount an effective market challenge to high performance machine tools from abroad, a 'failure' reflected in a dependency on imports and declining shares of world export markets. Away from the public gaze, the MTTA confidential report on exports agreed: 'in technical design we have taken the line of least resistance, relying on the momentum of the past'.[87] Modern machine tool design required the industry to co-ordinate its R&D policy, and from the late 1950s the industry came under increasing pressure to respond to government attempts to create institutional co-operation. This, as we shall see in the next chapter, fundamentally changed the rules of the 'game', but what factors constrained the industry's R&D performance? To examine this question there is a need to focus on another key source of productivity growth identified by Nelson, 'educational attainment' and investment in human resources.

---

[83] MTTA, 6 October 1960, Report on British Machine Tool Exports; *Engineer*, 29 January 1960.

[84] See Broadberry, *Productivity Race*, p. 78.

[85] MTTA, Council Minute Book, 13 December 1956.

[86] Astrop, 'The Rise and Fall', pp. 19-20; MTTA, Council Minute Book, 30 March 1960.

[87] Mitchell Report, p. 23; MTTA, 6 October 1960, Report on Machine Tool Exports.

R&D and Investment in Human Resources

The Mitchell Report raised public awareness of the industry's shortcomings in R&D, its findings supported by a Federation of British Industry survey that observed the relatively small research expenditure per unit of turnover by machine tool makers.[88] Key factors identified as inhibiting R&D were shortages of skilled personnel, compounded by the fragmented business structure of the industry, and the small turnover of individual firms. Machine makers all too frequently lacked the resources to build and sustain research teams, and this was a consequence of their small size. A survey in 1963 by the Manpower Research Unit found that two-thirds of the machine tool firms consulted did not provide systems to forecast their labour requirements.[89] Deficiencies in the industry's potential knowledge base can be gauged by a comparison with other industrial sectors, whose competitive capabilities were closely related to their R&D effort, and the employment of highly skilled personnel (Table 7.9). Machine tool firms registered the lowest proportion of QES employed on R&D activity. In 1958, a survey of 90 machine tool firms employing some 30,000 workers found that they employed only 28 graduate engineers, and only 3 per cent of the industry's personnel were engaged on design work, significantly less than the 6.6 per cent in Germany and the 7.2 per cent in Switzerland. International comparisons made dismal reading, and the DSIR concluded that the relative employment of graduate engineers by British makers, compared to Switzerland and Germany was of the same proportion as for design workers.[90] Indeed, according to the *Engineer* in 1958 German makers recruited some 500 graduates compared to just two in the British industry.[91]

Nelson's emphasis on educational attainment as a key source of productivity growth is important. As Metcalfe observes, the firm is a collection of evolving competencies, and this means that the quality of its human resources is essential to the effectiveness of its technical capabilities.[92] The employment of technically qualified R&D personnel in the British machine tool industry was at a threshold level, which seriously threatened its competitive advantage. Thus, 'in the markets for high performance machine tools U.K. designers are becoming increasingly uncompetitive with those of Germany and Switzerland, where stronger teams of qualified design engineers are employed'. The *First Census of Production of Machine Tools* conducted in 1961 by the MTTA and the Machine Tool Advisory Council confirmed the fact that 59.2 per cent of Britain's metal-working machine tools were over 10 years old, a period representing an 'accepted international

---

[88] Mitchell Report, pp. 24, 33; B. J. A. Bard, 'Some Aspects of R&D in the 1960s in the U.K.', *Research and Development for Industry* (1962), p. 41.

[89] Evans, 'Some Problems of Growth', p. 35; *Economist*, 13 June 1964, p. 1274; *Hansard, Proceedings of the House of Commons*, 14 June 1965, pp. 32-3.

[90] Mitchell Report, pp. 26-7.

[91]; *Engineer*, 29 January 1960, p. 161.

[92] S. Metcalfe, 'Technology Systems and Technology Policy in an Evolutionary Framework', in D. Archibugi and J. Michie (eds), *Technology, Globalization and Economic Performance* (Cambridge, Cambridge University Press, 1997), p. 278.

yardstick for obsolescence'.[93] Shortages of highly trained personnel, such as designers, were of considerable concern to the MTTA. In 1959, the President, J. C. Robinson, announced the formation of an Expert Committee on education and training, and the establishment of MTTA Design Scholarships linked to the introduction of an Advanced Design Course at the Manchester College of Science and Technology. By the beginning of 1960, there were 10 scholarships of £500 per annum, and thereafter the intention was to recruit a cohort of 20 students per year. The initiative had more to do with public accountability, than it did with the needs of the industry for trained personnel. Thus, Robinson inferred that the scheme was more vital for enlisting public sympathy for the industry 'than could ever be achieved by ... a contentious and spasmodic advertisement campaign'. Robinson's initiative appeared to pay dividends, *The Engineer* endorsing it as a sign that on the technical front 'the industry is ... well aware of its responsibilities'. Education initiatives was also given the backing of the DSIR, which supported the policy of the MTTA in late 1959 to forge closer cooperation between engineers and designers in industry with the research work of universities, colleges and research institutes. While the industry's leaders and the DSIR might extol the virtues of high levels of technical training and research expertise, the response of individual firms to these initiatives was another matter. In June 1960, *The Engineer* informed its readers that it could still detect a 'smell of complacency', with only 14 candidates submitted by firms in the whole of the machine tool industry to the scholarship established at Manchester.[94]

Table 7.9
Comparison of Qualified Engineers and Scientists (QES) in 10 Selected Industries (QES as % of Total Employees in the Industry), 1958-59

	Employed for All Purposes	Employed on R&D
Oil Refining	7.0	2.3
Chemical and Allied	3.7	1.8
Aircraft	2.7	1.4
Heavy Electrical	2.3	1.2
Electrical Engineering	2.2	1.25
Electronics	2.1	1.4
Precision Instrument etc.	1.7	1.0
Plant and Machinery (not electrical)	1.5	0.4
Machine Tools	1.3	0.3
Marine Engineering	1.1	0.3

Source: Mitchell Report, p. 27.

[93] Mitchell Report, p. 27; 'First Census of Production', in *Alfred Herbert News*, May/June 1961, p. 1.
[94] MTTA, Council Minute Book, 18 March 1959; *Engineer*, 25 December 1959, p. 868; 5 February 1960, p. 232; 3 June 1960, p. 924.

Table 7.10

Extent of Higher Level Training in Machine Tool Design in British Departments of Mechanical Engineering

	University of Birmingham		Manchester College of Science and Technology		Royal Technical College, Salford	
	1958	1960	1958	1960	1958	1960
Undergraduate Students (Mechanical Engineering)	111	117	190	164	84[a]	189[a]
Research Students (Total)	6	18	21[b]	26[b]	0	2
Of which on Machine Tools	0	10	5	6	0	2
Teaching Staff (Total)	16	19	19	19	31	40
Research Staff (Total)	0	3	6	6	1	3
Of Which on Machine Tools	0	2	6	6	0	2

Source: *Engineer*, 18 November 1960, p. 841.
Notes: a. Students working for Diploma of Technology in Mechanical Engineering. b. Postgraduates.

Not surprisingly, the industry's education and training record came under attack. A memorandum circulated to the Parliamentary Labour Party and TUC Economic Group in 1959 by the Labour MP Austin Albu, berated the industry's technological backwardness. In particular, the memorandum asserted that the British industry lacked the type of machine tool that reflected design leadership. According to the 1959 Report on Scientific and Engineering Manpower in Britain, QES represented only 1.3 per cent of the industry's workforce, this figure inflated by the fact that one-half of those classified as QES had reached that standard through their membership of a professional organisation, notably the Institute of Production Engineers, which had admitted members without examinations. A conference at the University of Birmingham in 1960 on machine tool design recorded the lack of synergy between practical designers and academic research teams. Few practical designers could understand the activities of research workers in their field, and the latter had minimal contact with the former, 'the two groups ... hardly able to comprehend one another'. This was of particular concern to an industry where technical demands were increasing rapidly. Adding to these concerns was the fact that with the exception of Manchester College very few British universities had departments dealing with machine design, and certainly had nothing to compare with the machine tool laboratories of the Technical University of Aachen.[95] Table 7.10 shows the provision for machine design in institutions designated as centres of this research. Britain's machine tool industry lacked a cadre of highly trained design engineers and scientific personnel compared to their main continental rivals, which lends support to the proposition

_____

[95] *Engineer*, 29 January 1960, p. 161; 18 November 1960, p. 823.

that this was an important contributory factor to the industry's poor R&D and productivity record.

Investment, Capacity and Markets

If the industry could be criticised for its limited investment in human resources, it also faced allegations that it under-invested in productive capacity. Complacency was a common accusation, the industry accused of being more concerned with supplying 'adequate' quantities of 'basic workshop tools it was already making'. Machine makers also gave the impression 'that the expansion of capacity beyond the moderate rate attained would not be an economic proposition'. A conservative investment strategy led to an inability to respond quickly to increases in demand, and this manifested itself in over-long and unreliable delivery dates. Data on the cycle between 1954 and 1960 is provided in Tables 7.11 and 7.12. The order cycle operated with wide fluctuations, emphasising the wide movements in demand, and while the industry had managed to expand production more evenly, the ordering fluctuations were much greater than output fluctuations. For example, in the upturn of the cycle in 1954-55 home orders increased by 33 per cent, and total orders by 25 per cent, while output rose by only 15 per cent. Correspondingly, in the downturn home orders by 1958 were 45 per cent lower than that for 1955, and total orders by 39 per cent, while output fell by only 2 per cent. In the economic upturn of 1960, home order fluctuations were even more marked, rising by 80 per cent over 1959, while output increased by only 21 per cent. The burst of demand from late 1959, both at home and abroad, led to extended delivery dates, and with new orders 'exceeding current deliveries by a large margin orders in hand have grown rapidly'. By April 1960 the value of orders in hand were 40 per cent higher than at the beginning of the year, and some 59 per cent higher than at the low point at the end of July 1959. During upturns, a widening gap appeared between orders and output, only closed, as shown in Table 7.12, by rising imports. According to Mitchell, 'Experience shows that whenever a major increase has arisen in the demand for machine tools heavy recourse has had to be made to imports to meet it'. For example, the re-equipment programme in the car industry of 1955-7, when imports rose to 25 per cent of total consumption in 1956. Despite a steady increase in production, imports were still 20 per cent in 1957. This was 'due primarily' to a sudden concentration of demand and insufficient productive capacity to meet demand with the consequence that 'valuable orders went abroad'.[96]

---

[96] *Engineer*, 23 January 1959, p. 125; 15 July 1960, p. 924; Mitchell Report, pp. 20-1.

Table 7.11
Consumption of Machine Tools, 1954-60 (£ 000)

	A	B	C	D	E
	Home Deliveries	Imports	Consumption	Imports – % of Consumption	Exports
	Manufacturers Returns	Customs-Excise	A+B	B as % of C	Manufac-turers Returns
1954	47,397	13,044	60,441	21	18,198
1955	56,794	13,901	70,695	19	18,590
1956	64,103	21,433	85,536	25	21,376
1957	70,795	17,588	88,383	20	24,440
1958	63,164	13,926	77,090	18	20,751
1959	60,216	13,159	73,365	18	20,751
1960	70,626	19,153	89,779	21	24,310

Source: MTTA, Machine Tool Directory, 1966, p. 17.

Table 7.12
New Orders for Machine Tools and Total Output, 1954-60 (£ 000)

	Home Orders	Export Orders	Total New Orders	Actual Total Output
1954	57,870	20,991	78,861	65,595
1955	76,887	21,337	98,224	75,384
1956	61,216	22,508	83,724	85,479
1957	54,582	20,723	75,305	95,253
1958	42,333	17,465	59,798	83,915
1959	62,058	18,217	80,275	78,768
1960	111,879	32,868	144,747	94,936

Source: MTTA, Machine Tool Directory, 1966, p. 18.

As we saw earlier, however, imports were actively encouraged by British firms who factored foreign machine tools. Imports were a strategic response by the industry to the cyclical pattern of demand. Thus, C. W. Clark, the Chairman of Alfred Herbert, referred to the importance of foreign transfers of machine technology to the advancement of British industry. It was 'farcical', he claimed, that in all cases 'British designers should be able to produce designs equal to or better than those of foreign specialists'. The industry was pursuing a rational policy premised upon the recognition of international competitive advantage:

the equipment of overseas makers is available to British factories, suitability for British purposes being the main consideration ... Many of the types of machines concerned are highly specialised and the whole world demand may be easily satisfied by the output of a few specialist manufacturers who are so firmly established that it would be quite uneconomic to divide the market.[97]

At the MTTA, a policy of importing to meet the peak of the cycle was fully accepted, and this also related to the industry's commitment to maintain export markets.[98] In 1960 A. B. Morgan of EMI, and E. W. Field, Secretary and President of the MTTA respectively, informed members that exports should be maximised, and thus 'The industry should follow its declared policy of meeting fluctuations in demand by fluctuations in imports'. Curtailing exports would lead to a decline in market reputation, and Field reminded members of how difficult it had been to get back into the Canadian market since the war.[99] Endorsement of importation came from the Board of Trade in 1958, who believed that specialist foreign machine tools enabled 'a full range' to be offered to domestic users, a condition of trade that could be regulated by the industry itself to ensure that they did not compete with domestic types.[100]

In the market environment of the 1950s, the industry faced acute problems. For example, in defending the industry against allegations that it had failed to meet the needs of the car industry, the MTTA informed Sir Leslie Roberts, Second Secretary to the Board of Trade, in 1957 that there was a bunching of demand during the re-equipment phase between 1955-7. If the demand from 'the motor car industry was spread over a longer period', the MTTA argued, the machine tool industry could have increased its 'output of special and tooled up machines'. However, when 'replacement programmes' for a number of large car plants were 'executed simultaneously, the machine tool industry cannot cope with the level of demand, which is inevitably followed by a relatively slack period'.[101] Indeed, the investment phase of 1955-7 was followed by a sharp reversal, and the machine tool industry was thrown into a deep recession, and in these 'lean years' stockpiled machines to ensure the full operation of plant and the retention of skilled workers. During the subsequent upswing, makers 'liquidated' machine stocks, but now ran into labour supply problems, especially in terms of the recruitment of skilled workers, and this placed a major obstacle in the way of increasing output. When demand was low makers laid off workers, and then faced recruitment problems in the upturn of the cycle when rapidly rising levels of activity in engineering industries created intense competition for skilled men.[102] At

---

[97] *Economist*, 1 April 1961, p. 64; *Machine Tool Review*, Vol. 49, 1961, p. 49.

[98] Guy Chesham , 'The Machine Tool Industry, *Manager*, Vol. 27, (1959), pp. 43-4.

[99] MTTA, 6 October 1960, Report on British Machine Tool Exports.

[100] John Rodgers, Parliamentary Secretary to the Board of Trade, in *Hansard*, Vol. 594, 25 November 1958, pp. 210-11.

[101] MTTA, Council Minute Book, Report of Meeting with Sir Leslie Roberts, 31 January 1957. See also *Economist*, 17 August 1963, p. 374.

[102] *Economist*, 30 January 1960, p. 441; Mitchell Report, pp. 21-2; *Machine Tool Review*, Vol. 48, 1960, p. 118. The industry required abnormally high proportions of skilled workers, according to one estimate 40-60 per cent. PEP, Report on 'The Machine Tool Industry', pp. 183-4.

the height of the motor vehicle re-equipment phase in 1956, for example, the MTTA informed the Machine Tool Advisory Council that despite increased investment by machine tool firms the major constraint they faced in raising output and improving delivery times was 'the scarcity of skilled labour, especially in the drawing office'. Again in 1960, the industry was swamped by rising orders, and shortages of capacity were evident not only in production but in design and drawing office requirements.[103] This is a reminder of Nelson's point that the sources of productivity growth are complementary, and it would seem that a shortage of skilled labour constrained the entrepreneurial incentive to invest in new and additional plant in the machine tool industry. Indeed, over the long-run, investment in 'production capacity was tailored to survive the troughs in demand rather than meet the peaks, so when demand revived capacity was insufficient to meet it'. In this scenario, it was inevitable that imports would fill the gap between demand and supply, and the long-run trend was that at each successive peak of the cycle the share of imports in the home market increased. Between 1956 and 1959 imports on average contributed 23 per cent of British machine tool production compared to only 8 per cent in both West Germany and the U.S.A.[104]

Investment, it is plausible to argue, was inhibited by the volatility of demand as machine makers pursued a risk aversion strategy. Consequently, a conservative set of habits towards investment, innovation, and labour recruitment became embedded in the industry.[105] However, an appeal to the vagaries of the demand cycle is not altogether convincing, for this was not a market phenomena that was unique to Britain. American, German and Swiss producers faced a similar pattern of demand, and yet the productivity record of their makers out-performed those in Britain during the 1950s. A report by MinTech in the mid-1960s concluded that in the machine tool industry 'A peak to trough ratio of 3:1 is certainly troublesome, but no worse than any other capital goods industry, and not much different from overseas experience'.[106] Moreover, American machine tool makers in the mid-1950s complained that the biggest difficulty facing them was 'first and foremost ... the acute shortage of all staff for the engineering departments which now have so much work to do'.[107] The business environment had common patterns, but it was the British, compared to their continental rivals who experienced a relative decline in the share of the world market for machine tools.

A more convincing case for the defence of the British machine tool industry is less to do with the volatility of demand and more to do with its structure. For example, *The Engineer* asserted that in the industry investment in R&D and advanced products could only be justified by expanding markets. It claimed that 'many industrial firms and government establishments in the country seem to go on quite happily using a deal of out-of-date plant'. Consequently,

---

[103] MTTA, Council Minute Book, 27 September 1956, 30 March 1960.

[104] Mitchell Report, p. 23.

[105] See R. Hamilton, 'Early British Machine Tool Automation: The Road to Numerical Control', *Journal of Industrial History*, Vol. 2 (1999), p. 99.

[106] Cited in *Economist*, 11 June 1966, p. 1,221.

[107] MTTA, Council Minute Book, 20 June 1957, Report on visit to Canada.

indicative of the difficulties makers experienced when they did develop an improved design was the 'fact that relatively few high precision machines equipped with automatic control have been sold to British firms'. Users were 'not giving the machine tool manufacturers the assurance of a receptive and expanding market for improved products', and held back productive investment in the machine tool industry by their 'reluctance to purchase other than tried and proved machines'. The blame was equally proportioned, the user deserving 'a substantial share of the criticism levelled at the industry'.[108]

In its editorial in 1957 *The Machine Tool Review* referred to the deficiencies of British engineering in enhancing 'plant efficiency', which included high taxation, restrictive practices, poor tooling equipment, abuse of machines, low standards of maintenance, and continued use of obsolete equipment. Engineers were 'prepared to watch their plants drift into obsolescence, unmindful of the fact that on the modernity of machines and methods rests their only hope of combating rising labour costs'. In the upswing of 1960, criticisms of lengthening delivery times were based on the assumption 'of a stable demand', but as the *Review* reminded its readers, they could not influence 'a factor which is so completely in the hands of our customers'.[109] Following this line of argument the country got the machine tool industry it deserved, and as pointed out earlier the fragmented structure of Britain's engineering industry, with a high number of small producers, created a structure of demand that may well have acted as a constraining factor on the pattern of investment and innovation. The problem of slow productivity growth, which sharply decelerated by the early 1960s, may not be laid entirely at the door of the machine tool industry. This begs the question, however, of what remedies the industry sought to tackle the challenge it faced, and how successful they were in overcoming them. The next chapter explores the responses of the industry to the growing criticisms it faced, in the context of initiatives aimed at modernising Britain's manufacturing industries in the 1960s.

---

[108] *Engineer*, 8 January 1960, p. 42.
[109] *Machine Tool Review*, Vol. 45, 1957, p. 114; Vol. 47, 1959, p.1; Vol. 48, 1960, p. 118.

CHAPTER EIGHT

Responding to the 'Game': Modernisation and the British Machine Tool Industry in the 1960s

'Make no mistake about it, ours is today an embattled industry' [J. C. Robinson, President, MTTA, 1959].[1]

Introduction

By 1960 a decade of 'rapid changes in the scientific and industrial scene', together with the rising competitive challenge, had altered the nature of the 'game', and industries such as machine tools took centre stage in the growing political debate over modernisation.[2] Foreshadowing the policies of Harold Wilson after 1964 epitomised in the slogan the 'white heat of technology', the Conservative Governments from 1959 to 1964 attempted to reform the institutional framework governing industry-state relations.[3] One of the fundamental objectives of modernisation was institutional reform aimed at the supply side of the economy,[4] and for machine tools this involved attempts to induce inter-firm cooperation on R&D to raise productivity. Given the importance of the industry to the manufacturing economy it was seen as a vital sector in raising the long-run rate of economic growth, the planning for which was co-ordinated by the National Economic Development Council (NEDC) of 1962. Central to government plans was the cooperation of the industry itself. Tory modernisation signalled a change in the rules of the 'game' and this was expressed not only in terms of the technical and competitive challenge facing the industry, but also included a political dimension. Makers perceived their industry as an 'embattled' one, under political

---

[1] MTTA, Council Minute Book, 18 March 1959.
[2] See Reports from Commissioners, Vol. XX, Session 1960-1 (cmnd. 1365), DSIR, *Report of the Research Council for 1960*, pp. 9, 21-2.
[3] See D. E. H. Edgerton, 'The "White Heat" Revisited: The British Government and Technology in the 1960s', *Twentieth Century British History*, Vol. 7 (1996), pp. 53-82; A. Ringe and N. Rollings, 'Responding to Relative Decline: The Creation of the National Economic Development Council', *Economic History Review*, Vol. 53, No. 2 (2000), pp. 331-53; Tomlinson, 'Inventing Decline', p. 764.
[4] Modernisation implied demand management, competition, as well as supply side policies. J. Tomlinson, 'Conservative Modernisation, 1960-1964: Too Little Too Late', *Contemporary British History*, Vol. 11, No. 3 (1997), p. 19.

siege. The Tory modernisation policies will be examined in terms of the cyclical pattern of demand, and the response of the industry to institutional reform targeted at raising the level of R&D as a precursor to raising economic growth. As will be shown, governments faced constraints in instigating reform in an industry with entrenched values which militated against cooperative action. Nevertheless, increasing pressure for modernisation, involving policies of rationalisation, were heaped upon the industry by the Labour Government's National Plan of 1965. Describing the industry as 'the crucial sector of the whole mechanical engineering industry', acknowledging that the bulk of the industry's output supplied the investment needs of the engineering and allied industries, the Plan projected a rise in the growth rate of machine tool output from 2 per cent per annum, 1960-64, to 8 per cent during the second half of the 1960s.[5] In examining the response of the industry to increased intervention by Labour, the chapter will evaluate relations with agencies such as the Ministry of Technology (MinTech). Under Labour, the industry's leaders saw a direct challenge to the 'freedom' of individual firms 'to run our business in the way that experience has taught us best'.[6]

Tory Modernisation and the Machine Tool Industry

Business firms are only one of the organisational forms that operate in the 'game' of industrial capitalism. There is a system of innovation, which includes not only business firms but also trade bodies, educational institutions, and government agencies. How this system works, the degree of cooperation and 'trust' between the different organisations may be crucial in determining national performance.[7] Institutions encompass a set of rules, both formal and informal, which act to reduce uncertainty, and the effectiveness of enforcing these rules 'shape the whole character of the game'. This institutional approach provides the framework for analysing the relationship of the machine tool industry to the growing political emphasis on technological change and modernisation, which emerged at the national level from the late 1950s.[8] To understand the process of technological change requires not only an examination of the role of the firm in the process of innovatory change, but also a consideration of the political and institutional environment in which firms operate.[9]

---

[5] Reports from Commissioners, Vol. XX, Session 1959-60 (cmnd. 1049), DSIR, *Report of the Research Council for 1959*, pp. 16-17, 22; *National Plan*, 1965, p. 104.

[6] MTTA, Council Minute Book, H. Potts, Presidential Address, 21 March 1956.

[7] Nelson, 'The Role of Firms in Technical Advance', pp. 168-9.

[8] D. C. North, *Institutions, Institutional Change and Economic Performance* (Cambridge, Cambridge University Press, 1990), pp. 3-4, 6-7. See also M. Casson and M. B. Rose (eds), *Business History*, Vol. 39, No. 4 (1997), Special Issue on *Institutions and the Evolution of Modern Business*; J. J. Vromen, *Economic Evolution: An Enquiry Into The Foundations of New Institutional Economics* (Routledge, London, 1995).

[9] K. Lipartito, 'Innovation, the Firm, and Society', *Business and Economic History*, Vol. 22, No. 2 (1993), pp. 92-104.

Modernisation implied 'a major reconstruction of British society, its institutions and its values with a view to improving economic performance and reducing lost esteem'.[10] Studies of relative economic decline in the 1950s and 1960s, in particular in manufacturing, have emphasised the lack of appropriate institutional arrangements to promote industrial development. From this viewpoint institutions do matter.[11] However, studies of institutional initiatives, such as the creation of the NEDC in 1962, have emphasised the limitations on what governments can actually do to bring about change. 'Those at the centre of government', claim Ringe and Rollings, 'cannot dictate policy but are dependent on others, both in government and beyond, to achieve their goals'.[12] Accepting this caveat, institutional reform was central to the ideals of modernisation from the late 1950s, and involved a critical review and configuration of the rules of the 'game'. Modernisation was set within the context of the growing realisation by the Conservatives of 'declinism', and pressure was exerted from a number of directions. The Labour party attacked the failings of the industrial economy, the FBI in 1960 took up the challenge, and civil servants and economists focused attention on breaking the 'stop-go' cycle, and raising the long-term growth rate of the economy. After 1960, when the balance of payments turned sharply into deficit, the government was forced to push the economy into a 'stop phase', which undermined its credibility in economic policy making. Concerns over increasing economic 'growth gave a prominence to industrial policy which was previously absent'. A clear single industrial policy to encourage growth never emerged, and this was reflected in the range of institutions devised to coordinate and plan industrial output.[13] Nevertheless, the push towards modernisation had implications for industries such as machine tools, which were identified as key sectors in raising aggregate growth through co-operative action.

Public criticism of the industry intensified, with the publication of the Mitchell Report in 1960, which identified the problems of the industry in meeting increased orders during the upturn of economic activity. In the upturn of the cycle in 1960, domestic and export orders accelerated leaving the industry 'once again

---

[10] D. Porter, 'Downhill All the Way: Thirteen Tory Years, 1951-64', in R. Coopey, S. Fielding and N. Tiratsoo (eds), *The Wilson Government, 1964-70* (London, Pinter, 1993), p. 23.

[11] See Ringe and Rollings, 'Responding', pp. 331-5; N. F. R. Crafts, 'Institutions and Economic Growth: Recent British Experience in an International Context', *West European Politics*, Vol. 15 (1992), pp. 16-38; Elbaum and Lazonick, 'An Institutional Perspective on British Decline', pp. 1-17; M. Kirby, 'Institutional Rigidities and British Economic Decline: Reflections on the British Experience', *Economic History Review*, Vol. 45, No. 4 (1992), pp. 637-60; R. Middleton, *Government Versus the Market* (Aldershot, Ashgate, 1996).

[12] Ringe and Rollings, 'Responding', p. 335; S. Wood, 'Why Indicative Planning Failed: British Industry and the Formation of the National Economic Development Council', *Twentieth Century British Industry*, Vol. 11 (2000), pp. 431-59.

[13] Tomlinson, 'Inventing Decline', p. 747; J. Tomlinson, *Public Policy and the Economy Since 1900* (Oxford, Oxford University Press, 1990), p. 252; Porter, 'Downhill All the Way', pp. 18-19. For an excellent account of 'stop-go', see Pollard, *Wasting*, pp. 31-55.

'extremely embarrassed through the over-filling of capacity'.[14] On the export front, an MTTA report in 1960 called for cooperative action on technology to implement improved production methods, increased use of common standardised components, and more advantageous buying out of materials and semi and finished components. The report also recommended collective action on marketing, which was found to be woefully inadequate, with a failure to develop adequate advertisement, dilatory handling of enquiries, and poor technical servicing of machines to customers. Groups of firms marketing similar product lines could pool information and develop joint marketing strategies for market forecasting, licensing, and the financing of export credit. Self help was the order of the day, and the MTTA recommended the formation of an outside company, financed by a bank or finance corporation, which would be responsible for developing groups of makers to improve technical and marketing co-ordination and enhance the industry's export performance. It was recognised, however, that such an initiative could not be applied on an 'industry wide' basis, which 'would either fail or be so cumbersome as to make it valueless'. Proposals for group collaboration was to be initiated on a small-scale with the longer term objective of creating an influential group of makers 'willing to subscribe to common principles and to put them into action even at the cost of sacrificing some small degree of autonomy and independence'.[15]

Recommendations for industrial collaboration remained on the planning board, and, as we shall see, market forces were to dictate the formation of groups of companies by absorption into larger manufacturing organisations. Indeed, proposals for group collaboration were a purely defensive reaction to the Mitchell Report which the MTTA feared would lead to government action to force rationalisation through amalgamation, and so interfere in the legitimate rights of individual business. As the MTTA Report on Exports concluded, cooperation between firms, and not amalgamation was the desired policy, but they recognised that this 'will not take place unless someone from outside organises it. We do not want that someone to be the government'.[16] This dilemma was evident in the industry's poor relationship with the DSIR on the formation of collaborative research institutions. As was shown in the previous chapter, an important factor identified with growth was appropriate levels of R&D to enhance industrial productivity. At an official level, reports in the early 1960s by the FBI Research Committee, the Advisory Council on Scientific Policy, and the Zuckerman Committee on the Management and Control of R&D, all identified R&D as a key factor in promoting national efficiency. At the same time, the National Research Development Corporation (NRDC), an organisation funding private research, appealed for a great national effort to raise R&D to increase industrial productivity.[17] The government's attempt to link with firms at the micro level was

---

[14] MTTA, Council Minute Book, 30 March 1960.

[15] MTTA, Council Minute Book, 6 October 1960, Report on British Machine Tool Exports.

[16] Ibid.

[17]*Research and Development for Industry*, 1962, p. 40; Reports from Commissioners, NRDC Report and Statement of Account for 1 July 1958-30 June 1959,

based on the encouragement of industry-wide research associations; cooperative institutions designed to support and stimulate the development of R&D, which already existed. Research associations had first been established in 1916, and came under the direction of the DSIR formed in 1918. In 1959, 49 grant aided industrial associations covered 55 per cent of British industry, and between 1950 and 1960 their combined income rose from £3.1 million to £7.9 million.[18] Machine tools had no dedicated research institution and channelled its cooperative activities through consultation between the MTTA and the Production Engineering Research Association (PERA), founded in 1947. Consequently, the DSIR, and its Advisory Council on Scientific Policy, identified the industry as a 'problem sector' with a low propensity for R&D, and targeted it as a 'a pilot' for collaborative activity as part of a national strategy to increase productivity.[19]

Constructive talks between the DSIR and the MTTA for a 'devoted' research association for machine tools commenced in 1959. The MTTA responded positively, and there was general agreement for closer cooperation between the industry and academic and research institutes.[20] Agreement, however, disguised apprehension by the MTTA over government motives, and their concerns heightened with the realisation that the industry was a pawn in the wider public debate on modernisation. In 1959 the DSIR produced a confidential report which condemned the industry as 'deficient' in research, but its publication was delayed because of grass root objections from the industry, and the need to pacify the MTTA during negotiations. Sensitivity over the publication of the report was defended by the industry in terms of its technical content, which could be valuable to foreign competitors, but suppressing publication hardly appeased critics who voiced the view that the MTTA was engaged in special pleading and were 'covering up' a negative assessment of R&D performance.[21] While this episode signalled a complacent response by the industry, there were key figures who took a more pragmatic outlook to the politicisation of the industry. In 1960, R. W. Asquith, Chairman of the MTTA Economic Policy Committee, claimed that his 'committee ... had long been of the opinion that they should centralise research', and gave full backing to the creation of a Machine Tool Industry Research Association (MTIRA), an 'information led organisation to apply research to production'. He noted, however, that 'efficient research' was no longer merely an

---

Vol. XIX, pp. 1-2; D. E. H. Edgerton, *Science, Technology and the British Industrial Decline, 1870-1914* (Cambridge, Cambridge University Press, 1996), p. 43.

[18] D. E. H. Edgerton and S. M. Horrocks, 'British Research and Development Before 1945', *Economic History Review*, Vol. 47, No 2 (1994), pp. 213-38; D. W. Hill, 'The Research Associations – Essential Link between Science and Production', *Research and Development for Industry* (1962), p. 36.

[19] Reports from Commissioners, *Annual Report of the Advisory Council on Scientific Policy*, (PP 1959-60, XX); Reports from Commissioners, DSIR, *Report of the Research Council for 1959* (PP 1959-60, XX), p. 2; Reports from Commissioners, DSIR, *Report of the Research Council for 1960* (PP 1960-1, XXI), pp. 21-2.

[20] MTTA, Council Minute Book, 27 August 1959; *Engineer*, 28 December 1959, p. 868.

[21] *Engineer*, 5 February 1960, p. 211.

economic imperative, but was now 'also essential politically'. Sending the right message to government would signal the industry's recognition of 'the political need for some action'.[22]

Political pressure on the industry was intensified by the publication towards the end of 1960 of the Mitchell Report which endorsed the creation of the MTIRA. Seizing the initiative, Reginald Maudling, President of the Board of Trade, gave a personal endorsement 'to the establishment and future strengthening of the new co-operative Research Association'. The development of specialised machine tools was a prerequisite for industrial modernisation and in such a diverse industry this could only be achieved by cooperative action 'in which small firms have a part to play as well as the giant'.[23] Appeals to a collective spirit, however, were somewhat premature. Asquith, for example, forewarned of the 'difficulty in securing the support of some of the large firms, which were already carrying out their own research, and ... that of small firms who might entertain some doubt on the advantages such a scheme could offer to them'. Despite this, he believed that it was politically expedient, in the light of the government's modernisation strategy, to be doing something. Asquith's pragmatism was not easily accepted, and in March 1960 the President of the MTTA, E. W. Field, thought that the government's repeated message to face the reality of 'technical advance' was a 'cliché'. Public criticism was 'ill founded', and he defended the inability of firms to meet the upturn in economic activity by accusing users of bunching investment in periods of prosperity. Nevertheless, he was forced to concede, on the urging of Asquith's committee, that cooperative research was a political expediency. Accordingly, the DSIR initiative to establish the MTIRA was endorsed, the MTTA underwriting the new research association until it received government funds.[24]

Incorporated in December 1960, a year later the MTIRA had 85 members, including 64 machine tool firms, representing half the total output of the industry, and 21 manufacturers in allied industries, including electronics firms that were innovating numerical control (NC) technology. The long-term strategy of the MTIRA was to establish 'university departments of research teams with machine tool interests', coordinate, stimulate and initiate machine tool research, and disseminate technical information to the industry. Its ultimate goal was to educate 'providers and users of machine tools'. From the outset, this was an over-ambitious programme, given the resources at its disposal and the problems of coordinating disjointed research projects, a fact noted by A. A. De Barr, the first director of the MTIRA in 1961. An initial income of £104,500 was insufficient to provide specialist laboratories and workshops, forcing the MTIRA to use the facilities of member firms, which delayed the start of prioritised long-term projects. Working under 'considerable difficulty', the MTIRA had launched only 27 projects,

---

[22] MTTA, Council Minute Book, 28 January, 30 March, 17 November 1960.
[23] *Hansard, Proceedings of the House of Commons*, 10 November 1960, pp. 1210-11; *Board of Trade Journal*, Vol. 153, 1961, p. 508.
[24] MTTA, Council Minute Book, 28 January, 30 March 1960.

employing 40 research personnel, by 1962, and only £150,000 worth of research contracts had been allocated.[25]

Two constraints limited the actions of government in instigating institutional cooperation in the industry. On the one hand, there was a lack of trust between the MTTA and officials at the DSIR; on the other hand, the individualism of leading machine tool makers, firms in allied industries, and industrial users, militated against collaborative action. Despite Field's political platitudes that the Mitchell Report represented 'a new era in the understanding of the industry's difficulties', relations between the MTTA and the DSIR were fraught. A major issue concerned the control and direction of the R&D effort, and the supporting role of the MTIRA. The MTTA viewed the activities of the MTIRA as completely separate from its own, the main link being in the field of 'education'. The function of the MTIRA was to coordinate cooperative R&D projects, while the MTTA would forward research projects through the DSIR's Machine Tool Research Council. Immediately, cooperation broke down on how DSIR funded development projects were to be allocated. For example, the MTTA complained about the 'unsatisfactory' action of the Economic Division of the DSIR in employing private consultants to provide information on the design needs of the industry, as a prerequisite to granting research contracts. The 'most objectionable aspect' of these arrangements was 'the lack of co-operation evidenced between the DSIR and the Association'. A meeting of industrial trade associations under the auspices of the FBI, and instigated by the MTTA, concluded that the 'modus operandi of the Economic Division, DSIR, left much to be desired'. Deep concern in the industry persisted over DSIR interference in its business, and only after several meetings, presided over by the FBI, was 'harmony' restored, the DSIR guaranteeing to inform the MTTA of its actions 'to a much greater extent'.[26] Consultative problems still remained, and in 1962 the Zuckerman Committee lambasted the DSIR for its refusal to appoint MTTA representatives to their Machine Tool Projects Advisory Council, which appropriated development contracts. The MTTA believed that 'the direction and control of the R&D effort was out of their control', the Advisory Council consisting 'entirely of users'. It was not until 1963 that Viscount Hailsham, Britain's first Minister of Science, finally conceded to MTTA demands, following their threat of non-participation in his new committee to consider British engineering design. The cost of procrastination was to delay the granting to the industry of development contracts which could have been fed to the MTIRA, and it was not until March 1963 that the MTTA was given representation on the Advisory Council through the creation of a separate Machine Tool Development Committee, which consisted of makers, users, and the directors of the MTIRA and PERA.[27] This episode in industry-state relations was symptomatic of the secondary

---

[25] *Research and Development for Industry*, 1962, p. 99; MTIRA Annual Reports, 1961, pp. 1-2, 4, 6-7; 1962, p. 3; 1965, p. 4; *Economist*, 13 June 1964, p. 1274.

[26] MTTA, Council Minute Book, 17 November 1960; 26 January, 29 March, 25 May 1961.

[27] MTTA, Council Minute Book, 29 March, 27 September 1962; 31 January, 26 March 1963.

role of the MTTA in the institutional 'game' of modernisation. The industry, in its relations with the DSIR, was relegated to a junior partner and the MTTA believed that user industries were given priority. Also, it is questionable whether the policy of the DSIR was a sensible one, lacking in the diplomatic skills which were likely to elicit a positive response from the industry's leaders.

However, problems of effective collaboration between the industry and government institutions were compounded by the individualistic attitude of members of the MTTA to cooperation on R&D. In 1960, J. E. Hill, of Landis Lund, an American subsidiary of the Landis Co. based at Keighley, and the General Manager of the MTTA, complained that certain member firms had withdrawn from the MTIRA because of the high level of subscriptions. Asquith was also 'appalled' by the fact that only £40,000 per annum had been pledged to the MTIRA. 'What was needed', he claimed, 'was 100% backing [to] prove to the DSIR that the industry was truly concerned about its future development'. Reluctance was also noted by J. W. Morgan of EMI, who claimed that many companies could not see the benefits of cooperation, or 'they were waiting for a lead from the larger companies'. Hopes of a proactive lead from the large companies were in vain. For example, H. V. Hodgson of Wickman Ltd. and J. G. Bailey of Jones & Shipman felt that their research facilities were adequate to meet the technological challenge. More damning were the views of W. Core, Sales Director of Britain's largest producer, Herbert's, who reminded the MTTA that 'members might have their own views, particularly with regard to carrying out their own research'.[28]

The antipathy of the Herbert management led them to reject MTIRA membership until 1968, the company concentrating research in a new department formed in 1961. This rejection drew contradictory responses from government ministers. On the one hand the President of the Board of Trade, Reginald Maudling, was full of praise for a management which understood 'the need for R&D within their organisation' and was determined 'to allocate sufficient resources for that purpose'. On the other hand Hailsham at the DSIR viewed the actions of the company as symptomatic of an individualistic spirit, which hardly provided a lead for the industry. Indeed, he condemned the Herbert research facilities as 'little more than a prototype machine testing station'.[29] As we shall see in the next chapter, the governance style of the Herbert management determined proprietorial control over R&D capabilities, but if Herbert's did not provide a lead for collaborative action, much the same can be said of firms in complimentary activities such as electronics, and in the general engineering industry at large.

Collaboration with electronics firms was a key recommendation of the Mitchell Report in 1960. There was a need to evaluate electronic control systems, and standardise their design for application by machine makers, and this was a priority recognised by the MTIRA to expand the demand for NC machines. To facilitate this, and under directions from the Board of Trade, an approach was

[28] MTTA, Council Minute Book, 26 May, 6 October, 9, 17 November 1960.
[29] *Research and Development for Industry*, 1961, p. 108; *Board of Trade Journal*, Vol. 153, 1961, p. 1,508.

made by the MTTA in 1960 to the Electronic Forum for Industry (EFI), a panel formed in 1958 to link electronic gear manufacturers with user industries. The MTTA immediately found itself playing second fiddle, representatives from the Association being invited to the EFI on a random basis merely as advisors to a forum dominated by electrical companies and large engineering concerns. In September 1961 the EFI was disbanded, the gear control manufacturers questioning its feasibility as a 'co-ordinating centre' for manufacturing industry at large. Electronics companies looked to their own trade body, the British Electrical and Allied Manufacturers' Association (BEAMA) to coordinate joint industrial action on standardisation and R&D. This opened up opportunities for the MTTA to co-ordinate directly through BEAMA's Electronic Equipment Section, chaired by J. W. Morgan of EMI who was also a member of the MTTA. Proposals for such a cosy relationship found little support from officials at the Board of Trade. A more focused approach on developing electronic control, they believed, would result from collaboration between the machine tool industry and Plessey, a leading electronics firm, through a joint commercial venture. Supported by the DSIR, however, the MTTA signalled its support for cooperation with electronics firms on an industry-wide basis, and a MTTA Liaison Sub-Committee was established to coordinate with the Electronic Equipment Section of BEAMA. Board of Trade suspicions were justified, the Liaison Sub-Committee, to the annoyance of the MTTA, confined its activities to standardisation, largely ignoring cooperative action on R&D. In the view of the MTTA there was a need 'to seek closer coordinated action on the basis of parity, neither industry being regarded as inferior or superior to the other'. In September 1962 the Sub-Committee broke up in disarray, due to MTTA 'frustration' with their relations with BEAMA, and was resurrected in 1963 with a limited agenda to concentrate on coordinating a standardisation policy through the British Standards Institute.[30] Committees spawned committees, but the impression remains that left to their own devices inter-industry collaboration created little positive outcomes. Further, the conflicting positions of the DSIR and Board of Trade in this episode, was symbolic of their different views on the degree of collective action required in the planning process.

Institutional initiatives for collaboration had mixed outcomes for the machine tool industry, but what were the expectations of the industry concerning the role of the government in economic affairs? The key issue for the industry was the promotion of demand side policies, rather than supply side polices relating to institutional collaboration for R&D. In an environment conditioned by a cyclical pattern of demand, outside the control of individual enterprise, the role of government should be to instigate macro economic policies to smooth out the cycle, allowing the industry to forecast for future investment decisions. The pattern of orders and output between 1960 and 1965 is given in Table 8.2. Responding to the surge in both domestic and export orders in 1960, coinciding with the government's expansionary policies, output was expanded but was insufficient to

---

[30] MTTA, Council Minute Book, 26 May 1960; 26 January, 23 February, 29 March, 27 July, 28 September, 16 November 1961; 28, 29 March, 27 September 1962; 28 March 1963.

meet total orders. However, by late 1960 the Manufacturers' Committee of the MTTA was reporting on the actions of domestic car manufactures 'to cancel or retard the delivery of machine tool orders for standardised machines'. Consequently, there was a sharp downturn in domestic demand between 1961 and 1963, and the industry was caught in the familiar cyclical trap. With falling domestic orders output was 22.6 per cent and 19.5 per cent above the level of total orders in 1962 and 1963 respectively. In both years, orders were substantially below capacity, which had been built up to 'overtake the peak demand of earlier years, and as the backlog dwindled away, the trade has had to struggle to keep its teams together and employed'. At the same time there was evidence of 'suppressed demand' with user industries making 'undiminished' enquiries for machine tools. In the downturn of the domestic cycle, maintaining export demand became a key priority, a policy reinforced by the Board of Trade who urged an expansion of exports to stabilise a declining balance of payments. J. C. Snow, the President of the MTTA in 1962, was in no doubt that the strongest 'political' emphasis is given to exports, which 'are essential to the economic well being of the United Kingdom'. However, the value of imports rose substantially in the upturn of 1960-61, stabilised during the next two years, but by 1963 accounted for 26 per cent of consumption (Table 8.1).[31]

Table 8.1
Consumption of Machine Tools, 1959-65 (£ 000)

	A	B	C	D	E
	Home Deliveries	Imports	Consumption	Imports % of Consumption	Exports
	Manufacturers Returns	Customs-Excise	A+B	B as % of C	Manufac-turers Returns
1959	60,216	13,149	73,365	18	18,552
1960	70,626	19,153	89,779	21	24,310
1961	87,085	27,620	114,705	24	28,627
1962	91,702	27,632	119,334	23	35,471
1963	74,974	26,196	101,170	26	39,188
1964	83,908	33,179	117,087	28	37,801
1965	98,300	33,640	131,940	25	40,500

Source: MTTA, Machine Tool Directory, 1966, p. 17.

The rising proportion of imports in total consumption brought the industry under further political scrutiny between 1961 and 1964, and reinforced government calls for an expansion of exports. The Economic Policy Committee of the MTTA viewed with deep concern the appointment of Board of Trade independent

---

[31] MTTA, Council Minute Book, 17 November 1960; 29 March 1961; *Machine Tool Review*, Vol. 52, 1964, p. 25.

consultants to the shipbuilding industry to investigate criticisms that it had become a net importer, and warned that machine tools were next to be targeted. Consequently, MTTA policy on exports involved an increasing call for government subsidies for exports. Government support for exports, via the services of the Board of Trade and the Export Credit Guarantee Department (ECGD), were felt to be inadequate and information was not disseminated to the large number of small-scale makers in the industry. At regional meetings between makers and representatives from the Board of Trade and ECGD, instigated by a newly formed MTTA Export Committee, the industry strongly presented their view that government initiatives were no more than 'soft words'. Referring to higher levels of government assistance in the U.S.A., the MTTA called for direct subsidies and the issuing of Industrial Development Certificates for export projects, both proposals leading to a rejection by the Board of Trade. A report by the Manufacturers' Committee of the MTTA in 1962 observed a failure to maintain world export shares, and condemned the Board of Trade and the ECGD for a failure to investigate the individual needs of the industry. Calls for direct export subsidies were resisted by the Board of Trade, but the industry did receive a boost from government incomes policies. In March 1962, Snow referred to the opportunities opened in export markets due to rising wages abroad, especially West Germany, and welcomed 'the Chancellor's standstill in wages [which] may yet give our industry ... just that edge in price which will enable it to improve even further its export potential'. Price competitiveness was a crucial factor in the competitive game, and Snow called for cooperation from trade unions in restraining wage demands.[32]

Table 8.2
New Orders for Machine Tools and Total Output, 1959-65 (£ 000)

	Home Orders	Export Orders	Total New Orders	Actual Total Output
1959	62,058	18,217	80,275	78,768
1960	111,879	32,868	144,747	94,936
1961	90,509	36,420	126,929	115,713
1962	60,469	38,074	98,523	127,172
1963	61,267	33,653	94,920	114,162
1964	101,085	38,172	139,257	121,709
1965	117,879	40,500	157,500	138,800

Source: MTTA, Machine Tool Directory, 1966, p. 18.

Reinforcing the industry's commitment to exports was a continuation of its rejection of protectionist policies on imports. This view represented a long

---

[32] MTTA, Council Minute Book, 27 July, 16 November 1961; 25 January, 28 March 1962; MTTA, Manufacturers' Committee Report, The Challenge to the Machine Tool Industry, 31 May 1962.

tradition in the industry and its leaders expressed the importance of the reciprocal relationship between exports and imports. In late 1959 the Board of Trade had accepted the MTTA case to abolish the duty free entry on imported machines, and in line with the GATT agreement to reduce the standard rate of duty from 17.5 per cent to 10 per cent, a reduction which was extended to the import of machine parts in 1962, following an extensive campaign by the MTTA during 1961.[33] Supporting low import duties, the Export Committee of the MTTA argued that reciprocal trade in machine tools was as essential to the development of British engineering 'in terms of importation as it was to the Exchequer in terms of exports'. Such a view symbolised the long held principal of an international division of labour, the British concentrating on standard lines and importing specialist machine tools from abroad, but also reflected the constitution of the MTTA which incorporated merchanting firms and manufacturers who factored foreign machine tools. Moreover, under Board of Trade initiatives, the industry had targeted exports towards lesser developed areas and Eastern bloc markets. Given the balance of payments problems that these countries faced, it was an 'established' position 'that exports cannot occur in the absence of trade'.[34]

In the downturn of the cycle, government pressure from the Treasury and the Board of Trade was directed towards the industry's export performance, which was related to the problem of alleviating the balance of payments deficit. In March 1962 Snow informed the MTTA that exports had helped sustain orders for the industry, but warned members that 'We must not allow ourselves to be blinded too much by the blandishments of ... Government for increased exports; these cannot, in themselves, maintain a healthy machine tool industry'. The home market was also important, and there was a need 'to preserve a reasonable balance between the two outlets'. On the domestic front, Snow called for a 'vigorous replacement policy' by user industries that were presently operating 'obsolete equipment', and fiscal action by the government to raise demand. The Manufacturers' Committee of the MTTA reached similar conclusions in 1962, the Committee observing a serious decline in the domestic market, and recognising the need for 'harmonisation of sales effort between the home and export' sectors. Each machine tool firm operated at 'an optimum level of production, and this must be supported from somewhere'; with falling domestic demand there was inadequate throughput which inevitably raised overhead costs and detrimentally affected profits. Recognising that export markets acted as a counter-cyclical device with the home market, and therefore could provide relief from domestic recessions, the Committee nevertheless advocated the need for government to alleviate the stop-go cycle and to provide the machinery for the forecasting of future demand.[35]

---

[33] MTTA, Council Minute Book, 30 March 1961, 28 March, 27 September 1962; Annual Report of the Board of Trade 1960, p. 10; Revisions to Customs Duties (Dumping and Subsidiary Act), 1957, Parliamentary Reports, Vol. 20, No. 336.

[34] MTTA, Council Minute Book, 29 March 1961.

[35] MTTA, Council Minute Book, 28 March 1962; Manufacturers' Committee, The Challenge of the Machine Tool Industry, 31 May 1962.

The emphasis on the demand cycle and forecasting defined the Tory government's initiatives for growth, symbolised by the creation of the NEDC in 1962, and its operational arm the National Economic Development Office (NEDO) formed in 1961. NEDC planning for growth was based on consultation between industry, unions, and government and this involved the collection and 'exchange' of information to identify the obstacles to growth and 'the implications of faster growth, with an underlying belief that if everyone accepted that goal this would be nine-tenths of the way to achieving it'.[36] The consultative function of the NEDC was outlined by T. C. Fraser, its Industrial Director:

> We said to industry ... 'If the national economy grew at an annual average of 4 per cent between 1961 and 1966 what would your output, exports, imports ... and employment be in that year? What do you reckon will be your annual investment figure between now and then?'

This was all 'part of the work of the economists to devise a model for 1966',[37] and machine tools were one of 17 industries selected by the NEDC. As an autonomous agency from government the NEDC was positively received by the MTTA as a platform for projecting industrial policy to both the public and to government ministries. In May 1962 top level negotiations commenced with Sir Robert Shore, Director General of the NEDC, followed by working level discussions with NEDO staff on the procedures for collecting information. Recognising the dearth of information for industrial forecasting, the MTTA Council urged members to supply information on output, R&D expenditure, exports, skilled technical workers, and the age of machine tools. The initial response to the survey was described as 'pathetic', only 11 firms replying. Failure to respond, claimed Snow, was 'detrimental to our interests', and negated an opportunity to 'keep the industry in the public eye'. In 1963 the MTTA complained about the lack of statistics on a range of indicators, including exports, imports, and employment, and in March 1964 the President, J. G. Petters, was still urging firms to complete statistical questionnaires. The problem of statistical data was strikingly demonstrated in the crucial areas of costs and prices, when in January 1964 NEDO approached the Engineering Employers Federation (EEF) for information in relation to the effects of recent economy-wide pay awards sanctioned by the National Incomes Commission. The MTTA response showed the limits of their influence on individual firms. In 'a competitive industry', the MTTA argued, 'prices were not increased unnecessarily', and 'the MTTA had never had any hand in questions concerning its member's prices and costing and was not prepared to enter that field'.[38] This is a reminder that planning can be seen as a solution to 'market failure', but this can be frustrated when there is a need for 'access to detailed micro

[36] Tomlinson, *Public Policy*, pp. 252-3; Tomlinson, 'Inventing Decline', p. 748.
[37] T. C. Fraser, 'How NEDC Works with Industry', *The Manager*, Vol. 31 (June 1963), pp. 37-9.
[38] MTTA, Council Minute Book, 31 May, 26 July 1962; 30 May 1963; 30 January, 25 March 1964.

economic information', and this was clearly the case in Britain's attempt to instigate 'indicative planning' in the early 1960s.[39]

At a more general level, the formalisation of the planning system for industrial forecasting was slow to materialise. During 1963 discussions with NEDO took place to formalise relations with the industry, by creating a Machine Tool NEDC Committee, which included representatives from the MTTA and the unions. Eventually inaugurated in March 1964, under the directorship of Sir Steuart Mitchell, this was one of nine 'Little Neddies' to consider and advice on the problems and obstacles to industrial growth. The protracted nature of the negotiations demonstrated the problems of formalising institutional arrangements at an industry level. At meetings with Fraser in May and June 1963 the MTTA raised serious concerns about the formalisation of institutional arrangements. There was a general feeling by members that 'Little Neddies' had no specific function, and the inclusion of the unions, generally accepted by the MTTA, raised issues concerning the discussion of wages outside the confines of the EEF. Further sticking points concerned the constitution of the Committee, and the costs of administration. For example, the MTTA objected to the inclusion of a permanent member from the Board of Trade, the industry's 'sponsoring department', arguing that this undermined 'the jealously guarded independence of NEDO from Whitehall', and claimed that members would be unwilling to finance increased administrative costs unless they saw 'tangible outcomes flowing from NEDO'. In March 1964, with much reluctance, the MTTA formed a secretariat, which consisted of economists and statisticians, and cost £4,000. The reluctance of the MTTA reflected a deep concern about NEDO 'pressure' to force 'a closer adherence ... to the current way of ordering industrial life – through an economist'. The MTTA viewed this as 'undesirable', and from the industry's perspective the 'game' was entering a more dangerous phase. If the MTTA committed the industry to full participation in the NEDC machinery, the risk of the industry being absorbed into the 'central controls' of a future Labour Government was increased. 'One cannot ignore the suggested intentions of the Socialist Party with regard to the NEDC', the MTTA informed Fraser, and 'If it should be absorbed by Whitehall', it would be difficult to disassociate the industry, irrespective of a shift from relative autonomy to centralised control.[40]

Nevertheless, NEDO offered the industry the opportunity to put forward their policy vision for the industry, and in 1963 Snow outlined the objectives of the MTTA. Referring to the trend towards the absorption of firms into larger industrial organisations, he attacked the critics of the industry who saw rationalisation as the only solution to meeting the 'foreign challenge'. In a free market economy, he argued, it was impossible to substantially reduce the number of types of machine tools produced, given the demand of users, both at home and abroad, for a wide

---

[39] Metcalfe, 'Technology Systems', p. 270; Wood, 'Indicative Planning', pp. 435, 450.

[40] MTTA, Council Minute Book, 30 May, 25 July 1963; 30 January, 24 March 1964; *Department of Economic Affairs, Industrial and Regional Progress Reports*, No. 1, January 1965, p. 4.

range of machines. Replying to Labour Party calls for nationalisation, he attacked direct state interference in the legitimate operations of business. Britain was not a 'monolithic state' and 'we are convinced that the god of rationalisation must not be worshipped to the exclusion of all other considerations'. Such a view, he claimed, was supported by NEDO, which had taken on board MTTA suggestions for the government to provide a 'fiscal carrot'. MTTA policy proposals related to a government stimulus to investment demand, through reductions in profit tax, leasing schemes on machine tools for industry, and lower interest rates. The aim, claimed Snow, was to boost home demand which 'required a period of prosperity to occur before it can become effective'. On this issue the solution lay with government who 'should think about controlling cyclical demand through fiscal action'.[41]

Advice to the Chancellor through consultation with NEDO assumed, of course, that such proposals would be acted upon, and NEDO had no statutory powers, being autonomous from government.[42] For example, MTTA and NEDO suggestions to stimulate home demand through the provision of fixed incentive payments for confirmed orders and financial assistance to firms for accumulating stocks of standard machine tools was rejected by the Treasury in 1963, the Chancellor believing that he had 'stimulated the economy sufficiently from a capital investment point of view'. Indeed, the problem of the cyclical nature of demand for machine tools was deeply embedded in the industry, and related to the investment decisions of users. What government fiscal policy could actually do to alleviate the cycle was constrained. As the Economic Policy Committee of the MTTA concluded, the 'blocking of orders' occurred in the 'board rooms' of British industry, and under a NEDO initiative launched a survey of the 'age of machines' in user industries. There was a need to persuade 'users to help eliminate the peaks and troughs of demand', and NEDO was seen as a means of achieving this. For example, Snow attacked the conservative replacement policy of user industries in 1963, who had offered the 'excuse' of the uncertainty of future trade caused by negotiations over British entry into the Common Market. The breakdown of the Brussels Talks on entry in 1963, Snow claimed, meant that 'the die is cast' and the prospect of higher European tariffs necessitated NEDO to encourage user industries to modernise equipment to meet the competitive challenge. Such views were reciprocated by Britain's largest producer, Alfred Herbert. The company's *Machine Tool Review* predicted that the 'freeze up' in engineering will finally 'crack', now that the decision over the Common Market had been reached, and that government policy, in preparation for a general election, was orientated towards expanding demand. It went on to warn, however, that 'we shall be back to the long order books and extended deliveries which are no good for neither buyer nor seller, nor for the productivity of the country as a whole'. The problem lay with user industries who were delaying investment decisions for re-equipment, thus leading to the usual bunching of demand in the upturn of the cycle. Reiterating the views of the MTTA, there was a call for a major re-equipment of British industry, and a

---

[41] MTTA, Council Minute Book, 26 March 1963.
[42] Tomlinson, *Public Policy*, p. 253.

government leasing programme to alleviate the shortages of financial capital in engineering industry.[43]

In the upturn of the cycle in 1964 and 1965 orders expanded, and although output increased there were extended deliveries. As Table 8.2 shows, output fell short of new orders in both years, the industry facing the usual problem of skilled labour shortages in the upturn of demand, and the bunching of orders, especially from the motor vehicle industry.[44] The difficulties in meeting supply in the upturn of the cycle prompted the Machine Tool NEDC to instigate an industry led survey of investment patterns in user industries, conducted by the Management Consultants' Association. Despite this initiative, the industry again faced criticisms of its technical performance, especially from the Labour Party, and in the run up to the general election of October 1964 there were growing fears in the industry that the potential for a Labour victory would bring nationalisation and the increasing politicisation of NEDO. The spectre of Labour planning persuaded the MTTA to move closer to 'co-operation' with the Conservative Party Headquarters in 1961, Robert Asquith denouncing the Labour Party pamphlet on 'Science and the Future of Britain', presented at the Party Conference of that year, as an 'experiment in socialism'. In March 1964 the President, J. G. Petters, circulated an MTTA policy statement 'against undue interference from government or any other agency in the affairs of our industry', but also reminded members that the public expected the industry 'to take a leading part in the scientific and industrial revolution now occurring'. In this respect, the NEDC, as an autonomous institution, was a shelter against government intervention. As Petters informed members, 'Whatever happens at the Elections we are going to have national planning and national examination of our affairs, whether it's by the NEDC or some other body'. Referring to 'incursions into their affairs', Petters urged that 'we must use NEDO to have our say', and the accumulation of statistical data will allow the industry to 'talk with strength and accuracy at the right levels'. Improving public relations, Petters naively believed, 'will do much to protect us from the dead hand of bureaucracy in its worst forms'. At the same time, he was well aware that the industry faced rapid technical change and intense competition, 'in which some may not survive'.[45] Despite this recognition, the attempts by the Tory government to forge closer links with the industry remained unfulfilled. The leaders of the industry did accept that some form of government intervention was going to occur, and that they needed to respond, but the majority of machine tool firms were indifferent to the request for basic economic and technical information, and the industry continued to resist the idea of rationalisation, never mind nationalisation. The election of a Labour Government in October 1964 'led to both a new enthusiasm for growth and new agencies for its increase',[46] but before examining

---

[43] MTTA, Council Minute Book, 25 January 1962; 30 May, 26 September 1963; *Machine Tool Review*, Vol. 51, 1963, p. 1.

[44] MTTA, Machine Tool Directory, 1966, pp. 18-19.

[45] MTTA, Council Minute Book, 25 May, 16 November 1961; 25 March, 28 May 1964.

[46] Tomlinson, *Public Policy*, p. 253.

the relations of the industry to Labour modernisation, the next section assesses the international performance of the industry in the 1960s, and the competitive challenges it faced.

Table 8.3
Percentage of Total Machine Tool Output Exported, 5 Leading Western European Countries, 1962

Switzerland	W. Germany	Italy	U.K.	France
77	47	42	31	28

Source: *Machinist*, 9 December 1963, p. 90.

Table 8.4
World Production of Machine Tools for 5 Leading Makers, 1962-70

	Output ($ Millions)		% Increase in Money Value of Output per annum	% Increase in Real Value of Output per annum[a]	% of World Output	
	1962	1970	1962-70	1962-70	1962	1970
U.S.A.	867	1,443	8.3	3.75	19.6	18.5
W. Germany	821	1,479	10.0	5.1	19.0	19.0
U.S.S.R.	715[b]	1,073	6.2	2.2	16.4	13.8
U.K.	356	477	4.2	0.7	8.7	6.1
Japan	310	1,109	32.3	22.5	6.4	14.2

Source: *Machinist*, 25 January 1963, p. 90, 18 January 1965, p. 133, 25 January 1971, p. 70.
Notes: a. Real values based on index of American machine tool prices of 1959-70, which show an average increase of prices of 3.5 per cent. b. Cutting tools only.

The International Machine Tool Industry in the 1960s

During the 1960s the British machine tool industry continued to face a rapidly changing market-cum-technological environment. In international markets, countries constituting the European Committee for Co-operation in the Machine Tool Industry[47] produced on average 36 per cent of total world output of machine tools, with the U.S.A. contributing one-fifth. A characteristic of the Western European industry was a significant level of inter-trading with 45 per cent of total exports being consumed within the European Committee bloc of countries, the second largest export area, Asia, taking only 15 per cent. The British industry reaped the benefits of inter-trading, and in 1960 was the third largest supplier to

---

[47] West Germany, Austria, Denmark, Spain, France, Italy, U.K., Netherlands, Portugal, Switzerland, and Belgium.

EEC markets, behind West Germany and France, but was outsold by the Germans in a ratio of 8:1.[48] There was also considerable variation in the machine tool export capacity of the leading Western European nations, with West Germany exporting 47 per cent of its total output compared to Britain's 31 per cent in 1962 (Table 8.3). In the international league table (Table 8.4), the British industry was the fourth largest producer in 1962, although it significantly lagged behind the leading three, and by 1970 was fifth, relegated by the emerging Japanese. British machine tool production per annum grew at the slowest rate of the leading five makers, 1962-70, and as Table 8.5 shows British output in proportion to the four leading producers fell significantly over the decade, most dramatically in relation to Japan. Rather than closing the gap, the British machine tool industry fell further behind.

Japan's breakthrough was the most dramatic, its machine tool industry rapidly overtaking Britain and significantly catching up to that of the U.S.A. and West Germany. The Japanese surge began from the mid-1960s, and between 1965 and 1969, the value of its machine tool output increased at 10 times the rate of West Germany, and 50 times the rate of Britain. Inter-country differences in performance were also marked in the case of the U.S.A., which was overtaken by West Germany as the world's largest machine tool producer in 1970 and experienced rising import penetration with the proportion of imports to total output increasing from 3.9 per cent in 1965 to 9.9 per cent in 1970. The West German growth record in the 1960s, although significantly slower than Japan, nevertheless remained impressive, the real rate of output growth rising by 5.12 per cent, 1962-70. In a matter of just 25 years, the West Germans had by 1970 'established an immensely strong machine tool industry' through inter-firm collaboration in contrast to the strong individualistic ethos of American and British makers. This is not to suggest that the West German industry did not experience problems. The Japanese were rapidly catching up, and similar to the U.S.A. the West Germans experienced increasing import penetration, imports rising by 71 per cent between 1968 and 1969 and by a further 48 per cent between 1969 and 1970. Moreover, in the late 1960s, inflationary pressures further eroded the competitive position of West Germany. This culminated in an 11 per cent pay increase to workers in the metal working industries in 1970, forcing German makers to raise prices.[49] Nevertheless, what impressed most about German performance was its hold on export markets (Table 8.6). Between 1962 and 1970, German exports grew in money value by 13.4 per cent per annum and, despite the spectacular rise of Japanese exports, it remained the dominant machine tool export economy in the world, the value of exports in 1970 being greater than the combined value of her four nearest rivals. Britain, despite falling back in terms of overall output, recorded a similar growth rate of exports to that of West Germany, and maintained her position as the world's third largest machine tool exporter. From this perspective,

---

[48] MTTA, Council Minute Book, 6 October 1960, Report on British Machine Tool Exports.

[49] *Machinist*, 14 September 1964, p. 71; 12 October 1964, p. 75; 19 May 1969, p. 2; 25 January 1971, pp. 70, 72.

the performance of the British industry in the 1960s was a mixed one, an issue we shall return to later.

Table 8.5
British Machine Tool Output as a % of 4 Leading Makers, 1962-70

	1962	1970
U.S.A.	41.1	33.0
W. Germany	44.5	32.2
U.S.S.R.	49.8	44.4
Japan	115.1	43.0
Average for		
4 Makers	13.1	9.3

Source: Calculated from value of output in Table 8.4

Growing Western European competition and the rise of Japan as a major machine tool producer in the 1960s coincided with the first phase of the rapid diffusion of numerical controlled machine tools (NCMT's) at an international level. The first half of the 1960s was 'a time of rapid expansion of numerical controls', enabling improved accuracy in machining, new engineering product development, and the evolution of multi-function and multi-purpose machining centres, combining turning, boring, milling etc. During the 1960s, 'Most of the industrialized countries started national programs to ... accelerate and intensify the development and introduction of NC'.[50] The rate of diffusion of NCMT's varied across countries, with the U.S.A. leading the way. Estimates indicate that there were 2,800 NCMT's in use in the U.S.A. in 1963, rising to 5,000 in 1964 and 7,000 by 1965, at which time they produced approximately 2 to 4 per cent of 'metalworking output'. In contrast, there were approximately 400 NCMT's in Britain in 1964, and in 1965, there were 600 out of a total machine tool population of 250,000. Using the U.S.A. as the benchmark, NC diffusion was slower in Western Europe, which was in all probability about five years behind the Americans in 1964. The Western Europeans, however, were already 'making up for lost time'. In contrast to the European Machine Tool Exhibition of 1959, the Milan Exhibition of 1963 included a wide range of NCMT's, and the development of NC 'was the talk of the British International Machine Tool show' of 1964.[51] NC represented the new technological horizon for the industry, a fact not lost on British makers and government modernisers. Innovation in NC, set within the context of an increased competitive environment associated with European competition and the rapid emergence of Japan, posed new challenges, and these forces dovetailed with changes in the institutional environment reflecting the more interventionist industrial policies of the Labour Government after 1964.

[50] Arnold, 'The Recent History of the Machine Tool Industry', pp. 18-19, 31.
[51] MTTA, Machine Tool Directory, 1966, pp 34-5; *Machinist*, 26 October 1964, p. 3; *Engineer*, 19 June 1964, p. 1,062.

Table 8.6
Value of Machine Tool Exports, 5 Leading Makers, 1962-70 ($ millions)

	1962	1970	% Increase in Money Value of Output per annum 1962-70
W. Germany	385.6	800.4	13.4
U.S.A.	182.1	305.1	8.4
U.K.	99.7	206.2	13.4
U.S.S.R.	35.7	86.7	17.9
Japan	12.4	90.9	79.1

Source: *Machinist*, 18 January 1965, p. 133, 25 January 1971, p. 70.

British Machine Tools and the White Heat of Technology, 1964-70

There were few illusions concerning the competitive challenge the industry faced in the 1960s. Harold Wilson's Labour Government of 1964 was committed to a policy of industrial modernisation.[52] The Department of Economic Affairs (DEA) of 1964, headed by George Brown, was 'the ministerial counterpart' to a National Plan for economic growth.[53] Published in 1965 the Plan allocated the machine tool industry, as did the Conservative Government before it, a key role in the process of modernisation, and defined it as a 'crucial' sector supplying 'the investment requirements in the engineering and allied industries'. Under the Plan the industry was expected to raise the rate of growth of output per annum from an average of 2 per cent, 1960-64, to a projected 7.8 per cent, 1964-70. The Plan also reflected on the industry's poor productivity record, and targeted for a productivity increase of 4.8 per cent per annum, 1964-70. Reflecting concern with the 'stop-go' cycle and its relationship to the balance of payments, the planners at the DEA also prioritised import penetration as a key failure. Increased imports, which were rising 'at about the same rate as exports and are about equal in value', reflected technical deficiencies 'to develop and produce machine tools of advanced design as well as its failure to expand capacity sufficiently to meet demand for home industry and for exports'. What concerned planners most was the advanced type of machine tools imported, and the Plan cited the usual suspects for the industry's shortcomings; a fragmented industrial structure and insufficient trained engineers and technicians were obstructing faster growth.[54] Under Labour the DEA was to assume the key responsibility for planning, although the NEDC with its links to the unions and industrialists, through the little neddies was retained, as well as the creation of MinTech charged with the modernisation of British industry.[55]

---

[52] See R. Coopey, 'Industrial Policy in the White Heat of the Scientific Revolution', in Coopey, Fielding and Tiratsoo (eds), *The Wilson Government*.
[53] Tomlinson, *Public Policy*, p. 250.
[54] *National Plan*, 1965, pp. 104-5.
[55] Tomlinson, *Public Policy*, pp. 252, 262.

The performance of the industry in relation to the National Plan was a mixed one. The most positive aspect was in the foreign trade sector, where the rate of growth of exports in real terms reached their planned target of 10 per cent (Table 8.7), while the real growth of imports was only 3.2 per cent per annum.[56] Consequently, the trade surplus rose from $12.8 million in 1964 to $72.2 million by 1970, the proportion of exports to total output increased from 31.1 per cent to 43.2 per cent, while the proportion of imports remained more or less stable (Table 8.8). The most disappointing outcome was in the projections for total output, the real rate of increase attained being only one-third of the planned target (Table 8.7). Although this represented an improvement over the early years of the 1960s, the average growth rate disguised the sharp volatility in output, shown in Table 8.8, which replicated the long-term cyclical pattern of demand. As output slowed down in 1966-7 the trade surplus in machine tools turned into a deficit, and even with a sharp fall in output in 1968, the surplus was only $27 million. Between 1966 and 1969, output growth was negative, before it again surged ahead in 1970.[57] This relatively weak output performance was compounded by the fact that by 1971 59 per cent of British machine tools were 10 years old plus compared to 35 per cent West Germany, 37 per cent Japan, and 40 per cent Italy.[58] As shown in Table 8.9, the number of British-made machine tools operating in domestic industry actually fell by 30.5 per cent between 1961 and 1971.

Table 8.7

Targets and Outcomes: Machine Tools and the National Plan, 1964-70

	National Plan Target	Outcomes 1964-70		% of Target Achieved	
		Money Values	Real Values	Money Values	Real Values
Average rate of output per annum	7.8	6.7	2.63	85.9	33.7
Average rate of export growth per annum	10.0	15.8	10.2		100
Output per worker per annum	4.8		-0.6		0

Source: *National Plan*, 1965, p. 28; *Machinist*, 25 January 1971, p. 70.
Notes: Productivity based on $ values of worker output assuming 80,000 workers in the industry in 1964 and a projected 16 per cent increase by 1970.

---

[56] *Machinist*, 25 January 1971, p. 70.
[57] It fell again 1970-72.
[58] *Machinist*, 21 February 1972, p. 67.

Table 8.8
British Output, Exports, and Imports of Machine Tools, 1964-70 ($ millions)

	Output	Exports	% Exports to Output	Imports	% Imports to Output	Trade Surplus
1964	340.5	105.9	31.1	93.1	27.3	+12.8
1965	394.2	136.2	34.5	94.0	23.8	+42.2
1966	414.0	98.0	26.7	106.0	25.6	-8.0
1967	420.1	118.5	28.2	141.8	33.7	-23.3
1968	367.4	135.4	36.8	108.2	29.4	+27.2
1969	410.0	145.0	35.4	91.2	22.2	+53.8
1970	477.0	206.2	43.2	134.0	28.1	+72.2

Source: *The Machinist*, 16 January 1967, p. 130, 20 January 1969, p. 121, 26 January 1970, p. 138; 25 January 1971, p. 70.

Table 8.9
Number of Machine Tools in British Industry, 1961-71

	1961	1971
Metal Cutting	1,034,536	727,856
Metal Forming	199,221	128,826
Total	1,273,757	856,682

Source: *The Machinist*, 21 February 1972, p. 67.

What the government believed it could achieve by planning was not, in turn, reciprocated by the actual performance of the industry, and this set the context for the dialogue between machine makers and government institutions from 1965. As this dialogue unfolded, business-state relations became more fraught. Concern over planning was the subject of J. G. Petters' Presidential address in 1965. Petters had high hopes that, despite the 'immense challenge' facing the industry, 'governmentally inspired action' through NEDO and MinTech, would alleviate the competitive problems of the industry. Praising the industry's contribution to the Olympia Machine Tool Exhibition of 1964, where 61 per cent of British exhibits were of new designs, he warned his fellow manufacturers against complacency with 'the phenomenal success of West Germany in the export field', and the potential of Japan as a formidable competitor. Business leaders should pursue 'deliberate management for change', prioritising 'expansion – expansion of thought, expansion of capacity, of production, and, of course exports'. In overseas markets a more aggressive sales policy was required to raise exports to counteract periodic balance of trade deficits. His rhetoric fitted the tone of Labour policy, and he urged members that 'there must be planning ... to stabilise the economy', both by business and government. The full machinery of planning should be implemented, and the key to success was the collection and management of industrial information. Business information was the platform on which planning rested, but on this point Petters was less than optimistic. Planning, he claimed, was obstructed by the continued reluctance by individual firms to provide information, leading to a scarcity of 'detailed knowledge' by MinTech staff of the 'operating' procedures of the industry. Nevertheless, he urged the acceptance of a corporatist solution, the 'intention' of government being for 'co-operation and consultation', and the industry should not assume that ministers were 'hostile' to the creation of 'an effective machine tool industry'. Positive overtones signified that the MTTA resigned itself to the fact that government intervention was unavoidable, but it also recognised that firms remained suspicious about government intentions. To reassure members, Petters pointed out that effective planning was 'based on knowledge and understanding', and they now had the opportunity to 'influence' government policy. For example, the NEDC was 'looked to by the [DEA] more as an instrument of policy than the sounding board which it was regarded as by the Conservative Government'. Aware of the government's drive for exports, Petters referred to the 'immense technical know-how' of the industry and its potential to compete with foreign rivals, but the key constraint facing the industry remained the need to increase capacity. As he argued, increasing exports would create a larger 'vacuum' in the home market which would be filled by imports, and this would negate any improvement in the industry's balance of payments position.[59]

Breaking the capacity constraint was the key to successful planning; a fact that Petters believed the industry had been 'too slow in recognising'. This, he related to the cyclical pattern of demand in user industries which deterred long-term investments by machine makers. 'If planning reaches the high level of development which seems to be the intention of the DEA', he insisted, 'this will substantially alter the pattern of investment in capital goods and will go a long way to securing a levelling of our order input', providing the 'spur' for 'a higher productive capacity to meet a higher demand'.[60] Expanding the capacity of the industry was a central theme of the Machine Tool NEDC Action Plan, sponsored by NEDO and published in June 1965, which recommended 13 action points. These included a substantial increase in capacity to meet foreign competition at home and in export markets. An enhancement by the industry of its R&D effort, coupled with the import substitution of high-technology machines, and a re-evaluation of the advantages of factoring foreign machine tools. The rationalisation of design and production, and the encouragement of 'a pioneering spirit on the part of customers by making widely known the advantages and potentialities of more productive, more advanced machines', including NC. On the government side, there were promises of fiscal incentives to promote the modernisation of the nation's machine tool stock, and to remove the cyclical fluctuations in demand. At the same time the unions agreed 'in principle' to support the increased use of more modern equipment by both machine tool makers and users. This all added up 'to a comprehensive programme for reform and advance on the part of a key, if small,

---

[59] MTTA, Council Minute Book, 24 March 1965.
[60] Ibid.

industry which has had its share of troubles and criticisms in the past'. The aim of the Machine Tool NEDC was 'not to provide global answers to national problems ... but rather to identify and tackle the specific obstacles to maximum efficiency and growth in the individual industries with which they are concerned, on a basis of mutual agreement and joint commitment'.[61]

Appeals for mutual co-operation, however, were somewhat optimistic, and Ralph Gabriel, managing director of Charles Churchill & Co. and Chairman of the MTTA Manufacturers' Committee, was disappointed 'with the paucity of reaction by members of the industry' to the recommendations of the Action Plan. As the head of the Action Plan Working Group of the Machine Tool NEDC, Gabriel was conscious of the need to promote a spirit of co-operation between firms and government officials. An obstacle towards a more positive reception by the industry was clearly the vexed question of import substitution, explicit in the Action Plan. The MTTA executive, for example, firmly held to the principles of free trade, and tabled a motion calling for 'government action' to stimulate 'a better climate for the more intelligent use by the mechanical engineering industry ... of machine tools of all types'. They added the proviso that this should include 'the more exotic, from whatever national source they originate'. A commitment to free importation demonstrated the industry's hostility to Labour's imposition of an import surcharge of 15 per cent in November 1964, the MTTA informing the Board of Trade that British industry should have 'free' access 'to choose the source of its machine tools' so that it 'may secure the equipment most suitable to provide optimum production'.[62]

Resistance to plans for import substitution reflected the MTTA constitution, and the structure of the industry itself, with specialist machine tool merchants and manufacturing factorers of foreign machine tools. For example, in March 1966, the Machine Tool Importers' Committee of the MTTA called for a meeting with MinTech to register their deep concern over recommendations calling for phased import substitution to reduce dependency on foreign machines. Endorsing the action of importers, the MTTA General Council reaffirmed its policy of 'fair competition', and its continued 'support of factoring by British manufacturers'.[63] Additional support for the position of the MTTA was forthcoming from the Action Plan Working Group of the Machine Tool NEDC. While accepting an investigation of the costs and benefits of factoring in the British machine tool industry, they nevertheless announced that the 'interchange of specialised machines between technically advanced countries will continue and ... imports are likely to be a rising trend in a technically advanced economy'. This could be sustained, it was argued, by improving the competitiveness of exports to alleviate the trade deficit. The Working Group, however, did spell out the disadvantages of factoring. These included a disincentive to invest in R&D to

---

[61] DEA, Industrial and Regional Progress Reports, No 6, June 1965, pp. 5-6; MTTA, Council Minute Book, 19 November 1964; 24 March, 2 June 1965.

[62] DEA, Industrial and Regional Progress Reports, No 6, June 1965, pp. 5-6; MTTA, Council Minute Book, 19 November 1964; 24 March, 2 June 1965.

[63] MTTA, Council Minute Book, 8 March 1966.

develop competing products, underselling by factorers of new machines developed by British makers, and a discouragement to the development of 'all-British' machine tool systems, makers complementing British machines with those imported through factoring. The Machine Tool NEDC considered that these disadvantages should be minimised and there was a broad agreement by manufacturers to curtail imports where they could be identified. A logical starting point was to pinpoint import substitution through factoring, as firms engaged in this activity possessed detailed technical knowledge of the imports. Where the development of British products on similar lines was not feasible, then the possibility of producing under licence, or through an operating company, was to be an option for the industry to explore.[64]

Nevertheless, import substitution clashed with the long-held principle of free importation. H. B. D. Kearns, the President of the MTTA in 1967, rallied importers, manufacturers and factorers to the cause, boldly announcing that intentions by MinTech to reduce imports was not acceptable, 'importation will continue indefinably to fill a part of the U.K's consumption of machine tools'.[65] Rising imports in 1966 and 1967 and a worsening trade deficit (Table 8.8) was a major concern of the Action Plan Working Group of the Machine Tool NEDC,[66] but its efforts to persuade the industry to accept import substitution fell on deaf ears. Indeed, the success of planning import requirements was problematic in an industry in which information was limited. As the Importers' Committee of the MTTA noted in 1967, following a request for information from MinTech on the effect on imports and prices caused by the ending of surcharges, the revelation of detailed information 'is not likely to be acceded to on the grounds of confidentiality ... which we have argued should be observed'.[67] A failure to plan adequately import policies resulted in an inevitable increase in imports. During the first four months of 1967, there was a 50 per cent increase in imports over the concurring period in 1966, due to orders made 15 months previously when domestic engineering industries had been extended. This was particularly true of the automobile industry, and the import of German machines was noted due to a substantial decrease in price.[68]

With depressed economic conditions in 1967 and 1968, the industry relied on exports to sustain output, especially in the latter year when there was a sharp drop in total production, as shown in Table 8.8. The Machine Tool NEDC reported in 1967 that the way out of the 'recurring stop-go' was to substantially increase capacity and pursue 'export-led growth'. This reflected general trends between

---

[64] *Engineer*, 18 February 1966, p. 288.
[65] MTTA Council Minute Book, 9 March 1967. This was in marked contrast to the views of the American Machine Tool Builders' Association who campaigned vigorously against foreign import penetration, opposing in 1964 reductions in the machine tool tariff, and again in 1968 lobbied against an agreed reduction of 50 per cent by the U.S.A. as a result of GATT negotiations. *Engineer*, 8 March 1968, p. 418.
[66] MTTA, Council Minute Book, 9 June 1966.
[67] MTTA, Council Minute Book, 25 January 1967.
[68] MTTA, Council Minute Book, 9 March, 11 July 1967.

1967 and 1975 predicted by NEDO, which called for a 6 per cent annual growth in British machine tool production to provide a 'massive improvement' in the industry's trade balance, backed up by an intensive selling and marketing programme by makers. By 1968 export growth was the central plank of a revised NEDC Action Plan that envisaged a long-term export target of 50 per cent of total output.[69] The performance of exports demonstrates the commitment of the industry to fulfilling national planning targets and, by 1970, there was a substantial trade surplus. However, to meet the revival in domestic industry in 1970 there was also a substantial rise in imports, suggesting that the problems of meeting domestic demand in the upturn of the cycle remained persistent. The persistence of the cycle was noted by the MTTA in 1967 who predicted that the industry will be faced by the usual problem of insufficient capacity to meet the upturn of domestic demand. As Kearns argued, the usual importation occurred as economic activity increased, capacity being constrained by shortages of skilled workers, technicians and designers. Further, he questioned the quality of managerial recruitment into the industry, especially the limited supply of junior managers who were qualified in production methods and personnel management techniques vital to raising productivity on the factory floor.[70] *The Machine Tool Review* in 1968 told a familiar gloomy story, and at the same time highlighted the failure of industrial planning to overcome the cycle:

> all trade is cyclical ... In our trade ... the cycle of demand takes five years to swing from peak to peak, three years of decline followed by two years of comparatively rapid rise. Over the years we have cast the statistical bones time and time again without finding an acceptable answer. Outside influences, new inventions, all have been plotted and to none can we confidently point to as the direct cause. The sole remaining factor is the event itself'.[71]

The persistence of the cycle provided the opportunity for the industry to launch a counter attack against the inadequacy of government economic policy. In May 1968 Ralph Gabriel, the new President of the MTTA, although welcoming MinTech initiatives to provide incentives for customers to invest in new production equipment, attacked the government's failure to 'create a climate of stability'. Voicing deep suspicion concerning government intentions, he argued that interventionist policies were acting as a substitute for effective macro economic management. Consequently, a proposal to provide financial assistance to industry in the Industrial Expansion Bill was seen as a means of enabling political intervention, and recommendations in the Bill to form Industry Boards with 'extreme power' was condemned as an assault on industry 'as a commercial entity'. Earlier in 1968, the Economic Policy Committee of the MTTA condemned the inauguration of the government's Industrial Reorganisation Committee as a

---

[69] DEA, Industrial and Regional Progress Reports, No 32, September 1967, p. 8; No. 46, November 1968, p. 8.

[70] MTTA, Council Minute Book, 9 March 1967.

[71] *Machine Tool Review*, Vol. 56, 1968, p. 1.

form of 'back door nationalisation'. The persistence of the cycle, however, could not be ignored, and the usual scapegoat was blamed, namely the replacement policies of user industries.[72] As the MTTA observed in 1967, the cause of cyclical ordering was a result of the liquidity problems facing domestic users who consequently exercised prudence in the downturn of the cycle. Again, the MTTA made the standard appeal for fiscal incentives to provide cheap finance to induce users to take orders during downturns in economic activity, taking advantage of shorter delivery times to re-equip with modern machinery.[73] Identifying the problem as a demand-side phenomenon shifted the onus towards users. A report by a Working Party of the Machine Tool NEDC in 1966 concluded that the cyclical ordering of machine tools was a phenomenon of 'fluctuations in the outputs of the industries to which the machine tool makers supply tools'. In this respect, more progressive machine tool firms viewed the cycle as 'a fact of life', and could, with careful 'management' of stocks especially of standard lines, ensure that the fluctuations of output need not be as sharp as that of orders. For the majority of firms, however, lacking the financial resources to invest in inventories, the cycle was highly damaging. On this point, the Working Party rejected government proposals for an insurance scheme to build-up stocks in the machine tool industry, concluding that it would encourage inefficient firms to shelter behind government grants. However, the Working Party did accept the need for a campaign to persuade users to plan replacement orders three or four years ahead.[74] In its assessment of these recommendations, *The Engineer* exonerated machine tool makers from past criticisms, praising the industry for its efforts to vigorously expand output and raise the level of R&D, while condemning users for their resistance to British machine tool designs.[75]

From this perspective the main problem facing the industry and government planners related to the weak collaboration between domestic makers and users. As Kearns argued, users needed to consider the use of more domestic sources of machine tools 'than is customary and to plan requirements ahead in order to avoid bunching in the upturn of the cycle'. But initiatives to induce co-operation met with limited success. For example, attempts by NEDO and MinTech to create co-operation between representatives of the Machine Tool NEDC and the automobile and aircraft industries in early 1966 failed to arrive at any practical solutions to the ordering problem, both sectors being reluctant to invest forward given uncertainties over the economic outlook.[76] The NEDC Working Party of 1966 observed that 'orders for machine tools may be four times as high at the peak of the typical five year cycle as they are at its trough'. Consequently, the Working Party opened discussions with major firms in automobiles, an industry that had a long history of bunching orders for machine tools. While automobile

---

[72] MTTA, Council Minute Book, 8 March, 23 May 1968.

[73] MTTA, Council Minute Book, 9 March, 11 June 1967.

[74] *Report of Machine Tool NEDC Working Party on the Problems Arising from the Cyclical Pattern of Machine Tool Orders* (London, HMSO, 1966), p. 7.

[75] *Engineer*, 10 June 1966, pp. 877-8;

[76] MTTA, Council Minute Book, 13 January, 10 February 1966; 9 March 1967.

manufacturers recognised the need for consultation, they were not prepared to implement practical policies for 'forward ordering policy ... in the down-turn of the cycle'.[77] In June 1969, *The Engineer* commented that

> If machine tool manufacturers are not to slide towards the pattern of domination by American-owned firms as in the car industry the users must be quicker off the mark in supporting advance by British designers. And manufacturers must do better in letting production engineers know exactly what they can offer.

Attempts to promote user-maker co-operation tended to attract the interest of mainly larger engineering concerns, at the cost of damaging overall industrial efficiency and the loss of orders and future growth to the machine tool trade. A maker-user conference in London, a collaboration between the Machine Tool EDC and PERA, was attended by mainly 'highly sophisticated firms, such as Rolls-Royce, G. & J. Weir, and Automotive Products'. Institutional initiatives by government could set a framework for cooperation, but in a highly volatile economic environment, and in an atmosphere of business individualism, what government could actually achieve was contingent. With the revival of domestic trade in 1969 *The Engineer* presented its readers with the usual headline: 'Machine Tool makers swamped with orders'. A surge of orders in the first quarter of 1969 placed increasing pressure on existing capacity, leading to lengthening delivery dates, and the journal predicted that 'valuable exports ... will be lost if the industry does not increase its capacity quickly'. The position of the industry, it was claimed, was 'made worse by the resulting rise in machinery imports'.[78]

High, and rising import penetration, brought into question the technical competency of the British machine tool industry. The revised Machine Tool NEDC Action Plan of 1968 observed that 'Britain's propensity to import machine tools is high', and attacked the attitude of the industry based on 'the axiom that no one country can be best at everything'. Recognising that rising imports accelerated with the upturn of activity, and accepting that this was 'tolerable' if exports could be expanded, the Action Plan nevertheless warned that the pattern of trade reflected 'the fact that Britain in general is making the less complex goods and importing the more complex'. Earlier, in 1966, a NEDO report had concluded that the majority of users purchased machine tools based on performance and delivery rather than price, which gave an advantage to foreign imports. Two years later the Action Plan cited the same report, and concluded that 'what buyers were looking for was a product to meet their needs. Price was a secondary consideration'.[79] In 1969, Sir Richard Way, Chairman of Lansing Bagnall and chair of the Machine Tool NEDC, condemned both users and makers for the increasing importation of sophisticated machine tools. Users, he argued, were accustomed to 'pick up a German or Swiss catalogue and order straight out of that', while makers, through firms acting as agents for foreign machine tool

---

[77] DEA, Industrial and Regional Progress Reports, No 21, October 1966, pp. 6-7.

[78] *Engineer*, 22 May 1969, p. 9; 5 June 1969, p. 56.

[79] DEA, Industrial and Regional Progress Reports, No 21, October 1966, pp. 6-7; No 46, November 1968, pp. 7-8; No. 47, December 1968, p. 6.

concerns, found it more profitable to promote overseas lines where prompt delivery could be ensured from existing stocks. At regional conferences between makers and users in 1969, complaints abounded that the British machine tool industry was concentrating on standard lines and had not exploited 'the most advanced techniques and highly specialised applications'. In particular, the conferences noted the limited advance in high precision and automated machines.[80]

Empirical studies of the process of technological diffusion suggest that there is considerable user uncertainty about the application of new technology. Business managers frequently 'differ in the speed with which they evaluate new options, the judgements they arrive at, and even the range of options of which they are aware'.[81] Such uncertainty characterised the diffusion of NC in Britain; a survey by PERA in 1964 concluding that very few users of the technology could supply evidence that justified its economic use. This was important, because in the 1960s NCMT's could cost up to four times as much as conventional machine tools, and consequently users needed to be certain that their application would produce direct and indirect cost savings.[82] Decision making was further complicated by the existence of competing NC technologies in the 1960s. Input information systems, for example, were characterised by two broad types. At the lower level there was plug-board information input, where information (a programme) for a full cycle of operations was prepared on plugged locations and punched cards. At the higher level, taped controlled machines, using coded information on magnetic tapes, allowed computers to be used for this process. Under the plug-board system only a limited number of machine operations were possible, the information storage being limited, while with tape control the memory was almost unlimited allowing a wide variation of machine actions. Consequently plug-board was more conducive to 'Positioning Control', which placed the 'workpiece and tool in the correct position, and then advances the tool' for specific operations, for example drilling holes or by positioning the spindle, which held the tool, in a vertical or horizontal position without having to manually re-set it. Alternatively, tape control was most used for 'Continuous Path Control', where 'the path of the tool is controlled while machining is in progress, so that complicated shapes may be machined automatically'. Control systems, themselves, also varied between 'digital control', where information was fed between the control unit and machine by electrical signals, and 'analogue control, where information was fed by varying the strength of the electric current'.[83]

With the variety of systems, and potential applications for NC, as the PERA survey indicated, it was disappointing that while papers and articles on the subject had stimulated some general interest there was only limited information diffused to potential users concerning the economic advantages of installing the

[80] *Engineer*, 5 June 1969, pp. 56, 58.

[81] Nelson, *The Sources of Economic Growth*, p. 36.

[82] *Engineer*, 6 March 1964, p. 437.

[83] P. Blackburn, R. Coombs and K. Green, *Technology, Economic Growth and the Labour Process* (Basingstoke, Macmillan, 1985), pp. 52-3; MTTA, Machine Tool Directory, 1966, pp. 34-8; *Machine Tool Review*, Vol. 56, 1968, pp. 50-2.

new technology. PERA, however, was positive that there was considerable 'scope' for the application of NC in British engineering, and the growth of technical knowledge since the late 1950s had proved that NC machines had the potential to raise productivity in manufacturing, justifying 'their purchase on economic grounds'.[84] As a report by economists at Ford in 1967 concluded, the productivity of machine tools would have to increase four fold in the next 10 years if production targets were to be maintained.[85] The potential of NC was not lost on the machine tool industry. At the Olympia Machine Tool Exhibition in June 1964 control systems were displayed by a number of makers, demonstrating to *The Engineer* that NC, 'considered but a few years ago applicable only to machines for the larger, specialised, high production factories, are being regarded by smaller establishments now that their capacity for economic small batch production is increasingly appreciated'.[86] Increasing interest in NC was demonstrated by the fact that of the 400 NC machines in use in Britain 40 per cent of them had been purchased between January 1963 and February 1964, and it was predicted that NC machines in operation would double by the end of 1965.[87] Diffusion was still in its infancy, but optimism was high and this was enhanced by the increasing use by machine tool makers of NC systems designed in collaboration with electronic firms. At Olympia, Ferranti, Airmec, Plessey, EMI, AEI, and Staveley Industries from the U.K., Acramatic (Cincinnati Milling), Giddings & Lewis Fraser, Pratt & Whitney, Sperry, SEL from the U.S.A., Olivetti from Italy and SAAB from Sweden, all exhibited NC systems.[88] At the MTTA, the potential of NC raised new optimism about inter-industry collaboration, which had proved so difficult to achieve in the early 1960s. Petters, for example, informed the MTTA in March 1965 that it was crucial that they work closely with BEAMA in the industrial application of electronics to create 'the best atmosphere in which numerical controlled machine tools can be conceived and built as a entity in themselves'.[89] A joint conference between the MTTA and BEAMA provided Kearns in November 1965 with the opportunity to proclaim that this was an important step towards launching 'the advanced type of numerical controlled equipment so much needed by the British engineering industry'.[90] Indeed, in his own company, H. W. Kearns Ltd., they had invested 'considerably in the development of numerical control', believing that they were 'in advance of world competitors'.[91] Commitment to the acceleration of NC technology seemed to be confirmed in 1966 when Britain hosted the world's first international all NCMT exhibition, an event which was

---

[84] *Engineer*, 6 March 1964, p. 437.

[85] MTTA, Council Minute Book, 25 January 1967.

[86] *Engineer*, 19 June 1964, p. 1,062.

[87] *Machinist*, 4 January 1967, p. 3.

[88] *Machinist*, 12 October 1964, p. 76.

[89] MTTA, Council Minute Book, 24 March 1965.

[90] *Engineer*, 26 November 1965, p. 891.

[91] MTTA, Machine Tool Directory, 1966, p. 169.

heralded as providing the 'weapon in the British government's fight to solve the nation's critical shortage of skilled labour'.[92]

Euphoria concerning NC technology dovetailed with Labour government planning to increase productivity in British manufacturing and MinTech made two key announcements in relation to the show. Firstly, it made a commitment to purchase pre-production models of NC equipment either for testing in government factories or for installation in private concerns for industrial evaluation. Provided with a budget of just under £1 million, the scheme was intended to accelerate the diffusion process by promoting new designs to enter the market. Contracts were immediately placed with Churchill-Redman for its NC lathe, Mollins Machine Tool Ltd. for its multi purpose NC machine, and with Ferranti for a drawing, measuring and an inspection machine. Secondly, to facilitate the adoption of NC by industry, and to increase sales and protect makers from a fall in reputation and financial loss, a trial period scheme was introduced. Users buying a NCMT could return it within 6 to 24 months after purchase, the maker paying a guaranteed re-purchase price based on a small fixed charge deduction from the original selling price for each month the machine was in use. Management of this scheme was delegated to the NRDC, which would negotiate contract terms with suppliers of machine tools who voluntarily wished to participate.[93]

It was not the case that there was a lack of NCMT's on the market, and at the 1966 International NCMT Exhibition at Olympia 18 British makers displayed machines as well as a number of merchant firms who displayed NCMT's, especially from Germany and the U.S.A.[94] As Appendix A, Table A1 shows, a small but influential number of firms were engaged in developing NCMT's in Britain by 1966, although there was also a significant influence made by subsidiaries of American makers. Indeed, observers at the exhibition informed the MTTA that some visitors expressed the view that the British had 'stolen their thunder' in NC application to machine tools.[95] The vast majority of British makers used control systems developed by electronic firms, with Ferranti and General Electric being prominent.[96] As Table 8.10 shows, mainly British and American electronics firms supplied the NC control systems for installation on machine tools. There were, however, some noticeable exceptions of British machine firms integrating machine tool building with the development of system controls. Charles Churchill & Co, which had a number of subsidiary manufacturing companies, had developed hydraulic and electronic control systems at its research laboratories at Daventry since 1963, and, together with outside suppliers, incorporated these into its machine tool designs.[97] Founded in 1960, Marwin, Britain's only machine tool maker specialising solely in NC, developed in the 1960s machining centres especially for the aircraft industries in Britain and America. At the Exhibition of

---

[92] *Machinist*, 23 May 1966, p. 106.

[93] *Engineer*, 20 May 1966, pp. 770-1.

[94] *Engineer*, 26 April 1966, p. 675.

[95] MTTA, Council Minute Book, 26 May 1966.

[96] *Engineer*, 29 April 1966, p. 675; 6 May 1966, p. 682.

[97] MTTA, Machine Tool Directory 1966, p. 101.

1966, it displayed a number of machines fitted with its own NC designs, and in the 1960s developed versatility in machines to meet the needs for batch work in engineering.[98]

Table 8.10
Numerical Control Systems (CP= continuous path, PP= point-to-point)
Available in U.K., 1966

Supplier	System		Origin	Firm type
Ferranti	CP/PP		U.K.	Electronics
International GE of New York	CP/PP		U.S.A.	Electronics
Plessey	CP/PP		U.K.	Electronics
EMI	CP		U.K.	Electronics
Staveley-Smith Controls	CP		U.K.	Subsidiary of Staveley Industries
Airmec	PP		U.K.	Electronics
AEI	PP		U.K.	Electronics
Douty Moog	PP		U.S.A.	Electronics
Nicholas Automatics	PP	for lathes	Unknown	Unknown
Kearney and Trecker	PP		U.S.A.	Machine Tools
Marwin Machine Tools	PP		U.K.	Machine Tools
E. K. Cole	PP		Unknown	Unknown

Source: MTTA, Machine Tool Directory, 1966, p. 37.

In-house design was also a feature of the products displayed by firms in the Machine Tool Division of Staveley Industries.[99] A horizontal spindle milling, drilling and boring machine, manufactured by George Richards Ltd., one of the Staveley companies, was fitted with NC systems designed and developed by the Staveley Research Department, and built on specifications based upon the results of a national survey of user requirements. The machine was designed to be fitted either with a Staveley 3-axis continuous path control or a General Electric Mark Century NC system. James Archdale & Co., another Staveley company, displayed its taped controlled milling and drilling machine, incorporating both Plessey Mark 3 equipment and Staveley continuous path control. In 1966, Staveley extended its NCMT capabilities by purchasing the Asquith Machine Tool Group, which comprised Drummond Bros. (auto lathes and gear cutters), George Swift & Sons (heavy duty lathes), Swift & Summerskill (planning machines), Kitchen & Wade (drilling, boring and special-purpose machines), Ormorod & Sharpe (shapers and

---

[98] *Engineer*, 29 April 1966, p. 675; 19 February 1970, p. 47; 25 June 1970, p. 35.
[99] Staveley originated as a steel and coal company outside Chesterfield, and began to acquire machine tool firms in the 1950s as it extended the functions of its holding company.

slotters), and Asquith Electronics (Colne) Ltd. a producer of control panels and ancillary equipment. Asquith, a Halifax maker, was a valuable acquisition, having developed a reputation by the 1960s for building moderately priced drilling machines, fitted with either positioning or tape control and using digital control systems developed by AEI. In 1965, the company reported orders to the value of £400,000 for these machines. Staveley also supplied continuous path controls directly to British machine makers through its subsidiary Staveley-Smith Controls of Manchester, as well as possessing licences for manufacture through its association with the American companies Warner & Swasey and Norton.[100]

Group companies, such as Staveley, incorporated a number of machine tool firms in their acquisitions. This was a key trend of the 1960s, suggesting a pattern of increasing concentration, which of course had been a major recommendation of the Mitchell Report of 1960. The association between increased scale and R&D effort was made clear by Frank Cousins, the Minister of Technology in 1965, when he informed the Commons that 'The machine tool industry is too fragmented', and although he accepted that small firms made valuable contributions to the industry, 'Others cannot take full advantage of the ability of their highly skilled workers. The concentration of the industry into stronger units must therefore be encouraged'. Market forces, he argued, were unlikely to be sufficient to achieve concentration and rationalisation, and the industry, together with MinTech advisors, would give particular attention to the encouragement of larger-scale organisation. To this end, pre-production orders would be targeted at larger combines of firms.[101] MinTech support for large-scale was combined with a strategy of promoting extensive R&D facilities, a process central to the ideology of the Wilson government, with its belief that large resources were necessary to 'innovate and compete successfully on an international scale'.[102] Nevertheless, Cousin's remarks on the fragmentation of the industry by the mid-1960s needs to be re-evaluated.

A survey for 1965 registered 63 metal working machine tool companies that were still in private ownership, defined as having no public quotation. These small makers included notable pioneers of the industry such as Adcock & Shipley and F. Pollard. The vast majority of firms consisted of small makers absorbed into larger group organisations, either into those specialising in machine tools, such as Alfred Herbert Ltd., or into more diversified general engineering concerns such as Tube Investments (TI), BSA, George Cohen 600 Group, B. Elliot, John Brown Ltd., and Staveley Industries. Appendix A, Table A.2 contains the main group companies that were publicly quoted, together with their machine tool subsidiaries. Indeed, larger specialist groups of machine tool makers, such as Charles Churchill & Co., and the Asquith Machine Tool Corporation were in 1966 assimilated into general engineering concerns, the former by TI and the latter by Staveley. By far the largest specialist machine tool group, and the largest quoted holding company

---

[100] *Engineer*, 29 April 1966, p. 675; 6 May 1966, p. 682; MTTA, Machine Tool Directory, 1966, p. 37; *Engineer*, 10 December 1966, p. 974.

[101] *Engineer*, 25 June 1965, p. 1,114.

[102] Coopey, 'Industrial Policy', p. 111.

in the list provided in Table A.2, with a market capitalisation of £45.9 million was Alfred Herbert. This, for example, was significantly higher than that of the machine tool interests of Charles Churchill, within the TI group, or that of Asquith within the Staveley group. Small firms, even within the expanding Herbert organisation, sheltered under the umbrella of large group organisations, and as we shall see in the next chapter, this led to limited centralised control and problems of organisational coordination.

Nevertheless, the structure of the industry was changing rapidly in the 1960s. For example, the acquisition of Charles Churchill and its subsidiary companies by TI in 1966 led to a financial injection of £1 million for the expansion of Churchill Gear Machines Ltd. at Blaydon, Newcastle, for modern flow production techniques. Staveley's acquisition of Asquith in the same year led in 1967 to the formation of a wholly new company, Staveley Machine Tools Ltd., to co-ordinate the policies and operations of all the parent companies machine tool subsidiaries. In 1966 the George Cohen 600 Group could claim to be amongst the largest machine tool companies in the country, and was increasing capacity and planning future investment programmes in manufacturing and marketing. Alfred Herbert, Britain's premier producer, acquired the machine tool division of BSA in 1967, with a workforce of 4,000 and including BSA Broach Co., Redditch, BSA Small Tools Ltd., and the Churchill Machine Tool Co., Altrincham.[103] In 1968, Gabriel contended that increasing concentration had been progressing for 20 years, and he estimated that 75 per cent of total metalworking machine tool production was in the hands of some 30 groups of companies, in some cases these constituted small specialist companies of high international reputation. This, he claimed, did not represent a contraction of the industry, but rather a consolidation into larger units to provide economies of scale in investment and plant utilisation. Of more importance, Gabriel made a direct correlation between increasing concentration in groups and R&D in advanced machine tool design. Group organisations, he asserted, were now well aware of the need for corporate planning utilising 'long range forecasting techniques that hitherto have been used solely by the very large supranational trading and manufacturing companies'. This was vital, he claimed, as R&D requirements had escalated as the frontiers of machine tool technology had widened with the advance of NC. Gabriel concluded by suggesting that only by long-term planning in large units and continued investment in R&D can the industry's competitive future be secured.[104]

In terms of the diffusion of NC in Britain the development of group organisations hardly speeded up the process. In 1966, the number of NC machine tools in use in the U.K. was equivalent to just 0.03 per cent of Britain's machine stock of 1961. By 1970, there were an estimated 3,000 NCMT's in operation, representing 0.3 per cent of the total machine tool stock, in comparison to 20,000 NCMT's in the U.S.A.[105] The diffusion of NC encountered three inter-related

---

[103] *Engineer*, 1 July 1966, p. 12; 11 November 1966, p. 730; 3 February 1967, p. 122; *Machine Tool Review*, Vol. 55, 1967, p. 49.

[104] MTTA, Council Minute Book, 23 May 1968.

[105] *Engineer*, 25 June 1970, p. 35.

obstacles: the low take-up of NC by user industries, the growing association of British companies with foreign technological imports, and the ineffectiveness of the industry's relationship with MinTech.

In November 1967, Kearns urged user industries to 'investigate machines in this country before going abroad, and was highly critical of the 'sporadic methods of placing orders' by British users which jeopardised long-term planning in advanced machine tool design.[106] The same theme was repeated by Gabriel a year later when he claimed that makers had embraced the technological revolution of the Labour Government since 1964 by accelerating the pace of R&D, only to be frustrated by the low demand for NCMTs. The more progressive user was the exception rather than the rule, and he contrasted this with the more positive attitude towards NC in the U.S.A. and West Germany. Unless the situation improved, he concluded, 'the outlook for manufacturers of advanced machines would be very poor'.[107] Problems of integrating NC into manufacturing systems had been raised at the time of the Exhibition of 1966, where it was argued that these were essential to raise productivity but 'prejudice' abounded because users did not appreciate that prior poor results from such technology was due to limited re-organisation of their production plant and insufficient training of technical personnel. Yet the 'fund of knowledge' was available. Forecasts in the U.S.A., for example, predicted that although NC would account for only 35-40 per cent of the machine tools in operation by 1975, because of higher productivity they would undertake approximately 80 per cent of the production currently conducted by general-purpose machines.[108] In contrast, however, British engineers had limited planning systems to integrate higher productivity machine tools. R. D. Young, the managing director of Herbert's, was well aware of this when he observed that NC brought high productivity to the batch and jobbing industries, but its advantage depended largely in planning the manufacturing programme which fell to production control staff which were in short supply.[109] The *Machine Tool Review* proclaimed in 1968 that 'In industry at large the greatest development in recent years is the expansion of the control element into all phases of the factory'. 'Control' related to the planning process for production, divorced from the 'shop floor', but also related to the 'control' of individual machines by plug-board and tape systems and by automatic transfer which enabled 'efficient machine and manpower utilisation and use of skills at all levels without wastage'. However, there was a growing awareness that the installation of NCMT's alone did not necessarily raise productivity, but rather were the means 'to promote new planning techniques that lead to greater productivity with less manpower and ... less floor space'. The relationship between NC technology and planning engineering production, claimed the *Review*, was not fully appreciated in British industry. A MTIRA report in 1968, for example, had found that machine tools used in industry were generally not conducive to the specific tasks that they were designed for, and the conclusion was

---

[106] *Engineer*, 25 November 1966, p. 778.

[107] *Engineer*, 24 November 1967, p. 708.

[108] *Engineer*, 21 January 1966, p. 139; 29 April 1966, p. 633.

[109] *Engineer*, 15 July 1966, p. 75.

that the total cost of machining could be cut by 20-30 per cent. As the *Review* claimed, 'With the pace of modern development the installation of an isolated machine tool without a new appraisal of production needs has become a sure recipe for inefficiency'.[110]

Production engineering, involving systems of planning, was, of course, a central feature of mass production industries, but in general engineering, which made up a large part of British industry, this 'discipline' had not been appreciated. NCMT's were specifically designed to meet the requirements of general engineering, with its batch production requirements, and thus it reinforced the 'need to consider complete manufacturing systems and to avoid piecemeal plant replacements and additions'. Surveying 'Ten Years of NC' in 1970, the *Machine Tool Review* concluded that modern designs of conventional machine tools were as efficient as NCMTs, cost considerably less, and were 'potentially capable of machining at more competitive rates'. Comparison between NC and conventional machine tools was considered 'understandable but hardly logical', as 'NC is more a tool of economics than an extension of the conventional machine'. NC allowed the advantages of 'mass production economics', with automatic and systematic machining, but for batch production systems these economies could only be realised with a full appraisal of its merits.[111]

User resistance to NC related to the problems of investment appraisal in British engineering industry, an industry populated by large numbers of small and medium sized firms. A survey in 1964 by the Management Consultants' Association, sponsored by NEDO and the MTTA found that despite substantial tax concessions for purchasing high productivity machinery increased sales were limited because the methods of investment appraisal in use in engineering were either non-existent or 'misleading'. A follow up survey by the Consultants in 1966, commissioned by the Machine Tool NEDC, reported that the majority of companies purchasing machine tools did not make an accurate and comprehensive assessment of the investment, and missed the opportunity to install advanced machinery.[112] In 1969 Dr Jeremy Bray, Joint Parliamentary Secretary to MinTech, urged that 'Firms should ask themselves ... Will we increase our profits by replacing old machines with new?' but concluded that the answer was not often in the affirmative. Peter Marshall, who had served with PERA's Numerical Control Advisory Service (NCAS) since 1964, gave a frank assessment of the problem in 1970. Dismissing the assertions that unions were restricting advanced machine technology, and rejecting claims that NC was too expensive to install, Marshall condemned British engineering managers for a 'lack' of formal plant replacement policies, designed to indicate when machines were obsolete and the funds available. Engineering, he claimed, failed to assess investments in terms of the potential productivity gains, and in relation to the potential that NC offered for

---

[110] *Machine Tool Review*, Vol. 56, 1968, pp. 50-1, 176-7.

[111] *Machine Tool Review*, Vol. 58, 1970, pp. 71-3.

[112] MTTA, Council Minute Book, 28 January 1965; DEA, Industrial and Regional Planning Reports, No. 21, October 1966, p. 7; National Economic Development Council, *Investment in Machine Tools*, pp. 2, 15, 21.

placing control of the shop floor in the hands of managers. His reserved judgement was that British industry under-invested, spending less than 10 per cent of the total machine tool budget for 1969 on NC, and this 'is just not enough if productivity is to expand at more than 3 or 4% a year'.[113]

MinTech were acutely aware of the problems of enhancing capital replacement in industry. For example, in 1968 it established the Numerical Control Advisory and Demonstration Service in collaboration with the Royal Aircraft Establishment, PERA, and the newly merged Airmec-AEI Ltd. Opened by the Minister of Technology, Tony Benn, the demonstration centre run by Airmec-AEI at High Wycombe provided a consulting service to the engineering industry. As Benn accepted, the expansion of NC in British industry was a long-term process.[114] MinTech also copiously produced information on risk assessment and replacement investment planning.[115] In particular, the NCAS, subsidised by MinTech, offered free appraisals to industry, and small firms only paid 10 per cent of the cost. Nevertheless, as Marshall admitted, the economic benefits of NC were not easy to disseminate, because despite considerable savings the figures were not always 'presented in a way that the firm's accountant will understand and recognise'. Further compounding these information problems were the diverse and competing range of NC systems offered, especially in terms of 'proven software'.[116] Market constraints, relating to the structure and business decision making in British engineering, had clear implications for the diffusion of NC technology, but the machine tool industry itself should not be exonerated from blame. In 1969, regional conferences between users and makers highlighted the fact that while the industry had developed standard lines of machines, they 'have not gone fast enough with developments exploiting the most advanced techniques and highly specialised applications'.[117] F. W. Craven, of Craven Bros., a large engineering concern that also produced machine tools, was even more scathing of the performance of the industry in 1967. In a letter to *The Engineer*, he claimed that the development of NC lathes were more advanced in West Germany, and that German makers had high sales in the U.K. Unlike their British counterparts, the Germans were aware of developments in computer programming for machines, and offered a complete package of tape controlled lathes backed up by computer programming. In Britain, there were few types of NC lathes available, the minority who did supply paying insufficient attention to making readily available economic computer programming facilities. In Craven's view there was no coordination of policy to rationalise planning and he called on MinTech for action on 'group' cooperation between British lathe manufacturers who were interested in the application of full tape control.[118] By 1970, there was also evidence that makers, with the exception of Marwin, were not meeting the requirements of users for

---

[113] *Engineer*, 5 June 1969, p. 57; 25 June 1970, pp. 34-5.

[114] *Engineer*, 16 February 1968, p. 268.

[115] *Engineer*, 26 May 1967, p. 768.

[116] *Engineer*, 25 June 1970, pp. 34-5.

[117] *Engineer*, 5 June 1969, p. 58.

[118] *Engineer*, 28 April 1967, p. 645.

machines capable of meeting the versatility of batch production.[119] The slow diffusion of NC and its impact on the competitive strength of the British machine tool industry was demonstrated by *The Engineer* in 1969. Responding to the announcement of Massing & Co., a subsidiary of Robert Bosch, the giant West German electrical company, that it had set up manufacture to supply a 'comprehensive system of numerical controls in Britain', it pronounced that 'the German and American pincer movement' was a blow to any hopes of a revival of competitive advantage of the British industry in NC technology.[120]

From the industry's perspective, there was a growing unease with the Labour Government's modernisation strategy, and this manifested itself in a general negative attitude towards MinTech. As a 'sponsor' of four major industrial sectors, computers, electronics, telecommunications, and machine tools, MinTech was the vital institution linking government to industrial modernisation.[121] However, as Kearns argued in 1966, the impact of policy on the machine tool industry was far less effective than the rhetoric of government ministers implied. While private industry strived to raise productivity, according to Kearns MinTech 'had been lamentably slow in preparing action'. Taking as his example a joint memorandum by the MTTA and BEAMA to the government in November 1964, which called for the urgent need for the wider application of NCMTs in industry, Kearns was dismayed by a 16-month delay in formulating action. He condemned MinTech officials for their 'desire to take from the industry any credit for the initiative'. For example, in December 1965, after repeated pressure for action, MinTech had questioned the arguments advanced by the joint memorandum, and then in February 1966 had launched its own informal talks 'to secure the same objectives'. Kearns was also deeply dismayed by the limited progress on pre-production contracts for NCMTs, which had been raised by the Machine Tool NEDC in May 1965, and had been included in their Action Plan of June. Indeed, as we saw earlier, the trial period scheme was not launched until the summer of 1966 and by September the Manufacturer's Committee of the MTTA was registering its frustration that no progress had been made by the NRDC in implementing the scheme, 'apparently because of their desire to get as much harmony between individual cases as they could before making any assessment'. The Committee believed, however, that harmonisation would be difficult to achieve, because of the differing circumstances of individual buyers, and they pressed the NRDC 'to deal with the matter on an individual basis, in order that potential business, which is currently hanging fire, could be completed'. Substantial progress on this issue was not recorded until January 1967, when a meeting of the Manufacturers' Committee of the MTTA noted that the NRDC had considered it possible to move ahead with the full implementation of the scheme, subject to the signing of an administrative agreement with MinTech.[122]

---

[119] *Engineer*, 19 February 1970, p. 47; 25 June 1970, p. 35.

[120] *Engineer*, 20 November 1969, p. 12.

[121] Coopey, 'Industrial Policy', p. 112.

[122] MTTA, Council Minute Book, 2 June 1965; 8 September 1966; 12 January 1967.

According to Kearns, a window of opportunity was closing against the British industry. The 1966 NCMT Exhibition, for example, had 'set a standard for the industries of the world', but MinTech initiatives to widen their application in British industry had proved 'complicated and difficult to implement'. A number of makers regretted the delays, and as Kearns concluded, the initial 'enthusiasm of many of us ... has become weakened'. He hoped that the announcement by MinTech of the signing of the first of nine agreements for trial schemes with NC would encourage 'British suppliers' to 'reopen discussions with the NRDC'. Concern over the delays and low take-up of the trial scheme was also expressed by the Machine Tool NEDC, who criticised the lack of coordination between MinTech and the NRDC in organising the details of the arrangements. Further anxiety arose following the announcement that six of the nine agreements signed with the NRDC were by foreign makers, particularly American. When the MTTA itself set up its own Machine Tool Control Committee in 1966, three of its original members, including the chair, were representatives from the American firms of Kearney & Trecker, Cincinnati Milling Machines, and Giddings, Lewis-Frasier, a fact that was received with much 'pleasure' by the MTTA Importers' Section. In 1967, the Machine Tool Control Committee, recognising a breakdown in communication with MinTech, invited their officials to attend meetings, with the intention of overcoming 'the evident gap in understanding between industry and the government in relation to the wider use of techniques associated with numerical control'. The gap could not be closed, and at the end of 1967 the trial scheme was 'in abeyance', the NRDC proposing 'yet another scheme aimed at securing the wider introduction of numerical controlled machine tools to user industries'.[123]

Procrastination and excessive bureaucracy were certainly features of MinTech relations with the MTTA, and added to frustrations over the delays in practical policy. Nevertheless, the machine tool industry itself displayed a thinly disguised contempt for the aims and objectives of MinTech. 'Socialist policy' and Socialist technology' were common euphemisms for the institutional arrangements of the Labour Government, and the MTTA demonstrated a considerable reluctance to supply relevant business information. For example, its Manufacturers' Committee in January 1966 recorded its reluctance to supply data to MinTech, 'Statistics' having 'long been a bone of contention within the industry because of their inadequacy', and it was felt that the only incentive to accumulating additional information was to 'keep ahead of those who otherwise might have appeared to be hounding us'. In late 1966 and early 1967, the Manufacturers' Committee refused to supply MinTech with any information on a machine tool comparison exercise undertaken by member firms, defending this on the need to retain 'complete confidentiality'. Yet the MTTA itself accepted that this information was vital for market research, and provided a 'vital management tool'. The low level of trust between the industry and government agencies was demonstrated by Ralph Gabriel in January 1969, when he announced that the MTTA would do everything possible to fight against MinTech proposals to form an 'Expert Committee', incorporating

---

[123] MTTA, Council Minute Book, 10 May, 28 September 1966; 9 February, 7, 23 March, 16 May, 12 October, 16 November 1967.

not only users, makers, and MinTech officials, which was acceptable, but also management consultants and the Unions, which was not. Launching a direct attack on Government interference, Gabriel concluded that the Expert Committees were a back-door to Industry Boards, and he did not care whether his criticisms 'were not very popular'.[124]

What really got at the members of the MTTA was the continuation of allegations over the industry's technical and managerial failings. A confidential report commissioned by MinTech in 1967 on the problems associated with the introduction of a pre-ordering scheme for NCMT's, depressingly concluded that British makers 'had limited design expertise' in this 'crucial area', inferior management controls, 'and very limited market intelligence'. It also condemned the reluctance of makers to take part in the pre-production programme, because although MinTech underwrote the costs of developing new prototype machines, 'it did not guarantee a profit'. This in turn led to frequent complaints by MinTech officials that makers were attempting to disguise profits within their costing estimates and this often led to multiple submissions before a project was approved.[125] Both parties had reason to blame each other, not least because the machine tool industry could be represented as an example of the more general problems confronting Britain's manufacturing sector. While the evidence does point to ideological forces frustrating attempts at government-industry cooperation, it is important to note that the capacity for such cooperation was not simply reducible to ideological influences, as the failure of the BEAMA-MTTA initiatives testify. It would also be unfair to suggest that the industry's leaders were simply complacent, but there is nonetheless a hint of fatalism about their response to modernisation. Thus, the repeated complaints against users for their lack of symmetry in ordering patterns leading to demand volatility could be used by makers to legitimise the avoidance of hard decisions concerning investment in new capacity. This level of uncertainty tested the quality of top management, and the latter too had to confront the lack of investment in human resources that manifested itself in shortages of skilled operatives, designers and middle managers during the upswing of the cycle. These problems manifested themselves at the level of the firm, and the next chapter examines Britain's premier maker, Herbert's, and assesses the extent to which it possessed the managerial and organisational capabilities to successfully respond to the increasing competitive challenge of the 1950s and 1960s.

---

[124] MTTA, Council Minute Book, 13 January, 23 March 1966; 12 January 1967; 29 January, 19 March 1969.

[125] Coopey, 'Industrial Policy', p. 118.

CHAPTER NINE

Business Strategy and Business Structure: Alfred Herbert 1950-70

'The bell wether of industries capital investment plans.'[1]

Introduction

Alfred Herbert was by far the largest specialist machine tool maker in Britain, and, it also marketed the machine tools of both foreign and domestic makers via its extensive factoring business, as well as producing under licence a range of foreign designed machine tools. Given the need to confront foreign competition in the 1950s, and the challenge of modernisation in the 1960s, the strategy of the leading 'player' in the industry is obviously important in examining how firms responded to the cyclical pattern of ordering and the crucial issue of technological development and institutional pressures for change. The central role given to the company by *The Economist* in 1963 signified its strategic importance as a vital supplier of capital goods to British engineering. This chapter will firstly examine the strategy of the company in response to the cyclical nature of the market from the mid-1950s to 1964, analysing the persistence of capacity constraints on the company in the upturn of the cycle. Secondly, it will examine the company's R&D strategy in the context of increasing demands for modernisation from the late 1950s. Finally, from 1965 the company, under the leadership of Richard D. Young, undertook an ambitious expansion strategy, which involved the acquisition of the machine tool interests of BSA and a venture with the American Ingersoll Co. to manufacture special-purpose machine tools, incorporating NC, in Britain. This required structural adjustments in the organisation of the company, and raised issues concerning the capabilities of the executive to develop effective strategies to modernise the company. At the same time, the firm faced growing foreign competition, increasing labour unrest, and as the cycle progressed a deteriorating financial performance. As a starting point, there is a discussion of the company's expansion in the 1950s, and the changing governance of the organisation following the death of Sir Alfred in 1957.

---

[1] *Economist*, 6 April 1963.

Business Expansion and Executive Management, 1950-64

In 1965, the market capitalisation of Herbert's was greater than the combined value of all the other main specialist makers in the industry, and its average trading profits between 1954 and 1961 was greatly in excess of its major domestic competitors (Table 9.1). Stimulated by the Korean War, output expanded rapidly and, in 1955, the company had three factories. Exhall, Coventry, manufactured a range of small tools, the head works at Edgwick, Coventry, produced lathes, milling and drilling machines, and Lutterworth, Leicester, originally acquired as a shadow factory in 1941, augmented the company's production of lathes. The company had also acquired in 1951, for £77,475, Sigma Instruments, Letchworth, a manufacturer of special-purpose testing machinery for the automobile industry, an 'extremely competitive field of engineering'. These production centres in 1955 employed 5,700 workers and operated 2,000 machine tools, and management could claim that the company 'had achieved a reputation as the largest machine tool organisation in the world'.[2]

Table 9.1
Market Valuation, 1965, and Average Trading Profits, 1954-61, of Major Specialist Machine Tool Companies (£ million)

	Market Capitalisation, 1965[a]	Average Trading Profit, 1954-61
Alfred Herbert & Co.	43.4	3.784
Charles Churchill & Co.	8.4	0.919
B. Elliott & Co.	6.2	0.375
Coventry Gauge & Tool Co.	6.1	0.511
Wadkin & Co.	5.8	0.472
Jones & Shipman	5.6	0.408
Asquith Machine Tool Co.	4.3	0.841
Newall Machine Tool Co.	2.4	0.294
Kerry's (Great Britain)	1.5	0.294
Greenwood & Batley	1.1	0.253
H. W. Kearns & Co.	1.1	0.259
Butler Machine Tool Co.	0.6	0.173

Source: *Economist*, 10 June 1965, p. 247; MTTA, *Machine Tool Directory*, 1963.
Note: a. Market capitalisation records the value for machine tool manufacturing firms only, and does not include sales and importing companies.

The term 'organisation' reflected the company's historical evolution, its reputation as a machine tool builder, and its development of external networks. In

---

[2] 926/1/1/1, Alfred Herbert, Minute Book of the Board of Directors, 1944-60, 30 October, 6 December 1951; 27 February 1952; *Machine Tool* Review, Vol. 43, 1955, p. 113; Vol. 49, 1961, pp. 16-17; Astrop, *The Rise and Fall*, pp. 16-18.

1955, the company's Factored Department at Red Lane, Coventry, handled machines manufactured by 'all the worlds' leading makers'. Consistent with a strategy of meeting customer need, factored supplies covered all aspects of production 'from the machining of the smallest watch component to the heaviest class of work in the electrical and shipbuilding industry'. At the Machine Tool Exhibition at Olympia in 1956, the company exhibited the machines of British makers such as Archdale, Cunliffe & Croom, George Richards, Lumsden, Brown & Ward, and Pullmax, American makes such as Devlieg and Landis, and the German maker Fokker-Eckold. Factoring enabled the company to market a wide range of machines, and supporting its sales drive were associate companies in France, Italy, India and Australia, as well as private merchant firms, in 65 countries, with agency contracts. In Britain, Herbert's had eight regional branch offices, providing demonstrations of the company's machines. Networking, via its factoring business, also led to collaboration in the production of machine tools under licence.[3] By the mid-1950s, 'one of the company's greatest strengths' was the combination of factoring with its own in-house production, offering 'probably the most extensive product range of the time'.[4] The management identified manufacturing and factoring with the company's tradition of providing a complete service function to engineering. Red Lane provided demonstrations of the machines for which it acted as agents, and provided re-conditioning and repair services to customers. As the management commented in 1956, 'The function of the machine tool organisation is not only to supply machine tools, but to provide effective service, both before and after sales, to ensure that customers obtain the most efficient production from any equipment supplied'.[5]

Between 1955 and 1963, the Herbert organisation grew rapidly, employment increasing by 21 per cent to 7,500, and the number of machine tools in operation by 67.5 per cent to 3,350. At the same time, the number of machine tools in operation per worker rose from 0.351 to 0.450, a 28 per cent increase.[6] During this period, the company converted and expanded Lutterworth to manufacture under licence American Devlieg precision boring machines, the factory employing 500 in 1960. Capacity expansion intensified in 1960-1, the management investing in a new foundry and extensions to machine shops at Edgwick, as well as enlarging space at domestic branch offices. In 1963, a new light engineering shop at Edgwick opened, accompanied by further extensions to branch office capacity during 1964. To augment its capacity and product range, the company acquired between 1957 and 1961 three complementary small machine tool companies, Holbrook, Berridge, and Whiteley, and one electrical company,

---

[3] *Machine Tool Review*, Vol. 43, 1955, p. 113; Vol. 44, 1956, p 22; *Engineer*, 15 July 1966, p. 75; Astrop, *The Rise and Fall*, p. 18.

[4] Astrop, *The Rise and Fall*, p. 17.

[5] *Machine Tool Review*, Vol. 44, 1956, p. 123.

[6] *Machine Tool Review*, Vol. 48, 1960, p. 1; *Economist*, 6 April 1963, p. 76; Astrop, *The Rise and Fall*, p. 18.

Mudie.[7] From the mid-1950s, Herbert's also expanded its factoring business opening agencies with domestic and foreign suppliers, the company in 1959 having 36 sole agencies, including prestigious British makers such as Asquith and Richards, and leading American suppliers such as Pratt & Whitney, Devlieg, and Heald. Factoring, according to the management in 1965, was a profitable business activity supporting the company's sales in the downturn of the trade cycle. By the mid-1960s, the company had also become a major licensed producer of mainly American machine tools. These developments reflected the manufacturing strategy of the company in the 1960s, a programme designed to build general-purpose machine tools, supplemented by extensive factoring and licensing agreements.[8] As shown in Appendix B, Table B1, the company was engaged in an extensive range of activities, including manufacturing, licensing, factoring, and selling.

To finance expansion, the directors periodically increased share capital by issues from undistributed profits. For example, in 1951, nominal capital increased from £1.1 million to £2.1 million by the capitalisation of profits and the issue to shareholders of a two for one scrip, and, in 1954, £4,751,879 from the company's general reserve was capitalised through distributing bonus shares to existing holders of ordinary shares in a ratio of two to one. Redistributed profits raised nominal capital to £6 million in 1954, £12 million in 1958, and £18 million in 1964.[9] Colonel C. W. Clark, the chairman, summed up the financial policy in 1964:

> It is the profits saved from earlier years which we propose to convert into capital and ... such profits have always belonged to the shareholders. These profits have already been used to finance the growth of the Company's business and will therefore be more appropriately designated as capital.[10]

Internal financing was a tradition stretching back to the origins of the company, but the profit record of the company was a mixed one between 1950 and 1965 (Table 9.2), reflecting the cyclical pattern of demand. Profits rose steadily to 1957, but net profits fell sharply during the severe recession of 1957-9, and trading profits crashed. The cyclical pattern of ordering in the industry, and increased competition, was to present management with difficult decisions from the mid-1950s.

Meeting the challenge from the mid-1950s required effective executive control and, as Toms and Wright claim, effective systems of governance and the talent of management are important determinants of successful corporate

---

[7] *Machine Tool Review*, Vol. 49, 1961, p. 51; Vol. 51, 1963, p. 48; Vol. 52, 1964, p. 48; Astrop, *The Rise and Fall*, p. 17.

[8] MTTA, Machine Tool Directory, 1966, pp. 147, 151; *Machine Tool Review*, Vol. 49, 1961, p. 49; Vol. 53, 1965, p. 47; *Economist*, 1 April 1961, p. 61.

[9] Herbert, Board of Directors 1944-60, 18 October, 6 December 1951; 21 July 1954; 25 April 1958; 1558/1/1/1-5, Minute Book of the Board of Directors of Alfred Herbert, 1960-80, 6 March 1964.

[10] *Machine Tool Review*, Vol. 52, 1964, p. 47.

development, as governance may shape the strategic direction of the organisation.[11] The dominant personality in the company's history was Sir Alfred Herbert, who, on his death in 1957, still held 25 per cent of the issued share capital.[12] The system of governance was authoritarian, reinforced in 1944 with the appointment of Sir Alfred, then aged 77, as 'sole chairman and managing director', replacing his previous title of 'sole governing director'. Age and experience went together, and following the Companies Act of 1947 the executive passed a special resolution enabling managers to continue beyond the retirement age of 70. The establishment of a Finance Committee in 1944, chaired by Sir Alfred, and consisting of D. M. Gimson, who had worked for the company's auditors from 1903 before joining the board in 1917, and J. W. Ellson, chief accountant, who had arrived in 1919, further consolidated his authority. The Committee had powers to allot shares, appoint and control staff other than departmental heads, the sole prerogative of Sir Alfred, and to authorise the financial business undertaken by the company. Sir Alfred's control over the appointment of department directors reinforced his policy of selecting company men for promotion. For example, in 1952 he appointed S. H. B. Muirhead, deputy works director since 1950, to a full directorship in recognition of his services to the re-organisation of the Lutterworth factory. The Finance Committee potentially created a two-tier executive management structure, the Committee setting strategic direction, reporting to the departmental board of directors 'for approval and confirmation of all decisions of importance', and then the board implemented policy.[13] In effect, the Committee was the means by which the ageing managerial elite sanctioned the actions of directors at the board level.

Table 9.2
Alfred Herbert Ltd. Net and Trading Profits, 1950-65 (£ million)

Year	Net	Trading	Year	Net	Trading
1950	0.76		1958	1.42	3.33
1951	0.93		1959	1.34	2.71
1952	1.19		1960	1.74	3.69
1953	1.35	3.07	1961	1.80	4.18
1954	1.48	3.48	1962	1.99	4.75
1955	1.77	3.98	1963	1.85	4.45
1956	1.80	4.32	1964	2.21	4.77
1957	1.82	4.61	1965	3.11	5.40

Source: MTTA, Machine Tool Directory, 1966, p. 146.

---

[11] S. Toms and M. Wright, 'Corporate Governance, Strategy and Structure in British Business History', *Business History*, Vol. 44, No. 3 (2002), p. 98.

[12] Evans, 'Some Problems of Growth', p. 47; Breeley and Troup, 'The Machine Tool Industry', pp. 363, 378.

[13] Herbert, Board of Directors, 1944-60, 29 March 1944; 7 April 1948; 4 October 1950; 11 June 1952; 30 October 1958.

Sir Alfred's age, however, eventually caught up, and by 1955, the issue of managerial succession was a major concern. In August, Clark tended his resignation as a director, and then withdrew it after a 'lengthy discussion'. Confrontation arose over the selection of younger managers to director status, and in 1955 this focused on the retirement of Joseph Pickin, after '60 years of loyal and devoted service', and the decision to replace him with K. W. Norman, against Clark's wishes, an episode which was a preliminary to a growing power struggle in the boardroom. In February 1956, the directors announced the death of A. H. Lloyd, the Director of Design, after 50 years of service, resulting in Clark again questioning the replacement of directors. Given Sir Alfred's advanced age, the board appointed Gimson deputy chair, and Clark and J. C. Blair as joint managing directors, to act in a supporting role. Succession, however, remained the prerogative of Sir Alfred, the board extending his sole powers of appointment to include the right to appoint and dismiss the deputy chair, and managing directors. Sir Alfred had no surviving sons, but his two grandsons, Walter Alfred Herbert Allen, and John Herbert Hollick held middle management positions. In April 1957, Alfred, with 'much pleasure', announced the appointment of his grandsons as deputy directors of the company, with rights to attend the board on invitation by the directors. Continuing the family line was clearly an issue, but the succession belonged to Gimson. Under instructions from Sir Alfred's executors, after his death on the 26 May 1957, Gimson was nominated chairman, a request which Clark put to the board as a formal resolution which was unanimously passed.[14]

In the managerial shake-up, Gimson's succession to the chair raised a number of issues concerning the executive authority of the Finance Committee, and senior positions on the board. J. C. Blair warned that 'the eyes of the business world were upon us', and he pleaded for 'a strong and united board', but at the same time he directly confronted the authority of the Finance Committee. Supported by J. H. Mahler, Blair tabled a resolution to devolve executive policy making from the Finance Committee to the full board. Supporting the resolution, the design director, B. C. Harrison, commented that the devolution of authority was crucial to the 'unity' of the board. On this matter, the future executive roles of Clark and Blair became paramount, with both the managing directors insisting that Sir Alfred's instructions to his executors to appoint them in the first place implied that they should have a prominent position in executive decision-making. Accepting this interpretation, Gimson confirmed the appointment of the joint managing directors, and to appease Clark proposed his appointment as deputy chairman, an offer that Clark duly accepted. Having made this decision, Gimson acceded to a discussion on the 'wide powers' of the Finance Committee, compromising by widening its constitution to include Clark and Blair. This decision represented a departure from the concentration of executive authority in the hands of a single individual, backed up by a small committee, and although the Committee retained its authority, under the 1944 resolutions, it nevertheless

---

[14] Herbert, Board of Directors, 1944-60, 9 August, 13 September 1955; 9 February 1956; 26 April, 5 June 1957.

represented a widening of participation at an executive level. Responding to Gimson's suggestion that the Committee should maintain the authority for the purchase of new plant, 'previously authorised by Sir Alfred', Blair insisted that they were a 'Board of engineers' who could provide valuable insight into capital investment policy. This strong stance by Blair led to an alteration in the powers of the Committee ensuring 'that matters of policy should be decided by the Board as a whole'. Effectively, the directors re-organised the board in its own image, and despite the fact that Sir Alfred's will had expressed the wish that his grandsons should be appointed to full directorships this was rejected, the board deferring the decision for future consideration.[15]

Table 9.3
The Herbert Board of Directors, 1957

Director	Responsibility	Years of Service
D. M. Gimson	Chairman	54
C. W. Clark	Joint Managing Director	50
J. C. Blair	Joint Managing Director	45
W. Core	Sales Director	37
O. S. Townsend	Technical Director	59
K. W. Norman	Factored Division Director	22
J. W. Ellson	Chief Accountant	38
B. C. Harrison	Design Director	33
J. H. Mahler	Combustion Engine Dept	29
S. A. B. Muirhead	Works Director	38
L. J. Hugo	Factored Division Director	27

Source: *Machine Tool Review*, Vol. 45, 1957, p. 56.

The succession of 1957 represented a break with the excessive authority represented by Sir Alfred and the Finance Committee within the organisation. In this respect, Gimson's tribute to the career of Sir Alfred, presented at the AGM in 1958, was full of irony. The 'great founder and Chairman ... while maintaining the keenest interest in the company's business ... appreciated the importance of delegating authority to the fullest extent, and thus ensured that the administration of the business will be continued with the same vigour and efficiency'.[16] Nevertheless, a persistence with a personal style of governance continued well after Sir Alfred's demise, reinforced by the rise of Clark to executive authority and the maintenance of the existing elite of long-serving directors. An elite board had evolved through a combination of merit and reward for long service, and the internal promotion system militated against the creation of extensive managerial hierarchies of professional managers. At the time of Sir Alfred's death, the accumulated service of the directors totalled 432 years, an average of 39 years for

---

[15] Herbert, Board of Directors, 1944-60, 5 June, 2 July 1957.
[16] Herbert, Board of Directors, 1944-60, 4 March 1958.

each (Table 9.3). O. S. Townsend, for example, the technical director, had joined the company in 1898, and continuity of executive management through internal promotion, often on the retirement or death of an existing director, remained a fundamental principal of the company until the mid-1960s. Thus, in 1958, Gimson vacated the chair due to ill health, although he was to continue as a part-time consultative director, paving the way for the accession of Clark, who had himself joined the company as a junior apprentice in 1908. Clark now became chairman and sole managing director, with Blair taking on the mantle of deputy chairman.[17]

As the business expanded from the late 1950s, the board were well aware that the company's organisational capabilities were being stretched. In order to maintain control some degree of reform was required, and the board acted by appointing consultative directors and promoting younger managers to deputy directorships to support the existing executive. Thus, Sir Halford Reddish, a director of Portland Cement and Hawker Sidley, was appointed in a consultative role in 1959. Responding positively to this appointment, Clark observed that 'The company would receive considerable benefit from an outside mind looking in'. Following Reddish's appointment, V. N. Brailsford, a prominent member of the Coventry Chamber of Commerce, joined the board in 1960, to provide expertise on general engineering affairs. Managerial overload was a clear problem for the board by 1960, and in a frank discussion on the policy for the retirement of directors, Clark stated that he was well aware of the 'personal situation' of directors, he himself being 'overburdened'. As a short-term solution, he extended the responsibility of Muirhead to include those for the company's main subsidiaries, although Clark was aware that the board was in desperate need of new blood. Consequently, he promoted B. C. Harrison to deputy managing director in a supporting role. In doing so, Clark reinforced the tradition of internal promotion. Apprenticed to Herbert's in 1924, Harrison became a section leader in the design office, factory-planning manager in 1940, works manager on the board in 1947, and design director in 1955. Aware of the increasing financial complexity of the business, Dereck Allen joined the board, providing assistance for Gimson and Ellson on financial matters. By the early 1960s, internal candidates for directorships were scarce, and in 1961 Ellson and Blair, 'in a public spirited action' offered their resignation from the main board, continuing as directors of the subsidiaries, 'to make way for a younger man'. This resulted in Clark appointing an outsider, E. A. Smith, 43 years of age, and a partner in a leading firm of international management consultants, and a financial director of a public company in civil, electrical and mechanical engineering, as deputy financial director.[18] Executive repositioning emphasises the limited managerial scope of the Herbert organisation, but as we shall see, it also had clear implications for the formulation of strategies to deal with the changing technological and market environment from the mid-1950s.

---

[17] Herbert, Board of Directors, 1944-60, 30 October 1958.

[18] Herbert, Board of Directors, 1944-60, 28 August 1959; Herbert, Board of Directors, 1960-80, 2 December 1960; 24 July 1961; *Machine Tool Review*, Vol. 49, 1961, p. 99.

Strategy and Structure, 1954-65

In August 1963, Clark presented a graph to the board displaying the order pattern over the past nine years. Orders dropped from an average of 214 machines per month in the financial year 1954-5 to 92 by 1957-8, and then rose to 263 in 1959-60. The average for 1962-3 was just 109.[19] In nine years, the company had traversed the cycle on two occasions, moving from full capacity and lengthening delivery dates to under-capacity utilisation. This uncertain future was hardly on the mind of Sir Alfred in 1954 when he predicted a rising demand for machine tools, both in domestic and overseas markets, although he was well aware of the need for vigilance in the face of rising competition and technological advance in machine tool manufacture. Between 1954 and 1957, demand remained buoyant, and trading profits rose from £3.48 million to a peak of £4.61 million (Table 9.2). In 1957, economic expansion came to a sharp end, and while Clark could proclaim in June that 'All our hearts are in the development of this wonderful business', he was deeply concerned that 'For months now we have not sold our output and on the factored side he was surprised to see how stock was building up'. By the end of 1957 orders were only one-third of estimated output, cancellations and machine stocks rising, the factories working short time, and the management confronting the stark choice of cutting the manufacturing programme further and enforcing redundancies. The downturn of 1957, according to Muirhed, stood in sharp contrast to the extended deliveries and increasing subcontracting of work, which characterised the expansion of 1954-6. By late 1957, the order backlog at Edgwick was down to only 1.8 months and at Lutterworth to 1.7 months, and 'practically all subcontract-work had now been brought back to our own shops'. Prospects in export markets provided little consolation, and Blair informed the board that the American and Canadian trading position was bleak, there was intense competition, and in the Soviet bloc there was a limited demand for the company's core products, capstan and turret lathes.[20]

Depressed conditions continued into 1958, and the company faced 'the most difficult period ... for more than twenty years', sales falling by 20 per cent during the financial year to October, and the backlog of orders 'practically' disappearing, leading Ellson to forecast reduced profits 'unless there was a substantial trade recovery'. In early 1959, Clark 'authorised' a 25 per cent reduction in the manufacturing programme, and Muirhead announced that this would involve adding one-third of the reduced output to stocks. To avoid rising overheads the management introduced a four-day week at Edgwick and Lutterworth, orders being insufficient to 'justify maximum production'. Forced redundancies followed, the number of direct productive workers falling from 4,386 to 3,347 in the 13 months to January 1958. The severe downturn in domestic industrial activity also affected the demand for factored products, which was 'at a lower level than normal'. To maintain full capacity utilisation required orders of 200 machines per month, two-thirds (133) of which originated from the domestic

---

[19] Herbert, Board of Directors, 1960-80, 9 August 1963.
[20] Herbert, Board of Directors, 1944-60, 4 March 1954; 5 June 1957; 7 January 1958.

market, but during the 1957 calendar year home orders averaged only 90 per month, marginally rising to 92 in 1958, and then falling to a low of 39 in January 1959. In 1958, orders accounted for only 46 per cent of the full capacity level, and stocks peaked at 636 machines in January 1959. Despite an upturn in orders between February and May, averaging 70, stocks were still 585 machines in June 1959. Fortunes improved from the middle of 1959, stocks falling by 8 per cent in May and by a further 17.5 per cent by September, leading, as Muirhead emphasised, to the usual outcome that 'the works were striving to meet the increased demand' by December. Rising demand in 1960 led to the usual scenario that by September 'the increasing of output is one of our biggest problems'. During the first half of 1961 buoyant orders continued, and in May the company received orders for 243 machines with only 185 dispatched. However, in the last quarter of the year, domestic demand slowed, orders approaching levels of productive output, only compensated by rising exports in early 1962. Domestic demand continued to weaken, and by mid-1962, despite the introduction of a hire purchase scheme and a management sales drive, Clark reported orders falling 'off rather badly', with customers cancelling at short notice, a common characteristic of 'a lack of confidence by industry for the immediate future'.[21]

Reddish had no doubts about the reasons for declining confidence. Political uncertainty required 'some quick action ... by the government', unless '1963 could be very uncertain'.[22] This mirrored the industry's call for government fiscal action to stimulate demand, discussed in Chapter 8, and Clark reinforced this at the company's AGM in 1962. Condemning overspending by government on bolstering nationalised industries, Clark attacked the Tory's alleged high corporation tax on profits, which was reducing re-investment in industrial expansion, and urged a revaluation of financial incentives to increase the application of new machine tools in engineering.[23] Falling business confidence at the end of 1962, leading to low orders, again necessitated stockpiling, although 'thriving' export demand, accounting for over 50 per cent of the company's output, acted as a temporary buffer. Nevertheless, a four-day week came into force early in 1963, the management deciding to accumulate stock to ride out the downturn. The expansionary budget of March 1963, provided some hope, but Clark noted that despite substantial enquiries there was no appreciable up-take of orders. Low orders persisted, and by the middle of 1963 rising enquiries were still not being converted into firm orders. In August, Clark extended the four-day week, claiming that this was not a 'calamity', orders predicated to recover within six to 12 months. The severity of the downturn intensified in August, with 'keen' competition in export markets adding to the demand problem. Not until the end of 1963 did the order cycle recover, demand continuing to fluctuate until October 1964, with

[21] Herbert, Board of Directors, 1944-60, 30 October, 2 December 1958; 2 January, 18 February, 16 June, 5 October, 4 December 1959; Herbert, Board of Directors, 1960-80, 9 September 1960; 17 February, 19 June, 29 August, 24 November 1961; 9 February, 22 June 1962.
[22] Herbert, Board of Directors, 1960-80, 22 June 1962.
[23] Machine Tool Review, Vol. 50, 1962, p. 47.

orders for small machines rising, but that for heavy equipment remaining low. During 1964, declining demand from the Common Market and the U.S.A. placed increasing pressure on orders, and as Clark observed, despite signs of improved domestic demand, the company's investment in increased capacity since the late 1950s now required even larger orders to sustain full output.[24] At the company's AGM in 1965, Clark confronted the political criticisms of the industry, and the allegations of a conservative response to the 'cyclical problem'. Government, he claimed, had failed to create the conditions for sustained economic expansion, and user industries continued to bunch investment demand in the upturn of the cycle.[25] This, as we have seen in previous chapters, was the usual scapegoat for the industry's problems, but how did the company respond to the volatile markets it faced?

A major constraint in managing cyclical demand was the strategic deployment of labour. Labour retention was crucial during downswings and its recruitment vital during upswings. Potentially, as Clark claimed in 1961, they could raise output by 25 per cent, but at present 'the shortage of skilled labour was a serious break on production', which led to lengthening delivery dates.[26] Shortages in 1961 related to the cutting of output during the downturn of 1957-9, and although they implemented the usual expedient of short time working to retain labour, this backfired in early 1959 as skilled workers found alternative employment in the region's engineering sector. In late 1958, Muirhead reported a severe shortage of skilled labour, and by early 1959 there were loud complaints that firms in the Engineering Association were poaching skilled workers who were attracted by full-time work. This break down of informal arrangements between the machine tool industry and the Association led the management to concede that further redundancies were inevitable. By the end of 1959, however, trading conditions had changed dramatically, the company 'striving' to meet demand, which was constrained by the 'problem of attracting labour', and this problem intensified during 1960.[27]

A tight labour market for skilled workers, as we saw in Chapter 8, was a common characteristic of the industry generally, but retention problems at Herbert's were exacerbated by the established policy to set pay rates under the average district rate, a feature demonstrated in negotiations with the shop stewards. In April 1959, cuts in production reduced the weekly piece work, day work, and monthly output bonuses, and Herbert's hourly earnings were 1s 6d below the Coventry district average. Not surprisingly, the Shop Stewards Committee demanded a flat rate payment for skilled workers, the maintenance of present monthly bonus rates, the elimination of piece rates, and their replacement by a standard day rate. However, as Muirhead argued, given the policy of stock-

---

[24] Herbert, Board of Directors, 1960-80, 14 December 1962; 26 April, 21 June, 9 August, 13 December 1963; 2 October 1964.

[25] *Machine Tool Review*, Vol. 53, 1965, pp. 47-8.

[26] Herbert, Board of Directors, 1960-80, 21 April 1961.

[27] Herbert, Board of Directors, 1944-60, 2 December 1958; 18 February, 4 December 1959; Herbert, Board of Directors, 1960-80, 2 December 1960.

building in anticipation of an upturn in demand, piece rates and bonus schemes offset the costs of holding large inventories, the latter being paid on sales not output. Holding firm on the principles of piece rates, the company reached a compromise settlement in June; the monthly bonus payment applied to production, not sales, but spread over six months to account for the value of machines held in stock. As Clark admitted, management would need to review this after six months, but 'The important point is that the basis of calculation is still under our control, and the principal of piece work payment is maintained'. Nevertheless, as Muirhead pointed out in December, the company was still paying 8d per hour below the district average, a factor that now affected the recruitment of skilled workers as trade recovered. Parsimony was demonstrated by Muirhead in 1960 when he calculated that while scarce tool room workers in the Midlands were averaging 10s per hour the rate at Herbert's was just 9s 8d, and although they were attracting about 20 workers per week, 'labour recruitment of the right type was still difficult'.[28] Labour recruitment difficulties extended to administrative and technical staff, leading to pressure on the accounting and commercial departments during busy periods. In 1961, the company employed 1,560 staff, but lost 100, 16 per cent, largely female employees, during the first six months of that year. High staff turnover, as Harrison noted, reflected upon the company's provision of holiday entitlement, compensation for redundancies, and poor quality accommodation, relative to other local companies. Top management, however, reacted with indifference and vacillation to the high turnover problem. Union proposals for providing an additional one week holiday to workers who had served three continuous years was constantly deferred, and extra expenditure on improving office accommodation thwarted by a cost-conscious management, and by directors whose own departments would have been affected by a scheme of re-location. On the matter of redundancy payments, for example, despite intense union pressure, Clark was insistent that the costs were too high, and dismissed proposals out of hand.[29]

Human resource management difficulties reflected on the limited organisational capabilities of the company. An example of this was the failure to co-ordinate production engineering with customer services. In 1957, leading sales engineers were scarce, the earnings differential between them and engineering draughtsmen being too narrow to ensure a sufficient supply. This was crucial to the company for, as L. J. Hugo reminded the board, they were not simply a manufacturing organisation, but sold 'engineering and tooling services', and he insisted that there should be adequate remuneration for 'these specialised technical engineers'. It was not until 1964 that the company announced the appointment of a senior manager to co-ordinate the personnel records of the company, in order to enable a more effective selection of staff for training for sales, commercial and technical positions. The manager was also responsible for recruitment as required by the various departmental directors, and in the training of apprentices.

---

[28] Herbert, Board of Directors, 1944-60, 3 April, 16 June, 4 December 1959; Herbert, Board of Directors, 1960-80, 2 December 1960.

[29] Herbert, Board of Directors, 1960-80, 24 July, 29 September 1961.

Demonstrating a rather cavalier attitude to the appointment, the directors suggested that 'he may ultimately become their personnel manager'. Management lacked the necessary foresight to administer an effective training and recruitment scheme, and the antiquated personnel management system reflected the limited supply of quality professional middle managers. As E. A. Smith argued, undoubtedly reflecting his own experiences outside the company, there was a need to obtain higher trained staff, at the expense of larger numbers, by paying enhanced salary grades, and he registered his deep concern about the capabilities of middle management within the organisation.[30]

The inability of management to co-ordinate the various activities of the company frustrated the implementation of strategies to deal with the expansion of the organisation. This was evident in the administration of factoring and sub-contracting within the business. In 1960, for example, Gimson reported arrangements with Ransone, Sim and Jefferies Ltd. of Ipswich to manufacture small batches of auto-lathes, which freed up capacity and labour at Edgwick. Sub-contracting was crucial to reduce excessive delivery times, which were resulting in cancelled orders. However, recourse to sub-contracting brought with it increased transaction cost problems, the management reporting delays in supplies of Ransone machines, 'which was usual with a new sub-contractor'.[31] A similar problem of ensuring a sustained supply confronted the Factoring Department, a profitable business, which cushioned the firm in the downturn of trade. Herbert's factoring activities included Archdale and Richards, both members of the Staveley Industries Group, and accounted for one-fifth of the total factoring business in 1965.[32] In 1962, Norman complained that 'their production is very badly behind programme and there are strings of broken promises'. Backlogs of deliveries from Richards stretched back to 1960, and cancellations to the value of £85,000 had 'a very bad effect on the Herbert name'. Deliveries from Archdale were more reliable, but as Blair noted both companies were subject to the 'Staveley influence', and their main priority, given the rush of orders, was to supply to the parent company.[33] Nevertheless, factoring did bring reciprocal advantages. For example, in 1963 the 'Herbert influence' secured orders for Archdale from Chrysler and agency agreements with the Newall Machine Tool Co. opened the way for contacts with the American Hammond Machinery Co. and Sach of Germany, both networked through sales to Newall.[34]

In order to reduce dependency on supplying customers via the Factoring Department, the company took the decision to launch a more aggressive acquisition policy. In July 1957, attention turned to the Holbrook Machine Tool

---

[30] Herbert, Board of Directors, 1960-80, 6 March, 22 May 1964.

[31] Herbert, Board of Directors, 1960-80, 2 December 1962.

[32] MTTA, Machine Tool Directory 1966, p. 147.

[33] Herbert, Board of Directors, 1960-80, 27 July 1962. Richards, for example, had large obligations under Staveley contracts for Bhopal, India. Herbert, Board of Directors, 1960-80, 29 September 1961.

[34] Herbert, Board of Directors, 1960-80, 18 October, 9 July 1963.

Co., which had factories at Stratford, London, and Harlow, Essex. Holbrook, a firm with an 'excellent' reputation as a batch producer of precision lathes, had an average turnover of £500,000, pre-tax profits of £130,000 and total assets, excluding plant, of £600,000. Operating plant included 250 machine tools, the Stratford and Harlow factories each producing 12 lathes per month. As Blair acknowledged, with additional investment Holbrook could increase output, its lathes would sell 'without interfering with other lines', and it would provide additional capacity when trade recovered. Announcing the financial settlement in December 1958, at a purchase price of £700,000, Clark assessed Holbrook as a cost effective producer, which 'would broaden the interests of Alfred Herbert ... in the Machine Tool Industry ... to the mutual advantage of both companies'. Rationalisation envisaged the utilisation of the joint production and sales 'facilities' of the two companies to enable a coordinated manufacturing programme for lathes to avoid duplication.[35]

Rising economic activity led, in June 1960, to offers for the share capital of I. L. Berridge, Leicester, totalling £469,375, the deal finalised in April 1961. Potentially, Berridge provided experienced labour and additional capacity, allowing capstan lathe manufacture at Lutterworth to be re-located. In 1963, conversions to the Berridge plant, aimed at manufacturing a new small Keller lathe produced under licence, was designed to utilise Berridge's 'spare draughtsmen capacity'.[36] Further acquisitions came in 1961 when Mudie Electrical, Birmingham, employing 35 workers making control gears, and Whitley, Son & Co., Huddersfield, makers of textile machinery and planing machines, were incorporated into the Herbert manufacturing and sales organisation. Mudie was eventually to make electronic controls for the licensed Devlieg programmed machines, and Whitley's experienced workforce took on responsibility for the building of licensed Fellows gear shapers, and provided additional capacity from its two modern foundries. Herbert's were selling agents for Whitley, and, in 1958 had under-wrote a 170,000 debenture deal loan to the company [37]

Acquisition complimented the ideals of modernisation through rationalisation, espoused by the Labour Government in 1965. At the company's AGM in that year, Clark focused on 'Rationalisation', acknowledging that 'Our group has had some experience of bringing together smaller plants with products that fit our range or with a technique which we have felt we could help them to widen'.[38] The 'group' symbolised the ideal of an integrated organisation, a 'board of engineers', with central co-ordination by the Herbert board. Group organisation implied a more direct control over both manufacturing and sales, including acquired subsidiaries, and the executive also saw this as an alternative to a holding

---

[35] Herbert, Board of Directors, 1944-60, 2 July, 3 September 1957; 2 January 1959.
[36] Herbert, Board of Directors, 1944-60, 9 June 1960; Herbert, Board of Directors, 1960-80, 17 February, 21 April 1961; 26 April 1963.
[37] Herbert, Board of Directors, 1944-60, 9 September 1960; Herbert, Board of Directors, 1960-80, 21 April, 24 July, 29 September 1961; *Machine Tool Review*, Vol. 49, 1961, p. 99; Vol. 50, 1962, p. 48; Vol. 52, 1964, p. 48.
[38] *Machine Tool Review*, Vol. 53, 1965, p. 48.

company format. In January 1958, Gimson informed the board that the Finance Committee had been considering the question of 'hiving off' parts of the business to protect the company against possible nationalisation, which involved creating a holding company, with two subsidiaries for manufacturing and selling. Rejecting the scheme, Clark and Gimson concluded that holding companies entailed significant administrative costs, and the duplication of functions 'now carried out for the benefit of the company as a whole'. Consequently, a holding company would have, according to the Herbert executive, a decentralising function, in contrast to a centrally co-ordinated group.[39] Discussing the issue for a second time in 1963, again in the context of paranoia over nationalisation, the directors similarly rejected a holding company, but Clark did raise serious concerns about the capability of executive management to co-ordinate the activities of acquired companies within the group. In particular, the balancing of production between the subsidiary factories and the Herbert works were stretching the resources of the top management team to the limits.[40]

Illustrating the limited scope of management was the problems encountered in reorganising the newly acquired group subsidiaries. Whitley, for example, lacked 'dynamic management',[41] had no proper system for cost accounting, and its textile machinery business sustained substantial losses. Although Clark remained optimistic that they could develop the company into a profit-making concern within two years, it ultimately proved a financial liability. There were serious delays in converting the plant to the full production of planing machines, 'workmanship' was of a poor quality, plant antiquated, and overhead costs rising. Attempts to introduce small lathe manufacture at the company, to fill a 'gap' in the Herbert sales programme, were frustrated, the technical staff unable to adapt Herbert designs. In 1961, the company recorded a loss of £52,600, rising to £80,000 in 1962 and £134,000 in 1963, at which date the textile machine business was sold off at a knock down price of £6,000, the company resuming trading as Lockwood Machine Tool Ltd. By that stage Herbert's had sunk £343,000 in the venture, £184,000 for the purchase of shares and £195,000 in the form of a debenture loan, and liquidation would have proved a costly affair.[42]

To effect central control over subsidiaries, the executive appointed cross directors. At Mudie, Clark, Harrison, and Smith became directors in 1961, serving on the board with D. R. Mudie. Direct control enabled the monitoring of financial performance, and the concentration of effort upon work commissioned by Herbert's. Thus, extensive surveys were made of the manufacturing facilities and accounting procedures, and prices were raised by 10 per cent to enable Mudie to

---

[39] Herbert, Board of Directors, 1944-60, 4 March 1958.

[40] Herbert, Board of Directors, 1960-80, 13 December 1963.

[41] Under the acquisition agreement Whitley's long-serving chairman, H. Charlesworth, retired, but his son, T Charlesworth, was retained to help in putting the company 'on its feet'. Herbert, Board of Directors, 1960-80, 21 April 1961.

[42] Herbert, Board of Directors, 1960-80, 21 April, 21 June, 24 July, 29 September 1961; 14 December 1962; 21 June, 18 October 1963; *Machine Tool Review*, Vol. 49, 1961, p. 99; Vol. 50, 1962, p. 48; Vol. 52, 1964, p. 48.

operate at a 'break-even' point. However, as Harrison observed, management was inefficient and costing systems unreliable. By July 1961, output had risen by 25 per cent, and factory extensions were under consideration to enable the transfer of work from Coventry. However, profits remained small, £400 in 1961 and £10,000 in 1962, and by 1963 Mudie was highly dependent upon contracted work from Herbert's for electrical control panels.[43] More serious problems were confronted at Holbrook, Clark acknowledging that 'Administration of the company is peculiar', and there had been difficulties in persuading the long serving family managers to retire. To install direct supervision of the business, Blair became chair, with Ellson a co-director, but although the company's Harlow operations were concentrated in modern premises, providing a potential to speed up output, its Stratford plant was obsolete. The company also relied on 11 outside suppliers for castings, providing problems for quality control. As Clark conceded, 'Many changes would have to be made'. Rapid change, however, proved problematic, the technical staff at Holbrook resisting interference from Herbert staff, forcing Blair to appoint a Holbrook man, G. L. Kaye, as general manager of the company. Urging the need for a 'close liaison' with Holbrook, Clark sanctioned the transfer of Edgwick lathe manufacture to the company's Stratford works. Further, the factory at Harlow was converted to manufacture a new tool room precision lathe, expected to sell to the value of £500,000 in 1961, while at the same time the Herbert Factored Department assumed responsibility for export sales from Harlow. However, as early as 1959, problems appeared in the design capabilities of Holbrook, production constrained by shortages of skilled workers. Nevertheless, the demand for precision lathes persuaded management to invest in improved plant in 1961, a programme supervised directly by Muirhead. In 1962, Blair reported that Holbrook's speciality precision lathes had a real potential, but Muirhead remained sanguine, emphasising that output had fallen short of targets, labour was in limited supply, and delays occurred in re-configuring designs to Herbert standards. Moreover, intense competition from the lower priced and superior designed lathes of Dean, Smith and Grace posed serious marketing problems. From a financial perspective, Holbrook profits in 1962 were just £41,000 and rose to only £45,000 in 1963.[44]

The acquisition strategy, rather than economising on scarce management resources, actually stretched them even further, and problems in reorganising the subsidiaries raised concerns over managerial capabilities within the group. For example, Muirhead found himself also appointed to the boards of Berridge, Sigma, and Whitley, raising concerns over the weight of responsibility placed on individual directors. His role was to coordinate the production programme of the subsidiaries, and in 1964 Harrison joined him in a supporting capacity. As Blair commented in 1961, Muirhead's involvement in the management of subsidiaries conflicted with his primary function of developing economic production systems at

---

[43] Herbert, Board of Directors, 1960-80, 21 April, 24 July 1961; 18 October 1963.

[44] Herbert, Board of Directors, 1944-60, 2 July, 3 September 1957; 2 January, 18 February, 3 April, 16 June, 4 December 1959; Herbert, Board of Directors, 1960-80, 29 September 1961; 27 July 1962; 17 July 1964.

the Coventry factories.[45] Management problems at the subsidiaries distracted the Herbert executive, and this was even the case at their oldest subsidiary, Sigma. In 1957, Sigma management had contracted for one off special testing machines at 'liberal prices' and under agreements to share design costs with users, but when orders fell in 1958 this proved a financial miscalculation, leading to substantial losses. As Mahler concluded, this was a sign of ineffective control by the Herbert board, and despite efforts to develop more profitable designs, Sigma was still recording a loss on specials in 1961, which reduced its overall profits to just £29,400, although this recovered to £52,300 in 1962.[46] More successful was Berridge, which in 1961 was producing two types of Herbert designed capstan lathes. This enabled an increased production of Devlieg and Keller programme controlled machines at Lutterworth, and in 1962 the manufacture of the newly designed Edgwick lathe was also transferred to Berridge. Nevertheless, substantial investment programmes, and plant re-balancing which disrupted sales, reduced profits to just £3,000 in 1962, although they rose substantially to £56,000 in 1963, sales rising by 25 per cent.[47] At the Herbert AGM in 1963, Clark endorsed the overall acquisition strategy. Subsidiaries provided valuable 'additional capacity', but Clark also admitted to delays in bringing them 'more into line with the methods and standards of the parent concern', despite the transfer of Herbert technical personnel and the installation of modern equipment.[48]

Consequently, despite the acquisitions, capacity constraint remained a perennial problem in the upturn of the cycle, affecting the company's competitive position. By May 1960, increased demand had already lengthened delivery time beyond 12 months, and by 1961 Clark thought it inevitable that that there would be a loss of business. Similar problems were encountered by the Factoring Department, Norman reporting in September 1961 of his deep concern over the late deliveries and broken promises from Heald, Archdale, Richards, and Cunliffe & Croom which seriously damaged 'The Herbert goodwill'. In September 1961, production was up 38 per cent on the previous year, but stocks were 'exhausted'. In response, Clark urged that they must maintain adequate stocks of materials to ensure no break in production, despite the inventory costs involved. In this situation, Clark resisted the pressure to raise prices, insisting that they would lose competitiveness, and alternatively they 'need to carefully watch expenses'. By February 1962 there was a further acceleration of output, machine stocks recovering to £1 million, but by April they were again 'exhausted', leading to advanced delivery dates for Herbert and factored machines. In July, the sales director, Core, referred to serious delays in delivery, which affected competitiveness, compounded by rising costs, which finally forced Clark to concede a 5 per cent increase on the price of all Herbert machines, to come into

---

[45] Herbert, Board of Directors, 1960-80, 24 July 1961; 2 October 1964.

[46] Herbert, Board of Directors, 1944-60, 18 February, 5 October 1959; Herbert, Board of Directors, 1960-80, 29 September 1961; 14 December 1962.

[47] Herbert, Board of Directors, 1960-80, 29 September, 24 November 1961; 27 July, 14 December 1962; 18 October 1963.

[48] *Machine Tool Review*, Vol. 51, 1963, p. 48.

force in October 1962. Price increases were an attempt to dampen demand and improve delivery times, and consequently to halt the cancellation of orders due to declining customer confidence. In June 1963, with economic activity falling, the management reviewed its previous decision, observing the loss of orders for capstan and turret lathes to their competitors because of high prices. Nevertheless, in December 1963 Clark announced further price increases, scheduled for February 1964, forced on the company, despite customer criticisms, by rising labour and raw material costs, which had been accelerating since 1961.[49] Even in the mid-1950s, wage differentials for skilled labour in the Coventry area were 37.7 per cent above the national average, and between 1961 and 1964 there was increasing pressure on wage costs.[50] Price rises, clearly affected export sales, especially to America and Europe. In November 1965, higher prices, coupled with tariffs, meant that 'we are not really getting our share of business from highly competitive and sophisticated markets', one-quarter of exports destined for India and one-fifth for Australia. Austral-Asian markets were conditioned by the high demand for Herbert general-purpose machines, but in European and American markets, as well as in the home market, there was intense competition against the company's limited range of specialist machines. In 1962, for example, Clark complained of their poor export performance in the German market, and at home there was intense competition from Warner & Swasey auto lathes, despite their selling price being extremely high. The realisation that competitive performance was not simply a question of price was made clear in December 1963, when the board insisted that customers 'were not paying much attention to price', the key determinant being 'new designs' affording improved productivity and the simplification of set-up routines.[51]

Market repositioning of their machine designs was emphasised by leading executives in the company in 1963. Core felt that the company was lagging behind its competitors, Allen emphasised the challenge from the new automatics, incorporating NC systems, developed by Warner & Swasey, and Hugo admitted that they had no machine in the current programme to match this 'formidable competitor'. Between 1960 and 1963, Herbert's lost an estimated £2.25 million of business to American makers such as Warner & Swasey, Monfort, Tarex, and other competitors. At the opening of the company's new London salesroom in December 1963, customers were impressed by the display of licensed manufactured machines, and the new Herbert tape controlled drill, but the appearance of 'older machines', notably capstan and turret lathes, raised considerable criticism.[52] Three

---

[49] Herbert, Board of Directors, 1960-80, 9 May 1960; 17 February, 29 September 1961; 9 February, 27 April, 27 July 1962; 21 June 1963; 13 December 1964.

[50] E. Wigham, *The Power to Manage: A History of the Engineering Employers Federation* (Macmillan, Basingstoke, 1973), pp. 209-10.

[51] Herbert, Board of Directors, 1960-80, 14 March, 27 April 1962; 13 December 1963; 8 November 1965. Increasing prices was not unique to Herbert's. American makers, such as Norton and Landis, also raised prices in 1964, but unlike Herbert's this was not a cost consideration, but a decision based on compensating for the prevailing low prices of previous years. *Machinist*, 25 May 1964, p. 47.

[52] Herbert, Board of Directors, 1960-80, 9 August, 18 October, 18 December 1963.

interrelated factors influenced design strategy, and led to competitive problems by the mid-1960s. First, organisational constraints limited the co-ordination and centralisation of R&D within the company. Second, the long association of the company with general-purpose machines focused design effort on traditional products, to the detriment of a more rapid advance in automatic and NC machines. Product development reflected the existing knowledge base of the organisation, the limited technical capabilities and human resource inputs to the organisation, but also the way that the pattern of cyclical demand constrained the strategic action of the executive. This related to the third factor, the supplanting of technical knowledge by a closer association, via its factoring department, with foreign machine makers through manufacturing licensing agreements.

As Metcalfe argues, innovation within organisations is dependent 'upon the individuals involved and the ways in which their creative endeavours are organised and connected with the rest of the firm'.[53] This would suggest the need for integrating and co-ordinating the operations of the firm to maximise organisational capabilities. Indeed, Clark made a direct connection between the company's performance, in both engineering production and factoring, and the knowledge embedded in executive management. Insisting on the need for 'first class' design, quality and marketing, he recognised that 'No one member of the board could expect to be conversant with all aspects of this vast business. Our job is to look ahead, to be active, keeping up-to-date and making changes where necessary'.[54] To achieve these outcomes, Clark was appreciative of the necessity to deliver economies of scope, which relates to the effective administration and utilisation of resources across a diverse range of products.[55] As Clark informed the board, 'the internal organisation of the company will require very careful consideration' to co-ordinate the 'wide variety of products we are selling'.[56] The core organisational challenge was the co-ordination of activities between manufacturing and factoring, the third factor identified above, and this related to the decision in 1957 to appoint two managing directors. De facto, this accepted the existence of two separate business activities, nominally residing in one company, and reflected the knowledge and experience of Blair and Clark. The former had begun his career in the company's Glasgow showroom in 1913 and he acted as a sales representative in Canada and the U.S.A. between 1914 and 1924. He was a 'leading figure' in the development of factoring operations. In contrast, Clark was a production engineer, with a long service in the machine shops.[57]

The management restructuring of 1957 implied a divorce of function between the two managing directors, and gave credence to the belief that Herbert's

---

[53] Metcalfe, 'Technology Systems' p. 278.
[54] Herbert, Board of Directors, 1944-60, 5 June 1957.
[55] See D. Teece, 'Economies of Scope and the Scope of the Enterprise', *Journal of Economic Behaviour and Organisation*, Vol. 1, No. 3 (1980), pp. 223-47.
[56] Herbert, Board of Directors, 1944-60, 5 June 1957.
[57] Herbert, Board of Directors, 1960-80, 27 July 1962.

was in fact two separate companies. In the mind of Clark, however, the firm was a unitary organisation: 'Alfred Herbert and Factored were not two separate businesses, but two parts of one whole, and he was looking forward to an even closer relationship with Mr Blair in the joint management of both sides'. Despite Clark's protestations, it is not clear what he meant by the term 'one whole', and the fact that the executive toyed with the idea of a holding company, with two separate divisions for manufacturing and factoring, suggests a deep ambivalence over the organisational structure of the company. Clearly, Clark was concerned that the existing separation was jeopardising 'a closer liaison between engineering and development' and he pleaded that 'the best brains of our technical staff', in both the production plants and the factored division, 'should get together to help one another with ideas and avoid any duplication'. The issue of duplication involved the creation of agency agreements with outside manufacturers who competed with Herbert's own machines, and in the view of the sales director, Core, this needed to be co-ordinated so that the technical capabilities of the organisation should be maximised. The organisational problems at the company involved the inability to forge a close co-ordination between production, factoring and sales and this problem became more acute as competitive pressures increased. Co-ordination problems weakened the knowledge base of the company and consequently its ability to compete effectively. In an attempt to address these issues, an internal Engineering Committee was formed in June 1957, comprising four leading directors, Hugo, factoring, Harrison, design, Townsend, technical, and Muirhead, works, to assess strategies for integration to 'take advantage of the technical skills available to the company'.[58]

Reporting in July 1958, the Committee recommended a new purpose-built 'Development Department', which would integrate technical staff from both the factoring design department at Red Lane and the engineering design department at Edgwick. Clark's enthusiasm for the recommendation was tempered. On the insistence of Blair, the board deferred a decision until the implications for the factored department of establishing a Development Department with the intention of providing an integrated programme for R&D had been fully considered. In October 1958, Clark succeeded Gimson as chair, and given low orders there was a general agreement to concentrate the company's 'efforts on development and research, in conjunction with new designs'. Unfortunately, this decision coincided with a worsening of the company's financial position, net profits falling by 26 per cent between 1957 and 1959, and trading profits by 41 per cent (Table 9.2). Despite cuts in manufacturing and a 'critical review' of expenditure, Clark insisted on the priority of gearing their tool room and experimental departments to develop new models in anticipation of revitalised demand, and in December 1958 he announced a capital expenditure programme for a new integrated Applied Research Department (ARD). Administrative problems, however, concerning the re-location of the small tool department, delayed its opening until 1961.[59]

---

[58] Herbert, Board of Directors, 1944-60, 5 June 1957; 7 January 1958.
[59] Herbert, Board of Directors, 1944-60, 1 July, 30 October 2 December 1958; 2 January 1959; *Alfred Herbert News*, Vol. 35, 1961, pp. 69-74.

Delays in developing a centralised design policy had implications for the planning of the manufacturing programme in the late 1950s, which takes us to the second interrelated issue concerned with the firm's focus on traditional product lines. In December 1958, Hugo complained about the lack of coordination between the factoring and manufacturing departments and the sales department, with only limited technical information provided to customers. More worrying was problems of devising its manufacturing programme for 1960, which was high on the boardroom agenda during 1959. In February, the management noted the difficulties of devising a programme to ensure that the company could provide a range of machines to customers, there being a limited coordination between the design teams in the factored and manufacturing departments concerning the development of new machines. The key issue was the design of new machines, incorporating automation and NC systems, a feature of the technological environment, which Clark saw as 'a new era in the manufacturing history of Britain'. Management were well aware of the technological challenge, and in June Hugo warned of competition from the new Warner & Swasey automatics, and their intention to license them to Asquith. Consequently, he asked, 'what their policy was concerning the future development of automation?' Clark's response was to defer to the Engineering Committee for further deliberation, a decision reached in October to manufacture two new designs. A batch of 24 modified Herbert turret drilling machines, and 24 sets of components to convert the Herbert 2D Capstan Lathe to automatic programme control, marketed as the 2D Robot, were sanctioned. The executive also authorised an increase of Herbert 3A Auto Lathes from 6 to 24, to ensure sufficient stocks. This was a highly conservative programme, the drilling machines were simply modifications of earlier designs, and the auto lathes, originally launched in 1956, were not fully automatic. Summing up the general manufacturing programme for 1960, Clark confirmed that there would be no substantial revision.[60]

Partly, conservative forward planning at the company is explained by the outcome of investment decisions made in the recession from 1957. As Clark made clear in October 1959, the company had maintained stocks of existing designs during the downturn, especially general-purpose capstan and turret lathes, in anticipation of meeting orders in the upturn, and they now faced the stark reality of having to sell to cover costs. As Clark informed the 1961 AGM, this had been a 'prudent' policy 'when we were far from busy, but confident, nevertheless, that demand would improve'. Prudent, perhaps, but to adequately explain the nature of forward design planning requires an assessment of the technical knowledge of the organisation and the market potential of general-purpose machine tools. As *The Machine Tool Review* conceded in 1959, the largest demand in Britain was for general-purpose 'capstan, turret and engine lathes, plain horizontal and vertical milling machines, drilling machines ... and machines for grinding and broaching'. This represented the Herbert product range, the company adapting general-purpose machines to the variety of special requirements of users. For example, the

---

[60] Herbert, Board of Directors, 1944-60, 2 December 1958; 18 February, 16 June, 5 October 1959; *Machine Tool Review*, Vol. 44, 1956, p. 43; Vol. 47, 1959, p. 25.

company's No. 4 Senior Capstan Lathe was available in over 2,000 different specifications, not including the actual tooling. Clark outlined the company's engineering philosophy:

> although our manufacturing facilities are very extensive they must be employed in producing few of the many types and sizes of machines and equipment which are needed to meet the requirements of the engineering industries. Only by such a policy of specialisation, can our designers and production engineers acquire the knowledge and experience which are essential if our products are to meet the full blast of competition in the world's markets. Too much diversification in a machine tool factory results in a mediocre product.

Engineering specialisation was a deeply embedded 'policy to use our sales and service organisation to meet our customers' varying needs by offering a far wider programme of machines than that produced in our own shops'. This was the province of the Factored Division 'which handled machines produced by British and foreign firms who again specialise on definite types for which they have an established reputation'.[61] Such a strategy, of course, reduced the capability to develop effectively a range of special automatic and NC machines.

The company's limitations in automatic and special-purpose machines was common knowledge in the motor industry. In the early 1950s Leonard Lord, the chair of the British Motor Corporation (BMC), carried out a series of studies on machining efficiency. Conducting a group of trade unionists around the factory, Lord picked up a connecting rod, emphasising that it took five different machining operations to manufacture, and required five separate machines purchased from Herbert's. What they 'really wanted was a single machine', specially built as in Germany, 'to do the entire operation'. Herbert's do not 'make that kind of tool. This won't last long. Either they'll go bloody bust or we'll go bloody bust'.[62] In 1966, *The Engineer* concluded that since the 1950s Herbert's had not sufficiently developed their 'scope for automatic or automated' machine tools, especially incorporating NC.[63] Yet, Herbert's did develop automation and NC in the 1950s, and its management were well aware of the significant changes this represented. As shown in Chapter 7, a number of research projects were undertaken by electronics firms in Britain, and by Herbert's itself in the machine tool industry. Hamilton suggests that the company was a victim of the exaggerated expectations associated with automation and NC in the 1950s. Such were the 'wild claims' made for NC systems that Herbert's attempt to enter the field 'appeared out of date before it even got beyond the prototype phase'. In particular, Hamilton criticises Herbert's technological choice, the management developing record playback systems rather than integrating this with pulse manipulation, an innovative development associated with American producers and followed by electronics

---

[61] Herbert, Board of Directors, 1944-60, 5 October 1959; *Machine Tool Review*, Vol. 47, 1959, p. 25; Vol. 49, 1961, p. 49.

[62] M. Adeney, *The Motor Makers: The Turbulent History of Britain's Car Industry* (London, Collins, 1988), pp. 202-3.

[63] *Engineer*, 17 June 1966, p. 913.

companies in Britain. Although Hamilton does recognise the 'ingenious features' of the Herbert technology, he claims that record playback technology was considered out-dated by the time the company applied it in the mid-1950s.[64]

Nevertheless, Hamilton's observations fails to take account of how top management at Herbert's perceived the innovatory process, and also the association of the company with outside firms and agencies in the development of advanced machine tools. At Herbert's, management viewed innovation as an evolutionary process, and central to this was 'specialised "know-how" acquired by long experience' in building quality machines.[65] In developing strategies to meet the challenge of automation and NC decisions were based not only on a consideration of the costs and benefits of the technology to themselves and to the industry, but also by a perception of how knowledge had evolved to shape the capabilities of the organisation. In this sense, and contrary to Hamilton, the top management at Herbert's were not at all convinced that the assimilation of automation and NC into machine tool design was going to produce radical change. Sir Alfred typified this cautious approach: 'Automation will come gradually and will apply to a limited field of industry', notably in the development of mass production technology requiring 'long-runs without resetting'. Assuming that the technology would have limited application for general engineering, he concluded that 'The fully automatic factory is still a long way from realisation'.[66] Clark, too, was sanguine about the diffusion of NC technology. Focusing in 1956 on the theme of skilled labour shortages, he registered his dismay over 'that wretched, over-worked subject, Automation, for despite the pipe dreams of some of our technical workers, I cannot encourage the thought that this is the likely direction in which to look for the answer to our employment problems'.[67] Reflecting the technical uncertainty associated with NC, he observed in 1963 that 'Despite the considerable economies that can be achieved', the acceptance of the advantages of NC 'has come relatively slowly', especially in terms of appreciating a 'tangible ... reduction in work piece costs'.[68] Interestingly, the company was conspicuous by its absence from the MTTA Sub-Committee on Automation of 1956, which made positive overtures on the potential for increasing the use of automatic machine tools incorporating NC systems.[69]

The vision articulated by the company's dominant leaders, and its absence from the Sub-Committee, does not suggest that the executive were actively embracing NC technology. Instead, the position of management tended to reflect an 'adaptive' rather than an innovating organisation, one which lives 'off rather than creatively 'build upon the organisational capabilities that have been

---

[64] Hamilton, 'British Machine Tool Automation', pp. 96, 98-9, 106.

[65] Clark, cited in *Economist*, 1 April 1961, p. 64.

[66] *Machine Tool Review*, Vol. 43, 1955, p. 74; Vol. 44, 1956, p. 21.

[67] Coventry Archive, 12701/7/31, Business Papers of Colonel C. W. Clark, Speech to Leicester District of the Engineering and Allied Employers Association, 28 November 1956.

[68] *Machine Tool Review*, Vol. 51, 1963, p. 99.

[69] MTTA, Council Minute Book, 28 November 1956.

accumulated from its prior investment in productive resources'.[70] Given low market expectations for automation and NC, the Herbert design strategy, in the short-term, adapted traditional product lines to the needs of customers, reinforced by the cyclical pattern of ordering. Further, there was overwhelming support of the general industry position on the importation of specialist machine tools from abroad, which provided Herbert's with a diversified product range and benefited users at large. With unstable demand conditions, industrial buyers could use imported specialist machine tools not manufactured domestically, and by doing so could accumulate technological knowledge.[71] However, in the 1950s the company extended its factoring operations with American and foreign makers, including those 'to the fore' in the development of NC, and increasingly substituted factored imports by manufacturing under licence. Over half of Herbert's sales were of their own make in 1966, offering a 'very wide range ... some produced under licence'. Licensing evolved via the marketing networks developed by the factoring department, and as Clark claimed in 1961, the company built machines to the designs of foreign makers, whose products they had long been familiar with as importing agents. The 'special merit' justifying the making of these in Britain, was that 'The design and operating techniques are the fruits of close study of a definite group of machining problems by men whose experience we cannot readily match'.[72] The assimilation of American technology was vital to the accumulation of this knowledge, and this requires an examination of the third interrelated factor mentioned earlier, the contribution of factoring and licensing arrangements to the company's design capabilities.

In 1957, Herbert's began the manufacture of chasers, licensed from the Landis Machine Tool Co., at Exhall, employing 18 workers with an output of £90,000 per annum. At the same time, Landis, with a long association with Herbert Factoring, proposed a joint venture to manufacture chasers, dies and thread rollers, Herbert's acquiring sole agency rights for their sale in the U.K. As Muirhead pointed out, Landis would bring knowledge of 'American methods of manufacture', as well as sole rights to manufacture over British competitors. The potential advantages from association, however, were outweighed by the competitive effect of Landis products on the Exhall small tool range, and duplication with the manufacture of dieheads licensed by Tangye, Birmingham. Rejecting the joint company, the executive negotiated in 1958 a licence to manufacture Landis dieheads and thread rollers at Exhall. They also decided to transfer the work on chasers to Landis Machine Maiden, a new Landis subsidiary at Hyde, Cheshire. Work on Landis components at Exhall began in early 1959, 'using American ... techniques', and Herbert Factoring obtained exclusive selling rights for Landis dieheads and chasers in the U.K. for 10 years. To reinforce

[70] W. Lazonick and M. O'Sullivan, 'Governance of Innovation for Economic Development', Research Paper to European Commission, (March 1998), p. 5.

[71] *Machine Tool Review*, Vol. 47, 1959, p. 121; Vol. 49, 1961, p. 9; *Economist*, 1 April 1961, pp. 61-4.

[72] *Machine Tool Review*, Vol. 43, 1955, p. 118; Vol 49, 1961, p. 49; MTTA, Machine Tool Directory 1966, p. 147.

collaboration, a joint Herbert-Landis Maiden service provided consultation to customers.[73] During the same period a joint selling company was launched with Pratt & Whitney, Hertford, Connecticut, to market their Keller BG 21 milling machine, manufactured in Britain by Herbert's who provided the patterns, jigs and tools from engineering data supplied by the American company. The technical capability and market potential of the BG 21, equipped with fully automatic control, certainly impressed Muirhead, as a machine capable of delivering 'considerable reductions both in indirect labour and inspection costs'. In 1959, Pratt, Whitney & Herbert was formed, with a nominal capital of £125,000, 25 per cent subscribed. The Americans held 55 per cent of stock, decision making based on a two-third majority, Pratt & Whitney nominating three and Herbert's two of the company directors. Keller machines, manufactured at Edgwick, were sold to the new company, which had exclusive selling rights in all foreign markets outside North America, through the existing agents of Pratt & Whitney, while Herbert Factoring obtained exclusive sales rights in the U.K.[74] The potential for an American domination of the product range of the company was not lost on Hugo, who 'hoped that the proposed expansion of the American interests ... would not overshadow the vital development of the true Herbert product', and this caution was supported by Core and Mahler. Nevertheless, although accepting that adapting American designs to Herbert production methods raised technical problems, Clark made clear the advantages accruing from technical knowledge to the engineering potential of the company, and to the expansion of factored sales.[75] In reality, Keller machines proved a disappointing commercial venture, the BG21 facing stiff competition from larger type models produced by competitors, and by insufficient capacity at Edgwick to manufacture the new larger type BG22 Keller in 1962. With low demand at home and abroad in 1965, only one Keller was built every 3 months at Edgwick. Landis Maiden, however, made an important contribution to the Herbert range of accessory tools, providing an input of technical knowledge on high tensile cutting steels, applied to Herbert components.

External networks also proved valuable in the development of NC systems. In 1946, Sir John Black of Standard Motors advised Sir Alfred to secure the selling agency for high precision boring and milling machines manufactured by Devlieg of the U.S.A. By 1952, a joint venture for building tape controlled jig mills in the U.K. was formalised, which led to the introduction of Datarol, a NC system developed by Herbert's in collaboration with a British electronics manufacturer. The Herbert/Devlieg 2B-36 Jigmill, launched in 1959, incorporated a number of complementary machining operations, minimised overall machining, and reduced associated costs. Initially, Herbert's supplied Datarol separately to customers as a fixture to be fitted to their machines, but, in 1961, the Herbert executive extended the Lutterworth factory to manufacture Datarol on a production basis, the system

---

[73] Herbert, Board of Directors, 1944-60, 3 September, 5 November 1957; 26 February, 1 July, 30 October 1958; 3 April 1959; *Machine Tool Review*, Vol. 49, 1961, p. 116.

[74] Herbert, Board of Directors, 1944-60, 30 October, 2 December 1958; 18 February, 3 April 1959.

[75] Herbert, Board of Directors, 1944-60, 30 October 1958.

fitted to both Devlieg and Keller machines. Also in 1960, the British makers Cri-Dan, based in Croydon, finalised a licence for high-speed tape controlled threading machines, filling a gap in the Herbert range, and eventually manufactured at the Berridge factory in 1962. At Olympia in 1960, the company exhibited from three stands: Herbert capstan and turret lathes, drilling and milling machines; licensed Devlieg jigmills, Keller automatics, and Cri-Dan machines; and factored machines, such as Norton and Heald precision grinding machines. The majority of factored machines, it was claimed, 'were of British manufacture, exact duplicates of the maker's model or incorporating new features of Herbert designs, developed to meet the particular requirements of Britain's industries'. In 1961, the Herbert 'reputation', Clark accepted, rested on its engineering knowledge of general-purpose machines, supplemented by factored machines. By 1965, Herbert's was also manufacturing licensed Fellows gear shaping machines, and Clark positioned the company as an initiator in Britain 'of machines formerly imported'. Through their own initiatives, or by 'association with friends overseas', they had steadily expanded the range of both standard and specialist high precision machines to British manufacturers. In 1964, well over half of factoring agencies were for British makers, and imported machines were only 4 per cent of total sales.[76]

Did factored sales and licensing arrangements, however, enhance the organisation's own design capabilities? As Nelson claims, a central task of management 'is to make decisions regarding R&D allocation', and technological sophistication by management is a prerequisite for doing the job well'.[77] The role of factoring in the company disguised serious weaknesses in the technical capabilities of the organisation. At the same time, it placed Britain's largest machine tool maker at the centre of the growing criticism of the industry's competitive performance. On the opening of the Herbert ARD in 1961, Clark defended the industry against the allegations of the Mitchell Report that there was significant under-investment in R&D, leading to a loss of competitive advantage. The ARD cost the company £2.75 million, and in the early 1960s, according to Clark, Herbert's was spending £350,000 per annum on R&D, approximately 19.5 per cent of net profits in 1961. The number of qualified engineers engaged on R&D work was 0.5 per cent of the total workforce in 1961, the proportion engaged directly on design was 4 per cent, and this was significantly higher than the average for the industry. Through *The Machine Tool Review*, the management positioned itself as a leading player in the industry: 'The machine tool is not wholly an end product in itself but is a means to an end', to facilitate increased productivity and efficiency in general engineering. Consequently, the company directed its R&D provision towards meeting the diverse demands of general engineering, a 'task' made 'complicated' by the problems of 'anticipating its future

---

[76] Herbert, Board of Directors, 1944-60, 5 October 1959; Herbert, Board of Directors, 1960-80, 24 November 1961; 9 February, 27 July 1962; 1 March 1965; *Machine Tool Review*, Vol. 43, 1955; Vol. 48, 1960, p. 29; Vol. 49, 1961, p. 49; Vol. 52, 1964, p. 48; Vol. 53, 1965, p. 47; Vol. 58, 1970, pp. 71, 113; Astrop, *The Rise and Fall*, p. 18; MTTA, Machine Tool Directory, 1966, p. 151.

[77] Nelson, *The Sources of Economic Growth*, p. 43.

needs'. Three basic principles summed up the R&D approach: an in-depth assessment of components manufactured in customer factories to predict future demands, 'developing the existing functions of the machine', and 'by close association with outside bodies such as Research Organisations, cutting material manufacturers, and manufacturers developing new materials to be cut'. This symbolised the firm as a service organisation, providing qualified production and machinery engineers to solve the manufacturing problems of their customers. R&D clearly relied on external feedback mechanisms, involving, as Clark emphasised, engineering firms who undertook 'costly research work on materials, electric and electronic components' which 'can be justified by much wider markets than the machine tool industry can offer'. Cooperation with outside agencies included the company's long association with the National Physical Laboratory, the National Engineering Laboratory, and the College of Aeronautics, who were 'readily available to help with the more basic problems'. Tied to this was the external links through the factoring and licensing of machine tools, which 'provided information of the latest developments in machine tool practice'. External networks, claimed Clark, were necessary, but not sufficient. The technology was applied by 'Herbert men' with deep knowledge of machine tool theory and practice in adapting general-purpose machines to the needs of engineering. The ARD was thus 'designed for the express needs of development projects, which will not necessarily be limited to our own organisation'.[78]

In the political game of modernisation of the early 1960s, there was a mixed reaction to the provision of R&D by Herbert's. As discussed in Chapter 8, Reginald Maudling, at the official opening of the ARD, praised the company for its commitment to R&D in the interest of the machine tool industry generally. This was contrary to the position of Hailsham at the DSIR who viewed the company's actions as propriatorial, providing no lead for the industry, and condemned the ARD as 'little more than a prototype machine testing station'. The ARD was no more than a minimalist alternative to the government's promotion of the MTIRA, which Herbert's did not join until 1968.[79] The Economist described the company's decision not to join industry level initiatives on R&D as a 'curious and bitter disappointment'.[80] The state might provide the opportunity for collaborative R&D, but the decision of the Herbert directors not to participate is indicative of the limitations of the government's modernisation strategy in the early 1960s. The actions of the 'leading player' in the industry supports our general perception of individual interests taking precedence over wider collective arrangements, but also crucially reflects on the evolution of the company's external networks. Business performance was linked to their capabilities to design new models through their ARD, Clark publicly announcing in 1962 that this was 'adequate' and could be

---

[78] *Machine Tool Review*, Vol. 49, 1961, pp. 50-1, 53, 56; *Engineer*, 30 June 1961, p. 1,097.

[79] *Research and Development for Industry*, 1961, p. 108; *Board of Trade Journal*, Vol. 153, 1961, p. 1,508.

[80] MTTA, Council Minute Book, 26 May, 6 October, 9, 17 November 1960; *Economist*, 13 June 1964, p. 1,274.

supplemented through long established networks outside the formal government initiative of the MTIRA.[81] This seems to support the verdict of the NEDC that 'The current system of research in isolation within firms ... increased the proportion of irrelevant and unproductive research and increased the duplication of research'.[82]

Ironically, this was the exact same position that the Herbert executive took of the MTIRA, an institution that it felt replicated its own research initiatives through its external relations. To demonstrate this we can consider the rational behind the formation of research associations put forward by Sir Christopher Goodere, Chairman of the Committee of Directors of Research Associations in 1963. 'A company joining a Research Association' he claimed 'joins a club with access to knowledge and assistance in many spheres'. Research associations occupied an intermediary position between university and industry, an institution providing an opportunity for high-class original research, 'with contracts with the universities on the one side and a comprehensive mental picture of the central problem of the industry on the other'. In 1962, Goodere's predecessor, D. W. Hill, outlined the practice of applied research. In the process of industrial research 'fundamental science must form the basis of applied research', but this was not a unilinear process, and instead involved the accumulation of knowledge through learning by doing. The transition from research to commercial development evolved as a process of trial and error as new problems arose.[83] This may well have been a description of the approach to research at Herbert's, and is reflected in the notion of organisational learning. Metcalfe defines three broad types of organisational learning: learning by doing, learning involving external sources of knowledge, and internally directed learning 'which is typically organised around a formalised R&D programme. These different forms of learning 'will generate different patterns of innovation'.[84] The company's decision to invest in its own ARD clearly prioritised the third form of organisational learning. Indicative of this was the fact that when a decision was finally taken, in 1967, to join the MTIRA the Herbert executive still raised serious doubts about the potential benefits to the company. Indeed, it would seem that the prime motive for joining was related to the acquisition by Herbert in 1967 of the machine tool division of BSA, a company with a strong affiliation to the MTIRA, and consequently leading to the registration of Herbert's as a member in 1968.[85]

While the company projected the image of an organisation that had developed a formalised R&D programme by the early 1960s, paradoxically this reinforced a process of learning by doing. Indeed, learning by doing typified R&D

[81] *Economist*, 7 April 1962, p. 85.

[82] Wood, 'Why Indicative Planning Failed', p. 451. On research duplication, see Nelson, 'The Role of Firms in Technical Advance', pp. 165-9.

[83] Sir C. Goodere, 'Research Associations and Collaborative Networks', *Research and Development for Industry*, (1964), p. 33; D. W. Hill, 'The Research Associations: Essential Links Between Science and Production', *Research and Development for Industry*, (1962) p. 37.

[84] Metcalfe, 'Technological Systems', p. 277.

[85] Herbert, Board of Directors, 1960-80, 9 June 1967.

in British machine tool firms, a key factor in the public allegations of technical backwardness. *The Economist* described R&D in the industry as a process of trial and error, no longer 'capable of infinite extension', with a limited conversion of research projects into commercial developments.[86] Despite Clark's praise of the ARD in 1961, commercial application of research projects was slow to materialise, and the main problem of co-ordinating design policy between factoring and engineering remained. In 1961, the company received 18,000 enquiries for machines, but Core complained that their sale service was inadequate and Blair noted confusion in advising customers on factored machines in relation to machines of their own design. Promoting Harrison to Director of Design in 1961 Clark insisted that he needed to become more closely involved with the Factored Division, which contributed over 50 per cent of sales. To implement this Harrison was appointed deputy managing director, and in 1962 headed a newly formed Group Design Policy Committee, with Muirhead, Hugo, and Norman, 'to ... co-ordinate design for the group as a whole'. This was the opportunity, claimed Clark, to develop standard practices in design, communicating technical knowledge between the factored and engineering divisions. Co-ordination problems persisted, and in July 1962 Norman referred to the placing of factored business to the value of £600,000 with various companies, including those licensed machines produced within the Herbert group, but argued that much more could be manufactured internally if they could get more assurance from the works that there would be a continuity of production. In the past, he claimed, contracts placed by the Factored Department with the Edgwick works had only been delivered when business picked up, and this had caused severe embarrassment to the Factored Department and its customers. Despite the work of the Design Committee to co-ordinate policy for 'engineering design at Herbert's and its subsidiaries', as well as monitoring orders for factored agencies and licensing agreements, there were constant complaints in 1963 over a failure to integrate design with the Sales Department, and on the overlap between factored products and Herbert machines.[87]

At the AGM in 1963 Clark could boast that 'Our heavy investment in Applied Research is proving well justified', but this was followed up by the damning statement that 'Much of our Research Work will be embodied in new designs not yet introduced'. Of equal importance, he concluded, 'are modifications to existing models, which make for enhanced productivity with improved reliability'. The inadequacies of the design programme were the focus of boardroom discussions in 1963. Using the barometer of the automobile industry, Core cited the authorisation of a replacement programme by Leyland Motors, and predicted that Herbert's 'should have its share'. Herbert technicians reviewed the Leyland machine utilisation routines, a practice devised to provide information on the type of machines demanded for plant replacement. Generally, Herbert sales staff were engaged in 'drawing the attention of the customer to the age of the

---

[86] *Economist*, 17 July 1963, p. 374; 13 June 1964, p. 306.

[87] Herbert, Board of Directors, 1960-80, 17 February, 24 July, 29 September 1961; 27 July, 14 December 1962; 15 February, 21 June 1963; *Machine Tool Review*, Vol. 49, 1961, p. 56.

machine'. Core, however, raised serious concerns about the design and manufacturing programme, warning that they should avoid decisions based on past trends in the cyclical pattern of demand. 'After the Suez recession', he argued, 'plant was largely replaced on a like for like basis', but, in contrast, a restoration of business confidence after 1963 would entail a demand for more advanced machines with a labour saving bias. 'Many of their good customers', he claimed, who had previously replaced capstans and turrets are now giving attention to automatics'. Recognising that the company had put in place a new design programme, which would be 'competitive' when in production, Core nevertheless concluded that 'we are certainly behind at the moment'. Following up on this, Allen criticised the quality of design staff. The 'foundation of our future programme', he claimed, should be premised upon 'original design', and although they had sufficient draughtsmen there was a need to strengthen their capabilities by employing 'top level' designers from outside the company 'with advanced engineering thinking'. Allen concluded that they should 'import new blood, free from Herbert conditioning, who would supplement knowledge within the company'. To support his indictment of the company's design capabilities, and the adaptive approach to technological change, Allen gave the example of the Herbert 2D Robot, originally designed in 1959 to incorporate programmed control. Problems in applying NC to the machine caused 'heavy modification costs at the production stage', and by 1963 had proved commercially unsuccessful, leading the board to agree that there was a fundamental need to reconsider their design effort and the quality of their technical personnel, 'even to the extent of attracting senior personnel from abroad'.[88]

Design problems particularly affected the new Progmanto machine of advanced design, in its final stages of development in 1963, but originally scheduled for the Olympia Show of 1960. The delay, as Clark argued, had seriously undermined the commercial potential of the machine, and he urged Harrison to deliver a completed batch immediately, as the machine was the forerunner in a programme for developing three larger types. In response, Harrison emphasised that the cause of delays related to the need for continual modifications at the prototype stage. At the same time, he assured Clark that the machine would definitely be ready for exhibition at Olympia in 1964. While the executive could celebrate its investment in internal R&D, the company still pursued a development policy that typified the process of learning by doing, resulting in delays to the commercialisation of machines. Constant experimentation, in conjuncture with technical feedback from customers, was illustrative of the process of R&D, a process that, as shown in Chapter 4, was entrenched in the company during the 1920s. Thus, the company finally displayed its No. 1 Progmanto, a tape-controlled machine, at Olympia in June 1964, the product receiving favourable reviews from customers. However, production beyond the prototype stage was put back until November, Clark taking Harrison to task on the continued modifications needed to the electric and clutch systems. As Clark observed, this was causing

---

[88] Herbert, Board of Directors, 1960-80, 9 August, 18 October, 13 December 1963; *Machine Tool Review*, Vol. 51, 1963, p. 48.

'embarrassment' with customers who had pre-ordered, and causing bottlenecks in the workshops where plant was lying idle. Indeed, technical problems on the No. 1 was not solved until the end of 1965, when experimental work on the larger No. 2 Progmanto allowed the ARD to develop working specifications for the electrics, which could then be applied to prototypes of the No. 3 and No. 4 versions. Concentration of effort on experimentation on the Progmanto, in turn placed 'a huge pressure on the R&D block', leading to delays in the development of new prototype vertical and horizontal milling machines with tape control.[89]

In 1963, Clark still insisted on the 'wisdom' of the policy pursued in 1957-8 to hold stocks in the downturn of the cycle. Predicting an upturn in 1964, he concluded that stocks were now only half of what they were in 1958, and would be rapidly absorbed by rising orders as 'they were of the right type'. Caution remained the order of the day, Clark referring to the fact that in 1961 the company's older automatics, such as the 3A Auto, were still selling extremely well, and this should be kept in mind when considering the policy of withdrawing older types of machines as new designs were developed. Consequently, in 1962, Clark reaffirmed his cautious machine replacement programme, despite the fact that the company's development work on new designs of automatic lathes had received encouraging comments from customers. Observing that their existing range was selling well, he concluded that they would have to consider the production of both old and new types in their manufacturing programmes. The 3A Auto, he emphasised, 'was still very popular in spite of the fact that its basic design was of a mature age'. In 1964, Clark delivered the same message. At Olympia, their automatic and tape controlled machines had aroused considerable interest, but there was also a market for 'simpler' types of turret and capstan lathes 'for a long time ahead, particularly for manufacturers who were not able to justify a high degree of automation'. In the industry generally in 1964 there was considerable despondency, and at Olympia 'New and tempting models have been introduced and displayed', but makers were 'examining the whiteness of each other's wash, and searching the halls for customers'.[90]

A New Direction, 1966-70

In February 1964, Clark appointed B. C. Harrison to support him as joint managing director, a prelude to eventual retirement from an executive position on the board. Aware of the need for a smooth succession, Clark was also concerned about the need to inject 'new blood' into top management, and in October 1964, following the retirement of the sales director, W. Core, he proposed the appointment of an outsider, Richard Dilworth Young as deputy chair. Young was a prominent engineer 'with a background of industrial administration at the highest level'. At

---

[89] Herbert, Board of Directors, 13 December 1963; 17 July 1964; 9 July, 13 September, 8 November 1965.

[90] Herbert, Board of Directors, 1960-80, 29 September 1961; 9 February, 14 March 1962; 9 August, 18 October 1963; 17 July 1964; *Machine Tool Review*, Vol. 52, 1964, p. 25.

the same time, Clark affirmed his intention that Harrison should succeed him as sole managing director. By December, Clark had worked out the route to the succession. He was to continue 'to be fully executive' and with Young as deputy 'will establish policy after appropriate discussion with the Board and Managing Director'. Surprisingly, the board deferred a confirmation of Harrison as sole managing director, when he raised concerns over the authority of Clark and Young to 'establish policy'. Harrison objected to the fact that in the managerial reorganisation his own position as managing director was relegated to that of a consultative role. Executive responsibilities, he claimed, had been determined without due consultation with the board. As he emphasised, 'they should act as a board and have time to discuss policy'. Taking up this point, J. H. Mahler hoped to see Harrison as sole managing director within six months, and to have a board 'working together'. Confirming the appointment of Young, Clark deferred his resignation as joint managing director, to enable 'a settling down period during the changes in top management'. Consequently, Young became deputy chair in January 1965, and in May, the board confirmed Harrison as sole managing director. In March 1966, Clark retired as chair, effective from June, retaining a non-executive role as president, and Young succeeded him. The senior executive role of Young was confirmed by Harrison, who acknowledged that he had 'won the admiration and whole-hearted support of all members of the Board, and shall undoubtedly lead the company to even greater heights of achievement'. [91]

Executive re-organisation set the context for an ambitious acquisition policy, announced by Young in February 1966. A first target was the machine tool interests of Staveley Industries, an association already existing through the factoring of Archdale and Richards machines, agencies scheduled to terminate in January 1967. Preliminary negotiations for the sale of four Staveley subsidiaries, Archdale, Richards, Craven (Manchester) and the Stavley Canadian Machine Tool Sale Co., for £9 million commenced, but a deal was rejected after a survey by S. G. Warburg & Co., financial consultants, on the grounds that the purchase would entail substantial investment in low efficiency manufacturing plant.[92] A more promising opportunity arose in June 1966, when Clark announced discussions for a merger with the machine tool and small tool division of BSA.[93] Consequently, a detailed cost benefit analysis was prepared, and presented in a report delivered by Young to the board in July. Positive gains arose from increased capacity and skilled labour resources. The BSA machine tool division encompassed 11 companies, with total assets of £9.5 million and employing nearly 4,000 workers (Appendix B, Table B.2). BSA Tools and BSA Churchill employed 1,560 and 1,340 respectively, and were both firms with a long tradition of quality production. Churchill, in particular, delivered low overhead charges, marketing their products through Associated British Machine Tool Manufacturers. In total, the factories added 1 million square feet of space, large office facilities, labour resources in a

[91] Herbert, Board of Directors, 1960-80, 2 February, 26 October, 11 December 1964; 7 May 1965; 4 March, 8 July 1966; *Machine Tool Review*, Vol. 53, 1965, p. 48.

[92] Herbert, Board of Directors, 1960-80, 7 February 1966.

[93] Herbert, Board of Directors, 1960-80, 3 June 1966.

location 'where they are scarce', and a widening range of products complementary to, but not conflicting with the Herbert range. Estimates of BSA sales included £3.5 million of lathes, taping and drilling machines, £0.5 million of broaching machines, £2.8 million of grinding machines, the speciality of BSA Churchill, and £1.2 million of small tools and components. Moreover, one-quarter of BSA sales went to export markets, and the company had built-up extensive overseas connections.[94]

Potential gains, however, needed to be 'balanced' against the heavy management tasks involved in improving designs, raising productivity and co-ordinating joint marketing. The efficiency of plant was 'average', capital equipment well laid out and maintained but productivity varying between different factories. In particular, the factories of BSA-Churchill were outdated with practically no use of automatic or NC machines. Managerial capabilities were also questioned, management being a mix of long and short serving staff, the senior managers being defined as 'about average', but overall 'not of the best'. Over the range of BSA machine companies, sales earnings were currently averaging just 10 per cent of asset values. Comparative estimates suggested that an average BSA worker produced £2,500 of total annual sales, compared to £3,500 for an equivalent Herbert worker, while BSA sales staff sold £80,000 per person per annum compared to £160,000 at Herbert's. The integration of BSA into the Herbert group also required careful co-ordination, Churchill grinders overlapping with Herbert factored sales of Newall and Heald grinders. Clearly, there were problems in integrating BSA into the Herbert organisation, but the acquisition also offered the potential for a rationalisation of the operations of the constituent BSA companies.[95]

Thus, a central thrust of Young's report was the opportunities for rationalisation, involving large-scale capital re-equipping, improved machine design, and the integration of BSA marketing into the Herbert organisation 'to increase group sales at home and abroad'. On the sales front, Burton, Griffiths had agencies with American makers such as Pratt & Whitney, as well as German and Swiss companies. This offered the opportunity to integrate the company into the Herbert factoring business, although it raised problems of conflicting interests with existing Herbert agencies. A final, but crucial consideration was the integration of R&D to provide additional scope to the Herbert design capabilities. BSA placed a high premium on R&D, the machine tool division spending an estimated £300,000 annually, and employing 120 experienced designers and draughtsmen, mainly on BSA Tools, BSA Electrics and Churchill development projects. Key priorities included pre-set tooling techniques, and the Batchomatic tape controlled lathe aimed at high productivity for small batch production, an important initiative in the advancement of NC for British engineering requirements. Young's report offered a set of positive and persuasive rationales for the merger, but there was also a defensive consideration. Acknowledging the emergence of group organisations involved with machine tools, the report concluded that increased concentration in

---

[94] Herbert, Board of Directors, 1960-80, 22 July 1966, Report Issued by R. D. Young on the BSA Machine Tool Companies.
[95] Ibid.

the industry represented a formidable competitive challenge. Thus, a deciding factor in the decision for acquisition was value for money in terms of the comparative purchase price of the BSA companies. On available information, the report concluded that a purchase price of £11.5 million, based on the profit to earnings ratio of the BSA machine tool companies, compared favourably with the buy-out of the Charles Churchill group by Tube Investment for £10.8 million and that of the Asquith group by Staveley for £8 million.[96]

While the report delivered a positive conclusion concerning the BSA purchase, the Herbert management entered negotiations in a cautious manner. A key consideration involved the relative profitability of Herbert and BSA machine tool lines, and the Herbert executive had no intention of propping up inefficient companies, Young announcing in July that 'scarce resources should not be unnecessarily diverted to BSA'. An agreement, 'in principal', was announced by Young in August; the new Herbert-BSA Co. was to be formed as a subsidiary of the Herbert group, the latter issuing to BSA £2.5 million in loan stock and £3.2 million in newly subscribed Herbert ordinary shares. The parties also announced the appointment of Eric Turner, the BSA chairman, and S. A. Roberts, the managing director of the BSA Tools Division, to the Herbert board, the latter becoming the managing director of Herbert-BSA, with Young as chairman. The aims of the merger were predicted to be higher productivity and efficiency in R&D, production and marketing, and the managements boasted that it would result in an organisation 'with as wide a range of machine tools as any other company in the world'. This early announcement, however, caused considerable embarrassment when Turner announced in October that the profits for the BSA machine tool group had collapsed from £1.25 million to £600,000, a figure which was £200,000 below the estimated returns made by the joint auditors involved in the negotiations. Despite a reassurance from Turner that profits would recover to £1 million in the forthcoming year, Young directed the auditors to investigate further the future profit potential. Agreement was finally reached in December, and in January 1967 Turner and Roberts joined the Herbert-BSA board.[97]

The BSA acquisition represented a significant expansion of the Herbert organisation, and a considerable challenge for executive management, a challenge which was intensified in February 1966 with the announcement of negotiations with Ingersoll, Rockford, Illinois, to establish a partnership in a new company, Herbert-Ingersoll, at Daventry, to manufacture special-purpose machines in the U.K. Ingersoll was America's leading special-purpose machine maker, a firm that had 'helped to forge the industrial giant that is modern America'. Driven by the enthusiasm of Young and Clark to incorporate American manufacturing and technical knowledge into the Herbert organisation, Herbert-Ingersoll was to mark a major investment decision by the company. At the company's AGM in 1967, Young outlined the basic business rational:

---

[96] Ibid.

[97] Herbert, Board of Directors, 1960-80, 25 July, 6 October, 9 December 1966; 13 January, 10 February 1967; *Engineer*, 12 August 1966, p. 250; 18 November 1966, p. 768.

> Their highly productive manufacturing systems are used not only in the automotive industry but also in other industries of both high and low volume output in the U.S.A. and Europe. Their expertise promises to combine admirably with Herbert's experience and marketing organisation at home and abroad.

In particular, Young praised the 'professional management drive' of the Americans, a factor in the successful manufacturing and marketing of advanced machine tools. Above all else, Young predicted that the venture would provide a new direction for the company, enabling them to manufacture special-purpose machines cost effectively, meeting what he saw as a rising future demand by industry for labour-saving machinery. Ingersoll also offered, as Clark made clear in July 1966, an opportunity for Herbert's to expand sales in the lucrative American market, which could only be accomplished 'with the right support'.[98]

On paper, the new company complimented the traditional Herbert strategy of meeting customer needs, an advancement of the commitment to provide a complete engineering production service from modern facilities. As Young claimed, by designing specials 'to meet customer needs' they could apply the 'accumulated knowledge of Ingersoll', which could be used to train 'British engineers and designers ... a proportion of whom will be trained at Herbert's works'. When the Daventry factory opened in January 1968, a modern factory layout accommodated advanced automatic NC machines from leading American and European suppliers. The building of specials complemented a production engineering 'service' offering 'advanced manufacturing systems developed to suit particular products'. Under the marketing slogan of 'A New Approach to Advanced Manufacturing Systems', Daventry was described as 'the most efficient and productive unit of its type anywhere in the world'. Partnership with Ingersoll brought knowledge and experience of building specials, machines that were adaptable either for the mass production of components, or to effect time saving in the production of batch components. The vision was to offer a complete manufacturing system, involving transfer machines for assembly line production, as well as several different designs of petrol and diesel engine blocks, multi-station machines for the volume production of a range of component parts, and heavy milling machines for specialised and precision work on large castings. A common principle of the systems approach, instigated at Daventry, was to deploy 'teams of experts to analyse, study and make recommendations for each individual set of manufacturing problems', on a fee paying basis. Solving production problems evolved through an 'in-depth study' of existing plant layout and 'forward design and production plans'. A 'systematic analysis' and review of the 'total production task', in consultation with customers, enabled the compilation of alternative solutions, which could then be tested through an examination of required production loads and accuracy to recommend to users an optimum solution. Theoretically, a 'total system' could be developed, including metal cutting, control, material handling and scheduling, devised to meet the specific task facing customers. Effectively, this was a 'Marketing

---

[98] Herbert, Board of Directors, 1960-80, 7 February, 4 March, 3 June, 8 July 1966; *Machine Tool Review*, Vol. 54, 1966, p. 61; Vol. 55, 1967, p. 49.

Approach', the equipment 'sold always on the basis of a detailed concept', and guarantees on accuracy, production rates, delivery dates, and prices provided.[99]

Herbert-Ingersoll, and its long-term vision, dovetailed with the Labour Government's commitment to modernisation, through the adoption of advanced manufacturing systems, and 'a creative approach to production problems'. Daventry, the Herbert executive believed, would provide an education to users, persuading them that the efficiency gains of automatic systems, coupled with a service to appraise long-term capital investment plans, could outweigh the high initial investment. Where possible, the use of standard machines, available in stock, were to be recommended to customers, but Daventry was equipped to supply specials and transfer lines, designed to operate with minimum maintenance and planned servicing. In early 1968, Daventry 'Stage 1' employed 200 workers, 115 engaged on production, with 102,000 sq. ft. of space allocated to 120 automatic NC machine tools integrated into an overall manufacturing system, providing production line efficiency with flexibility. In this early development stage, the emphasis was on 'one-off or small quantity manufacture', utilising NC machines intensively to eliminate expensive jigs and fixtures, and employing sophisticated material handling systems. Expansion was scheduled for 1969, employment rising to 500 and output to £5 million per annum, and this was to be consolidated by a 'stage 2' building and equipment programme in 1971, to be followed by 'stage 3' which would fully absorb the 1 million sq. ft. of the Daventry site. The ultimate aim was to provide an operation with a yearly productivity rate estimated at £8,000 per employee, compared to an 'average of £2,500 in the machine tool industry', and nearly three times the national average. As Young informed shareholders in 1967, 'The British machine tool industry is small compared to those of the United States and Germany; its latter day growth has not always been thought satisfactory. The association with BSA and Ingersoll will contribute to national growth and to the machine tool industry's export-import balance'.[100]

Table 9.4
Finance of Herbert-Ingersoll (£)

Finance Provided by:	Share Capital	Loan Capital	Total
Alfred Herbert	124,950	1,660,050	1,785,000
Ingersoll	120,050	1,400,220	1,520,270
Total Received	245,000	3,060,270	3,055,270
Plus			
Due from Ingersoll	-	194,730	3,305,270

Source: Herbert, Board of Directors, 1960-80, 14 June 1968.

---

[99] *Engineer*, 17 June 1966, p. 913; 8 March 1968, p. 406; *Machine Tool Review*, Vol. 55, 1967, p. 49; Vol. 56, 1968, pp. 70-3, 176-7.
[100] *Machine Tool Review*, Vol. 55, 1967, p. 49; Vol. 56, 1968, pp. 70-3, 176-7; Engineer, 8 March 1968, p. 406.

Incorporated in March 1967, Herbert-Ingersoll represented a substantial investment by Herbert's, involving the negotiation of a complex financial package between the two companies. This involved a combination of share capital and loan capital as shown in Table 9.4, Herbert's taking 51 per cent of the total capital of £3.3 million. To finance loan capital Herbert's received a bridging loan from Barclay's Bank, guaranteed by the conversion of £1.3 million gilt-edge securities held in Herbert investment reserves, the loan capital being scheduled for conversion to share capital by the end of 1968. American financial institutions remained cautious of investing in a joint British-American venture, refusing to bear the exchange risk in financing the Ingersoll part of the deal. Consequently, the Bank of England brokered the deal, consenting to the purchase of 'Investment Dollars' to finance the American side of the investment from London. Capital investment in Daventry was £3,546,000, £630,000 offset by a grant from the government's Industrial Reorganisation Corporation (IRC), formed in 1966 to encourage mergers and joint ventures. Government sanction for the project came with the granting of an Industrial Development Certificate, introduced under the Industrial Development Act of 1966, to ensure balanced regional employment growth.[101]

Both the Ingersoll and BSA ventures were major investment decisions, greatly enlarging the scope of the Herbert organisation, but at the same time exposing the managerial competencies of the Herbert organisation. Herbert-BSA, for example, incorporated in January 1967, from the outset presented top management with considerable problems in effectively integrating it into the Herbert operations. To facilitate integration, they constituted 11 working parties, headed by directors and senior managers from both concerns. The remit included a review and recommendation of policy for accounting and finance, integrated selling, co-ordination of manufactured and factored machines, the rationalisation of design, manufacture and sale of automatic machines and electrical components to avoid duplication. Reorganisation, however, proceeded in an ad hoc fashion. For example, in November 1967, domestic sales of BSA-Churchill were incorporated into the Herbert sales organisation, but the former still maintained control over its own sales staff, as well as retaining its agencies with Associated British Machine Tool Makers, a long-standing arrangement for sales in export markets. By February 1968, BSA Tools and Burton, Griffiths were integrated into the Herbert sales organisation, to create, it was claimed, a 'consolidated' group for the marketing of a range of machine tools in the U.K. In reality, both these companies continued to handle their own enquiries and orders from their offices in Birmingham, their own teams of specialists, demonstrators, and service engineers duplicating those at Herbert's. Sales integration was partial, but there was also a major capital investment programme at BSA-Churchill. This was a planned expansion to double output in four years, and included the modernisation of

---

[101] Herbert, Board of Directors, 1960-80, 22 July, 6 October, 8 December 1966; 17 March 1967; 14 June 1968. For the activities of the IRC, see Pollard, *Growth and Development*, pp. 310, 401.

existing plant, as well as a new factory at Runcorn costing £600,000, offset by a capital investment allowance from the IRC of 45 per cent on plant and machinery and 25 per cent on buildings. The large investment represented a considerable risk in the future profitability of the concern, a risk discounted by optimistic forecasts of gross profits, estimated to rise to £700,000 on sales of £4.5 million by 1970. Managerial optimism was based upon their belief in the reputation of the BSA companies, notably BSA-Churchill, a company with the potential to meet a growing demand for grinding machines through its extensive networks, established over 60 years. Indeed, in early 1967 the company acquired a large Russian order valued at £2.6 million, as well as selling 50 per cent of its roll grinding machines to the lucrative Canadian market.[102]

In the boardroom of Herbert's, optimism was high, yet by 1969 the company was in disarray, and faced serious financial problems. What went wrong? Plans for expansion coincided with rising economic activity in 1965-6, when the company had again experienced severe capacity shortages. Labour recruitment problems, with the persistence of the local wage differential between Herbert's and other employers, deteriorating industrial relations, delays in building machines for stock, and continuing problems of inefficiency at the Berridge, Holbrook and Lockwood subsidiaries all contributed to lengthening delivery times and a loss of competitive advantage. Nevertheless, optimism prevailed, and in March 1966 Clark announced rising profits, the fruition of a considerable investment in new and improved productive capacity, and a continued emphasis upon high quality design and workmanship. At the same time, he announced the company's commitment to a plant replacement programme throughout the organisation, designed to reduce direct labour costs. By July, however, the tone had changed, and Young, occupying the chair for the first time, reported the damning news that sales for the first seven months of the year had fallen by £1 million while overheads had increased by £400,000. Although the executive agreed to maintain output, Young, in a press release to the stock exchange, registered deep concerns over the uncertainty of government policy, and with rising costs predicted that group profits would fall short of the record of 1965. Uncertainty partly related to the delayed confirmation of a wage freeze, which the Labour Government had announced the intention of implementing in June under its prices and incomes policy. Consequently, Herbert's froze wages until the government clarified the situation, but of more concern to Young was the current decline of profits and future uncertainty of demand given Labour's deflationary policies to control the balance of payments deficit.[103]

---

[102] Herbert, Board of Directors, 1960-80, 10 February, 10 March, 13 October, 8 December 1967; *Engineer*, 24 November 1967, p. 717; 9 February 1968, p. 255; *Machine Tool Review*, Vol. 55, 1967, p. 129; Vol. 56, 1968, p. 41.

[103] Herbert, Board of Directors, 1960-80, 1 March, 8 November 1965; 4, 11 March, 8, 22 July 1966. For an examination of price and income policy, see Pollard, *Growth and Development*, p. 335. Between October 1964 and June 1966 wages in Britain increased by 7.5 per cent.

By August 1966, orders had fallen by 5.7 per cent and sales by 2.8 per cent since January, and gross profits by 15.3 per cent. Stock had risen by £1.1 million, the usual sign of an oncoming downturn, and overheads were rising sharply. Wage pressure now caused serious concern, especially as falling order books restricted an increase in prices. In March, the executive had acceded to a national increase of 5s. per week for all workers, on top of a company award of 30s per week for skilled, and the introduction of a sliding scale for semi and unskilled. The confusion over pay negotiations, in the light of the government's wage freeze was all too obvious, the management agreeing to a further company increase in November, aware of the need to bring their rates in line with local rates, but restricted from implementing it under the existing wages and price freeze. Herbert's average wage per hour was now 13s 1d, compared to the tool room district rate of 14s 5d, which Herbert's was obliged to pay under an agreement reached with the unions by the Employers Federation, despite the existence of the pay freeze. Young acknowledged that reductions in operating profits was partly due to rising wage costs and materials, but also noted a substantial rise in costs of non-productive employees. This prompted Clark to insist on strict monitoring by departmental directors of all non-productive costs. Adding to these problems was falling factored sales, down from £14 million to £10 million, especially for imported machines as customers cut capacity. The potential for re-directing output to export markets was also limited. Buoyant demand in American and Canadian markets offered some relief, but as Muirhead made clear, this was temporary, and a fall would have serious repercussions. Further, the important Indian market was in decline, a poor market for 'Coventry made' machines, and sales in Europe substantially reduced due to price competition.[104]

The company's poor competitive performance in export markets was emphasised by a major internal report on the Common Market in 1967. Commissioned as an investigation of the impact on the company of an EEC common external tariff on machine tools of 12 per cent, scheduled for implementation in July 1968, and the Labour Government's negotiations for entry, the report covered a wide range of Herbert's export markets. Consequences of British entry, it concluded, would result in 'an onslaught by present Common Market countries on our home market whilst exports from the U.K. into the Common Market will be difficult and highly competitive'. As the report argued, the British machine tool industry had enjoyed a protective duty of 10 per cent on machine tools, and 17.5 per cent on spares 'and against these duties Germany imported substantial quantities into the U.K.' Prior to the harmonization of the EEC tariffs, the principle machine tool using countries in Europe allowed free entry of British machine tools, but 'very little success was achieved'. The report, in considering potential disadvantages of non-entry, concluded that 'Britain would be outside a large economic bloc to its serious disadvantage', it being essential that British manufacturing exported 'sophisticated products' to large markets. This necessitated heavy capital investment in 'advanced technological knowledge and

---

[104] Herbert, Board of Directors, 1960-80, 6 October, 9 December 1966.

economies of large-scale production', only achievable if Britain required 'a large un-closable market'. These conclusions on the potential of the EEC represented a change of opinion to those of the late 1950s, discussed in Chapter 7, the Herbert report of 1967 dismissing Commonwealth markets as viable alternatives. As the report observed, 'The Commonwealth is not an economic entity present or potential', imports from those countries falling to a new low of 26.3 per cent of total British imports in 1965, while EEC imports rose to 18 per cent. The success of British industry, and consequently the performance of the machine tool industry, 'will depend more and more on mass markets'.[105]

Pro-European in its stance, the report also pointed to the potential loss of U.S. capital investment in the British market, and the effect on arrangements for distributing and manufacturing American machines under licence. This would 'result not only in traditionally accepted machines of German origin and the greatly improved machines of French and Italian makers coming into the U.K. without the protection of the present tariffs but also U.S. machines made in Europe at prices less than American makers were selling directly'. Surveying Herbert's export performance since 1964 (Appendix B, Table B.3), a damning indictment of competitive decline was presented. For example, in the lucrative German market, 'never a happy one for Alfred Herbert', there was a low demand for capstan lathes, Herbert's stock in trade. German 'engineering industries are not capstan minded; there is a very strong nationalistic preference for indigenous machine tools, which is backed up by a very strong machine tool making industry', with German machine tool importing agencies being reluctant to deal with British makers. Despite Herbert's efforts to improve sales through exclusive rights for both Herbert and factored machine tools, there was considerable sales resistance, despite the fact that Germany had no significant tariff, before EEC harmonization, on imported machines.[106]

By July 1968, the company was well aware of German competition in the British market, Harrison reporting a rising trend towards imports exceeding exports, a problem that he predicted would intensify when the government removed its surcharge on imports later in the year, inevitably opening the industry to further public criticism. Furthermore, a slow-down in domestic economic activity, coupled with rising costs, had a serious impact on the company's financial performance between 1967 and 1969. In February 1967, in his review of trading conditions, Young pointed to a significant decrease in orders, and together with increased overhead expenses this had a marked effect on profitability. He also reminded the board that an increase of 3d per hour to hourly paid workers, due in November but postponed because of the freeze, was now due to be implemented in May. Given severe American and German competition, the margin to raise prices was limited, and thus rising costs had to be absorbed at the expense of profits. Cuts in department expenses of 10 per cent were imposed in May, departmental directors urged to monitor costs closely to avoid the layoff of staff, 'which are the backbone of the business'. The target was a reduction of £500,000 per annum in

---

[105] Herbert, Board of Directors, 1960-80, 5 June 1967, Report on the Common Market.
[106] Ibid.

indirect labour, involving reductions in overtime and the number of basic clerical staff. By June, the downturn was also having severe repercussions for BSA, Young insisting on expenditure cuts of £75,000. The seriousness of the cost situation led to discussions with MinTech, who agreed to price increases on Herbert machines of between 2.5 and 12 per cent, similar rises applying to BSA Tools, Churchill, Holbrook, and Cri-Dan machines.[107]

During 1967, external consultants undertook major reviews of overhead costs, especially in clerical staff, leading to substantial reductions in expenses. However, stocks continued to escalate, both for Herbert and factored machines, and the executive again faced a major downturn of the cycle. Young reported discussions between the MTTA, the IRC and MinTech to extend credit to stimulate demand, but the IRC withdrew its support, and Herbert's decided to launch its own credit scheme, financed through its normal overdraft facilities with Barclay's. Group net profits in the first six months of 1967 fell to £1.1 million, compared to £1.3 million for the comparable period in 1966, and orders declined from £22.6 million to £19.3 million. Home orders fell rapidly, prompting Young to condemn government policy:

> Against this background of falling orders, Government pronouncements have repeatedly stressed that increased investment in new capital equipment in private industry is crucial for our industrial future. However, Government actions have engendered a sharp reduction in private capital investment and nothing has yet been done to reverse the trend. Unless Government tackles this, the vigorous growth to which this company, like so much of the rest of the machine tool industry, has set its hand, is bound to be held in check.

While Young might condemn government policy, Herbert's own internal problems began to multiply. A major concern was the serious order problems at BSA Tools, BSA-Churchill, and BSA Small Tools, together with those of Lockwood and Holbrook. The limited organisational capabilities at Herbert's had failed to integrate these companies' sales facilities into the larger group, and the acquisition strategy had not delivered the increasing orders anticipated by the executive management. Neither could Young draw much comfort from the factored department; although it did offer a 'wide spread of lines' it too was not immune from the negative impact of falling domestic demand. As a somewhat rattled Young warned in October 1967, 'the staff and other cost reduction programmes would go onto the verge of cutting into the essentials of the business'.[108]

The severity of the domestic recession forced Young to introduce a four-day week for 1,100 workers in early 1968. With a crisis looming on the horizon, the executive decided to ride-out the downturn. Predicting stocks rising to 700 to 800 machines at Edgwick alone by mid-1968, Young emphasised that if business

---

[107] Herbert, Board of Directors, 1960-80, 10 February, 8, 12 May, 9 June 1967; 8 July 1968.

[108] Herbert, Board of Directors, 1960-80, 6 June 1967, Consultant's Report on Sales and Equipment Department, and board meetings, 1 March 1965; 13 January, 14 July, 13 October 1967.

activity improved by the end of the year, sufficient stocks would then be available, and workers retained at a reasonable level to meet rising demand. If demand did not revive, the management would reverse the policy. To effect this, Young urged all directors to 'rigorously' reduce expenditure, and redouble efforts to increase orders at home and abroad. Little relief, however, was forthcoming from export markets, although there were expectations that the government's devaluation of 1967 would stimulate demand. Export demand for Herbert and factored machines remained depressed, German makers reducing selling prices to counteract the effects of devaluation. In the American market, which the executive had pinned high hopes on, sales fell by 40 per cent in the 12 months to March 1968, due to severe price competition.[109]

In mid-1968, sales for the Herbert Group recorded an all-time low, accompanied by declining profits and rising wage pressure. These problems intensified in 1969, Young reporting in July of the great uncertainty of demand, a sign of a continuation of the declining trend in domestic orders. Consequently, he called for an 'urgent' need to expand exports, and, acknowledging that the company faced mounting liquidity problems, he advocated a policy 'to retrench, throughout the group ... to restore profitability at lower levels of activity'. In particular, trading performance at the Herbert and BSA factories was 'grave', the 'break-even level being now unacceptably high, for the level of present or prospective business'. As Young admitted, planned economies were unlikely to improve the situation, 'a fundamentally new approach was needed'. Planning for this 'new approach' had started in early 1968, when the executive produced a report advocating immediate structural re-organisation. The key aim was to restore profitability, to at least the levels of 1965, on the enlarged assets of the group, enabling the company to develop 'its full potential in the world's machine tool markets', which it was predicted would expand by at least 50 per cent over the next three to five years. Re-organisation required an exploitation of the core capabilities of the organisation. These included 'a great spread of market knowledge all over the world.' 'A long history of engineering competence both in design and manufacturing, coupled with a recognition, if not yet a full expertise, in the rapid changes developing in these fields'. On the management front, 'A body of men at all levels throughout the organisation with good knowledge and high loyalty – and with undoubted purpose to succeed individually and co-operatively'. Finally, the company possessed adequate financial resources to modernise productive resources. Reorganisation, as the report made clear, did present a major managerial challenge. Low demand, intense competition, the 'obsolete and obsolescent' condition 'of group's fixed assets and main products', together with an ageing management elite, with 6 of the 10 executives due to retire by 1972, all provided substantial obstacles to radical re-organisation. In particular, management deficiencies were highlighted, the exploitation of the capabilities of the company restricted by a 'shortage of top management, a clear-cut profit responsibility for different sections of the group's work, and so they lack a sense of purpose and

[109] Herbert, Board of Directors, 1960-80, 12 January, 9 February, 8 March, 12 April 1968.

drive in middle management'. Illustrating this was the fact that the group consisted of 20 operating companies in Britain, each with its own 'individual company identity yet with no coherent market and product relationship'. A 'lack of coherence' resulted 'in an excessive number of individuals depending in effect on the managing director for policy direction and administrative action', and 'flows of management information to track performance, costs and earnings, in relation to the assets involved, are quite disparate in form and inadequate in context'.[110]

The major factor resulting in such managerial diseconomies was the costs of the rapid enlargement with the merger of BSA into the group.[111] Although there was no duplication of product type, the acquisition and limited integration of BSA resulted in a loss of central control, and too many small units making different types of products, with insufficient specialisation, which 'spread too thinly' the group's resources in design, engineering and marketing. Structural re-organisation, implemented from November 1968, consequently involved the creation of two functional divisions, one for services and one for production (Appendix B, Fig. B.1). The Production Division was sub-divided into product divisions, 'each responsible for maximising the profits on the assets allocated to each division, and each as a separate trading company', responsible to a managing director of the Production Division. Operating companies within each product division specialised on a particular range of machines, and were in turn responsible for the efficient 'design, manufacture and sale of its product'. The overarching theme was 'specialisation in production, design, marketing, and in the diverse management skills that are essential to the modern industrial enterprise'. Defined as a 'corporate scheme', each operating company would 'develop its own personality', the 'common thread' being a 'shared foundation of knowledge of machine tool technology and production engineering, a consistent use of the Herbert name and a common desire to satisfy the man who buys the machine tool'. Financial control and the discipline of operating companies rested in the 'authority' of the parent board, which would ensure that 'the highest autonomy will be given to each product division consistent with maintaining group policy and standards as defined from time to time'. In contrast to these operational divisions, the Service Division provided 'the functional services needed to carry out the board's policy and to maintain maximum professional competence in functions common throughout the production division', including sales, factoring, finance and accounting, and crucially management development. Summing up the reorganisation, *The Engineer* considered it an example of combined 'co-ordination from the centre, with wide freedom and responsibility for the operating companies'.[112]

---

[110] Herbert, Board of Directors, 14 June 1968; 18 July 1969, and 1 February 1968 for Report on Reorganisation into Product and Service Divisions; *Machine Tool Review*, Vol. 57, 1969, pp. 41-8.

[111] For a discussion of the problems associated with Merger, see Penrose, *The Theory of the Growth of the Firm*, p. 191.

[112] Herbert, Board of Directors, 1968-80, 1 February 1968, 'Report on Reorganisation into Product and Service Divisions'; *Machine Tool Review*, Vol. 57, 1969, pp. 41-8; *Engineer*, 8 November 1968, p. 717.

Reorganisation clearly recognised the need for increased managerial scope, especially in middle management, and increased flexibility for functional divisions, with overall strategy set by the centralised parent board. The managerial limitations of the firm had been forcefully emphasised by Young in December 1967, in a report following his visit to the U.S.A. to review Herbert factoring and licensing arrangements with their large American principals. His report presented a mixed picture of the advantages of these cooperative ventures to Herbert's future competitive success. For example, new orders for the Devlieg programmed jig mills were falling, the product facing stiff competition from Cincinnati and Giddings & Lewis. Young also visited Anocut, Chicago, manufacturers of electro chemical shaping machines, which Herbert's had been selling in the U.K. since 1962, and in 1967 manufacturing under licence. He also visited Ingersoll, emphasising the importance of this company to Herbert market networks, Anocut and Ingersoll conducting joint projects, sponsored by MinTech, at Bristol Aircraft, Rolls Royce, English Electric and Babcox. In particular, Young emphasised the direct financial interest of Herbert's in Ingersoll, which he viewed as a highly innovative enterprise attuned to the market. While celebrating the opportunities these connections offered for Herbert's competitive position in world markets, Young's observations raised serious concerns over his own company's organisational capabilities. Making comparisons to the American companies, including Norton and Cincinnati, which he also visited, Young suggested that the turnover of stock by U.S. makers was between 3.3 to 4 times higher than at Herbert's. Moreover, capital spending to compensate for depreciation was 60 per cent higher, and 'more spending on new plant' was a key feature of the American's general lead in productivity. With lead times, from batch to release to delivery, of six to eight months, 'they unquestionably get work through much faster'. In particular, the application of control gears to machine tools, which caused serious delays in the development of prototypes at Herbert's, was done far more efficiently by American makers. Noting the increased use of NC in the U.S., and the application of central computers for control, Young pointed to the backwardness of Herbert's in these crucial developments. Overall, in his assessment, one clear difference stood out. In the U.S., management was more 'concentrated', and, in what would be considered quite small concerns, with up to 1,000 employees, 'they have a quantity and quality of management that would be thought here adequate for 3,000 to 5,000'.[113]

Reorganisation on the scale of 1968 was clearly a longer-term solution, and did little to alleviate the short-term problems facing the company. This was emphasised by an internal working party set up in July 1969 to investigate the causes of low profitability. For example, the Herbert-BSA operating company was performing, at current levels of output, below the break-even point of £13.5 million. In formulating an action plan to restore profitability, the cyclical pattern of demand was a key consideration. Forecasting an upward trend in business activity over the next two years, the plan assumed that profits would adjust upwards, allowing the company to accumulate funds to meet 'the lean years', predicted for

---

[113] Herbert, Board of Directors, 1960-80, 8 December 1967.

1971 to 1973. This would provide a 'period of grace', during which longer-term strategies involving the possible closure of inefficient plant could be devised. Accepting that the future was uncertain, and that 'over-optimistic forecasts' had contributed to the company's present financial predicament, the plan concluded 'that a major reduction in manufacturing capacity at this point in time would be extremely unwise'. Consequently, action was required to simplify the management structure, reduce overhead expenses, and improve manufacturing output. In the short-term, the plan aimed to deliver a minimum rate of profitability of 15 per cent on capital employed by the end of the 1969/70 period, and achieve this without affecting the growth potential of the company over a two to three year period. In its assessment, however, of the causes of low profitability, the plan provided a damning indictment on past strategic failure. Factors inhibiting profitability concerned the limited co-ordination in the Herbert-BSA operating company, split between two main production sites, Edgwick and Mackadown, resulting in excessive inventory costs, unduly high manufacturing costs, excessive overheads, inequitable transfer pricing arrangements, and the duplication of management and administration. Most damning of all, was the observation that the Herbert-BSA product range consisted of too many low value and obsolescent lines, and too few up-to-date and technically competitive machines.[114]

Low productivity and design failures were key issues taxing the minds of the executive during 1969. Indeed, the need to raise productivity, in an environment of escalating wages, had been a central recommendation of a 'manpower report' in 1968, and a productivity deal was signed with the unions at Edgwick in February 1969, devised to produce cost savings of £200,000 over a 15 months' period. However, by June the deal had still not been implemented, the executive reporting delays due to shortages of work-study engineers needed to instigate flow production methods. Inefficiencies in production were also rife at BSA Tools, which recorded substantial losses in 1969. At BSA-Churchill, despite injections of capital for modernisation and expansion, there remained serious obstacles to increasing output because of low productivity and labour disruption. Attached to this were shortages of up-to-date designs, leading to a loss of the market for chucking machines. Accepting a three year investment plan for BSA-Churchill, Young was disappointed that the plan did not envisage higher efficiency and turnover from the capital injection. On the design front, the company faced acute problems. In 1967, a review of the group's R&D programme proposed the development of new machines, but highlighted continued problems in co-ordination between the drawing office and the design programme engineers, resulting in a break down of communication and delays in the proto-testing of machines. In an attempt to eradicate delays 'between the conception of new ideas and implementation', critical path analysis was used to enable 'the planning engineer to establish the logical inter-relationship of the many tasks and progress steps that make up the project'. However, a failure to co-ordinate design and engineering persisted, leading to delays in the commercial application of projects.

---

[114] Coventry Archive, 1270/2/5, Herbert-BSA Ltd. Profitability Investigation, 20 August 1969.

Attempts to improve production and design policy became the task of a 'small' Management Services Team, established in late 1967, and incorporated into the group's new Services Division (see Fig. B.1). Designated as a service to aid production staff to advance plans for expansion and cost cutting, and 'reviewing' the machine tool programme to ensure it met customer demand, it also took steps to reorganise the ARD as a Production Development Centre, charged with the key task 'to intensify co-operation between design, production, and sales'. Despite this initiative, forced cuts in expenditure substantially reduced the R&D budget, Turner emphasising in June 1968 that an expenditure of £129,000 over the last six months was 'too low' for an organisation of such size.[115]

In 1969, a report by the 'Marketing Services Director' condemned the failure 'to have new machines, both to up date traditional machines and to establish numerically controlled types; demand for the latter ... rising at about 40% p.a.' Admitting in June that there were severe deficiencies in the R&D budget, Young referred to the dilemma of developing new lines in the prevailing depressed climate, agreeing that more 'rather than less must be spent on development of machines, carefully selected to keep the product range competitive'. This was followed, however, in July by a further endorsement of 'stringent economies', a suspension of authorisation on new capital expenditure, and a consideration of 'major rationalisation', both in selling and manufacture to reduce overheads 'and realise under-utilised assts'. With declining profits, strict budgeting forecasting methods were introduced by the parent company, enforcing discipline on the management of operating companies, although realising that there was 'little past experience' of budget managing, and 'more realistic and conservative estimates' of forecasted performance 'would be essential'. By early 1970, continued losses at BSA led the executive to conclude that the management is now 'on trial, and knew it would be judged by results'. At BSA-Churchill, for example, which recorded losses and low output in late 1969, a recognition was given to a need for 'more dynamic management', and overall a reconsideration that the independence of the operating companies was not working, and 'that design and development was a crucial matter that might call for central direction and control'. As Young concluded, attempts to increase efficiency in the group, via information and procedures communicated by the Management Services Team had failed, because it 'depended upon management using the information, which was not always the case'.[116]

Adding to the mounting problems of the company was the disappointing launch of the new Herbert-Ingersoll consortium. In June 1966, *The Engineer* had applauded the new venture as a great opportunity to exploit a growing demand, especially in the automobile and electrical industries, for 'automated production of standardised ranges of products' using 'special numerically controlled tools'. In December 1967, the Rootes Motor Company placed the first contract for transfer

---

[115] Herbert, Board of Directors, 1960-80, 13 January, 13 October 1967; 14 June 1968; 14 February, 21 March, 20 June 1969; *Machine Tool Review*, Vol. 55, 1967, pp. 18-21.

[116] Herbert, Board of Directors, 1960-80, 14 February, 20 June, 18 July, 19 September, 17 October, 21 November 1969; 16 January 1970.

line equipment, valued at £900,000, Herbert's beating off 'stiff German competition'. A substantial order from Chrysler-Australia to design, manufacture, and install a manufacturing system for the machining of engine blocks, worth £1.75 million followed in February 1968. Despite this initial success, a report by J. H. Spur, the managing director with executive authority of Herbert-Ingersoll, told of an uncertain future in July 1968. With the high costs of acquiring technical staff for Daventry, which was running at 25 per cent above quoted prices, Spur thought that it would take two years to break even. Young, the chair of Herbert-Ingersoll, responded with little confidence: 'The prospect of orders ahead was one of hard competition and of inevitable variations of demand'. A year later, Young reported that the company was facing intense German competition, a resistance by domestic buyers to British equipment, and, given the trading recession, 'it would take longer to reach the break-even stage than had been envisaged'. Trying to remain up-beat, Young referred to the promising early orders for specials, and the potential growth of this market, but conceded that the company 'was still in the development stage, management was still learning, and profitability could not be predicted accurately until cost levels are better known'. Rough calculations for turnover, however, forecast £4.2 million for 1969 to 1970, while the break-even target was £5.6 million. Given this scenario, there was a crucial need for management to raise efficiency and prices to increase the rate at which capital was utilised, allowing the original planned profit of £4 million to £5 million to be realised. This was a damning indictment on the organisation's managerial capabilities, and its low level costing systems, the company having no clear understanding of its future profit potential. A progress report presented by Spur and E. I. Gaylord, the latter an Ingersoll representative on the board, in January 1970, spelled out the seriousness of the situation. Herbert-Ingersoll had a good order uptake, but contracts were confirmed at low prices, only averaging a 14 per cent margin for gross profit. Consequently, they were selling too many unprofitable machine lines, and they needed to refocus on more lucrative areas of demand. In technical terms the company was delivering high quality machines, but 'Management continued to be the key to ... development' especially in relation to learning 'commercial judgement', which was considered 'the most important single factor in reaching profitability quickly'. As the report acknowledged, 'the company had no past history of costs' to guide its commercial decision making, and at present costing could only be compared with the manufacturing systems at Rockford. Basic cost data had now been accumulated, and efficiency results were promising, but as the report concluded, losses were expected to reach £700,000 to £800,000 in 1970.[117]

The signs were evident of mounting financial distress, which hit crisis proportions in the first half of the 1970s. Accepting that management faced adverse market conditions, there is nevertheless a case to be made that Herbert's lacked high quality managerial resources, and these were stretched to breaking point by the acquisition of the BSA companies, and by the diversification into special-

---

[117] *Engineer*, 17 June 1966, p. 913; 29 December 1967, p. 868; 9 February 1968, p. 253; 8 March 1968, p. 406; Herbert, Board of Directors, 1960-80, 14 July 1967; 12 July 1968; 18 July 1969; 16 January 1970.

purpose machines by the Ingersoll venture in the mid-1960s. Young and Clark might be held accountable for an over ambitious expansion policy, which grossly overestimated the managerial capabilities of their firm. As Penrose has pointed out, 'if the ruling spirits of the firm do not possess the required managerial talent and have not the ability (including the good sense) to place others who do in responsible management positions, they will have to be replaced if the firm is to survive and prosper'.[118] Clark had already given way in 1966, and in 1973 Young was summarily dismissed, his reign ending in ignominy. This is the focus of the final chapter, which considers the demise of the firm in the context of the accelerating competitive decline of the British machine tool industry in the 1970s.

---

[118] Penrose, *The Theory of the Growth of the Firm*, p. 191

The 'End Game': The British Machine Tool Industry in the 1970s, and the Fall of Alfred Herbert

'There has been a considerable reduction in the U.K. manufacturing output of the Machine tool industry' [Kenneth Baker, Minister of Technology, 1983].[1]

'Herbert's remain a sad reminder for the U.K. machine tool industry'.[2]

Introduction

The 1970s were years of turmoil for the British machine tool industry. Rapidly left behind by the world's leading producers, particularly in high-performance machines, British makers faced increasing import penetration in the home market. In addition, the once dominant firm of Alfred Herbert lost its reputation, became financially unviable, and it was eventually acquired by the state in 1975. Although the company survived until 1980, when the Herbert group was dismantled, its name finally disappeared in 1983.[3] Reflecting on the performance of the industry during the 1970s, Kenneth Baker, giving evidence before the *Industry and Trade Committee* of 1983, had no doubts that the industry had suffered a severe decline. He also informed the Committee that in the highly competitive field of computer numerically controlled lathes and machining centres Japanese output was now 30 times that of the U.K., 'and their unit costs were one-third less'.[4] Thus, for every one dollar in value of machine tools made by British producers in 1971, Japanese makers produced an equivalent of $2, and by 1981, the productivity gap had widened to $5.14 in Japan's favour.[5] During the course of the 1970s, the number and size of companies in the British machine tool industry contracted, and the inability of its firms to meet demand had 'opened up the home market to importers, and had equally created problems for U.K. exports.'[6] This chapter will explore

---

[1] *Industry and Trade Committee: Machine Tools and Robotics*, 1982-3, p. 11.
[2] *Investors' Chronicle*, 4 July 1980, p. 48.
[3] *Alfred Herbert Ltd – A Coventry Firm: 1888-1983* (Coventry Environmental Educational Project, Coventry City Council, 1984), pp. 18-19.
[4] *Industry and Trade Committee*, 1982-3, pp. x, 11.
[5] *Machinist*, February 1972 and February 1982.
[6] *Industry and Trade Committee*, 1982-3, p. x.

these general trends in the industry, offer an assessment of its performance and the problems it faced, and emphasise the decline of the industry through an examination of the demise of its dominant 'player', Alfred Herbert.

The British Machine Tool Industry in the 1970s

In Tables 10.1 and 10.2, the trend of production in the machine tool industry is given, and comparisons made with the movement in total manufacturing output and GDP. The data confirms the volatility of the machine tool industry, a feature that we have continually identified in the long-run history of the industry. Indeed, the industry was characterised by far sharper short-term movements in output than that experienced by manufacturing industry generally, or in the figures for aggregate GDP. Following a short phase of rapid growth in the late 1960s, the industry's fortunes went into a sharp reverse at the beginning of the 1970s. While there was some recovery from a low level in 1972-4, the industry only enjoyed some degree of stability between 1976 and 1979, and even in that period output was nearly 20 per cent below the level achieved in 1975. Between 1980 and 1982, however, machine tool output collapsed, and by the latter date it was less than half of that achieved in the late 1960s and early 1970s. An important benchmark of the industry's decline was the level of import penetration, which, as Table 10.3 demonstrates, reached alarming proportions by the early 1980s. Between 1966 and 1982 import penetration increased by 151 per cent, imports accelerating rapidly between the late 1960s and first half of the 1970s, and again in the early 1980s. Clearly decline had set in before the OPEC induced oil price rise of 1973 and what worried the MTTA was the continuation of a trend, which had been identified as early as 1960 by the Mitchell Report, that saw Britain importing high technology machines and exporting 'standardised low technology tools'.[7]

Not surprisingly Britain's share of world machine tool production fell from 8.2 per cent in 1965 to a mere 3.5 per cent in 1981, while at the same time that of Italy rose from 2.6 per cent to 5.7 per cent. The negative aspects of the British machine tool industry can be over-stressed. For example, both West Germany and the U.S.A. lost market share between 1965 and 1981. The American decline was particularly severe with Japan in the process of overtaking it by the early 1980s. Britain's machine tool industry did make a determined attempt to maintain its export share and this met with some success, particularly in the second half of the 1970s. Between 1976 and 1980 Britain's share of world machine tool exports rose from 5.3 per cent to 6.1 per cent, and its export ratio also increased from 45 in 1972 to 50 in 1980. By 1982, British makers were exporting 66.6 per cent of their, albeit, smaller output compared to 29.4 per cent in 1966. This represented the sharpest rise in export to output figures of all the major exporting

---

[7] *Industry and Trade Committee*, 1982-3, p. xi.

countries, and by the early 1980s Britain's machine tool export proportion was only superceeded by Switzerland at 88.5 per cent of total output.[8]

Table 10.1
Index of Production Trends: Machine Tools, Manufacturing Industry, and GDP (1975 = 100)

	Machine Tools	All Manufacturing	GDP
1968	105.3	94.1	87.5
1969	118.0	97.6	89.3
1970	130.2	98.0	91.3
1971	109.5	97.5	93.0
1972	87.7	100	96.1
1973	98.0	108.4	103.0
1974	102.6	106.6	101.0
1975	100.0	100.0	100.0
1976	83.7	101.4	102.6
1977	80.0	103.0	105.1
1978	80.7	104.0	109.1
1979	80.9	104.4	111.2
1980	72.4	95.5	108.9
1981	50.4	89.6	105.5
1982	45.0	88.3	106.6

Source: *Industry and Trade Committee*, 1982-3, p. xviii.

Table 10.2
Growth Pattern: Machine Tools, Manufacturing, and GDP (% increase)

	Machine Tools	Manufacturing	GDP
1968-70	+12.45	+1.95	+4.34
1970-2	-21.25	+1.0	+5.25
1972-4	+7.45	+3.3	+5.09
1974-7	-7.53	-3.4	+4.1
1977-9	+1.125	+1.36	+5.8
1979-82	-44.4	-15.4	-4.1

Source: *Industry and Trade Committee*, 1982-3, p. xviii.

A focus on exports did not mean that the industry neglected the needs of domestic users. While the industry concentrated on making standardised general-purpose machines this did not appear to inhibit the diffusion of NCMT's across the

---

[8] E. Scriberras and B. D. Payne, *Machine Tool Industry, Technological Change and International Competitiveness* (London, Longman, 1985), pp. 31-2; *Industry and Trade Committee*, 1982-3, Annex A, p. 9.

British manufacturing sector. An international survey in 1976 estimated that there were some 114,000 NC machines distributed across the advanced industrial economies and that Britain was in fourth place (Table 10.4). Indeed, Britain had more NCMT's installed than any other Western European country, including West Germany, and their diffusion was widespread in British industry. For example, some 60 per cent of NCMT's were located in companies with fewer than 500 workers.[9] The rate of diffusion was a function of the factoring activity of U.K. machine tool firms and the process reinforced the historical specialisation of the industry with firms making general-purpose machines and facilitating the importation of special-purpose tools. The industry in this context, as we have seen in previous chapters, was not simply a producer of machine tools but a supplier of general engineering services. In this way, the industry served the needs of its customers, even if over the long-term such a strategy was not without its dangers.

Table 10.3
Level of Import Penetration in U.K. Machine Tool Market (% of machine tool consumption)

1966	24
1972	35
1975	41
1978	46
1980	49
1981	56
1982	61

Source: *Industry and Trade Committee*, 1982-3, Annex A, p. 9; Scriberras and Payne, *Machine Tool Industry*, p. 33.

Table 10.4
Distribution by Country of NCMTs, 1976

	No.	% of Total Machine Tools
U.S.A.	40,000	34.6
U.S.S.R.	24,000	20.8
Japan	14,000	12.2
U.K.	10,000	8.6
West Germany	8,000	7.0
Italy	3,000	2.7

Source: *Machinist*, October 1977, p. 121.

The industry also had capabilities that allowed some degree of adaptation to the rapidly changing business environment of the 1970s. For example, while

[9] *Machinist*, October, 1977, p. 121.

1972 was certainly an awful year for the industry, the U.K. falling from fifth to seventh place in the league of machine tool manufacturing nations, it had by the end of the year shown signs of recovery from the trough, and 1973 was to prove a more prosperous year in its fortunes. Orders rose steadily, backlogs fell, to approximately nine months on standard machines, and firms were able to curtail the making of machines for stock. Even Alfred Herbert, a company which had felt the full brunt of the recession of 1970-72, with a sharp fall in turnover and mounting losses, began to detect a turnaround in 1973, its chairman, now Sir Richard Young anticipating that the group would 'be trading at break-even by the end of the financial year'.[10] But Young's predictions and the industry's hopes were dashed by events at the end of 1973 when a miners' overtime ban, a government imposed three-day week, and an all out strike brought a major confrontation between organised labour and the administration of Edward Heath.[11] As the *Machinist* observed in January 1974, 'a pall has been cast over the outlook by the recent cut to a three-day week. Reduction in steel production, a ban by the miners on over-time and other restrictions make it difficult to see how the industry will be able to produce the machine tools that are currently on order'.[12] The battering the industry received at the tail-end of the Heath Government created an atmosphere of great uncertainty, and this intensified when the Labour Government entered office in February 1974, with certain elements in the party calling for industrial nationalisation. Tony Benn, the new Secretary of State for Industry, for example, made 'noises' concerning the possible nationalisation of part of the machine tool industry, and such rhetoric spread fear within the industry. Intentions and actions, however, are not necessarily the same thing and the *Machinist* considered Benn's proposals as premature, reassuring its readers that Labour was a minority government and consequently was not anxious 'to set the industrial sector against it'. Nationalisation was dismissed as little more than 'political rhetoric', but this American trade paper did acknowledge that the three-day week had not only 'cut into' the machine tool industry's output but it had 'also put a crimp that still persisted in their supplier's pipeline of components'.[13] The political conflicts of late 1973 and early 1974, left a legacy of uncertainty and during the first two years of the Wilson Government output in the industry fell sharply before a degree of stability set in during 1976-9.

Political strife, which led to business uncertainty, hardly created an environment conducive to sustained economic growth, and threats of nationalisation, feared by the machine tool industry, would add further pressure on the volatility of demand. Following a second narrow victory at the polls in October 1974, the Labour Government established the National Enterprise Board (NEB) with a remit to modernise the 'lame duck' firms it had brought under its wing, and

---

[10] *Machinist*, 22 January 1973, p. 78; 6 August 1973, p. 25.

[11] D Porter, 'Government and the Economy', in R. Coopey and N. Woodward (eds.), *Britain in the 1970s: The Troubled Economy* (London, UCL Press, 1996).

[12] *Machinist*, 21 January 1974, p. 75.

[13] *Machinist*, 27 May 1974, p. 39; J Tomlinson, 'British industrial policy', in Coopey and Woodward (eds.), *The Troubled Economy*, pp. 166-7, 175-6, 187-8.

this included British Leyland, nationalised in 1975. Altogether, the NEB distributed £777 million to the end of March 1979, approximately 85 per cent directed towards Leyland, and a significant proportion of the remainder to Rolls Royce, with smaller allocations to firms such as Ferranti.[14] The essential concern of the machine tool industry was its fear that it would be unable to fulfil the expected rush of orders for the machine tools needed by the modernisation programme. As *The Economist* observed, while Leyland might require some £40 million to £50 million a year in orders for new machine tools, this did not provide the boost that it seemed for domestic makers. They were 'too small or weak to cope'. Consequently, it was predicted that 'the bulk of these orders would go overseas'.[15] These fears were shared by Howard Barrett of the MTTA who, in meetings with Department of Industry (DI) officials, a ministry created by Harold Wilson in February 1974, and evolving from the Department of Trade and Industry (DTI), created by Edward Heath in 1970,[16] expressed his concern about the absence of a clear strategy. Deliveries of machines, Barrett concluded, would be 'stretched far into the future' and the likely outcome would be that domestic customers would 'turn to foreign sources'.[17] Nevertheless, on the investment front the industry made a positive response to the need for increased output. Tables 10.5 and 10.6 show that net capital expenditure in the industry increased sharply between 1976 and 1979, rising by 94.4 per cent, and on average by 47.2 per cent per annum. During these years net capital expenditure as a proportion of the industry's gross value added doubled from 6 per cent to 11 per cent.[18]

Behind this investment programme was increasing government financial assistance. In the summer of 1975, Eric Varley, who had succeeded Tony Benn as Secretary of State for Industry, introduced a scheme to enable machine tool firms to receive up to £20 million from the Treasury in investment grants. These were entitled to be used 'for the development of virtually anything aimed at improving efficiency and competition', but had to be spent by the 31 August 1978, the government also reserving the right to take a stake in the equity of a company 'where appropriate'. A key priority of government funding was the concentration of machine tool firms on applied research, rather than experimental design, which had been the intention of previous schemes. By accepting this principle, the government acknowledged the limited conversion of design projects into commercial development, a feature of the industry and its leading firm, Herbert's, noted in the previous chapter, as well as Department of Industry and Treasury concerns about the sharp decline in the foreign trade surplus for machine tools. Over the first half of the 1970s the surplus had contracted from £46 million to just

---

[14] Tomlinson, 'British Industrial Policy', pp. 177-8; *Machinist*, 15 June 1975, p. 31.

[15] *Economist*, 21 June 1975, p. 65.

[16] The DTI, formed in 1970, combined MinTech 'with much of the Board of Trade', before industry and trade were again split in 1974. Pollard, *Growth and Development*, pp. 405-6.

[17] *Machinist*, 15 June 1975, pp. 31-3.

[18] *Industry and Trade Committee*, 1982-3, Annex B, p. 9, Annex C, p. 10.

£8 million.[19] The initiatives of government to provide financial support for private enterprise in the machine tool industry provided a significant boost to the capital investment programme from the mid-1970s, but its impact upon the competitive performance of the industry, within the government's overall ambitions for industrial modernisation, was minimalist.

Table 10.5
Net Capital Expenditure of the Machine Tool Industry (Constant 1975 Prices)

	(£ million)
1970	19.8
1971	16.5
1972	9.2
1973	10.7
1974	16.6
1975	12.1
1976	14.4
1977	19.7
1978	23.8
1979	28.0
1980	14.5[a]

Source: *Industry and Trade Committee*, Annex B, p. 9.
Note: a. In 1980 the bases for comparison was changed reflecting the classifications contained in the 1980 Standard Industrial Classification, which excluded heavy gas cutting and welding equipment from the machine tool industry.

Table 10.6
Volatility Trends in Net Capital Expenditure in Machine Tools

	% change	% per annum
1970-2	-53.5	-26.75
1973-4	+80.0	+40.2
1974-6	-13.25	-6.3
1976-9	+94.4	+47.2
1979-80	-39.8	-39.8

Source: Calculated from Table 10.5.

Domestic machine tool makers failed to meet the demands of users, and import penetration rose by 19.5 per cent between 1975 and 1980 (Table 10.3). Nevertheless, as economic recovery gathered pace in 1976-7, there was increasing

---

[19] *Machinist*, September 1975, p. 35; *Economist*, 26 June 1975, p. 65; 9 August 1975, p. 25. As we shall subsequently see, Herbert's were excluded from the Government's scheme.

optimism concerning the future of the machine tool sector. In 1976, British Leyland announced the start of its new purchasing programme, expected to include an investment of approximately £42 million in machine tools in that year. The MTTA, planning for the September 1976 machine tool exhibition at Birmingham, observed that a 'prosperous period of business' lay ahead, but it seemed oblivious to the fact that there was 'a substantial increase in space taken by U.K. importers of machine tools compared to previous years'. No excuse was provided by the MTTA for the failure of domestic makers to close the supply gap, but rising imports offered good business opportunities for the factoring side of the British machine tool industry. Emphasising the government's continued support for the industry, the Prime Minister, James Callaghan, visited the exhibition, taking the opportunity for a photograph with the MTTA President G. W. T. Trowbridge. Callaghan promised that fiscal incentives would be maintained, the 100 per cent first year tax allowance for investment continuing into 1977, and he further announced that Varley's plan to spend £20 million to help modernise the machine tool industry would be broadened, although no specific details were provided. The lack of specificity was hardly surprising, the government aware of the fact that 'so few firms had applied for assistance that little of the money had been spent so far'. Government intentions and industry action were not necessarily the same, and there were clearly limitations on what government could actually achieve.[20] The culturally embedded individualism of machine tool firms made them suspicious of government 'assistance'. This was the case with government-industry relations generally, and more particularly, where a Labour Government, through the NEB, aroused suspicions of direct state intervention. This perceived threat was vocalised by left wing calls for wholesale nationalisation and the endorsement of a corporatist strategy based on strong links with the trade unions.[21]

Clearly, the industry had its own rationale for keeping at arm's length from the state's embrace. Whether closer ties between state and business would have improved the industry's fortunes remains in the domain of speculation. Nevertheless, Varley's plan was modest, certainly far removed from the ideas of the left, and aimed at plugging gaps in the industry's product range rather than pushing for major change in its business structure.[22] What was inescapable was the fact that by 1979 the machine tool industry, normally a net exporter of machine tools, was recording a trade deficit of over £50 million despite a vigorous export performance. This cast a dark shadow over the performance of the industry, a gloom reflected in MTTA projections of the future prospects for the machine tool sector. The Association's head of economics and statistics, Graham Shortell, predicted a bleak outcome for 1981, referring to sharp falls of up to 50 per cent in new orders, plants operating at 70 per cent capacity or less, and added the dismal

---

[20] *Machinist*, March 1976, p. 31; July 1975, p. 25; December 1976, p. 25.

[21] See C. Wrigley, 'Trade Unions, Strikes and the Government', in Coopey and Woodward (eds), *The Troubled Economy*; M. Artis and D. Cobham (eds), *Labour's Economic Policies, 1974-79*, (Manchester, Manchester University Press, 1991); A. Benn, *Against the Tide: Diaries 1973-76*, (London, Hutchinson, 1989).

[22] *Economist*, 21 June 1975, p. 65.

warning that 'Things are not going to get better in a hurry, that is for sure'.[23] In particular, the prospects of the industry's one-time dominant firm, Alfred Herbert, were dire. In 1980, after 5 years of NEB control it was broken-up and sold-off as separate components and finally disappeared in 1983. The next section examines the firm's demise as a private concern, focusing on its spiralling decline in the first half of the 1970s, which forced it into the hands of the NEB in 1975.

The Fall of Alfred Herbert: 1970-75

In July 1975, Varley announced a 'bail-out for the broke machine tool firm of Alfred Herbert'. The firm's financial situation (Table 10.7) deteriorated rapidly in the early 1970s, and in January 1975 *The Investors' Chronicle* reported the fourth 'hefty loss in a row' in 'our largest and least healthy machine tool manufacturer'. Mounting losses during the 1974 financial year, standing at twice the level of the previous year, came as no surprise to the *Chronicle*. A statement circulated by the company acknowledged that there was 'not likely to be any material improvement' for the current year, and given the financial strictures the management were 'pressing on with negotiations to secure funds for its long-term viability from the government'. Negotiations had actually been underway since November 1974, the desperate plight of the company recognised by the fact that investors had lost confidence in its shares. The value of Herbert shares in early 1975 was a paltry 4.75p., its market valuation estimated at a mere £800,000, compared to £43.4 million just ten years previously.[24]

Table 10.7
Financial Indicators: Alfred Herbert, 1970-74 (Year ending October)

	Turnover (£ million)	Pre-Tax Profit/Loss (000)	Gross Dividend per Share (pence)	Dividend Cover
1970	47.0	+1,257	0	N/A
1971	37.7	-3,345	0.5	0
1972	30.9	-3,592	0	0
1973	36.8	-2,039	0	0
1974	38.9	-5,096	0	0

Source: *Investors' Chronicle*, 11 April 1975, p. 134.

Discussions on the company's future followed a tripartite format, involving executive management, government officials, and trade union representatives, mainly from the Amalgamated Engineering Workers. Conspicuous

---

[23] *Machinist*, June 1980, p. 55; February 1981, p. 96; February 1982, p. 110.
[24] *Economist*, 12 July 1975, p. 51; 30 October 1975, p. 60; *Investors' Chronicle*, 10 January 1975, p. 114.

by their absence were the shareholders, a spokesperson for an institutional investor confiding in *The Investors' Chronicle* that 'If Alfred Herbert went under completely it would make little difference to (the) portfolio as the holding has been already written down to practically nothing'.[25] Such public condemnation was deeply humiliating for Herbert's, its assets now being worth less than its debts, and the finalisation of the government 'bail-out' compensated ordinary shareholders to the tune of 6p per share in cash, a payout which was considered generous in the circumstances.[26] *The Economist* certainly considered the deal a fair one, expressing little sympathy for ordinary shareholders who 'took dividends for years, put little back and tolerated years of bad results'.[27]

Problems at the company had manifested themselves in the 1960s, as seen in the previous chapter, and the company had attempted a major reorganisation in 1968 to rationalise operations (see Appendix B, Fig. B.1). Despite this, during the following decade the financial deterioration of the company was rapid and by 1975 it ceased to be a private concern. Why did this happen, what diagnosis did directors offer to explain the company's ills, what measures did they put in place in an attempt to stabilise the firm, and did they evolve a long-term strategy for survival? A major problem confronting manufacturing firms in the early 1970s, particularly in sectors such as engineering, was exposure to wage inflation. Although Herbert's had 'enjoyed' a long-term reputation of parsimony when it came to wage payment, a factor discussed in the previous chapter, by the late 1960s and early 1970s this had been lost in comparison to other machine tool firms. For example, in 1975 B. Elliott & Co. Ltd, a group organisation of similar size to that of Herbert's, had a turnover which was 9.2 per cent lower than that of Herbert's, but the Herbert wage bill totalled £22.04 million, which was a staggering 67.1 per cent higher than that at Elliott's. As indicated in Appendix B, Table B.4, Herbert's had a significantly greater wage to turnover ratio than any of the firms listed, and *The Investors' Chronicle* asserted that 'Alfred Herbert's 60 per cent wage/turnover figures supplies an important reason for that company's financial embarrassment'.[28] Industrial relations problems continued to weigh heavy on management time. In March 1970, the directors reported that 'much time is still having to be devoted to labour relations' at the company's two main production plants, at Edgwick Road, Coventry, and Mackadown, Birmingham, and in September the board noted that 'Labour conditions continue to be tense, absorbing much management time'.[29] There is little doubt that wage costs and deteriorating labour relations placed a strain on Herbert's financial and managerial resources, but a wage-cost argument does not explain fully the company's financial plight. Different types of machine tools, for example, had different labour contents, and machine tool makers generally acknowledged that there was 'no consistent link between low wage costs

[25] *Investors' Chronicle*, 14 March 1975, p. 786.

[26] *Machinist*, December 1975, pp. 23-7.

[27] *Economist*, 12 July 1975, p. 81.

[28] *Investors' Chronicle*, 28 February 1975, p. 615.

[29] Herbert, Board of Directors, 1960-80, 26 March, 18 September 1970.

and a good profit margin'.[30] High labour costs, therefore, constitute only part of the story of Herbert's rapid deterioration.

A consistent theme raised by directors during board meetings was their concern with the quality of management at the company. For example, in September 1970, they emphasised the need for 'present management to be given all possible assistance both from within, and, if necessary from outside the group to bring about the fundamental changes essential to achieving an adequate return on capital', which, as shown in Table 10.7, was zero in 1973. Faced with a mounting financial crisis, the directors accepted that the immediate challenge was to control liquidity, to improve profitability, to maintain the existing work load, and to monitor costs, especially of wages and of salaries, to effect a reversal in an escalating trend. Scrutiny of internal finances required detailed statistical information, but the board was forced to concede that managers within the group had supplied them with only partial information, which delayed the application of a set of economising measures aimed at preventing a further acceleration of what was already viewed as a downward financial spiral. In the short-term, attempts were made to address the liquidity situation through a negotiated loan of £6 million with the Finance Corporation for Industry (FCI), an institution originally established in 1946 to finance large industrial schemes. Attached to the loan, however, were heavy interest charges set at 2.5 per cent and 2.75 per cent above the prevailing bank rate during the first five years and the second five years of the loan respectively. Acceptance of such stringent terms had much to do with the worsening overdraft position with the company's bankers, Barclay's. In October 1970, the overdraft reached its limit of £8 million, forcing the directors to endorse the control of cash movements that were 'now being monitored from the centre to improve the position' of the company. In addition, the board requested that management rigorously control the accumulation of stocks, and give the issue of debtors and creditors a 'top priority'. At board level one gets the impression of increasing panic, an air of fire-fighting, as the short-term liquidity crisis absorbed the time of the executive, overshadowing considerations of longer-term solutions to the company's overwhelming financial problems. Adding to executive uncertainty, was a deteriorating external environment in 1970, with home demand 'continuing to weaken' and export markets stagnating.[31]

At the same time, the Herbert-Ingersoll venture proved a bitter disappointment, adding further to the company's financial burdens. Medium-term finance for Herbert-Ingersoll, which had failed to produce a profit, was forthcoming from the IRC, who contributed a total of £2.5 million, £1.5 million in fixed and £1 million in working capital. Half of the total provision was contained in a loan, and the remainder provided by a subscription on Herbert equity at £7 per share. The desperation of the board for injections of capital was demonstrated by the fact that the directors accepted, against their intentions, the IRC conditions that funds would not be used for expansion, other than that essential to reach

---

[30] *Investors' Chronicle*, 28 February 1975, p. 615.

[31] Herbert, Board of Directors, 1960-80, 17 April, 19 June, 18 September, 16 October 1970. For the FCI see Pollard, *Growth and Development*, p. 247.

profitability. The loan was also needed to persuade the management at Barclay's to hold the Herbert-Ingersoll overdraft at a ceiling of £4 million, subject to a £1 million guarantee given by Herbert and Ingersoll respectively.[32]

While liquidity was the immediate issue that demanded the attention of directors, the underlying problem facing the Herbert group was located in the performance of the operating companies, in particular Herbert-BSA, the Churchill Machine Tool Co., Herbert-Ingersoll, and to a lesser extent Herbert Control and Instruments. The problems identified by the board were associated with concerns about production, sales and overheads, and these, in turn, were identified with the quality of management. For example, the board was informed in March 1970 that at Churchill 'Production continued to be bad due to the shortcomings of management', and changes were promised 'at the top' of the operating company. A month later directors were again discussing problems at Churchill 'because of the breakdown in production management', the situation being so serious that they called in a firm of consultants, Production Engineering Consulting Group Ltd, who placed one of their own personnel in 'executive control' until a more permanent arrangement could be agreed. The consultants did not hold back on their assessment of the situation at Churchill. Articulating the view that short-term plans to economise were no more than 'first-aid' measures, the consultants concluded that the fundamental problem facing Churchill was an insufficient market share to justify levels of output that might break-even or make a profit. Despite gloomy predictions, the Herbert directors remained convinced that the long-term prospects for grinding machines, the Churchill speciality, were promising, and there was consensus that 'every effort should be made to remain in this business'. The board decided to discount the advice of the consultants, and instead they announced that management arrangements at the company should be simplified and capital commitments reduced, while they attempted to restore profits.[33] Churchill continued to be a problem, as will be seen, but more worrying were the difficulties experienced by Herbert-Ingersoll, and at the core operating company, Herbert-BSA.

As discussed in the previous chapter, a report on Herbert-Ingersoll in February 1970 maintained that 'management continued to be the key to the company's development'. The 'most important single factor in reaching profitability quickly', the report concluded, was the 'development of commercial judgement'. Young and his executive continued to sustain confidence in their heavy capital investment in the venture, referring to the potential for the joint development of a highly profitable business in special-purpose NC machine tools. Yet the report predicted recurring losses, questioned the lack of systematic costing procedures, and called into question the commercial judgement of the executive board, which had invested heavily in a speculative venture. There was to be no quick return to profitability, and as will be discussed subsequently, Herbert-Ingersoll became a financial albatross around the company's neck. Financial

[32] Herbert, Board of Directors, 1960-80, 19 December 1969; 16 January, 20 February, 17 April 1970.
[33] Herbert, Board of Directors, 26 March, 24 April, 19 June, 17 July 1970.

salvation was hardly to be found in the core Herbert-BSA operating company, where directors complained that adequate production controls had not been put in place by management which 'resulted in under utilisation of direct labour and to a rise in non-productive work'. In 1970, management devised an intensive sales campaign to fill the gaps in the order load, anticipating that the budgeted output for the year was achievable. This was followed by the caveat that the necessary orders continued to come in and there were no serious labour problems. A couple of months later Herbert-BSA were still complaining about problems with overheads, Young receiving a promise that shop-floor supervision was being strengthened to exercise 'better control' over production. A report by the Herbert group managing directors, however, acknowledged that at Mackadown 'management and technical competence on the control side of the business ... had shown little improvement', and the board remained concerned about the company's output levels, product mix and retrenchment for the next financial year. Consequently, the board instructed Herbert-BSA to avoid pursuing targets of high turnover and low margins, which they asserted 'could only add to the problems of management and liquidity', and they endorsed the need for 'yet stronger management at the company'.[34]

Although there were major concerns about the competency of management at the operating companies, the issue of low margins raised questions of pricing policy at the group level and this became increasingly important during a period of rising wage and price inflation.[35] For example, at a board meeting in April 1970 the importance of raising prices in anticipation of, rather than in response to, the effects of increasing wages and other costs, was stressed and a month later the board agreed to increase prices 'to the fullest extent the market can take'. Despite this seemingly aggressive move, directors were not comfortable with Herbert's role as a price leader and they called for cooperation with the MTTA to exchange information with other member firms and to ascertain how they handled the problems connected with the adjustment of prices to anticipated increases in cost.[36] Ten years previously the company had spurned the exchange of information associated with the establishment of the MTIRA, but in the more troubled business environment at the beginning of the 1970s, Herbert's was more accommodating when it came to sharing information on prices and costs. This was another indicator of the firm's declining reputation and its falling self-confidence.

According to Teece and Pisano, a key source of competitive advantage relates to the ability of a firm's strategic management to appropriately adapt, integrate, and re-configure 'internal and external organisational skills, resources, and functional competencies', in the context of a changing business environment. Such competencies are 'rooted in high performance routines operating inside the

---

[34] Herbert, Board of Directors, 1960-80, 20 February, 27 April, 17 July, 18 September 1970.

[35] See M. S. Schulze and N. Woodward, 'The Emergence of Rapid Inflation', in Coopey and Woodward (eds.), *The Troubled Economy*, pp. 106-35.

[36] Herbert, Board of Directors, 1960-80, 17 April, 18 May 1970.

firm, embedded in the firm's processes, and conditioned by its history'.[37] At Alfred Herbert, the monitoring of the financial situation, and the development of a coherent strategy to tackle the company's mounting problems, was not helped by the deficiencies of core competencies, which manifested themselves in inadequate accounting and executive management systems. For example, in May 1970 the board endorsed the 'establishment of essential accounting procedures in the operating companies, but seven months later directors acknowledged that 'Accounting procedures were weak in most cases' and made the astonishing admission that 'Herbert had never had any standard cost system or even plant costing'. By the beginning of 1971, plant costing was established, but standard costing was still awaiting instigation, leaving the company short of 'adequate controls'. In order to implement costing policies a set of executive management changes were put in place, including the abandonment of the group executive committee of managing directors established only in 1969, and the appointment of a single group-managing director from the end of 1970.[38]

H. Neale Raine, the new group-managing director, took responsibility for a recently appointed working party on group objectives, in addition operating companies and service divisions were required to report to him directly, and his specific remit was to secure a reduction in the overheads of the group as soon as possible. The board also took the decision to reconstitute the Finance Committee as the Finance and Policy Committee, and this body was required to focus on two key functions. Firstly, it had the right to approve annual budgets of capital expenditure for submission to the board. Secondly, the Committee was to provide reviews and recommendations to the board on matters of policy. This entailed a particular emphasis on the group's product range, availability of financial resources and their allocation to different parts of the product range, the supply of 'manpower' and adoption of effective personnel policies, the review of organisation and management, and the effective location of the various manufacturing activities of the group of companies. Despite this impressive range of responsibilities, the execution of policy would remain very much in the hands of the group-managing director, and the Committee would not be involved in matters of detailed management. The constituency of the Committee included the chairman, the group-managing director, the deputy managing directors (operating and service companies), and finance director, and the intention was to meet every two months. Finally, the board decided, following a review of the group's sales organisation, that there was a need to separate the two functions of selling and marketing. Responsibility for the former was to be located in a central sales organisation, while the operating companies would absorb the latter. Moreover, a small central corporate planning unit, including a market intelligence group, was to be formed, reporting directly to the group-managing director. The aim was to produce a corporate plan for the group, covering a three-year period, against which other

---

[37] D. J. Teece and G. Pisano, 'The Dynamic Capabilities of the Firm: An Introduction', *Industrial and Corporate Change*, Vol. 3, No. 3, (1994), p. 537.
[38] Herbert, Board of Directors, 1960-80, 18 May 1970, 16 October, 13 November, 18 December 1970; 15 January 1971.

policies could be considered, and it was expected that operating companies would become more market orientated in contrast to their historic focus on production.[39]

As the directors struggled to reform the company's internal organisational capabilities, they also now faced an increasingly volatile business environment, with deteriorating domestic orders and falling turnover. For example, in March 1971 Herbert-BSA reported a serious downturn in orders and the board responded by instructing the operating company to cut its production programme, only purchase supplies and manufacture in line with available orders, and reduce as far as possible overheads. A revised profit and loss forecast for the year ending 31 October 1971 was put before the board which estimated a loss for the financial year of £1.085 million, a gross underestimation; the company actually incurring a loss for the financial year of £3.345 million (Table 10.7) leading to the announcement of redundancies at the Churchill machine tool factory. In addition, Herbert Boring and Drilling was placed on a four-day week, and a warning given that further redundancies would follow if existing trends continued. Across the group as a whole, redundancies amounted to 2,270 by the end of May 1971; the board clearly aware that any further attempts to retrench was only achievable by closing plant and radically re-organising manufacturing procedures. Estimating a group turnover for 1971-2 within the range £37 million to £39 million, the directors concluded that overheads should be correspondingly cut by at least £1 million to £1.5 million in order to break-even. Imposing a financial discipline, the board announced that the 'saving' in overheads was to be 'mandatory for operating and service companies'. As it turned out, the actual turnover for the financial year to October 1972 was only £30.9 million (Table 10.7), well below the estimated forecast, and the drive to cut overheads proved counter-productive.[40]

In September 1971, Herbert's marketing division reported that the company's market share 'had declined rapidly over recent months'. Although marketing managers could not identify any 'clear' reasons for this, they nevertheless pinpointed the failure of the company's design strategy as a likely cause of declining market fortunes. Concentration of design effort on standard machines increased the vulnerability of the company during economic downturns. Thus, it was concluded that 'the preponderance of standard machines in the company's share ... in times of economic depression suffer to a greater extent than machines of a more specialist nature'. Over the long-term Herbert's product mix had been skewed towards standard makes, conditioned by its history, and this increased its vulnerability during downturns in the market. There was a growing fear that Herbert's was competing 'in a diminishing market', not least because of new entrants to the international machine tool industry from Eastern Europe who could build standard machines cheaper. Consequently, the board expressed 'the urgent need for the marketing function to indicate priority needs in design and development'. Directors wanted such information at the earliest possible date, as rather worryingly 'there were indications that the life of the older types of machines', of which Herbert's had many in its product range, 'were now very

---

[39] Herbert, Board of Directors, 1960-80, 15 January, 18 February 1971.
[40] Herbert, Board of Directors, 1960-80, 19 March, 16 April, 18 June 1971.

limited'. In early 1972, the company began to identify machines in low demand, contributing to a loss in their domestic market share, but solutions to this problem placed the directors in a dilemma. A re-vamping of the product range would require capital investment and an extended time period to deliver new machines, but such a policy ran up against the weak liquidity situation facing the company. Added to this constraint was the policies adopted to control expenditure to alleviate the liquidity crisis. Extensive economising to slash overheads, especially targeted at what the directors referred to as non-productive labour, produced unintended consequences in the form of a dilution of managerial and administrative capabilities. The company's sales division, for example, in early 1972 continued to report poor practices in making quotations, meeting delivery dates, and in the reception of products by customers. The underlying causes of these problems were reduced staffing, short-time working, overtime bans, inadequate administrative systems and quality control mechanisms. The drive to cut overheads had severe repercussions on the reputation and sales of the group, and 'These problems', it was concluded by the board, 'call for the most careful judgement when quoting short deliveries in order not to lose business. Such a policy could be self-defeating if taken too far'.[41]

The capabilities of business firms, according to Teece and Pisano may be understood in terms 'of the organisational structures and managerial processes which support productive activity',[42] and there is evidence to suggest that the consequence of the drive to cut overheads at Herbert's acted to weaken these systems. In particular, expenditure cuts began to undermine the accountancy reforms that were critical to bringing cost systems under control. In January 1972, J. H. David, the managing director of Herbert-BSA, recently appointed to the main board, warned directors that there had 'been a virtual breakdown in accounting' at the company and until the system was re-organised there would be 'no accurate forecasts of trading results for the year'. He further warned that 'because of the accounting problem there had been a substantial discrepancy between physical and book stocks as at the 31st October 1971'. The group finance director expressed his fear to the board that there was a 'risk of collapse in accounting' and this he put down to 'inefficient leadership and staffing in the accounting function, worsened by staff reductions and other pressures'. While he was quick to point out that he had warned the Herbert-BSA management about accounting problems before the end of the financial year, he conspicuously failed to acknowledge that the board had been continually pressing the operating companies to cut their overheads and 'non-productive' labour. Ignoring the irony of the situation, the board's response was to place Herbert-BSA under increased scrutiny, more time was to be devoted to the company's business during future board meetings, and it insisted on progress up-dates 'on the urgent correction of accounting management' at the company. Rather belatedly, the board also agreed that at the Edgwick plant of Herbert-BSA either the recruitment of, or changes in, personnel associated with production

---

[41] Herbert, Board of Directors, 1960-80, 24 September 1971; 21 January 1972.
[42] Teece and Pisano, 'The Dynamic Capabilities', p. 540.

management and quality control were needed.[43] The drive to cut overheads reduced knowledge routines at the company at a critical moment in its attempt to introduce accountancy reforms, and top management were culpable in their failure to grasp the strategic contradictions inherent in the policy.[44]

During 1972, the financial problems facing the company accelerated, although the failure of the accounting system distorted the accuracy of financial information available to the executive. For example, a recorded loss of £3.3 million in October 1971, was subsequently re-evaluated to £3.88 million, due to inadequacies in the standard costing system at Herbert-BSA. Nevertheless, continuing losses in the first half of 1972 led the directors to realise that the company's 'overall reserves' were 'virtually eliminated', a final, if somewhat belated acceptance of 'the overall gravity of the company's situation'. At the boardroom level agreement was reached, albeit reluctantly, to enter discussions with the DTI 'on the implications of a liquidity problem arising by the end of the year due to the current trading conditions'.[45] The company was entering the 'end game', and the executive were now faced with the challenge of devising contingency measures to keep the business afloat as long as possible, and this involved a realisation that the only chance of survival was a rescue package from the state. In June 1973, the board concluded that the only 'practical future strategy' would be the injection of new capital, considered essential for re-equipping the operating companies, rationalising the product range, developing new machine tool designs, and a possible diversification into new engineering products. Without new capital, the board concluded, 'no significant improvement in financial performance would be possible'.[46]

Financial reconstruction was the cornerstone of the survival strategy, and this, as we shall see involved a complex set of negotiations with the DTI and potential outside investors for a financial package. In the meantime, however, the executive attempted to get its own house in order through a policy of internal rationalisation, involving changes in production and organisational structure, and through an external policy based upon the possibility of a merger with one or more firms in the machine tool industry. Internal re-organisation involved the concentration of production in one machine tool company through the consolidation of Herbert-BSA, Churchill Machine Tool, Herbert Boring and Drilling and Herbert Associates. Endorsement for the integration of these companies into a 'single' entity, the Herbert Machine Tool Co. Ltd., came in September 1972, and the new company began trading in December. Integration into a consolidated business unit, however, remained only partial, with Herbert Small Tools, Herbert Control and Instruments, Herbert-Ingersoll, and the Herbert overseas agencies remaining as separate companies. Further, production at Herbert Machine Tool continued to be located in different factories; one each at

---

[43] Herbert, Board of Directors, 1960-80, 21 January 1972.

[44] The importance of knowledge and learning routines in the business organisation is emphasised by Teece and Pisano, 'The Dynamic Capabilities', pp. 544-5.

[45] Herbert, Board of Directors, 1960-80, 18 February 1972.

[46] Herbert, Board of Directors, 1960-80, 8 June 1973.

Birmingham and Lutterworth, and two at Coventry. Rationalisation through re-organisation seemed little more than a cosmetic exercise, and problems with manufacturing efficiency remained paramount. For example, in June 1973 the group-managing director reported that at Herbert Machine Tool there was a 'lack of motivation on the shop floor ... and a need for better quality, lower level management', and he went on to express his misgivings about the 'underlying weakness' of management at both Edgwick Road and Lutterworth.[47] A re-occurring theme at the executive level was the competency of middle and lower management, evidence of a historical lack of an extensive managerial hierarchy in the Herbert organisation. The consequence was that the company could not draw upon the range of managerial capabilities necessary to pull up the production side of the business even to a break-even point.

Not surprisingly Herbert's top management came in for heavy criticism, notably from *The Investors' Chronicle* who caustically remarked that there was 'no need to ask why Alfred Herbert got itself even more deeply into trouble in 1973/4, a year that was a good one for the machine tool industry at large'. In fact the turnover of the Herbert group increased by 5.8 per cent during 1973/4, and there was an encouraging rise in overseas sales, accounting for 44 per cent of total group sales. To meet increased activity the company's U.K. labour force rose during the year from 6,342 to 6,559. Rising employment, however, led to an escalation of £2 million to the company's wage bill over the previous year, and the bulk of the increased export sales came from the activities of the overseas subsidiaries. Indeed, U.K. based export sales increased only by £300,000, from £9.1 million to £9.4 million and, in addition, the group was required to pay £363,000 in foreign taxation despite the company's large overall loss. Not disguising its contempt for the Herbert directors, *The Investors' Chronicle* concluded that the company's shares were 'highly speculative and subject to exceptionally high political risks'.[48] Public admonishment, coupled with a dismal financial performance, weakened confidence in the company's leadership, a corollary to major changes in the governance of the company in 1973. The position of Sir Richard Young, appointed chair in 1966, became increasingly untenable. In a boardroom coup, in October 1973 he was removed from office, the day to day business conducted 'for the time being' by a General-Purpose Committee under the chairmanship of Professor Hugh Ford, who had been appointed a non-executive director in July 1971. Other members of the newly reconstituted board included the finance director, D. M. Davies, who had joined the board in April 1973, and H. Neale Raine, appointed group-managing director in December 1970, became the chief executive assuming the powers previously exercised by Young. The Finance and Policy Committee was disbanded and a salaries and appointment committee established, which, among other responsibilities, was to advise the company's General-Purpose Committee on possible candidates for the chairmanship prior to an individual being approached. Two new directors, appointed internally, joined the board: Douglas Lang,

[47] Herbert, Board of Directors, 1960-80, 7 September, 17 November 1972; 8 June 1973.

[48] *Investors' Chronicle*, 11 April 1975, p. 134.

managing director of Herbert Small Tools, and George Vincent Bloomfield, group director of engineering.[49] Herbert's search for a permanent chairman was long-drawn out, Ford taking on the role of acting chair from October 1973. Finally, in July 1975, the DI, exasperated by the prevarication at the company, insisted on the installation of J. W. Buckley of Davy International, who had joined the Herbert board in a non-executive capacity in March, as acting chair. Corporate governance is to do with providing 'overall direction' for the enterprise and supervising and controlling the 'executive actions of management'[50] and the lack of an agreed successor as chairman was not conducive to effective governance at Herbert. The board it would seem failed to grasp fully the need for clear and co-ordinated direction.

While internal rationalisation and re-organisation at the company proved ineffective, attempts at external solutions equally failed to resolve the problems. The partnership with Ingersoll Milling Machine through Herbert-Ingersoll turned into a financial fiasco, bleeding the company of much needed cash. In 1970, Herbert-Ingersoll experienced losses estimated at £700,000 to £800,000, but there was confidence that the situation could be turned around and E. I. Gaylord, the Ingersoll representative on the Herbert board, remained confident that 'in the light of the available evidence ... a profit could be earned in 1971'. This prediction proved to be hopelessly optimistic and Herbert directors were subsequently advised that for the financial year ending October 1971 Herbert-Ingersoll would incur losses of approximately £500,000, which in the event turned out to be near the actual loss of £540,000. In July 1970, the Herbert board had discussed the possibility of 'disengagement' from the Herbert-Ingersoll partnership 'as rapidly as possible in a financially advantageous way'. This was wishful thinking, and despite the board's apparent urgency it was not until the end of 1971 that they took the decision to provide no further financial support for Herbert-Ingersoll, with the added codicil that limited funding could be provided only if this was 'matched by Ingersoll, to enable the latter to continue the business in its own name'. Instructed to provide a decision on the Herbert offer by the end of January 1972, Ingersoll gave a firm rejection, leading to the Herbert executive opening talks with the DTI, Rothchilds, and Peat Marwick and Mitchell, to attempt to navigate a way out of the financial mess they found themselves. Indicating the desperation of the Herbert's executive, they agreed to a proposal to approach Staveley Industries, as a possible partner in an attempt to prop-up Herbert-Ingersoll, but this was not carried forward, the Herbert board quickly vetoing the move. In June 1972, Herbert-Ingersoll collapsed, Barclay's Bank were appointed receivers, and Herbert's requested by the DTI to repay a £500,000 IRC loan for which they and Ingersoll had given guarantees of £1 million. Herbert's share of the guarantee note was £650,000, and the company now became embroiled in a dispute with Ingersoll over the alleged reluctance of the American company to honour its share of the note. In the event,

---

[49] *Machinist*, 16 July 1971; Herbert, Board of Directors, 1960-80, 8 October 1973.

[50] S. Sheikh and S. K. Chatterjee, 'Perspectives in Corporate Governance', in S. Sheikh and W. Rees (eds), *Corporate Governance and Corporate Control* (London, Cavendish, 1995), pp. 5-6.

Herbert paid the DTI £241,852 in July, and in September Barclay's £500,000. This still left an outstanding balance of £150,000 plus the fact that Ingersoll continued to prevaricate over its share of the guarantee. Negotiations with Ingersoll continued into 1973, when the DTI advised the Herbert board that 'because of the uncertainty of the negotiations it would be probably necessary to write-off on the company's accounts at 31 October 1972 a large proportion of the Ingersoll note'.[51] The joint venture with Ingersoll, which seemed to promise a high-tech solution to Herbert's antiquated product range, quickly turned sour, and the directors did little more than wring their hands as the venture further bled the company's rapidly diminishing financial resources.

Other attempts at merger failed to inspire confidence in the board's judgement. For example, in June 1972, they had preliminary discussions with the Newall Machine Tool Co. Ltd., a business reported to be 'receptive to the idea of some form of merger'. Talks also ensued with H. W. Ward and Co., Raine informing the board that 'the possibility of further industrial rationalisation along these lines had been discussed informally with Mr [L. U. D.] Tindale of the DTI who had reacted favourably'. At discussions between Herbert's, Newall, and the DTI in July, both companies stressed that neither partner to the proposed merger could take on any additional secured borrowing, the merger depending upon DTI financial assistance. The negotiations with Ward proved abortive, but the Herbert directors hoped that there might be some cooperation between the two companies in terms of particular product markets. Neither was an agreement brokered with Newall, a proposed venture from which it is difficult to envisage what the directors of Herbert hoped to achieve. Newall was a small enterprise, with a turnover of £3.9 million in 1972/3, and was making losses with a negative cash flow. The rational behind these proposed mergers seems to have been a defensive one. That is, the Herbert board considered that because of the uncertainty of the machine tool trade 'it would be attractive to diversify', and they concluded that this should be borne in mind when considering any financial re-construction.[52] Again, this was wishful thinking, no coherent plan emerged, and the board's attempt at rationalisation and re-organisation failed to stem the financial haemorrhage. Consequently, between 1973 and 1975, the last two years of Alfred Herbert as an independent company, the board was preoccupied with financial restructuring and negotiations with the banks and government. This increasingly desperate attempt to keep the company afloat failed and, after 1975, the company entered a period of terminal decline.

Financial Reconstruction and Collapse

Apart from the temporary increase in employment of 1973/4, Raine, in order to reduce pressure on the company's finances, did cut the workforce of the Herbert

---

[51] Herbert, Board of Directors, 1960-80, 20 February, 17 July 1970; 31 October, 23 November, 17 December 1971; 17 March, 19 May, 16 June, 21 July, 31 October 1972; 15 January 1973.

[52] Herbert, Board of Directors, 1960-80, 16 June, 21 July 1972.

group of companies in a sequence of redundancies. These reduced the Herbert labour force from 11,000 in 1971 to just over 4,000 prior to the state take-over in 1975. There was also a drastic reduction in the company's product range as old models were phased-out.[53] Despite this surgery, the financial situation of the company proved intractable, and the directors desperately sought a rescue package that could preserve it as a private concern. Among the schemes considered was that of May 1973, entailing a new share issue underwritten by a syndicate led by Slater Walker Ltd, and brokered by S. G. Warburg & Co, a firm of financial consultants who had acted for Herbert's in the BSA merger of the 1960s. Credence to the scheme came from the DTI, the ministry agreeing to subscribe for 5.5 million preference shares at £1 per share, with an entitlement of a net dividend of 5.25 per cent. In addition, the scheme proposed to issue 15,730,400 ordinary shares at 25p each, of a special class with rights equal to the existing £1 ordinary shares of the company, and offered to existing shareholders at a ratio of 8 to 10. Concessions built into the scheme, included the rights of the Herbert directors to call for subscriptions to the preference shares in allotments of 500,000, at any time up to three years from the date of issue of the ordinary shares, and no dividend was payable on preference shares until £1.2m had been paid up fully.

The scheme, however, was not free of strings. In return for DTI backing, the Herbert board would guarantee to provide to the DTI full information, as requested, about its affairs, the DTI also proscribing the right, on the company taking up the issue of preference shares, to place a director of its own choice on the board. Additional changes were also required in the governance of the company, entailing a significant reduction in the power of the existing board, and this was a key aspect of the proposed financial package. As their price for heading the syndicate, Slater Walker, subject to discussions with Sir Richard Young, wanted Jim Slater on the Herbert board and installed as chairman. The latter was to assume responsibility for financial matters and control new appointments at the strategic management level. Increasing control of the Herbert board by Slater Walker found approval from the DTI, although there was no reference in the deliberations of the board to the dubious reputation assumed since for the role of Slater Walker as a company engaged in asset stripping. Indeed, R. C. Tarling of Slater Walker, justifying the arrangements to Tindale of the DTI, claimed that his company regarded the scheme 'In general terms ... as an opportunity for government, financial interests and the executive team at Alfred Herbert to work together in the development of an important element in a key sector of British industry'.[54] Slater Walker could not be faulted, at least by its rhetoric to the DSI and the board, but how long Herbert would have survived, or in what form, under the stewardship of Jim Walker it is not possible to gauge. In the event, the scheme went no further than the negotiating table. In August 1973, Warburg & Co. advised the Herbert board that the proposed re-financing operation 'would be deferred until the time was more opportune for approaching underwriters'. It would seem that such were the state of Herbert's finances that even Slater Walker were not tempted to indulge

[53] *Alfred Herbert, 1888-1983*, p. 18.
[54] Herbert, Board of Directors, 1960-80, 7 May 1973.

themselves in asset stripping and Warburg's cautioned the Herbert directors that a successful share float would 'seem unlikely' and certainly not before 1974 at the earliest.[55]

There was in fact no upturn in 1974, the financial position continued to deteriorate, not helped by the consequences of the three-day week and government prices and incomes policy.[56] The company did attempt to increase its secure borrowing rights, but in September 1974 Raine warned the board that the group's cash flow showed that the limits of the company's £8 million overdraft with Barclay's 'would be reached by early November and that the overdraft level would be built up to £11.25 million by July 1975'. Raine blamed 'threshold payments', introduced by Heath in 1973 as part of the phased incomes policy and honoured by the Wilson government in 1974, 'for the deterioration that led to 'lost deliveries and excess cost inflation'.[57] Herbert's chief executive warned the board that they should brief Warburg & Co. about the seriousness of the latest financial position, and that Barclay's 'should be immediately informed'. Raine did outline the options open to the company, but in practice these were confined to the disposal of assets and the familiar and rather pathetic plea 'to improve profitability'. In fact, Raine admitted that neither of these actions was 'likely to produce sufficient cash quickly enough to prevent the bank line being breached or to affect the cash flow materially until well into the next year'. Herbert's were, de facto, bankrupt, and while the board had not detected any change in attitude of their customers or suppliers, Raine agreed to discuss in detail the company's plight with the DI. The board also sought advice from Warburg's, and Raine undertook to inform the company's solicitors on the liquidity crisis 'so they can give full and proper advice on our present position'. At the next board meeting in October there was an 'extensive discussion on whether it was right and proper to continue to trade', and the directors were advised by the company's solicitors that pending a decision of government support for the company they were still 'responsible' for the continuation of trading. Alfred Herbert remained in business, but now subject to a constant review of its day-to-day financial position, the board being informed by Warburg's that they must ensure 'considerable care and prudence' in accepting customer deposits and creating new lines of credit. Later that month, Warburg's informed Raine that the government would provide assistance for the company allowing it to increase its guarantee with the bank. Nevertheless, negotiations were protracted and continued well into 1975.[58]

---

[55] Herbert, Board of Directors, 1960-80, 31 August 1973. For a discussion of the activities and reputation of Slater Walker, see C. Raw, *Slater Walker. An Investigation of a Financial Phenomenon* (London, Andrew Deutsch, 1977), pp. 222-42; M Hope, 'On being taken-over by Slater Walker', *Journal of Industrial Economics*, Vol. 24, No. 3 (1976), pp. 163-78; T Gourvish, 'Beyond the Merger Mania' in Coopey and Woodward (eds), *The Troubled Economy*, pp. 236-50.

[56] Herbert, Board of Directors, 1960-80, 26 April 1974.

[57] Herbert, Board of Directors, 1960-80, 23 September 1974. For incomes policy, see Schulze and Woodward, 'The Emergence of Rapid Inflation', p. 114.

[58] Herbert, Board of Directors, 1960-80, 23 September, 17 October 1974.

By March 1975, the company's management, government officials and the Amalgamated Engineering Union, were in detailed discussions over the form of the re-structuring. *The Investors' Chronicle* already saw this as a sign of the vultures picking over the bones, reporting that J. W. Buckley, newly appointed to the board, would need to draw the talks quickly to a conclusion or 'there would be soon nothing left to discuss'. A scheme for financial re-constructing was finally resolved in July 1975, when the DI increased its guarantee to the company's bankers to £15 million, and injected £25 million into the company's equity, to be held by the NEB. Ironically, shareholders must have been delighted with the deal, receiving just 6p cash for their shares, and realising that one of Britain's foremost engineering companies was now valued at a paltry £1.18m.[59] The nightmare scenario of Sir Alfred, the company founder, and C. W. Clark, who had both long preached the virtues of private enterprise and the iniquities of nationalisation, had come to reality.

While the helping hand of the state saved the company from oblivion, *The Economist* was under no illusion that most of the £25 million would 'go on paying off loans and reducing borrowing'. With total borrowing recorded at £17.4 million, with £15.7 million of it as an overdraft running up an interest bill of approximately £2 million per year, it would be difficult to disagree with *The Economist's* financial assessment. The journal also predicted that the nationalisation of Alfred Herbert, now renamed Herbert Ltd., 'will only be the start of the government's problems and more capital – possibly as much as £20 million will soon be needed if the son of Alfred is not to stagger from crisis to crisis, just as its unlamented father has for the past 6 years'.[60] *The Economist's* public assessment was privately shared by Herbert's new chairman, J. W. Buckley, and he informed the board in July 1975 that the £25 million injection 'was barely sufficient for the company's needs', and consequently as a matter of urgency they would need to 'achieve profitable trading in the shortest possible time'. In October 1975, Buckley announced forecasted financial requirements for the financial year ending in October 1976 at £34.1 million, including £2.5m for contingencies. He estimated that taking into account the government's long-term provision of £25 million and the facilities Barclay's were prepared to make available, there would be a shortfall of some £3.325 million Negotiations would be opened with Lord Ryder the chairman designate of the NEB.[61]

The period of state control between 1975 and 1980 did prove difficult. Even the loyal *Machine Tool Review* had to admit in 1980 that despite the influx of government money the cost of developing new machines on a broad front, at a time when the demand for current machines was falling, was too much for the company and that losses continued. There were some minor successes, Herbert Ltd. developing their Batchmatic turning machines to incorporate computerised numerical control, capable of simple programming by manual data input on the

---

[59] *Investors' Chronicle*, 14 March 1975, p. 786; 31 October 1975, p. 326; *Economist*, 8 November 1975, p. 100; Herbert, Board of Directors, 1960-80, 11 July 1975.
[60] *Economist*, 8 November 1975, p. 100.
[61] Herbert, Board of Directors, 1960-80, 11 July, 24 October 1975.

shop floor, and enabling versatile application both in the small sub-contract shop and in the large manufacturing complex.[62] While these machines were technologically sophisticated, and were in demand by customers, the advance was too little too late. By 1980, the company was again facing financial melt down, and there was no sign that the continued flow of public money would find its reward in a return to financial stability and profitability. For example, in March 1980, the Under Secretary of State for Industry, Michael Marshall, stated that since the initial injection in 1975, the NEB had invested in the shares of Herbert Ltd. £10 million in April 1978 and £8.3 million in March 1979. Additionally, the NEB had made a number of loans to the company between 1976 and 1978 amounting to a net maximum of £5.69 million.[63] In the first week of July 1980, the company collapsed and commenting on the general state of the British machine tool industry *The Investors' Chronicle* claimed that the escalation of machine tool imports was indicative of the fact that domestic makers had been left behind in high technology and specialist development. Despite 'record investment' they were 'not catching up on their foreign competitors'. Accepting that there were exceptions in the industry, such as B Elliott and Co., a firm that had undertaken extensive re-organisation and successfully introduced a range of high technology machines, the *Chronicle* nevertheless continued in its pessimistic tone. The main reason it provided for the decline in British machine tool manufacture was 'a lack of competitive products', a fact that had been all too evident at the firm of Herbert's since the 1960s.[64]

Herbert Ltd. was broken-up and sold to various bidders. For example, Devlieg purchased the Lutterworth plant where their machines were produced under licence. The Herbert Machine Tool Co., consisting of the main operating plants, was purchased by Tooling Investment Ltd. Regardless of the alleged reputation of Tooling Investment as an asset stripper, the workers at Coventry continued to hope that the return to private enterprise might save machine tool production in the city. The machine tools installed at Edgwick, alone, were estimated by the assessors to be worth £10 million, but the sum actually paid by Tooling Investment for the plant was nearer £2 million. By the early 1980s, it would seem that Tooling Investment had actually turned the company around, profits of £3.7m were announced, and the duo in charge Lynch and Wright received management awards for their contribution to the Herbert revival. In recognition of this success, the chairman's salary was doubled to £103,135 per annum, a substantial remuneration for the early 1980s. Success proved ephemeral. A 'scandal erupted in 1982 over a health insurance scheme', after facts emerged that 'the company had not paid in employees' contributions'. In 1983, Lynch and Wright were sued by the Industrial and Commercial Finance Corporation, who alleged that £1.25 million of shares had been allotted 'on the bases of ... an inaccurate and untrue business plan'. The company found itself in the hands of the receivers in August 1982, and a little over a year later in October 1983, 'the last 9 employees and redundant workers saw the Edgwick site go under the auctioneer's

---

[62] *Machine Tool Review*, Vol. 68, 1980, p. i.

[63] *British Business Index, Department of Industry*, 28 March 1980, p. 535.

[64] *Investors' Chronicle*, 4 July 1980, p. 48.

hammer'.[65] Scores of dealers came to Coventry to pick over the bones of the company; some of these were from overseas, and when they came to collect their bargains did they ever wonder, perhaps, what had brought down this great symbol of the British machine tool industry? In the end, the story was, indeed, 'a sad reminder for the U.K. machine tool industry'.

---

[65] *Alfred Herbert 1888-1983*, pp. 18-19.

Appendix A

Table A.1
Companies Engaged in NCMT Development in Britain, 1966

Company	NC Application	Country
BSA Tools	Lathes	British
Warner-Swasey-Asquith (Staveley Industries Group)	Lathes	Joint U.S.A.-British
Drummond Bros. (Staveley Industries Group)	Lathes	British
Asquith Machine Tool Co. (Staveley Industries Group)	Drilling, boring, broaching & milling	British
G. Richards (Staveley Industries Group)	Drilling, boring, broaching & milling	British
Charles Churchill Ltd. (Tube Investment Group)	Lathes	British
Alfred Herbert Ltd.	Lathes, drilling, boring, broaching & milling (plugboard and NC)	British
H. Ward	Lathes	British
D. Mitchell	Lathes	British
Alcock & Shipley	Drilling, boring, broaching & milling	British
Cincinnati Milling Co.	Drilling, boring, broaching, grinding & milling	U.S.A. (Birmingham)
Wadkin	Drilling, boring, broaching & milling	British
Kearney & Trecker CVA	Drilling, boring, broaching & milling	U.S.A. (Hove)
Kendall & Gent	Drilling, boring, broaching & milling	British
Brown & Sharpe	Drilling, boring, broaching & milling	U.S.A.
Giddings and Lewis Fraser	Drilling, boring, broaching & milling	U.S.A. (Arbroath)
H. W. Kearns	Drilling, boring, broaching & milling	British

Table A.1 Cont.

Company	NC Application	Country
High Precision Equipment Ltd. (Associated Engineering Group)	Drilling, boring, broaching & milling	British
Hayes Engineers	Drilling, boring, broaching & milling	British
Richmond Machine Tool Co. (George Cohen 600 Group)	Drilling, boring, broaching & milling	British
Verco Precision	Drilling, boring, broaching & milling	British
Kitchen & Walker (John Brown Group)	Drilling, boring, broaching & milling	British
Jones & Shipman	Drilling, boring, broaching, grinding & milling	British

Source: MTTA, Machine Tool Directory, 1966, pp. 29-31.

Table A.2
Main Group Companies with Machine Tool Manufacturing Subsidiaries, 1965 (Companies Compiled for 5+ Machine Tool Manufacturing Subsidiaries)

Holding Company	Machine Tool Subsidiaries	Market Capitalisation – Holding Co. (£ million)[a]
BSA:	BSA Tools	22.6
	BSA Churchill Machine Tools	
	BSA Small Tools	
	BSA Broach	
	BG Machinery	
John Brown & Co.	Wickman Ltd.	27.0
	Wickman Wimet	
	Wickman Scrivener	
	John Stirk	
	John Lang	
	Taylor & Challen	
	D. Walker	
	Webster & Bennett	
	Firth Brown Tools	
George Cohen 600 Group	George Cohen Machinery	18.2
	Colchester Lathe Co.	
	Selson Machine Tool Co.	
	Richmond Machine Tool Co.	
	Gamet Products	
	W. E. Sykes Ltd. – Subsidiaries:	1.3
	W. E. Sykes Manufacturing	
	Kendal & Gent	

Table A.2 Cont.

Holding Company	Machine Tool Subsidiaries	Market Capitalisation - Holding Co. (£ million)[a]
B. Elliot & Co.	Elliott Machine Tool	6.2
	Elliott Lathes	
	Snow & Co.	
	B. Elliott (Reading)	
	Adams Bros.& Burnley	
Alfred Herbert Ltd.	Alfred Herbert Ltd.	45.9
	Sigma Instrument Co.	
	Holbrook Machine Tool	
	I. L. Berridge	
	Lockwood Machine Tools	
The Kerry Group Ltd.	Qualters & Smith	1.45
	Broadbent-Schofield Ltd.	
	Kerry's Engineering Co. Ltd.	
	L. B. Stockdale (Melbourne)	
	Kerry Jost Tools Ltd. (Madras)	
Staveley Industries	James Archdale	16.51
	Craven Bros.	
	George Richards	
	Standard Modern Tool	
	Asquith Machine Tool	5.66[b]
	Corporation – Subsidiaries:	
	William Asquith	
	Drummond Bros.	
	George Swift	
	Swift-Summerskill	
	Kitchen & Wade	
	Ormerod Shapers	
	Warner-Swasey-Asquith	
	Norton-Asquith	
Tube Investments	Charles Churchill & Co.	10.9[c]
	Subsidiaries:	
	Churchill-Denhams	
	Churchill-Redman	
	Churchill Gear Machines	
	Churchill-Milnes	
	Churchill-Vertimax	

Source: Compiled from MTTA, Machine Tool Directory, 1966, pp. 43-264.
Notes: a. Market capitilisation records the value of the holding company and cannot be disaggregated for the individual machine tool subsidiaries. b. acquired in March 1966. Market capitalisation records the value for the Asquith group of companies, including sales and importing companies, which are not listed here. c. acquired in February 1966. Market capitalisation records the value for the Charles Churchill group of companies, including sales and importing companies, which are not listed here.

Appendix B

Table B.1
Alfred Herbert Ltd.: Structure of Group, 1965

Company	Factories/Offices	Product
Production Engineering		
Parent Co. Alfred Herbert:	Edgwick, Coventry	Capstan, turret, copy turning, precision, automatic lathes; planing, vertical drilling machines; injection moulding machines; plastic and die casting machines, Atritor Dryer-Pulvirisor
	Exhall, Coventry	Small tools, including taps, dies, chucks, and threading equipment
	Lutterworth, Leicester	Lathes, equipment and consumable small tools
Subsidiary Producing Co's.:		
Sigma Instrument Co.	Letchworth	Measuring equipment
Holbrook Machine Tool		Machine Tools
I. L. Berridge	Leicester	Machine Tools
Mudie Electrical	Birmingham	Control gear
Lockwood Machine Tool	Huddersfield	Planing and other machine tools
Machines and Equipment Built under Licence:		
Cri-dan	Herbert factories	high speed threading machine
Devlieg (U.S.A)	Herbert factories	Jigmill
Pratt and Whitney (U.S.A)	Herbert factories	Keller tracer-controlled milling machine
Fellows (U.S.A.)	Herbert factories	Gear-shaping machine
Factoring Division		
Herbert Factoring	Red Lane, Coventry	Agencies:
Archdale	Birmingham (U.K.)	Milling, drilling, and special purpose machine tools
Anocut	Illinois, U.S.A.	Electro-chemical machines

Table B.1 Cont.

Company	Factories/Offices	Product
Bechler	Switzerland	Swiss-type automatics
Brown & Ward	Walsall (U.K.)	High-speed automatics
Butterworth British Automatic Machine Tool	Rochdale (U.K.)	Bar automatics
Burrows & Smith	Leicester (U.K.)	Gear-deburring machines
Clarkson Engineers Ltd.	Nuneaton/Coventry (U.K.)	Chucks and cutters
Daniels	U.K.	Plastic and diecasting machines
DCMT	London (U.K.)	Diecasting machines
Fellows	Springfield (U.S.A.)	Gear shaping, gear inspection machines
Fokker-Eckold	German	Sheet metal working machines
Hammond	U.S.A.	Electrolytic grinding machines
Heald	Birmingham – Subsidiary of Cincinnati Co. (U.S.A.)	Internal and surface grinders and borematics
Hilger & Watts	Germany	Measuring equipment
Hilmor	U.K.	Tube bending machines
Landis	U.S.A.	Threading machines, centreless grinders
Lumsden	Gateshead (U.K.)	Surface and tool grinders
Mills, John	Llanidloes (U.K.)	Oilaulic presses
Newall	U.K.	External and universal grinding machines
Norton	U.S.A.	Grinding wheels
Pratt & Whitney	U.S.A.	Milling machines
Pullmax	Leeds (U.K.)	Sheet metal working machines
Richards	Manchester (U.K.)	Vertical and horizontal boring mills
Torrington	Halifax	Swaging machines
Waldrich-Siegen	Germany	Heavy lathes, planers, plano-millers, roll grinders

U.K. Branch Offices

	Newcastle, Manchester, Bristol, Leeds, Birmingham, Sheffield, Coventry, Glasgow, London	Sales

Table B.1 Cont.

Company	Factories/Offices	Product
Overseas Agents		
Merchanting companies	65 Countries	Sales
Foreign Associate Co's		
Alfred Herbert (Australasia)	Sydney, and others	Sales
Soc. Anon Alfred Herbert	Paris, Lyon	Sales
Alfred Herbert (India)	Calcutta	Sales
Soc. Per Azioni, Italiana Alfred Herbert	Milan	Sales

Source: *Machine Tool Review*, Vol. 54, 1966, p. xx, MTTA, Machine Tool Directory, 1966, pp. 151-2.

Table B.2
BSA Machine Tool Division, 1966

Company	Activity	Location	Direct Labour	Indirect Labour	Staff
BSA Tools Ltd.	Machine Tools	Birmingham	599	335	622
BSA-Churchill Machine Tools	Grinding Machines	Broadheath,	617	335	381
BSA Small Tools	Small Tools	Birmingham	114	106	145
BSA Broach	Broaches	Redditch	93	30	69
B. G. Machinery	Reconditioning Machines	Birmingham	3	1	6
BSA Electrics	Electrical Equipment	Birmingham	40	10	39
Burton Griffiths	Machine Tool Sales	Birmingham	0	2	39
Precision Alloy Castings	Castings	Birmingham	20	11	5
Jessop-Saville Small Tools	Small Tools	Rotherham	68	98	79
BSA Tools (Canada)	Sales	Toronto	0	0	6
Automatic Jig & Tool Ltd	Components	Dudley	0	0	14

Source: Herbert, Board of Directors, 1960-80, 22 July 1966, 'Report Issued by R. D. Young on the BSA Machine Tool Companies'.

Table B.3
Foreign Imports of Machine Tools Produced by Alfred Herbert Ltd.
(£ million)

Country	Total Imports	Capstan and Auto Lathes	Herbert Sales	Herbert Capstan and Auto Lathes	% of Herbert Sales to Total Imports
Belgium:					
1964	12.4	1.3	0.16	0.04	1.29
1965	11.0	0.8	0.05	0.02	0.45
1966	11.0	0.8	0.07	0.04	0.64
France:					
1964	35.4	3.7	0.17	0.12	0.48
1965	32.2	3.5	0.17	0.09	0.53
1966	34.8	3.9	0.21	0.08	0.60
W.Germany:					
1964	23.3	NA	0.05	0.02	0.21
1965	29.5	NA	0.06	0.01	0.20
1966	25.9	1.1	0.02	0.01	0.08
Holland:					
1964	10.6	0.5	0.10	0.04	0.94
1965	10.4	0.6	0.10	0.04	0.96
1966	10.3	0.7	0.13	0.08	1.26
Italy:					
1964	24.9	1.1	0.12	0.02	0.48
1965	12.1	0.7	0.08	0.01	0.66
1966	20.6	1.3	0.06	0.01	0.29
Australia:					
1964	6.8	0.7	0.80	0.47	11.76
1965	11.8	1.1	0.74	0.25	6.27
1966	NA	NA	0.80	0.16	NA
Canada					
1964	22.1	4.6	0.21	0.10	0.95
1965	29.0	5.1	0.32	0.18	1.10
1966	NA	NA	0.52	0.32	NA
New Zealand:					
1964	2.2	0.5	0.05	0.02	2.27
1965	2.3	NA	0.06	0.03	2.61
1966	NA	NA	0.7	0.03	NA
India:					
1964	22.0	1.5	1.02	0.30	4.64
1965	26.2	1.4	1.28	0.45	4.89
1966	NA	NA	0.81	0.31	NA
Mexico:					
1964	1.6	0.3	0.02	0.11	1.25
1965	2.1	NA	0.43	0.15	20.48
1966	NA	NA	0.16	0.10	NA

Table B.3
Cont.

Country	Total Imports	Capstan & auto lathes	Herbert Sales	Herbert Capstan and Auto Lathes	% of Herbert Sales to Total Imports
S. Africa:					
1964	8.2	2.5	0.48	0.26	5.85
1965	14.1	NA	0.43	0.23	3.05
1966	NA	NA	0.31	0.11	NA
Spain:					
1964	6.7	0.2	0.19	0.08	2.84
1965	7.4	0,4	1.03	0.09	13.92
1966	NA	NA	0.40	0.14	NA
U.S.A.:					
1964	13.0	3.2	0.26	0.12	2.00
1965	20.2	5.1	0.29	0.14	1.44
1966	NA	NA	0.97	0.47	NA

Source: Herbert, Board of Directors, 1960-80, 5 June 1967, 'Report on the Common Market'.

Table B.4
Financial Indicators: Main Machine Tool Groups (1973-74)

	Turnover (£ million)	Return on Assets (%)	Profit Margin (%)	Profit per Employee (£)	Total wages: turnover (%)	Cash Flow (£ 000)	Borrowing (£000)	Interest Cover
Abwood Machine Tools	0.4	0	0	-353	40.9	-13	59.7	0
Bronx Engineering	4.7	26.0	8.3	777	22.9	175	6.3	73.0
Brook Tool	2.3	0	4.0	-9	38.9	84	46.6	1.0
George Cohen 600	103.1	12.8	6.6	N/A	17.4	3,513	36.9	6.0
B. Elliott	33.4	22.2	8.5	N/A	21.7	1,229	59.8	7.0
Hartle, M.	6.6	21.3	7.1	N/A		182	168.8	2.9
Alfred Herbert	36.8	0	0	N/A	59.9	-1,687	56.2	0
Jones & Shipman	7.1	21.1	10.0	753	37.8	767	0	N/A
Megitt Holdings	2.9	27.9	9.3	933	17.1	132	41.0	77
Newall Machine Tool	3.9	0	0	N/A	N/A	-153	102.9	0
Redman Heenen International	22.1	12.6	5.3	N/A	40.9	841	75.3	2.1
Sheffield Twist & Drill	11.8	17.9	14.6	603	47.4	732	40.5	5.9

Table B.4
Cont.

	Turnover (£ million)	Return on Assets (%)	Profit Margin (%)	Profit per Employee (£)	Total wages: turnover (%)	Cash Flow (£ 000)	Borrowing (£000)	Interest Cover
Startrite Engineering	2.5	20.6	14.0	890	25.3	161	119.0	3.1
Staveley Industries	57.4	13.1	6.7	N/A	28.1	2,721	58.2	4.1

Source: *Investor's Chronicle*, 28 February 1975, p. 655.

Figure B.1 Re-organisation of Alfred Herbert Ltd., 1968, Divisional Structure

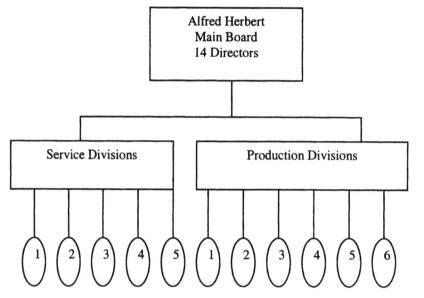

Production Divisions by Product

Product Division	1: Special Purpose
Name of Operating Company	Herbert-Ingersoll
HQ:	Daventry, Northants.
Managing Director:	J. H. Spurr
Manpower:	500
Estimated Assets (£ million):	4.5
Estimated Sales Potential (£ million):	4.5
Function:	Manufacture of advanced manufacturing systems for low and high volume industries, and 'general-purpose special machines'. Supplies also transfer machines, and service to engineering through teams of specialists who 'analyse systematically the total production task'.
Manufacturing Plant	Daventry

Product Division	2. Grinding and Milling
Name of Operating Company	Churchill Machine Tool Co.
HQ:	Altrincham, Cheshire
Managing Director:	D. P. Harris

Fig B.1 Cont.

Manpower:	1,500
Estimated Assets (£):	4.8
Estimated Sales Potential (£ million):	5.4
Companies forming the Division:	BSA-Churchill Machine Tool Co. and grinding activities of BSA Tools
Function:	Produce and market over 100 standard types of precision grinding machines formerly carried out by BSA-Churchill and the grinding section of BSA Tools.
Manufacturing Plant:	Altrincham, Runcorn

Product Division	3. Turning and Screw Cutting
Name of Operating Company	Herbert-BSA Ltd.
HQ:	Mackadown, Birmingham
Managing Director:	D. J. Lambert
Manpower:	5,600
Estimated Assets (£ million):	12.0
Estimated Sales Potential (£ million):	12.5
Function:	To combine activities mainly relating to turning machines formerly carried out by Alfred Herbert Ltd., BSA Tools, I. L. Berridge, Holbrook Machine Tool Co., and Precision Alloy Castings (Birmingham). To design, develop, manufacture, and market a 'comprehensive range' of machines, associated equipment and software for turning. The 'immense product group' includes capstan and monoslide lathes, turning centres, Batchmatic 50 NC machine, single and multi-spindle chucking lathes, bar lathes, precision centre lathes, copy turning lathes and specialist lathes such as Cr-Dan high speed threading machines. Machines equipped with plugboard and tape-controlled systems.
Manufacturing Plant	Coventry, Birmingham, Leicester, and licensed manufacture in France, Spain, India, and Pakistan

Product Division	4. Boring and Drilling
Name of Operating Company	Herbert Boring and Drilling Ltd.
HQ:	Lutterworth
Managing Director:	S. A. B. Muirhead

Fig. B.1 Cont.

Manpower:	1,000
Estimated Assets (£ million):	4.5
Estimated Sales Potential (£ million):	4.6
Function:	Combines activities mainly relating to boring and drilling machines, and electro-chemical machinery, previously undertaken by Alfred Herbert Ltd., BSA Tools, Servomatic (Guildford), and BSA Electrochemical Machines Ltd. Company designs, develops, manufactures and markets machines, associated equipment and software. Wide range of products, some with NC.
Manufacturing Plant	Altrincham, Runcorn

Product Division	5. Instruments and Controls
Name of Operating Company	Herbert Controls & Instruments Ltd.
HQ:	Mackadown, Birmingham
Managing Director:	F. G. Helps
Manpower:	650
Estimated Assets (£ million):	2.2
Estimated Sales Potential (£ million):	2.7
Function:	Combines activities relating to electrical control and measuring equipment formerly carried out by Herbert-BSA Electrics, Mudies Electrical Co. Designs, develops and manufactures wide range of standard and special types.
Manufacturing Plant	Coventry and Birmingham

Product Division	6. Equipment and Tools
Name of Operating Company	Herbert Associates Ltd.
HQ:	Red Lane, Coventry
Managing Director:	K. W. Norman
Manpower:	650
Estimated Assets (£ million):	2.75
Estimated Sales Potential (£ million):	3.2
Function:	Combines activities relating to factored machines, hitherto undertaken by Herbert Factoring, and Burton, Griffiths & Co. Also includes repair and recondition formerly undertaken by Alfred Herbert and BG

Fig B.1 Cont.   Machinery Ltd. Supplies and services many
                                    types of machine tools, ranging from those
                                    used in the production of miniature
                                    components for electronics to largest
                                    machines in heavy industry. Teams of
                                    specialists advise on a complete engineering
                                    system 'to customers' specific requirements'.
Manufacturing Plant   Coventry and Birmingham

Service Divisions

Service Division	1. Alfred Herbert World Sales
Function and Sub-divisions:	Home Sales: to co-ordinate home sales through 9 U.K. branch offices. Factored Sales: to co-ordinate factored sales. Equipment and Spares Sales Export Sales: overseas agents. Overseas Companies: Australia, India, France, Italy, Canada, U.S.A.

Service Division	2. Legal and Secretarial
Function and Sub-divisions:	Legal and secretarial

Service Division	3. Purchasing
Function and Sub-divisions:	Co-ordination of purchase of material and component supplies.

Service Division	4. Finance and Accounts
Function and Sub-divisions:	Co-ordination and planning of group finance, group accounts, divisional accounts, audits, capital appraisal, investments, taxation, salaries and pensions, insurance.

Service Division	5. Management Services
Function and Sub-divisions:	Management Services: value engineering, ordinance and maintenance, R&D and product development. Management Development. Resources Planning.

Source: Compiled from Herbert, Board of Directors, 1968-80, 1 February 1968, 'Report on Reorganisation into Product and Service Divisions'; *Machine Tool Review*, Vol. 57, 1969, pp. 41-8, *Engineer*, 8 November 1968, p. 717.

Bibliography

Primary Sources

Business Records and Other Archive Sources

Sir Christopher Addison MSS. Bodleian Library, University of Oxford:
 Addison MSS, C43/d2, Diary of Christopher Addison, 1916.
 Addison MSS, D2/1/c43, Report on the Utilisation of Labour in the Machine Tool Trade, 8 September 1916.
Joseph Beardshaw & Co. Sheffield City Archives:
 MD7091 (5), Records of Joseph Beardshaw, Minute Book of H. Spear.
Birmingham Small Arms (BSA). Coventry Archive:
 594/1/1/2/2-5, BSA Meetings File, 1918-22.
 594/1/1/3/1-78, BSA Board Minutes, containing the reports of subsidiary companies to the parent board, 1924-32.
Burton, Griffiths & Co. Coventry Archive:
 926/12/1/1, Burton, Griffiths & Co., General Minute Book, 1917-28.
Butler Machine Tool Co. West Yorkshire Archive Service (WYAS), Halifax Central Library:
 ASQ1/1, Accounts.
 ASQ33, Correspondence File of Butler Machine Tool Co., 1936-38.
 ASQ34, Minutes of Director's Meetings.
Churchill Machine Tool Co. Coventry Archive:
 926/17/1/2, Churchill Machine Tool Co., Minute Book of Board and General Meetings, 1924-39.
Churchill-Redman Ltd. (prior to 1934, C. Redman & Sons). WYAS, Halifax Central Library:
 CR2-CR4, Churchill-Redman, Director's Minute Books, 1919-60.
 CR8, Churchill-Redman, Director's Reports and Statements of Accounts, 1919-38.
Greenwood & Batley Ltd. WYAS, Leeds Archive:
 Box 47, Annual Reports and Accounts of Greenwood & Batley, 1889-1971.
 Box 53, Greenwood & Batley, Director's Minute Books, 1888-1925.
Alfred Herbert Ltd. Coventry Archive:
 586/11, Alfred Herbert, General Minute Book, 1894-1950.
 926/1/1/1, Minute Book of the Board of Directors of Alfred Herbert Ltd., 1944-60.
 926/1/4/1-3, Alfred Herbert Ltd., Minute Books of the Departmental Board of Directors, 1911-41.

926/1/5/32-51, Alfred Herbert Ltd., Annual Accounts and Schedules, 1918-37.
1270/1/7/31, Business Papers of Colonel C. W. Clark.
1270/2/5, 'Herbert-BSA Ltd. Profitability Investigation', 20 August 1969.
1270/4/1, Oscar Harmer for the Alfred Herbert Testimonial, 22 July 1917.
1558/1/1/1-5, Minute Book of the Board of Directors of Alfred Herbert, 1960-80.
Machine Tool Trade Association (MTTA). Privately held at offices of Association at Lancaster Gate, London:
Machine Tool Engineering Association (MTEA), Minute Books, 1910-19.
MTTA, Annual Reports and General Meetings, 1923-36.
MTTA, Council Minute Books, 1946-70.
MTTA, Director's Minute Books, 1919-42.
MTTA, Machine Tool Directory, 1966, produced by Miln and Robinson for private circulation, 1963 and 1966.
Scottish Machine Tool Corporation (SMTC). Glasgow University Archives and Business Research Centre:
UGD 175/2/1/1-5, Minute Books, 1937-61.
Arthur Scrivener Ltd. Coventry Archive:
1140/52/1, Records of Arthur Scrivener Ltd., Minute Books 1932-47.
Webster & Bennett. Coventry Archive:
1050/1/1, Webster & Bennett Minutes of Board of Directors.
1050/1/3, Typed History of the Company.
1050/5/1, Press Cuttings for Webster & Bennett.
1050/9/1, Webster & Bennett Sales Register.

Journals

Alfred Herbert News.
The American Machinist, 1880-1931 (thereafter *The Machinist*).
Board of Trade Journal.
The Cycle and Motor Cycle Trader.
The Economist.
The Engineer.
Engineering.
The Investors' Chronicle.
The Machine Tool Review (Published by Alfred Herbert Ltd.).
The Machinist, 1933-80 (prior to 1932 *The American Machinist*).
Ministry of Munitions Journal.
Research and Development for Industry.

Official

British Business Index, Department of Industry (London, H.M.S.O, 1980).
British Intelligence Objectives Sub-committee, Final Report No. 641, *The German Machine Tool Industry* (London, H.M.S.O., n.d.).

Committee on Industry and Trade: Survey of Metal Trades (London, H.M.S.O, 1928).

Department of Economic Affairs, Industrial and Regional Progress Reports.

Hansard, Parliamentary Debates of the House of Commons.

History of the Ministry of Munitions, Vol. 8 (London, H.M.S.O., 1921-22).

Machine Tool Industry Research Association (MTIRA), *Annual Reports.*

National Economic Development Council, *Investment in Machine Tools. A Survey by the Management Consultants' Association* (London, H.M.S.O, 1965).

National Plan (London, H.M.S.O, 1965).

Political and Economic Planning (PEP), Report on 'The Machine Tool Industry', in *Planning*, Vol. 15 (20 December 1948).

Productivity Team Report on Metalworking Machine-Tools by Anglo-American Council on Productivity (London, H.M.S.O., 1953).

Report of the Committee of the Privy Council for Scientific and Industrial Research for 1917-1918 (cd. 9144).

Report of Machine Tool NEDC Working Party on the Problems Arising from the Cyclical Pattern of Machine Tool Orders (London, H.M.S.O, 1966).

Reports from Commissioners, Vol. XIX, National Reconstruction Development Corporation, Report and Statement of Account for 1 July 1958-30 June 1959.

Reports from Commissioners, Vol. XX, Session 1959-60, *Annual Report of the Advisory Council on Scientific Policy.*

Reports from Commissioners, Vol. XX, Session 1959-60, DSIR, *Report of the Research Council for 1959.*

Reports from Commissioners, Vol. XX, Session 1960-61, DSIR, *Report of the Research Council for 1960.*

Revisions to Customs Duties (Dumping and Subsidiary Act), 1957, Parliamentary Reports, Vol. XX, No. 336.

Seymour Melman, Report on the Productivity of Operations in the Machine Tool Industry in Western Europe (European Productivity Agency, 1959).

Sir Steuart Mitchell, *The Machine Tool Industry: A Report by the Sub-Committee of the Machine Tool Advisory Council* (London, H.M.S.O, 1960).

Third Report of the Industry and Trade Committee: Machine Tools and Robotics, Session 1982-83.

Secondary Sources

Abe, E., 'The Technological Strategy of a Leading Iron and Steel Firm: Bolkow Vaughn & Co. Ltd.: Late Victorian Industrialists Did Fail', *Business History*, Vol. 38, No. 1 (1996).

Ackerman, C. and J. Harrop, 'The Management of Technological Innovation in the Machine Tool Industry: A Cross-National Regional Survey of Britain and Switzerland', *R&D Management*, Vol. 15, No. 3 (1985), pp. 207-18.

Adams, R. J. Q., *Arms and the Wizard: Lloyd-George at the Ministry of Munitions, 1915-16* (London, Cassell, 1978).

Adeney, M., *The Motor Makers: The Turbulent History of Britain's Car Industry* (London, Collins, 1988).

Aldcroft, D. H., 'The Performance of the British Machine-Tool Industry in the Interwar Years', *Business History Review*, Vol. 40, No. 3 (1966).

Alford, B. W. E., 'Lost Opportunity: British Business and Businessmen during the First World War', in N. McKendrick and R. B. Outhwaite (eds), *Business Life and Public Policy: Essays in Honour of D. C. Coleman* (Cambridge, Cambridge University Press, 1986).

Alfred Herbert Ltd – A Coventry Firm: 1888-1983 (Coventry Environmental Educational Project, Coventry City Council, 1984).

Archdale Machine Tools 1868-1948 (Birmingham, James Archdale Ltd., 1948).

Archibugi, D., J. Howells and J. Michie (eds), *Innovation Policy in a Global Economy* (Cambridge, Cambridge University Press, 1999).

Arnold, A. J., 'Innovation, Deskilling and Profitability in the British Machine Tool Industry: Alfred Herbert, 1887-1927', *Journal of Industrial History*, Vol. 1, No. 2 (1999).

Arnold, H., 'The Recent History of the Machine Tool Industry and the Effects of Technological Change', University of Munich, Institute for Innovation Research and Technology Management (2001).

Artis, M. and D. Cobham (eds), *Labour's Economic Policies, 1974-79*, (Manchester, Manchester University Press, 1991).

Astrop, A. *The Rise and Fall of Coventry's Machine Tool Industry* (Warwickshire, Warwickshire Industrial Archaeology Society, 2003).

Bard, B. J. A., 'Some Aspects of R&D in the 1960s in the U.K.', *Research and Development for Industry* (1962).

Benn, A., *Against the Tide: Diaries 1973-76* (London, Hutchinson, 1989).

Blackburn, P., R. Coombs and K. Green, *Technology, Economic Growth and the Labour Process* (Basingstoke, Macmillan, 1985).

Brayers, R. H. and E. Sandford, *Birmingham and the Great War, 1914-1919* (Birmingham, Cornish Bros., 1921).

Breeley, H. W. and G. W. Troup, 'The Machine Tool Industry', in D. Burn (ed.), *The Structure of British Industry: A Symposium*, Vol. 1 (Cambridge, Cambridge University Press, 1958).

Broadberry, S. N., *The Productivity Race: British Manufacturing Industry in International Perspective, 1850-1990* (Cambridge, Cambridge University Press, 1997).

Broadberry, S. N. and N. F. R. Crafts, 'British Economic Performance and Policy in the Early Post-war Years', *Business History*, Vol. 38, No. 4 (1996).

Broadberry, S. N. and N. F. R. Crafts, 'Competition and Innovation in 1950s Britain', *Business History*, Vol. 43, No. 1 (2001).

Brown, J. K. 'Design Plans, Working Drawings, National Styles. Engineering Practices in Great Britain and the United States, 1775-1945', *Technology and Culture*, Vol. 41, No. 2 (2000).

Burke, K. (ed.), *War and the State: The Transformation of British Government, 1914-1919* (London, Allen and Unwin, 1982).

Cain, P. J. and A. G. Hopkins, *British Imperialism 1688-2000* (Harlow, Longman, 2001).

Cairncross, A., *The Years of Recovery: British Economic Policy 1945-51* (London, Methuen, 1987).

Capie, F., *Depression and Protection: Britain between the Wars* (London, Allen & Unwin, 1983).

Casson, M., 'An Economic Approach to Regional Business Networks', in J. F. Wilson, and A. Popp (eds), *Industrial Clusters and Regional Business Networks in England* (Aldershot, Ashgate, 2003).

Casson, M., 'Regional Business Networks: An Economic Perspective', Paper presented to the International Conference on Business History and Theory, Glasgow, 24 July 1999.

Casson, M. and M. B. Rose (eds), *Business History*, Vol. 39, No. 4 (1997), Special Issue on *Institutions and the Evolution of Modern Business*.

'Charles Churchill 1865-1965', *Machine Shop and Engineering Manufacture*, (March 1965).

Chandler, A. D., *Scale and Scope: The Dynamics of Industrial Capitalism* (Cambridge, Mass., Belknap Press, 1990).

Chesham, G., 'The Machine Tool Industry, *Manager*, Vol. 27 (1959).

Church, R. A., 'Deconstructing Nuffield: The Evolution of Managerial Culture in the British Motor Industry', *Economic History* Review, Vol. 49, No. 3 (1996).

Church, R. A., 'The Family Firm in Industrial Capitalism: International Perspectives on Hypothesis and History', *Business History*, Vol. 35, No. 4, Special Issue on Family Capitalism, (1993).

Church, R. A., 'The Limitations of the Personal Capitalism Paradigm', *Business History Review*, Vol. 64, No. 4 (1990).

Coleman, D. C. and C. Macleod, 'Attitudes to New Techniques: British Businessmen 1800-1950', *Economic History Review*, Vol. 24, No. 4 (1986).

Coopey, R., 'Industrial Policy in the White Heat of the Scientific Revolution', in R. Coopey, S. Fielding and N. Tiratsoo (eds), *The Wilson Government, 1964-70* (London, Pinter, 1993).

Coopey, R., S. Fielding and N. Tiratsoo (eds), *The Wilson Government, 1964-70* (London, Pinter, 1993).

Coopey, R. and N. Woodward (eds), *Britain in the 1970s: The Troubled Economy* (London, UCL Press, 1996).

Crafts, N. F. R., *Britain's Relative Economic Decline, 1870-1995* (Oxford, Oxford University Press, 1997).

Crafts, N. F. R., 'Institutions and Economic Growth: Recent British Experience in an International Context', *West European Politics*, Vol. 15 (1992).

Craig, F. W. S. (ed.), *British General Election Manifestoes* (Chichester, Political Reference Publications, 1970).

Croucher, R., *Engineers at War 1939-1945* (London, Merlin, 1982).

Daley, A. and D. J. Jones, 'The Machine Tool Industry in Britain, Germany and the United States, *National Institute Economic Review*, No. 92 (1980).

Dewy, C., 'Military Recruitment and the British Labour Force during the First World War', *Historical Journal* (1984).

Dintenfass, M., 'Converging Accounts, Misleading Metaphors and Persistent Doubts: Reflections on the Historiography of Britain's Decline', in J-P. Dormois and M. Dintenfass (eds), *The British Industrial Decline* (London, Routledge, 1999).

Dormois, J-P. and M. Dintenfass (eds), *The British Industrial Decline* (London, Routledge, 1999).

Edgerton, D. E. H., *Science, Technology and the British Industrial Decline, 1870-1914* (Cambridge, Cambridge University Press, 1996).

Edgerton, D. E. H., 'The "White Heat" Revisited: The British Government and Technology in the 1960s', *Twentieth Century British History*, Vol. 7 (1996).

Edgerton, D. E. H. and S. M. Horrocks, 'British Research and Development before 1945', *Economic History Review*, Vol. 47, No. 2 (1994).

Elbaum, B. and W. Lazonick (eds), *The Decline of the British Economy* (Oxford, Oxford University Press, 1986).

Elbaum, B. and W. Lazonick, 'An Institutional Perspective on British Decline', in B. Elbaum and W. Lazonick (eds), *The Decline of the British Economy* (Oxford, Oxford University Press, 1986).

Evans, E. W., 'Some Problems of Growth in the Machine Tool Industry', *Yorkshire Bulletin of Economic and Social Research*, Vol. 18 (1966).

Feldman, G. D., *Army, Industry and Labour in Germany, 1914-18* (Princeton, Princeton University Press, 1966).

Ferguson, N., *The Pity of War* (London, Penguin, 1999).

Ferney, L. A., 'The European Machine Tool Trade OEEC, Paris', in *Engineer*, 8 September 1950.

Fieldhouse, D. K., 'The Metropolitan Economics of Empire', in J. M. Brown and W. Roger Louis (eds), *The Oxford History of the British Empire* (Oxford, Oxford University Press, 1999).

Floud, R., *The British Machine Tool Industry, 1850-1914* (Cambridge, Cambridge University Press, 1976).

Fraser, T. C., 'How NEDC Works with Industry', *The Manager*, Vol. 31 (June 1963).

Freeman, C., 'The National Innovation System in Historical Perspective', *Cambridge Journal of Economics*, Vol. 19 (1995).

French, D., 'The Rise and Fall of Business as Usual' in K. Burke (ed.), *War and the State: The Transformation of British Government, 1914-1919* (London, Allen and Unwin, 1982).

French, M., 'Public Policy and British Commercial Vehicles during the Export Drive Era, 1945-50', *Business History*, Vol. 40, No. 2 (1998).

Geiger, T., 'Like a Phoenix from the Ashes: West Germany's Return to the European Markets 1945-58', *European Contemporary History*, Vol. 3 (1994).

Goodere, Sir C., 'Research Associations and Collaborative Networks', *Research and Development for Industry* (1964).

Gourvish, T. R., 'Mechanical Engineering', in N. K. Buxton and D. H. Aldcroft (eds), *British Industry Between the Wars: Instability and Industrial Development, 1919-39* (London, Scolar Press, 1979).

Gourvish, T., 'Beyond the Merger Mania' in R. Coopey and N. Woodward (eds), *Britain in the 1970s: The Troubled Economy* (London, UCL Press, 1996).

Grierson, E., *A Little Farm Well Tilled* (Keighley, Dean, Smith & Grace, 1955).

Grodzinchi, Paul, 'Leipzig Machine Tool Exhibition', in *Machinist*, 19 March 1938.

Hamilton, R., 'Early British Machine Tool Automation: The Road to Numerical Control', *Journal of Industrial History*, Vol. 2 (1999).

Hannah, L., *The Rise of the Corporate* Economy (London, Methuen, 1983).

Hardach, G., *The First World War* (London, Allan Lane, 1973).

Hart, C. L., *History of the First World War* (London, Papermac, 1977).

Herbert, Sir Alfred, 'Trainees and the Machine Tool Trade', in *The Machinist*, 22 June 1940.

Herbert, Sir Alfred, 'Address at the 21st Anniversary of the Institute of Production Engineers', in *The Machinist*, 7 November 1942.

Hill, D. W., 'The Research Associations – Essential Link between Science and Production', *Research and Development for Industry* (1962).

Hogg, S. H., 'The Employment of Women in Great Britain, 1891-1921', unpublished D. Phil., University of Oxford, 1961.

Hope, M., 'On being taken-over by Slater Walker', *Journal of Industrial Economics*, Vol. 24, No.3 (1976).

Horne, J., *Labour at War: France and Britain, 1914-18* (Oxford, Oxford University Press, 1991).

Howard, M., *The First World War* (Oxford, Oxford University Press, 2002).

Howe, A., 'Free Trade and the Victorians', in A. Marrison (ed.), *Free Trade and its Reception, 1815-1960: Vol. 1, Freedom and Trade* (London, Routledge, 1998).

Hull, J. P., 'From Rostow to Chandler to You: How Revolutionary Was the Second Industrial Revolution?', *Journal of European Economic History*, Vol. 25, No. 1 (1996).

Hurwitz, S. J., *State Intervention in Great Britain: A Study of Economic Control and Social Response, 1914-1919* (N. Y., Columbia University Press, 1949).

Inscoe, S. A., 'Women and Machine Work', in *The Machinist*, 24 May 1941.

Ip, W. and K. Vowels, 'The Machine Tool Market in the U.K.' (June 1999), www.dfait-maecl.ca/english/geo/europe@4208-e.htm.

Jeremy, D. J., *A Business History of Britain 1900-1990s* (Oxford, Oxford University Press, 1998).

Jeremy, D. J., 'Gabriel, John Beresford Stuart', in D. J. Jeremy (ed.), *Dictionary of Business Biography* (London, Butterworth, 1984).

Keegan, J., *The First World War* (London, Hutchinson, 1999).

Keegan, J., *The Second World War* (London, Pimlico, 1989).

Kirby, M., 'Institutional Rigidities and British Economic Decline: Reflections on the British Experience', *Economic History Review*, Vol. 45, No, 4 (1992).

Lancaster, B. and T. Mason (eds), *Life and Labour in a Twentieth Century City: The Experience of Coventry* (Coventry, Cryfield Press, n.d.).

Lane, J., 'Herbert, Sir Alfred Edward', in D. J. Jeremy (ed.), *Dictionary of Business Biography* (London, Butterworth, 1984).

Langlois, R. N. and P. L. Robinson, *Firms, Markets and Economic Change* (London, Routledge, 1995).

Lazonick, W. and M. O'Sullivan, 'Governance of Innovation for Economic Development', Research Paper to European Commission (March 1998).

Lewis, M. J., 'The Growth and Development of Sheffield's Industrial Structure, 1880-1930', unpublished Ph.D., Sheffield Hallam University (1990).

Lipartito, K., 'Innovation, the Firm, and Society', *Business and Economic History*, Vol. 22, No. 2 (1993).

Lloyd-George, D., *War Memoirs of David Lloyd-George*, Vol. II (London, Odhams Press, 1936).

Lloyd-Jones, R. and M. J. Lewis, 'British Industrial Capitalism during the Second Industrial Revolution: A Neo-Schumpeterian Approach', *Journal of Industrial History*, Vol. 1, No. 1 (1998).

Lloyd-Jones, R. and M. J. Lewis, 'Business Networks, Social Habits, and the Evolution of a Regional Industrial Cluster: Coventry, 1880-1930s', in J. F. Wilson and A. Popp (eds), *Industrial Clusters and Regional Business Networks in England* (Ashgate, Aldershot, 2003).

Lloyd-Jones, R. and M. J. Lewis, *Raleigh and the British Bicycle Industry, 1880-1960: An Economic and Business History* (Aldershot, Ashgate, 2000).

Lloyd-Jones, R. and M. J. Lewis, 'Technological Pathways, Mode of Development, and the British National Innovation System: Examples from British Industry, 1880-1914', in L. Tissote and B. Veyrassat (eds), *Technological Trajectories, Markets, Institutions. Industrialised Countries Nineteenth and Twentieth Centuries* (Bern, Peter Lang, 2001).

Marrison, A., *British Business and Protectionism, 1903-1932* (Oxford, Clarendon, 1996).

McG Davies, J., 'A Twentieth Century Paternalist. Alfred Herbert and the Skilled Coventry Workmen', in B. Lancaster and T. Mason (eds), *Life and Labour in a Twentieth Century City: The Experience of Coventry* (Coventry, Cryfield Press, n.d.).

McIvor, A. J., 'Employers' Organisations and Strike Breaking in Britain, 1880-1914', *International Review of Social History*, Vol. 29 (1984).

Metcalfe, S., 'Technology Systems and Technology Policy in an Evolutionary Framework', in D. Archibugi and J. Michie (eds), *Technology. Globalisation and Economic Performance* (Cambridge, Cambridge University Press, 1997).

Middleton, R., *Government Versus the Market* (Aldershot, Ashgate, 1996).

Miller, H., *Tools that Built a Business. The Story of A. A. Jones & Shipman Ltd.* (London, Hutchinson Benham, 1972).

Mowery, D. C. and N. Rosenberg, *Paths of Innovation: Technological Change in Twentieth Century America* (Cambridge, Cambridge University Press, 1998).

Nelson, R., 'The Role of Firms in Technical Advance: A Perspective from Evolutionary Theory', in G. Dosi, R. Gionettie, and P. A. Toninelli (eds), *Technology and Enterprise in Historical Perspective* (Oxford, Oxford University Press, 1992).

Nelson, R., *The Sources of Economic Growth* (Cambridge, Mass., Harvard University Press, 2000), p. 104.

Nelson, R. and S. G. Winter, *An Evolutionary Theory of Economic Change* (Cambridge, Mass., Harvard University Press, 1982).

North, D. C., *Institutions, Institutional Change and Economic Performance* (Cambridge, Cambridge University Press, 1990).

Overy, R., *Why the Allies Won* (London, Pimlico, 1995).

Payne, P. L., 'Family Business in Britain: An Historical and Analytical Survey', in A. Okoch and S. Yasuoka (eds), *Family Business in the Era of Industrial Growth* (Tokyo, University of Tokyo Press, 1984).

Peden, G., 'Arms, Government and Businessmen, 1935-45', in J. Turner (ed.), *Businessmen and Politics: Studies of Business Activity in British Politics, 1900-45* (London, Heinemann, 1984).

Penrose, E., *The Theory of the Growth of the Firm* (Oxford, Basil Blackwell, 1959).

Pollard, S., *Britain's Prime and Britain's Decline: The British Economy 1870-1914* (London, Edward Arnold, 1989).

Pollard, S., *The Development of the British Economy, 1914-1980* (London, Edward Arnold, 1983).

Pollard, S., *The Wasting of the British Economy* (London, Croom Helm, 1982).

Porter, D., 'Downhill All the Way: Thirteen Tory Years, 1951-64', in R. Coopey, S. Fielding and N. Tiratsoo (eds), *The Wilson Government, 1964-70* (London, Pinter, 1993).

Porter, D., 'Government and the Economy', in R. Coopey and N. Woodward (eds) *Britain in the 1970s: The Troubled Economy* (London, UCL Press, 1996).

Postan, M. M., *British War Production* (London, HMSO and Longman and Green, 1952).

Quail, J., 'The Proprietorial Theory of the Firm and its Consequences', *Journal of Industrial History*, Vol. 3. No. 1 (2000).

Raw, C., *Slater Walker. An Investigation of a Financial Phenomenon* (London, Andrew Deutsch, 1977).

Reed, A., 'Employers' strategy and Craft Production, The British Shipbuilding Industry, 1870-1950', in S. Tolliday and J. Zeitlin (eds), *The Power to Manage? Employers and Industrial Relations in Comparative Historical Perspective* (London, Routledge, 1991).

Richardson, K., *Twentieth Century Coventry* (London, Macmillan, 1972).

Ringe, A. and N. Rollings, 'Responding to Relative Decline: The Creation of the National Economic Development Council', *Economic History Review*, Vol. 53, No. 2 (2000).

Rolt, L. T. C., *A Short History of Machine Tools* (Cambridge, Mass., MIT Press, 1965).

Rosenberg, N., *Exploring the Black Box: Technology, Economics and History* (Cambridge, Cambridge University Press, 1994).

Rosenberg, N., *Perspectives on Technology* (Cambridge, Cambridge University Press, 1976).

Saul, S. B., 'The Engineering Industry', in D. H. Aldcroft (ed.), *British Industry and Foreign Competition, 1870-1914* (London, Allen and Unwin, 1968).

Saul, S. B., 'The Machine Tool Industry in Britain to 1914', *Business History*, Vol. 10 (1968).

Saul, S. B., 'The Market and the Development of the Mechanical Engineering Industries in Britain, 1860-1914', *Economic History Review*, Vol. 20 (1967).

Schulze, M. S. and N. Woodward, 'The Emergence of Rapid Inflation', in R. Coopey and N. Woodward (eds), *Britain in the 1970s: The Troubled Economy* (London, UCL Press, 1996).

Schumpeter, J. A., *Capitalism, Socialism and Democracy* (London, Routledge, 1994).

Scriberras, E. and B. D. Payne, *Machine Tool Industry, Technological Change and International Competitiveness* (London, Longman, 1985).

Senge, P. M., 'The Leaders' New Work: Building Learning Organisations', in H. Mintzburg, J. B. Quinn and S. Ghoshal (eds), *The Strategy Process* (Hemel Hempstead, Prentice Hall, 1995).

Sheikh, S. and S. K. Chatterjee, 'Perspectives in Corporate Governance', in S. Sheikh and W. Rees (eds), *Corporate Governance and Corporate Control* (London, Cavendish, 1995).

Shenfield, A. and P. Sargant Florence, 'The Economies and Diseconomies of Industrial Concentration: The Wartime Experience of Coventry, *Review of Economic Statistics*, Vol. 12, No. 1 (1944-45).

Sigsworth, E. and J. Blackman, 'The Home Boom of the 1890s', *Yorkshire Bulletin of Economic and Social Research*, Vol. 16/17 (1965/1966).

Singleton, J., 'The British Engineering Industry and Commonwealth Development in the Early 1950s', *Journal of European Economic History*, Vol. 30, No. 2 (2001).

Smith, G. W., 'The Challenge to Automatic Control', *Manager*, Vol. 31 (1963).

Strachan, H., *The First World War, Volume 1, To Arms* (Oxford, Oxford University Press, 2001).

Teece, D. J., 'Economies of Scope and the Scope of the Enterprise, *Journal of Economic Behaviour and Organisation*, Vol. 1 (1990).

Teece, D. J. and G. Pisano, 'The Dynamic Capabilities of the Firm: An Introduction', *Industrial and Corporate Change*, Vol. 3, No. 3 (1994).

Thoms, D. and T. Donnelly, 'Coventry's Industrial Economy', 1880-1980', in B. Lancaster and T. Mason (eds), *Life and Labour in a Twentieth Century City: The Experience of Coventry* (Coventry, Cryfield Press, n.d.).

Thoms, D. and T. Donnelly, *The Motor Car Industry in Coventry Since the 1890s* (London: Croom Helm, 1985).

Tiratsoo, N. and T. R. Gourvish, '"Making It Like in Detroit": British Managers and American Productivity Methods, 1945-c.1965', *Business and Economic History*, Vol. 25, No. 1 (1996).

Tolliday, S., 'Steel and Rationalisation Policies', in B. Elbaum and W. Lazonick (eds), *The Decline of the British Economy* (Oxford, Oxford University Press, 1986).

Tomlinson, J., 'British industrial policy', in R. Coopey and N. Woodward (eds), *Britain in the 1970s: The Troubled Economy* (London, UCL Press, 1996).

Tomlinson, J., 'Conservative Modernisation, 1960-1964: Too Little Too Late', *Contemporary British History*, Vol. 11, No. 3 (1997).

Tomlinson, J., 'Inventing "Decline": The Falling Behind of the British Economy in the Postwar Years', *Economic History Review*, Vol. 49, No. 4 (1996).

Tomlinson, J., 'Mr. Atlee's Supply-Side Socialism', *Economic History Review*, Vol. 46, No. 1 (1993).

Tomlinson, J., *Public Policy and the Economy Since 1900* (Oxford, Oxford University Press, 1990).

Toms, S. and M. Wright, 'Corporate Governance, Strategy and Structure in British Business History', *Business History*, Vol. 44, No. 3 (2002).

Tweedale, G., *Sheffield Steel and America: A Century of Commercial and Technological Interdependence, 1830-1930* (Cambridge, Cambridge University Press, 1987).

Tweedale, G., *Steel City. Entrepreneurship, Strategy and Technology in Sheffield, 1743-1993* (Oxford, Clarendon Press, 1995).

Vromen, J. J., *Economic Evolution: An Enquiry into The Foundations of New Institutional Economics* (London, Routledge, 1995).

Walley, H. P. 'Shell-making in the Small Shop', *American Machinist*, 15 January 1916.

Wigham, E., *The Power to Manage: A History of the Engineering Employers Federation* (Basingstoke, Macmillan, 1973).

Wilson, J. F., *British Business History 1720-1914* (Manchester, Manchester University Press, 1995).

Wilson, J. F. and A. Popp, 'Districts, Networks and Clusters in England: An Introduction', in J. F. Wilson and A. Popp (eds), *Industrial Clusters and Regional Business Networks in England* (Aldershot, Ashgate, 2003).

Wilson, J. F. and A. Popp (eds), *Industrial Clusters and Regional Business Networks in England* (Aldershot, Ashgate, 2003).

Wilson, T., *The Myriad Faces of War: Britain and the Great War, 1914-18*, (Cambridge, Polity Press, 1986).

Wood, S., 'Why Indicative Planning Failed: British Industry and the Formation of the National Economic Development Council', *Twentieth Century British Industry*, Vol. 11 (2000).

Wrigley, C., 'The Ministry of Munitions, an Innovating Department', in K. Burke (ed.), *War and the State: The Transformation of the British Government, 1914-1919* (London, Allen and Unwin, 1982).

Wrigley, C., 'Trade Unions, Strikes and the Government' in R. Coopey and N. Woodward (eds), *Britain in the 1970s: The Troubled Economy* (London, UCL Press, 1996).

Zeitlin, J., 'The Labour Strategies of British Engineering Employers, 1890-1922', in H. Gospel and C. R. Littler (eds., *Managerial Strategies and Industrial Relations* (London, Heinemann, 1983).

Zollo, M. and S. G. Winter, 'Deliberate Learning and the Evolution of Dynamic Capabilities', *Organisation Science*, Vol. 13, No. 3 (2002).

Zysman, J., 'How Institutions Create Historically Rooted Trajectories of Growth?', *Industrial and Corporate Change*, Vol. 3 (1994).

Index

Modern Economic and Social History Series

General Editor
Derek Aldcroft, University Fellow, Department of Economic and Social History,
University of Leicester, UK

Derek H. Aldcroft
Studies in the Interwar European Economy
ISBN 1 85928 360 8 (1997)

Michael J. Oliver
*Whatever Happened to Monetarism?: Economic Policy Making and Social
Learning in the United Kingdom Since 1979*
ISBN 1 85928 433 7 (1997)

R. Guerriero-Wilson
*Disillusionment or New Opportunities?: The Changing Nature of Work in Offices,
Glasgow 1880–1914*
ISBN 1 84014 276 6 (1998)

Barry Stapleton and James H. Thomas
Gales: A Study in Brewing, Business and Family History
ISBN 0 7546 0146 3 (2000)

Derek Aldcroft and Michael Oliver
Trade Unions and the Economy: 1870–2000
ISBN 1 85928 370 5 (2000)

Patrick Duffy
The Skilled Compositor, 1850–1914: An Aristocrat Among Working Men
ISBN 0 7546 0255 9 (2000)

Roger Lloyd-Jones and M. J. Lewis with the assistance of M. Eason
*Raleigh and the British Bicycle Industry: An Economic and Business History,
1870–1960*
ISBN 1 85928 457 4 (2000)

Ted Wilson
*Battles for the Standard: Bimetallism and the Spread of the Gold Standard in the
Nineteenth Century*
ISBN 1 85928 436 1 (2000)

Andrew D. Popp
Business Structure, Business Culture and the Industrial District: The Potteries, c. 1850–1914
ISBN 0 7546 0176 5 (2001)

Bernard Cronin
Technology, Industrial Conflict and the Development of Technical Education in 19th-Century England
ISBN 0 7546 0313 X (2001)

Geoffrey Channon
Railways in Britain and the United States, 1830–1940: Studies in Economic and Business History
ISBN 1 84014 253 7 (2001)

Sam Mustafa
Merchants and Migrations: Germans and Americans in Connection, 1776–1835
ISBN 0 7546 0590 6 (2001)

Robert Conlon and John Perkins
Wheels and Deals: The Automotive Industry in Twentieth-Century Australia
ISBN 0 7546 0405 5 (2001)

Michael Ferguson
The Rise of Management Consulting in Britain
ISBN 0 7546 0561 2 (2002)

Scott Kelly
The Myth of Mr Butskell: The Politics of British Economic Policy, 1950–55
ISBN 0 7546 0604 X (2002)

Alan Fowler
Lancashire Cotton Operatives and Work, 1900-1950: A Social History of Lancashire Cotton Operatives in the Twentieth Century
ISBN 0 7546 0116 1 (2003)

John F. Wilson and Andrew Popp (eds)
Industrial Clusters and Regional Business Networks in England, 1750-1970
ISBN 0 7546 0761 5 (2003)

John Hassan
The Seaside, Health and the Environment in England and Wales since 1800
ISBN 1 84014 265 0 (2003)

Andrew Dawson
Lives of the Philadelphia Engineers: Capital, Class and Revolution, 1830–1890
ISBN 0 7546 3396 9 (2004)

Anne Clendinning
Demons of Domesticity: Women and the English Gas Industry, 1889–1939
ISBN 0 7546 0692 9 (2004)

Armin Grünbacher
Reconstruction and Cold War in Germany: The Kreditanstalt für Wiederaufbau
(1948–1961)
ISBN 0 7546 3806 5 (2004)

Joseph Harrison and David Corkill
Spain: A Modern European Economy
ISBN 0 7546 0145 5 (2004)

Lawrence Black and Hugh Pemberton (eds)
An Affluent Society?: Britain's Post-War 'Golden Age' Revisited
ISBN 0 7546 3528 7 (2004)

Marshall J. Bastable,
Arms and the State: Sir William Armstrong and the Remaking of British Naval
Power, 1854–1914
ISBN 0 7546 3404 3 (2004)

Robin Pearson
Insuring the Industrial Revolution: Fire Insurance in Great Britain, 1700–1850
ISBN 0 7546 3363 2 (2004)

Ross E. Catterall and Derek H. Aldcroft (eds)
Exchange Rates and Economic Policy in the 20th Century
ISBN 1 84014 264 2 (2004)

Till Geiger
Britain and the Economic Problem of the Cold War: The Political Economy and
the Economic Impact of the British Defence Effort, 1945-1955
ISBN 0 7546 0287 7 (2004)

Julian Greaves
Industrial Reorganization and Government Policy in Interwar Britain
ISBN 0 7546 0355 5 (2005)

Timothy Cuff
The Hidden Cost of Economic Development: The Biological Standard of Living in Antebellum Pennsylvania
ISBN 0 7546 4119 8 (2005)

Derek H. Aldcroft
Europe's Third World: The European Periphery in the Interwar Years
ISBN 0 7546 0599 X (2006)

James P. Huzel
The Popularization of Malthus in Early Nineteenth-Century England: Martineau, Cobbett and the Pauper Press
ISBN 0 7546 5427 3 (2006)

Richard Perren
Taste, Trade and Technology: The Development of the International Meat Industry since 1840
ISBN-10 0 7546 3648 8 / ISBN-13 978-0-7546-3648-9 (2006)

For Product Safety Concerns and Information please contact our
EU representative GPSR@taylorandfrancis.com Taylor & Francis
Verlag GmbH, Kaufingerstraße 24, 80331 München, Germany